T0313950

Transatlantic Economic Challenges in an Era of Growing Multipolarity

Jacob Funk Kirkegaard, Nicolas Véron, and Guntram B. Wolff, editors

PETERSON INSTITUTE FOR INTERNATIONAL ECONOMICS
BRUEGEL

Washington, DC
July 2012

FSC
www.fsc.org
MIX
Paper from
responsible sources
FSC® C005010

Jacob Funk Kirkegaard has been a research fellow at the Peterson Institute for International Economics since 2002 and is also a senior associate at the Rhodium Group, a New York–based research firm. He is author of *The Accelerating Decline in America's High-Skilled Workforce: Implications for Immigration Policy* (2007) and coauthor of *US Pension Reform: Lessons from Other Countries* (2009) and *Transforming the European Economy* (2004). He is a graduate of the Danish Army's Special School of Intelligence and Linguistics with the rank of first lieutenant; the University of Aarhus in Aarhus, Denmark; and Columbia University in New York.

Nicolas Véron is senior fellow at Bruegel and visiting fellow at the Peterson Institute for International Economics. A graduate of France's École Polytechnique and École des Mines, his earlier experience combines policy work as a French civil servant and corporate finance as a junior investment banker, chief financial officer of a small listed company, and independent strategy consultant. In 2006 he coauthored *Smoke & Mirrors, Inc.: Accounting for Capitalism* (Cornell University Press). He writes a monthly column on European finance, which is published by leading newspapers and online media in most Group of Twenty (G-20) countries.

Guntram B. Wolff is the deputy director of Bruegel. Prior to joining Bruegel, he worked at the European Commission and was an economist at the Deutsche Bundesbank. He was also an advisor to the International Monetary Fund and has taught economics at the University of Pittsburgh. His columns have been published and cited in the *Financial Times, New York Times, Wall Street Journal, Frankfurter Allgemeine Zeitung*, BBC, *Die Welt*, and CNBC. He is coeditor (with William R. Cline) of *Resolving the European Debt Crisis* (2012). He holds a PhD from the University of Bonn and has studied economics at the Universities of Bonn, Toulouse, Pittsburgh, and Passau.

PETER G. PETERSON INSTITUTE FOR INTERNATIONAL ECONOMICS
1750 Massachusetts Avenue, NW
Washington, DC 20036-1903
(202) 328-9000   FAX: (202) 659-3225
www.piie.com

C. Fred Bergsten, *Director*
Edward A. Tureen, *Director of Publications, Marketing, and Web Development*

Typesetting by BMWW
Printing by Versa Press

BRUEGEL
33 Rue de la Charité/Liefdadigheidsstraat 33
B-1210 Brussels, Belgium
Phone: +32 2 227 4210
Fax: +32 2 227 4219
www.bruegel.org

Jean Pisani-Ferry, *Director*

Printed in the United States of America
14 13 12   5 4 3 2 1

Library of Congress Cataloging-in-Publication Data
Transatlantic economic challenges in an era of growing multipolarity / Jacob Funk Kirkegaard, Nicolas Veron, and Guntram B. Wolff, editors.
    p. cm.
    Includes index.
    ISBN 978-0-88132-645-1
    1. United States—Foreign economic relations—European Union countries.
    2. European Union countries—Foreign economic relations—United States.
    3. European Union countries—Economic policy—21st century.   4. United States—Economic policy—21st century.
    I. Kirkegaard, Jacob F.   II. Véron, Nicolas.
    III. Wolff, Guntram.
    HF1456.5.E8T73 2012
    337.7304—dc23

                                        2012015638

Contents

Preface

The transatlantic political and economic relationship has shaped and dominated the global economy and its institutions since the end of the Second World War, but today the United States and Europe account for a smaller and diminishing share of world economic output. Transatlantic trade similarly represents a declining part of world trade. It is only in the field of finance that the relationship remains unrivaled.

The launch of the G-20 in the midst of the global financial crisis represented a natural evolution in the global governance architecture, which must at all times strive to include a critical mass of global actors to secure effective global policy cooperation. Global trends have, therefore, forced a rethink of not only how the United States and Europe act externally toward new rising economic poles but perhaps more importantly what the two partners see as the substantive contents of the transatlantic relationship itself.

How must the transatlantic relationship evolve to remain relevant in a multipolar world? Do policy areas still exist where the transatlantic relationship remains indispensable? Are there issues that the United States and Europe must still take the lead on? And if so, are Washington, Brussels, and other European capitals capable of successfully coordinating their respective positions, engage their domestic constituencies and interest groups, and rise to such occasions? The challenges are many: restore economic growth, reduce public and private debt overhangs, achieve financial-sector re-regulation, reform the existing global financial institutions, cope with ageing societies, and address climate change. These are some of the questions that transatlantic policymakers face, and the papers in this volume are intended to help facilitate discussion on and provide answers to these questions.

The papers, associated discussion, and topical addresses by key transatlantic policymakers in this volume were initially prepared for and presented at two policy conferences organized jointly by the Peterson Institute for International Economics and Bruegel, the first in Washington in October 2010 and the second in Berlin in September 2011.

Adam S. Posen and Jean Pisani-Ferry addressed the question of diverging macroeconomic perspectives in the United States and Europe. William R. Cline and Reinhilde Veugelers assessed the challenges to transatlantic climate change policies. Morris Goldstein and Nicolas Veron compared the terms of respective policy debates on too-big-to-fail banks on both sides of the Atlantic. Edwin M. Truman and Garry Schinasi tackled the outlook and requirements for effective reform of the global financial architecture and especially the International Monetary Fund. Ignazio Angeloni, Andre Sapir, and Joseph Gagnon examined the role played by, and challenges to, the international monetary system. Michael Mussa and Zsolt Darvas explored the outlook for restoring economic growth in the United States and Europe. Jacob Funk Kirkegaard, Alan Ahearne, and Guntram Wolff considered the scope and challenge of high postcrisis transatlantic debt levels.

The Peter G. Peterson Institute for International Economics is a private, nonprofit institution for the study and discussion of international economic policy. Its purpose is to analyze important issues in that area and to develop and communicate practical new approaches for dealing with them. The Institute is completely nonpartisan.

The Institute is funded by a highly diversified group of philanthropic foundations, private corporations, and interested individuals. About 35 percent of the Institute's resources in our latest fiscal year were provided by contributors outside the United States. This work has been supported by an EU-US Policy Research and Debate 2010–2011 grant from the European Commission Directorate General for External Affairs.

The Institute's Board of Directors bears overall responsibilities for the Institute and gives general guidance and approval to its research program, including the identification of topics that are likely to become important over the medium run (one to three years) and that should be addressed by the Institute. The director, working closely with the staff and outside Advisory Committee, is responsible for the development of particular projects and makes the final decision to publish an individual study.

Bruegel is an independent economic think tank. It contributes to European and global economic policymaking through open, fact-based and policy-relevant research, analysis, and debate. Membership is composed of EU governments, leading international corporations, and institutions. The Bruegel Board consists of 11 members, all with distinguished backgrounds in government, business, civil society, academia, and media. The Board decides on strategy and adopts the research program and budget. The Board does not bear responsibility for research results, this remains with individual researchers, under the overall editorial oversight of the director.

The Institute and Bruegel hope that their studies and other activities will contribute to building a stronger foundation for international economic policy around the world. We invite readers of this publication to let us know how they think we can best accomplish this objective.

The views expressed in this publication are the sole responsibility of the authors and do not necessarily reflect the views of the funders, the Institute, Bruegel, or any of their respective officers.

C. Fred Bergsten, Director
Peterson Institute for International
Economics

Jean Pisani-Ferry, Director
Bruegel

May 2012

Introduction
The Transatlantic Relationship in an Era of Growing Economic Multipolarity

JACOB FUNK KIRKEGAARD, NICOLAS VÉRON,
and GUNTRAM B. WOLFF

Shifts in global economic dominance are by nature tectonic and never precipitated by single events. The chain of events unfolding since 2007–08, however, if not an exception to this rule, has at the very least presented the European Union, its common currency the euro, and the United States with new global challenges. The transatlantic partnership has since the early 20th century dominated the world economy, and it has designed and sustained all its principal global political and economic institutions based upon its own values and interests.

But countries outside the European Union and the United States now account for about half of the world economy, and their share is growing rapidly. Hence their increasing role and concomitant demands for greater influence over global economic governance pose a series of challenges to and opportunities for the European Union and the United States, as illustrated by the eclipse of the Group of Eight (G-8) by the Group of Twenty (G-20).

The contributions in this volume, supported by a grant from the European Commission, were first presented at two policy conferences organized jointly by the Peterson Institute for International Economics and Bruegel, one in Washington in October 2010 and the other in Berlin in September 2011. Subject area experts were asked to ponder how or whether the rise of outside actors of potentially equal, or even greater, economic weight would force a re-

Jacob Funk Kirkegaard has been a research fellow at the Peterson Institute for International Economics since 2002 and is also a senior associate at the Rhodium Group, a New York–based research firm. Nicolas Véron is a senior fellow at Bruegel, the Brussels-based economics think tank, and a visiting fellow at the Peterson Institute for International Economics. Guntram B. Wolff is the deputy director of Bruegel.

thinking of two large issues: (1) the conduct of policy by the European Union and the United States toward the new rising economic poles and (2) the substantive contents of the EU-US bilateral economic and political relationship.

Participating authors were initially asked to look within their broad field of expertise for the most immediately pressing policy items and to contemplate whether respective US and EU priorities overlapped and might result in a deepened bilateral relationship. They were also asked to identify potential policy flash points that might arise bilaterally and to suggest how such flash points could best be managed.

Diverse detailed subject areas for individual papers were chosen with the intent to cover several angles of the deep transatlantic political and economic relationship. But as volume papers were written and conferences organized in 2010–11, when the euro area crisis was still accelerating, the attention of several authors shifted toward answering the paramount policy questions of the day: What will happen to the euro, and what is the impact of the euro area crisis on the transatlantic relationship and the global economy?

Substantial policy controversies have emerged in recent years as the United States and Europe seek to appropriately diagnose the causes of and provide solutions to the euro area crisis. On the one hand, partly based on successful early crisis interventions carried out in the United States in late 2008 and early 2009, US policymakers have tended to advocate the early forceful use of the central bank's balance sheet—either independently (through quantitative easing) or in collaboration with the fiscal authorities (through collaborative efforts such as the US Term Asset-Backed Securities Loan Facility, comprehensive banking sector recapitalizations and restructuring, and the creation of a very large euro area financial rescue entity to provide risk capital to restore private sector confidence). Euro area authorities, on the other hand, have in their crisis management tended to focus on the need to restore fiscal sustainability, implement structural reforms, reform the broader European institutional framework to strengthen the capacity for fiscal surveillance, and create a financial rescue mechanism for the euro area.

Given the differences in focus between these two crisis management strategies and the political capital already invested in them on both sides of the Atlantic, it seems improbable that the two will converge in the immediate future. Instead, perhaps the best hope for renewed vigor in transatlantic cooperation is that the crisis will ultimately take on a less acute character, enabling policymakers to turn their focus toward policy areas where more fruitful collaboration is possible.

The scope of this volume is wide. In addition to papers directly related to the crisis and transatlantic responses to it, the volume also includes papers on climate change, banking regulation, the global financial architecture, the international monetary system, the global postcrisis growth outlook, and the transatlantic debt challenge. We hope that its broad analysis and insights, offered in an empirically rigorous manner, will facilitate the strengthening of the transatlantic relationship in a rapidly changing global context.

2010 POLICY CONFERENCE, WASHINGTON, DC

Postcrisis EU Governance

MARCO BUTI

Opening address at the PIIE-Bruegel conference in Washington, DC, October 8, 2010

The European Union is currently in the process of a major broadening and strengthening of the existing system. I will outline this process along the lines of a triangle of challenges and solutions.

Let me start with the challenges. The crisis has revealed three main weaknesses:

- the banking sector,
- public finances and sovereign debt markets, and
- economic growth.

The first weakness is vulnerabilities in the banking sector. Banks were severely hit, and the public sector had to intervene to prevent the worst. Even after public interventions, however, banks have been significantly weakened in their capacity to provide financing to businesses and households.

The second weakness is public finances, which found specific expression in the sovereign debt crisis. The crisis took a heavy toll on public finances via two channels: the fall in economic activity and the need to support the banking sector. Average deficits in advanced economies are now reaching 7 percent of GDP, and debt levels have increased by 20 percentage points in two years, thus undoing 20 years of consolidation. Countries with weak fiscal positions,

Marco Buti has been director-general for economic and financial affairs at the European Commission since December 2008.

or with large exposure to the financial crisis, saw investor confidence wane and fell into a serious sovereign debt crisis.

The third weakness is growth. This economic crisis has been the most severe since World War II. World GDP saw the first outright fall on record. The European Union and the euro area were particularly hard hit, with GDP falling by 4 percent in 2009. The crisis set industrial production back to the level it was in 1990, two decades earlier, and increased the number of unemployed by 4.5 million. The crisis also had a large negative impact on the productive capacity of EU economies, which will probably have negative implications for potential growth.

The three sides of the triangle—banks, debt, and growth—interact strongly with each other:

- Weaknesses in the banking sector translate into sluggish credit growth and hamper recovery, but also pose further risks for the public sector.

- Public finances, faced by severe pressure from investors and the still-uncertain situation in the banking sector, are in strong need of consolidation, possibly delaying recovery and putting some constraints on growth.

- Finally, growth will not take off without fully functioning financial intermediation, which is the key element to ensure credibility and sustainability of fiscal consolidation.

I now consider the solutions to these challenges. In other words, How do we break the negative feedback loop? This is done by putting in place a new, stronger framework for economic and financial policy, addressing all three sides of the triangle.

First, starting with the banking sector, the European Union has agreed on a new architecture for financial regulation based on four priorities: development of a more efficient supervisory response, more and better capital in the banking system; extension of the perimeter of regulation and supervision, and completion of the tools to ensure financial stability.

Second, to safeguard the stability of sovereign debt markets, the European Union has created two new lending facilities for euro area countries in distress: the European Financial Stability Mechanism (EFSM) and the European Financial Stability Facility (EFSF). The EFSM has a volume of 60 billion euros. It is administered by the European Commission and is similar to the facility that had previously been set to help the non–euro area countries Latvia, Hungary, and Romania. The EFSF is a special-purpose vehicle set up to make loans amounting to 440 billion euros to euro area countries; it is supplemented with an International Monetary Fund commitment of 250 billion euros.

To secure the stability of public finances, the European Commission has recently proposed significant strengthening of EU fiscal surveillance. The proposed changes include the following:

- giving more attention to debt developments in fiscal surveillance. The focus over the past years has been very strongly on deficits, but more attention will now be paid to debt developments also;

- setting minimum requirements for national fiscal frameworks to align them with EU fiscal rules;

- putting in place a wider range of incentives and sanctions to strengthen compliance with the rules; and

- reinforcing the role of Eurostat to improve the quality of statistical information (proposed already in spring 2010).

Third, reinvigorating growth is the main aim of the so-called Europe 2020 strategy—Europe's strategy for sustainable growth and jobs. The strategy was agreed upon in summer 2010 and brings together reform efforts in various areas such as labor and product markets, innovation, and education while at the same time paying attention to climate change and social inclusion. To jump-start the strategy, member states have committed to frontload the implementation of key reforms that are likely to have a positive impact on growth in the short and medium terms.

An important part of the strategy includes the monitoring of macroeconomic imbalances such as large current account deficits or bubbles in housing markets. The crisis has also shown that these can be very harmful for growth and stability. This is why the European Commission has proposed a framework for monitoring imbalances, including an alert mechanism comprising a scoreboard of indicators and thresholds and the possibility of issuing policy recommendations and sanctions.

Finally, the European Union has instituted a so-called European semester, comprising the first half of each calendar year. The European semester has two major aims:

- *Integrated macrostructural surveillance of fiscal policies.* These key structural reforms address growth bottlenecks and macroimbalances as well as problems within financial systems.

- *Ex ante policy advice.* The Commission and Council prepare guidance, opinions, and recommendations at a time when important budgetary decisions are still in a preparatory phase at the national level.

I have sketched the triangle of challenges that faces the European Union and the triangle of policy solutions that it has instituted or is instituting. I thus see this crisis as an opportunity to advance the EU reform agenda and make inroads on structural reforms, permanent crisis resolution modalities for the euro area, and the economic governance framework. As a result, postcrisis EU governance should be deeper, stronger, and more comprehensive. We have learned the lessons from the crisis and will not allow it to happen again.

2

From Convoy to Parting Ways?
Postcrisis Divergence Between European and US Macroeconomic Policies

JEAN PISANI-FERRY and ADAM S. POSEN

The initial response in 2008–09 to the global financial crisis was in many ways a high-water mark for transatlantic policy coordination and, as important to crisis resolution, for common economic understanding. The major economies of the European Union and the United States came to rapid agreement on a series of measures to limit the crisis, including coordinated interest rate cuts by central banks, extension of deposit guarantees, provision of liquidity and in some cases capital to systemically important financial institutions, significant fiscal stimulus, increased resources for the International Monetary Fund (IMF), and resistance to trade protectionism or beggar-thy-neighbor exchange rate policies. These efforts, which paid off, were amplified through the establishment of the Group of 20 (G-20) at the level of heads of state and government and through the involvement of all its member economies, but they were undoubtedly driven by the common transatlantic approach.

The common EU-US approach to crisis response emerged in the few weeks after the Lehman Brothers debacle in September 2008, overcoming years of disagreement across the Atlantic on many issues (Cohen and Pisani-Ferry 2007). By the time the Group of Seven (G-7) finance ministers met on October 10–11, 2008, agreement on the immediate response to the banking crisis had essentially been reached. And by the time the G-20 leaders met in

Jean Pisani-Ferry is the director of Bruegel, the Brussels-based economics think tank, and professor of economics at Université Paris-Dauphine. Adam S. Posen is an external member of the Monetary Policy Committee of the Bank of England and a senior fellow at the Peterson Institute for International Economics. They are grateful to the European Commission for its support of this project and to Christophe Gouardo, Tomas Hellebrandt, and Neil Meads for excellent research assistance. The views expressed here are solely those of the authors and cannot be attributed to the Bank of England, Bruegel, Peterson Institute for International Economics, or the Commission.

November 2008, there was agreement on the desirability of a budgetary stimulus. And when the G-20 leaders met again in London in April 2009, all the building blocks of the common response were in place.

This response was forged as much by European leadership and creativity as by any initiatives from the US government, then in transition to a new presidential administration. Difficulties from divergences within the euro area that emerged in 2010 should not obscure the degree of previous cooperation. In particular, the UK government showed leadership on the response to banking problems, while the European Central Bank (ECB) set a model for other central banks in terms of rapidly finding means to provide liquidity to the banking system. On fiscal policy, there was certainly less intra-EU coordination than was advocated by the European Commission in autumn 2008, and the discretionary component of the stimulus was smaller in Europe than in the United States—but most economies with fiscal space went well beyond the automatic stabilizers. Certainly, there were differences in the form of the policy responses, such as the adoption of quantitative easing by the US and UK central banks, and its rejection by the ECB. But these differences were not a source of tension, let alone a cause of major divergence.

That agreement and common approach has since unraveled. Where the economic policymakers had been traveling in convoy in 2008–09, toward a common destination at a common velocity, protecting each other's flanks, in 2010 policy divergences between the United States and Europe emerged, and they have come to dominate the international discussion on macroeconomic policy priorities. This is most visible in the budgetary field, where transatlantic divergences dominated international discussions in the run-up to the Toronto G-20 summit of June 2010. US calls for a cautiously gradual exit from fiscal stimulus were rebuffed by the Europeans, who put emphasis on consolidation; and the summit itself confirmed this trend with its all-encompassing, G-7-style communiqué. On the monetary side, the central banks' stance also started to diverge, at least as regards announcements concerning inflation risks and the imminence of exit. True, the actual policies pursued to date were not as dissimilar as suggested by public statements. Germany in particular sounded very hawkish on fiscal policy in spring–summer 2010, but its actual consolidation program was markedly cautious for the short term. Nevertheless, words are indicative of differing policy directions.

Divergence was made all the more visible in Toronto in a context where discussions on policy priorities between advanced and emerging-market countries, which were expected to dominate the agenda, had become less pressing. Contrary to the initial assumptions behind the G-20-sponsored "mutual assessment process," it became evident in spring 2010 that domestic demand in the emerging-market world was in fact shockingly buoyant, and that there was no urgency to stimulate it. The absence of a North-South rift made room for a more traditional, G-7-like transatlantic divergence.

The question, however, is why the initial "London consensus" has not survived for much more than a year, making room for the "Toronto divergence." Several competing explanations are on offer. One emphasizes differentiated economic and financial structures as the origin of the dissimilar impacts of a common shock. According to this view, governments merely respond to different domestic economic developments—which a large part of the literature on coordination suggests is right as well as politically consistent. Another view stresses differences in the policy setup arising from institutional constraints, especially (though not only) as a result of the European Union's particular policy setup. A third one puts the onus on doctrine and ideology, which create different perceptions of the policy challenges and risks faced by policymakers. Which of these have mattered and still matter, and which have not and do not, is what we aim to clarify in this chapter.

From a policy standpoint it is indeed important to understand what motivates divergence, because different causes suggest different types of remedial actions, if any, and the desirability of those actions. To shed light on the issue, we start with an analysis of the different impacts across the Atlantic of the common shock from the financial crisis. We then take up successively monetary policy and fiscal policy. Next we summarize our findings and turn to international implications and policy recommendations in the last section.

Economic Developments

The first reason for policies to differ is that they have to deal with different problems. So the first question to ask is whether economic developments in the United States and Europe have warranted (or still warrant, going forward) asymmetric policy reactions.

Growth, Employment, and Productivity

To start with basic facts, figure 2.1 compares the evolution of GDP, employment, output per hour, and nonresidential investment in the United States, the euro area, and the European Union. Both the common character of the shock and some significant differences in later developments are apparent:

- First, US GDP declined less and recovered faster than GDP in either the euro area or the United Kingdom—though it remains early days for a recovery that seems to be weakening in the United States and perhaps strengthening in northern continental Europe.

- Second, US employment declined much more than European employment and did not start exhibiting feeble signs of recovery until early 2010. Consequently, the 2008-09 employment decline was exceptionally deep and prolonged in the United States, whereas in Europe (including the United Kingdom) it was by no means exceptional.

Figure 2.1 Impact of the crisis in the United States, euro area, and United Kingdom (movements in quarters from prerecession output peak)

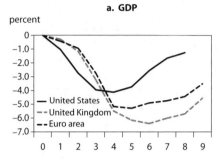

a. GDP

percent

b. Employment

percent

Note: Prerecession output peak is first quarter 2008 for the euro area and United Kingdom and second quarter 2008 for the United States.

Sources: Bureau of Economic Analysis (United States); Office for National Statistics (United Kingdom); and Eurostat (euro area). Data downloaded from Thomson Reuters Datastream.

Note: US measure is total civilian employment, UK measure is workforce jobs, and euro area measure is employment. Prerecession output peak is first quarter 2008 for the euro area and United Kingdom and second quarter 2008 for the United States.

Sources: Bureau of Economic Analysis (United States); Office for National Statistics (United Kingdom); and Eurostat (euro area).

c. Output per hour

percent

d. Nonresidential investment

percent

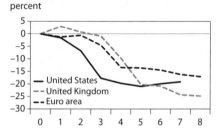

Note: US measure is output per hour of all persons, nonfarm business sector, UK measure is whole economy output per hour worked, and euro area measure is output/hours worked (whole economy). Prerecession output peak is first quarter 2008 for the euro area and United Kingdom and second quarter 2008 for the United States.

Sources: Bureau of Economic Analysis (United States); Office for National Statistics (United Kingdom); European Central Bank (hours worked [whole economy], euro area); and Eurostat (output, euro area). Data downloaded from Thomson Reuters Datastream.

Note: Euro area measure is based on individual country data for Belgium, Finland, France, Germany, Ireland, and the Netherlands only due to data availability. Prerecession output peak is first quarter 2008 for the euro area and United Kingdom and second quarter 2008 for the United States.

Source: Organization for Economic Cooperation and Development. Data downloaded from Thomson Reuters Datastream.

■ Third, as a result, productivity developments have been strikingly divergent. Eight quarters after the start of the recession, output per hour had increased by about 7 percent in the United States, whereas it was still below the initial precrisis level in the euro area and the United Kingdom.

- Fourth, there are no major differences as regards the behavior of investment, despite the differences in growth and in the financial system. It collapsed faster in the United States, but two years after the initial shock, it was in all three cases about 20 percent below its precrisis level.

It is not entirely clear why a large divergence in employment and therefore productivity can be observed between the United States and Europe (where the evolutions in the euro area and the United Kingdom are remarkably similar). Part of the explanation is that US companies, which are less constrained by firing restrictions, traditionally adjust their payrolls faster than European counterparts. But if this was the only reason the evolution in the United Kingdom, where the labor market is traditionally assessed as flexible, should mimic that of the United States.[1] Part has to do with specific shocks affecting the real estate and finance sectors, which had grown very large in the United States and on average much less so in Europe. And part results from the fact that in response to the crisis, several European governments introduced or strengthened schemes aimed at encouraging job preservation, such as the German *Kurzarbeit* (IMF 2010); those policies, however, did not include all countries with limited unemployment rises, such as the United Kingdom. The strength of the postrecession US productivity boom and the subdued productivity response in most of continental Europe (Spain being an exception) both remain puzzling (Wilson 2010).

Private Deleveraging

The strength of domestic demand in the short to medium run largely depends on the extent to which private agents will engage in deleveraging. To assess the comparative situation in the United States, the United Kingdom, and the euro area, table 2.1 shows the changes in levels of indebtedness from 1999 to 2007 and from 2007 to 2009. These data seem to tell a pretty clear story.

In the 2000s households went much more into debt in the United States and the United Kingdom than in the euro area. The contrast is striking, with the rise in household indebtedness as a share of GDP in the United States and the United Kingdom three times larger than for the euro area—and in 1999 the initial levels of household debt in the euro area were already significantly smaller than in the United States. The change in nonfinancial corporate indebtedness offers a more comparable picture transatlantically, though the initial level of debt was again much higher in the US economy.

There are signs that the deleveraging process for households and perhaps nonfinancial corporations has begun in the United States, yet on a limited scale. It is not clear that such a process is inevitable for the euro area as a

---

1. In Spain—a country where employment has evolved in a way that recalls the United States— employers have made use of the flexibility offered by temporary contracts.

Table 2.1   Changes in indebtedness, 1999–2009 (percent)

Year	Household			Corporate		
	United States	United Kingdom	Euro area	United States	United Kingdom	Euro area
1999	68.38	72.90	49.86	64.51	21.75	37.90
2003	85.31	92.13	53.22	65.86	24.15	40.35
2007	98.15	108.41	60.45	75.34	35.02	48.94
2009	96.34	109.94	62.88	77.15	35.11	52.73
Change 1999–2007	29.77	35.52	10.59	10.83	13.26	11.04
Change 2007–09	–1.81	1.53	2.43	1.81	0.10	3.80

Source: Authors' calculations based on data from national central banks and Eurostat database.

whole—though of course the divergences in indebtedness among member countries are quite enormous (and deleveraging has begun in Ireland and Spain). On the whole, balance sheet data do justify more concern about the risks of sluggish demand and recovery in the United States and the United Kingdom than in continental Europe, while also underlining the greater unsustainability of borrowing patterns on the American side of the Atlantic.

Supply-Side Optimism versus Supply-Side Pessimism

A key factor underlying policy reactions is the size of the negative supply-side shock resulting from the crisis—or at least the perceived size of this nonobservable shock. If policymakers believe—rightly or wrongly—that the GDP declines essentially result from a demand shock, leaving potential output unaffected, they will be naturally inclined to advocate further stimulus. If they tend to believe—again, rightly or wrongly—that the supply-side damage is significant, they will have less appetite for it.

Empirical evidence on the impact of financial crises strongly suggests that they tend to result in significant permanent output losses (see Abiad et al. 2009, Cerra and Saxena 2008, OECD 2010, Meier 2010, and Reinhart and Reinhart 2010). These losses are generally assessed to come through three different channels: first, through the downward revision of precrisis potential output; second, through recession-induced damages to potential output; and third, through damage to the sustainable rate of trend growth. These tend to occur over time, and in part depend on the effectiveness of initial policy response, as seen in the fact that there is considerable variance in country experience and that some countries succeed in minimizing such losses. In the 1990s Sweden, for example, succeeded in entirely recovering initial output losses. Economic analysis indeed suggests that the magnitude of losses depends on institutions and policies as well as on the global context.

Both official policy statements and available estimates from policy institutions suggest that supply-side optimism prevails in the United States, whereas the opposite holds in Europe. In the United States, the administration does not consider that the recession resulted in lowering potential output.[2] The Federal Reserve is more cautious in its assessment and does not rule out the possibility of an increase in structural unemployment, but it still regards the increase in unemployment as mostly cyclical.[3] The Congressional Budget Office (CBO 2010) is more pessimistic but even it considers that the medium-term output loss in comparison to precrisis projections should be lower than 2 percent, half of that as a consequence of forgone investment. The view put forward by Minneapolis Fed president Narayana Kocherlatoka, according to whom the equilibrium unemployment rate could have risen by three percentage points, remains a minority view.[4]

In Europe, by contrast, official statements indicate much more concern about the supply-side effects of the crisis. For the euro area, the European Commission (2010) asserted both that precrisis potential output had been overestimated and that the crisis would result in a permanent lowering of potential output. As a consequence, it has significantly revised estimates of potential growth in the euro area and other EU countries downward (and therefore has revised the structural deficit upward), as indicated by figure 2.2, which gives the evolution over time of the output gap estimates for 2007. In addition, the Commission expects postcrisis damages to potential output, and it therefore assesses the permanent output reduction to be of the order of magnitude of 4 percent of GDP, again in comparison to precrisis projections. In the United Kingdom, the new Office of Budget Responsibility[5] created by the current coalition government estimated in June 2010 that potential output in 2015 would be 8.75 percentage points below the level implied by trend growth of 2.75 percent from the end of 2006. This was a downward revision in comparison to the 5.25 percentage point loss assumed in the preelection March budget. These very large numbers, if determining policy, would significantly reduce the scope for demand-side policies and add to the urgency of consolidation.

Transatlantic differences in the evaluation of the impact of the crisis on potential output and equilibrium unemployment are first order in magnitude

---

2. This view was indicated by Assistant Secretary Charles Collyns of the US Treasury Department in response to questions after a talk given at Bruegel (Transatlantic Cooperation to Strengthen the Economy, remarks presented at Bruegel, Brussels, September 15, 2010).

3. Donald Kohn, The Economic Outlook, speech given at the Federal Reserve Bank of San Francisco Community Leaders Luncheon, San Francisco, April 8, 2010.

4. Narayana Kocherlatoka, Inside the FOMC, speech given in Marquette, Michigan, August 17, 2010.

5. The office was created on May 17, 2010, to "provide independent forecasts of the public finances and the economy to inform fiscal policy decisions." According to the chancellor of the exchequer, George Osborne, its creation implies that "the power the Chancellor has enjoyed for centuries to determine the growth and fiscal forecasts now resides with an independent body immune to the temptations of the political cycle" (Budget Statement by the Chancellor of the Exchequer, the Right Honorable George Osborne MP, June 22, 2010, www.hm-treasury.gov.uk [accessed on January 15, 2011]).

Figure 2.2 Evolution of European Commission estimates of the 2007 euro area output gap

a. Euro area as a whole

estimated output gap

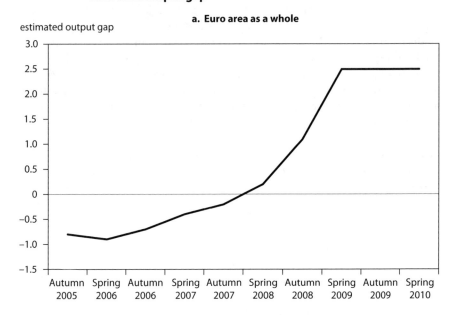

b. Selected euro area countries

estimated output gap

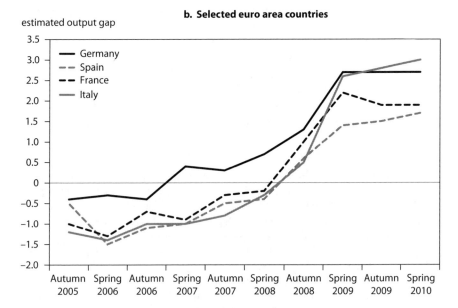

Note: Both figures give the evolution of estimates of the output gap for the same year (2007). Each point on the horizontal axis corresponds to the date when the estimate was published.

Source: European Commission, Economic and Financial Affairs, economic forecast for spring and autumn, 2007–10, available at http://ec.europa.eu.

Table 2.2 National estimate of potential output losses and structural unemployment increases

Country/economy	Source	Potential output loss (as percent of precrisis potential output)	Structural unemployment (percent)	
			Precrisis	Current
United States	Congressional Budget Office	−1.75[a]	4.80	5.00
United Kingdom	Office of Budget Responsibility	−8.75[b]	5.25	5.25
Euro area	European Commission	−3.70[c]	7.50	9.00

a. Estimate is for 2015–20.
b. Estimate is for 2015.
c. Estimate is for 2013.

Sources: Congressional Budget Office, *Economic and Budget Outlook*, August 2010; Office of Budget Responsibility, Budget Forecasts (Initial), March 2010, and Pre-Budget Report (Revised), June 2010; European Commission, Economic and Financial Affairs, estimates for June 2009 and economic forecasts for spring 2007 and spring 2010, available at http://ec.europa.eu.

(table 2.2). Taken at face value, they are bound to have profound implications for the setting of policy objectives and policy strategies.

Is this difference justified? According to the Organization for Economic Cooperation and Development (OECD 2010), the reduction in potential output arises from a combination of three main factors:

■ *A lower capital stock.* Forgone investment and a higher cost of capital negatively affect capital deepening and hence output per employee. The higher cost of capital is expected to result from a return of risk aversion to more normal levels and from the introduction of higher bank capital ratios. The latter effect, however, is likely to be small in the medium run (BCBS 2010). In a financially globalized context, there are few reasons why the magnitude of this effect should differ across countries—although the size of an economy's small and medium enterprises sector, with its dependence on collateralized bank lending for finance, may be one source of difference. In any event, figure 2.1d actually indicates that in the time since the crisis to date, capital expenditures have followed a similar evolution in the United States, the United Kingdom, and the euro area; the impact on capital stock would accumulate over time.

■ *Unemployment hysteresis affecting both equilibrium unemployment and force participation.* The magnitude of this effect depends on the size and composition of the unemployment shock. It is bound to be larger in countries that have suffered from larger and sectorally more concentrated employment losses and/or more regional divergences in employment markets. Going the other way, it is expected to be lower in countries with more responsive labor and product markets, where job reallocation takes place faster.[6]

■ *Reductions in total factor productivity resulting from sectoral reallocations from high- to low-productivity sectors, skill mismatches, and lower research and development expenditures.* The magnitude of this effect again depends on the size and the nature of the shock, as well as on the policies put in place to favor reallocation, skill acquisition, and retraining. The degree of financial dysfunction in a country would have a lasting effect via this mechanism.

Taking these three factors into account, the OECD (2010) assesses potential output losses to be about 3 percent in the United States, between 3 and 4 percent in the United Kingdom, France, the Netherlands, and Germany, and a little more than 4 percent in Italy—thus, importantly, comparable for most major Western economies. The estimated loss is 9 percent in Spain, where the bursting of the construction bubble is expected to result in a severe increase in structural unemployment and a significant lowering of the labor force participation rate. As to structural unemployment rates, estimates from the OECD 2010 spring forecast put their increase between 2007 and 2010 at 0.7 percentage points for the euro area and 0.3 percentage points for both the United Kingdom and the United States, hardly a policy-significant difference. We are skeptical of these latter estimates and expect them to rise over time, both in reality as hysteresis kicks in, and as data get updated—in fact, while the demand-driven rise in unemployment in the United States is the predominant share, the rise in unemployment is so high that it could well involve a one to two percentage point rise in structural unemployment, which longer-term persistence will worsen.

Differences in the nature and size of the shock, labor market institutions, and the functioning of labor and capital markets are therefore not sufficient to explain away the observed difference in policy assumptions. Greater supply-side optimism seems to be warranted in the United States, given both the recent productivity numbers (even heavily discounted) and a history of full recovery following shocks—but there is little evidence-based justification to rule out permanent effects altogether in the US economy. Conversely, European pessimism may well be exaggerated, especially given the lesser rises in unemployment and in private leverage, and the possibility that pessimism takes policy ineffectiveness for granted. In both cases, the policymakers' beliefs may in the end be self-fulfilling, as an active demand-side policy can help contain hysteresis and stimulate investment, whereas a policy that starts from the opposite assumption may be vindicated ex post (Posen 2010a).

---

6. Migration can also magnify employment shocks, as discouraged workers may migrate to other countries with better employment outlooks. This factor, however, is second order in a comparison between Europe and the United States.

In summary, differences in the magnitude and the character of the shocks and institutions may account for part of the contrast between US supply-side optimism and European supply-side pessimism. But beliefs about the supply-side effects of the crisis also matter, especially in how they will shape policy responses. Those differences in belief may help us understand why, in spite of having suffered an initially lower output shock than Europe, the United States has been consistently more in favor of stimulating aggregate demand through monetary and budgetary policies.

Political Economics

A last reason why policies may differ is that political economy constraints are not identical. Some of them are specific to policy fields, and they are addressed in the remainder of the chapter; but one is general: the political cost of mass unemployment. In this respect the US and European situations differ on two accounts:

- First, unemployment in the United States is back to levels not seen since the early 1980s, close to postwar highs. In Europe, however, the employment recession is by no means exceptional, and unemployment rates in the euro area or the United Kingdom are essentially back where they were in 1996–97, significantly below postwar highs.

- Second, US unemployment insurance does not cover long-term unemployment, whereas schemes to supplement the income of the long-term unemployed are widespread in Europe, making unemployment more tolerable.

In these conditions Joseph Stiglitz's remark that "our welfare state is our monetary policy" applies in the United States. It results in a call for action, including as regards fiscal policy, since monetary policy has hit the zero bound. In Europe, by contrast, the political urgency of action is not as great. Political economics may therefore also help to explain different policy attitudes.

Monetary Policy

We now turn to comparing the actual policy responses, starting with monetary policy, for which we first look at institutional constraints before comparing actual behavior.

Institutional Constraints

There were several reasons for the US Federal Reserve and the Bank of England (BoE) on one side, and the ECB on the other, to respond differently to the crisis. To start with, they had (and still have) different mandates, most clearly as regards output stabilization and financial stability (table 2.3). The ECB has a

Table 2.3 Main characteristics of central bank mandates

Central bank	Price stability	Exchange rate stability	Output stabilization	Financial stability
US Federal Reserve	Yes	No, but US Fed may intervene in foreign exchange markets, and New York Fed may also intervene on behalf of the US Treasury	Yes, on an equal footing with price stability	Yes, including supervision of major bank holding companies
European Central Bank	Yes	No, but may intervene on foreign exchange markets	Yes, secondary to price stability	Not explicitly
Bank of England	Yes, definition of price stability belongs to government	No, but may intervene in foreign exchange markets	Yes, secondary to price stability	Yes, but no direct supervisory responsibilities (until 2012)

Source: Adapted from Bénassy-Quéré et al. (2010).

more narrowly defined mandate than the other two central banks; it does not have explicit responsibility for financial stability nor a formal lender-of-last-resort role; and by its very nature, liquidity assistance is decentralized at the level of the national central banks.

The importance of stated mandates as determinants of central bank behavior, however, should not be overstated (Kuttner and Posen 2009). It is a general result of political economy that some institutions increase their mandates through activity in a crisis. It is well recognized that the Fed in fact did so during 2008–09, but so did the ECB. Its reach into financial matters has gradually strengthened throughout the crisis, as indicated by the following: the involvement of its president, Jean-Claude Trichet, in the rescue of the Fortis and Dexia banking groups in autumn 2008; the 2009 agreement to give it leadership in the European Systemic Risk Board in charge of macroprudential supervision; the role it played in the design of conditional assistance to Greece and provision of liquidity to distressed banks in spring 2010; and the launch of a government bonds purchase program in May 2010. Similarly, the BoE is regaining control over bank supervision and created new asset purchase facilities of various kinds over the course of the crisis.

Second, as reflected in the financial stability aspect of their mandates (and ex post in their relative willingness to exceed those limits), the three central banks have different relationships with their respective national governments and regulatory authorities. Times of acute financial stress require the sharing of information and the rapid making of unified decisions. In the United States and the United Kingdom, the central bank is part of the government, though independent from elected officials with regard to specific monetary policy decisions. There are institutionalized and informal channels of regular communication between these two central banks and their nations' treasuries and bank supervisors.[7]

The ECB, however, is not part of any member state's government and there are distinctly limited communication channels between it and the EU executives or national authorities.[8] When the crisis broke out, the ECB had no privileged access to needed information from national bank supervisors, nor even established channels of communication with them (Pisani-Ferry and Sapir 2010). Although some of these limitations have been overcome, ongoing consultations between ECB officials and euro area governments regarding financial stability remain much less intensive and continuous than comparable consultations in the United States or the United Kingdom.

Third, and most importantly, the central banks' monetary policies followed different strategies and had different priorities going into and now coming out of the crisis. The US Fed has much more room for discretion than the other two central banks, as it had neither been given nor adopted an explicit nominal target, and instead has a commitment to a "dual mandate" of output and price stabilization. The ECB has an inflation goal set by treaty, and a "two-pillar" approach based on both price developments and forecasts as well as on monetary developments. The BoE operates under a precisely defined inflation targeting framework.

Thus, the BoE is most tied to its inflation forecast, while the ECB can always justify a deviation from its inflation goal with reference to its monetary pillar, and the Fed can change its intermediate target as suits a majority of the Federal Open Market Committee, so long as at least either growth or prices are moving in the desirable direction.

Still, all three central banks behaved similarly during the decade of the Great Moderation (as estimated for example by reaction functions; see Belke and Polleit 2007), given the demonstrated ability to maintain low inflation at no apparent cost to growth or volatility. All three were committed to opposing the risk of outright deflation in autumn 2008, consistent with the clear assessment of the imminent danger and their common commitment to price stability. Their strategic approaches, however, have led to different plans for coping with uncertainty about inflation after the crisis.

Fourth, the three central banks' operational frameworks for providing liquidity to their respective banking systems differed as well. The ECB operated

---

7. This point should not be taken to indicate an absence of coordination failures. As illustrated by the calls for consolidation of supervisors in the United States and by the recently announced replacement of the "tripartite" regulatory system in the United Kingdom, there were breakdowns. But these were seen as failures rather than as inherent, as they would be in the euro area, and they notably did not extend to fiscal-monetary relations.

8. The president of the ECB attends the monthly meetings of the euro area finance ministers and the vice president attends the monthly meetings of the state secretaries (Economic and Financial Committee). Also, the European Commissioner for Economic and Monetary Affairs may attend the monthly meetings of the ECB Governing Council. But there are no high-frequency, multilevel meetings as in the United States or in the United Kingdom.

primarily through large-scale repo transactions prior to the crisis, and it was thus able to accept from the banks a very great quantity of a very wide range of collateral assets, which made particularly easy the provision of liquidity. The range of assets that are eligible as collateral for central bank lending was markedly narrower in the United States and the United Kingdom (where monetary policy essentially consisted only of buying and selling treasury securities on the open market prior to the crisis). The Fed and BoE had to play catch-up with the ECB, adding a host of acronymed "facilities" to try to achieve the same effect once the zero lower bound on nominal interest rates was reached.

Similarities and Differences

Against this background, the monetary and financial stability policies pursued by the three central banks have been in some respects remarkably similar, indicating that shared assessments of the risks to the financial system and the economy were strong enough to overcome institutional constraints. Interest rate policies were broadly identical, at least from the Lehman shock in September 2008 until summer 2010, as all three central banks brought policy rates de facto to zero within weeks (figure 2.3).[9] And responses to outbreaks of acute interbank market illiquidity were also remarkably parallel. Within hours after indications of paralysis emerged on the interbank market, all three central banks provided wholesale liquidity to the banking system. They expanded and rolled over their liquidity programs as much and for as long as necessary to ward off liquidity shortages. When interbank markets locked up again for several euro area banks in spring 2010, the ECB again intervened without hesitation.

There have, however, also been significant differences in the response, which have grown more important over time. The three most important are different attitudes toward quantitative and credit easing, different policies as regards partner countries, and different perspectives on the economic outlook.

Quantitative and Credit Easing

Probably the most notable difference among the three central banks is that the BoE and the Fed have undertaken significant *quantitative easing*, but the ECB has not undertaken any. The BoE and the Fed indicated in early 2009 that they considered it necessary to supplement interest rate cuts with loosening through unconventional instruments[10]; they both believed that the interest rate cuts were an insufficient response to the scale of the shock. The Fed has

---

9. Although the ECB's policy rate was only reduced to 1 percent, the adoption of a scheme for unlimited provision of liquidity in September 2008 implied that the 1 percent level become a ceiling rather than a reference for market rates

10. Ben Bernanke, The Crisis and the Policy Responses, Stamp Lecture, London School of Economics, London, January 13, 2009; Mervyn King, speech given at the CBI East Midlands Annual Dinner, Nottingham, England, January 20, 2009.

Figure 2.3   Policy rates in the United States, euro area, and United Kingdom, 2007–10

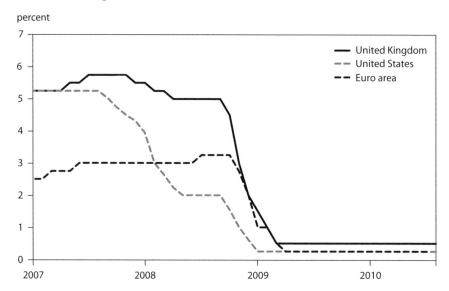

percent

Sources: European Central Bank; Bank of England; US Federal Reserve.

since proceeded to purchase vast quantities of mortgage-backed securities and agency paper as well as Treasuries, while the BoE has purchased essentially only gilts (long-term government bonds), reflecting differences in the respective economies' depth of markets and beliefs about which type of purchase would be more politicizing. Their general approach and scale of quantitative easing have been similar, however, and so are the estimated effects on interest rate spreads (Gagnon et al. 2010, Joyce et al. 2010).

At the same time, the ECB has consistently rejected the idea that it either had to go beyond the provision of liquidity to banks, to overcome the zero bound through purchasing of government bonds, or to attempt to influence the shape of the yield curve. The asset purchase programs it announced (a covered bonds purchase program in 2009 and a sovereign bonds purchase program in 2010) were intended to be of limited magnitude and to be sterilized so as to have no impact on aggregate money supply. Consistent with this approach, the ECB's balance sheet expanded by far less than those of the two other central banks (figure 2.4).

Also *credit easing* (i.e., specific asset purchase programs that aim to restore liquidity in asset market segments) was undertaken by all three central banks, but to an uneven degree. The Fed undertook early on to loosen clogged market segments such as the commercial paper as well as student loan and other securitization markets. The BoE offered a commercial paper facility, but had few takers. Through the early stages of the crisis, the ECB was satisfied with

Figure 2.4 Central bank balance sheets, 2007–10

index (January 3, 2007 = 100)

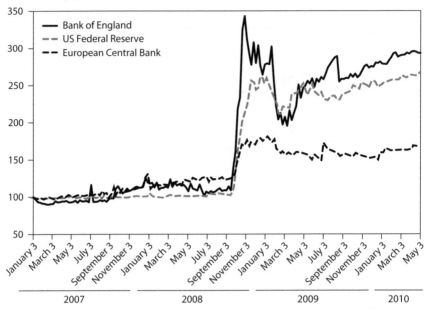

Sources: European Central Bank; Bank of England; US Federal Reserve; authors' calculations.

its measures providing liquidity to the banking system, perhaps because of the greater importance of bank lending versus securities markets in the euro area. As indicated already, the ECB did eventually undertake credit-easing actions, after the Greek crisis erupted in early 2010; however, it did so with evident reluctance, without having stated its aims, and only for a rather short period.

Such marked differences between the three central banks' responses to a common simultaneous shock—and to one for which at least initially all three had the same assessment and interest rate response—merit understanding. It could be argued that these differences result merely from structural rather than policy factors. Certainly, part of the explanation has to do with differences in the transmission of the shock through distinctive financial structures.

The US economy relies much more on securitized, market-based finance than the bank lending–centered economies of continental Europe, with that of the United Kingdom somewhere between the two.[11] As a result, it made sense that in 2008-09 the Fed gave priority to restoring liquidity in key securities markets, whereas the priority in the euro area was to ensure liquidity

---

11. Observers used to refer to more "arm's-length" financing in the United States and United Kingdom than in continental Europe, but developments in the 2000s leading up to the financial crisis indicate that the concept misleads more than it elucidates, both positively and normatively.

Figure 2.5 Growth in broad money aggregates, 1999 to August 2010

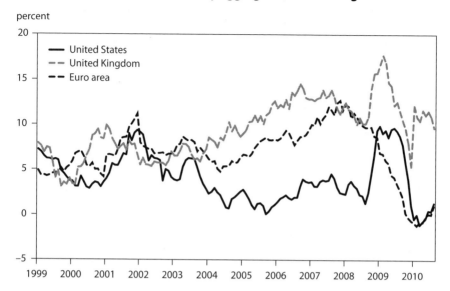

percent

Sources: European Central Bank; Bank of England; US Federal Reserve.

access for the banks and make sure that they were able to perform their credit distribution role.

For that reason, it is easier to explain the different approaches to credit easing than to quantitative easing. It is perfectly reasonable for the central bank to try end-run banks in an economy where a large number of nonfinancial agents borrow directly on the market, while it is just as reasonable for the central bank to act through the banking system in an economy that relies mainly on banks to channel credit to nonfinancial agents. Given that structural difference, it is clear that the money multiplier contracted more in the United States and the United Kingdom than in continental Europe—and as argued by Jürgen von Hagen (2009), this could help to explain why the base money response had to be more aggressive in the former case than in the latter.

Yet it is ironic that the one major central bank with a publicly declared monetary pillar has countenanced a large and sustained decline in broad money (i.e., credit) growth, without any use of quantitative measures to offset this decline. As seen in figure 2.5, for all three central banks, broad money growth went way down after the crisis (less so on this measure for the United Kingdom than for the United States or euro area). In fact, the largest sustained decline in trend monetary growth versus the precrisis average has taken place in the euro area, perhaps as a result of the lack of quantitative easing undertaken by the ECB. Remember, this is broad money and so is a measure of credit outcomes, not of an instrument like base money, which the central bank controls.

Quantitative easing is a substitute for interest rate policy when traditional monetary stimulus has reached its limits and/or been frustrated by financial instability. The pros and cons of its adoption do not depend on the specifics of the monetary transmission mechanism. So the difference between, on the one hand, the Fed and the BoE and, on the other hand, the ECB, is a genuine one. The ECB's rejection of quantitative easing cannot be attributed to conditions only, nor can it be a question of greater faith in monetarism in the Anglo-Saxon than in the continental central banks. Rather, the lesser degree of activism on the part of the ECB was first and foremost a matter of political doctrine.

The ECB could relatively easily embark on wholesale liquidity provision to the banking sector, but not on wholesale purchase of government bonds, because the former was not perceived as contradicting the spirit of the EU treaty, whereas the latter was seen as running against a fundamental treaty provision, the strict separation between monetary and budgetary policy.[12]

The Maastricht Treaty is very clear in the priority ascribed to protecting monetary policy from the consequences of budgetary policy. Although an outright purchase of government bonds on the secondary market does not violate the letter of the treaty, it is admittedly not in accordance with its spirit, and this acted as a constraint. In the United States, however, management of the yield curve by the Federal Reserve is merely a return to the early 1950s, when the Fed had an explicit mandate to ensure the stability of the long-term rates at low levels (Woodford 2001). Fiscal-monetary coordination is not alien to the US policy tradition, nor does it evoke dreadful times. Indeed the lack of clarity of the EU treaty about the financial stability responsibilities of the ECB can be ascribed to disagreements over the vertical distribution of tasks within the Eurosystem, not to disagreements over the doctrine of central banking. This lack of clarity was overcome at the height of the crisis. On quantitative easing, however, it seemed there was little room for reinterpretation, at least as a political reality.[13]

The same can be said of targeted asset purchase programs like the one undertaken by the ECB in May 2010. Although this program was explicitly framed as qualitative rather than quantitative (and all operations carried out within it were entirely sterilized), its adoption was controversial even within the ECB because it was regarded by some influential parties as implying the transformation of the ECB into a quasi-fiscal agent. Governor Axel Weber of the Bundesbank publicly opposed the measure. The ECB was quick to propose the creation of a European crisis management institution that would take over from the central bank the role of assisting sovereign issuers (ECB 2010). There

---

12. This argument was echoed in various ways in the United Kingdom (where the government gave an indemnity for the BoE's potential future losses on gilt purchase) and the United States (where some of the advocates of credit easing said extensive Fed purchases of government bonds would constitute an erosion of fiscal discipline), but too faintly to constrain policy.

13. Posen (2010b) makes a case that such bond purchases do not compromise central bank independence.

was no expansion of mandate or tools undertaken or even attempted by the ECB in the situation.

International Swap Agreements

Turning to international aspects, another significant difference is that only the Fed embarked on significant cross-border provision of liquidity through swap lines. In 2008–09 the ECB remained much more guarded in its approach to cooperation with central banks outside the euro area, including critically not providing euro cash to EU members that would be future euro area members and that had large outstanding euro-denominated (private sector) debt (Darvas 2009). Some other EU central banks, like the Swedish Riksbank, provided euro lines to banks exposed in Eastern Europe, and financed them through swaps with the ECB, but this did not fully substitute for direct ECB liquidity provision.[14]

Frankfurt's reluctance to embark on liquidity assistance outside the euro area in spite of evident needs and repeated requests from Central and Eastern European member states can be ascribed in part to institutional limitations. Unlike the provision of liquidity to banks, the provision of cross-border euro liquidity would have involved taking risks outside the remit ascribed to the ECB by the EU treaty, which does not envisage any financial responsibility for the ECB in the wider EU region. In the event of a loss, the ECB would have had difficulties giving a legal basis for its action. Only encouragement by the EU budgetary authority—i.e., the European Council—would have allowed the ECB to exceed its mandate, but this encouragement would probably have been considered in contradiction with the independence of the ECB. In the end the ECB entered into a semiclandestine swap agreement with the Bank of Sweden, which in turn provided euro liquidity to some of the new member states. The reluctance of the political authorities to have the ECB provide such swap lines in turn reflected a long-standing reluctance to have the euro play a stronger global or regional role.[15]

Policy Outlook

The last but certainly not the least of the differences among central banks has been their perspective on the economic outlook. Whereas their policy stance had been remarkably similar in 2008–09, by spring 2010 the ECB on the one hand and the Anglo-Saxon central banks on the other hand were beginning to have markedly different perspectives on their respective economic forecasts and to assess risk very differently. In the euro area, the focus gradually moved toward emphasis on the need to exit the period of exceptional support,

---

14. For the BoE, such swap lines are not relevant given the pound's limited global usage.

15. We do not pursue the discussion further here, as it is incidental to the theme of this chapter. For further discussion, see Pisani-Ferry and Posen (2009).

Figure 2.6 Market expectations of money market interest rates as of September 27, 2010

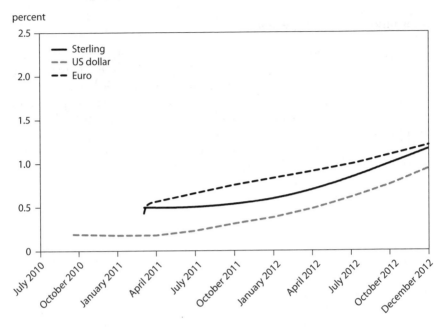

percent

Note: Figure shows predictions for dates on horizontal axis made on September 27, 2010.

Sources: Bank of England; Bloomberg.

whereas the Fed and the BoE were more willing to continue extending monetary support (or at least to hold off on exiting). This divergence had already emerged by early 2010, but it was overshadowed by mounting concerns over sovereign finances in the euro area and the ECB's need to respond to the resulting stress in financial markets. As market participants became concerned about the fallout of sovereign downgrades and the possible consequences of potential defaults for national banking systems, the ECB had to resume direct liquidity provision instead of winding it down as expected. But by autumn 2010 the ECB's focus was again on exit, and markets expected a rise in interest rates to take place in early 2011. By contrast the policy outlook in the United States and the United Kingdom remained markedly more tilted toward continued monetary support of recovery (figure 2.6).

Summing Up

In the end, central bank policy reactions to the crisis demonstrated remarkable initial convergence in view of dissimilar traditions and institutional constraints on either side of the Atlantic, as well as significant divergences in policy strategy, the instruments used, and ultimately the outlook once

Figure 2.7 Core inflation rates, 1999–September 2010

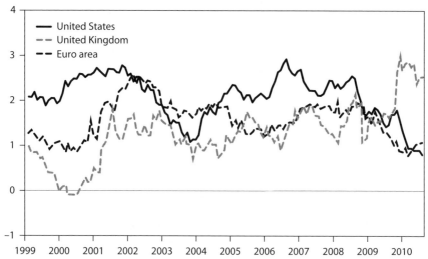

percent

Sources: European Central Bank; Bank of England; US Federal Reserve.

the worst had passed. Even the sovereign debt crisis of spring 2010 did not prompt greater activism from the ECB beyond immediate and targeted liquidity provision. On the basis of the track record thus far and the policy announcements made, we posit that divergences are likely to grow larger in the aftermath of the recovery.

Our reading is that two factors dominate. First, as documented in the previous section, central banks exhibit different stances as regards the desirability of stimulating demand. Analyses of supply-side developments and the assessment of the extent of slack that remains in the economy weigh significantly, as the magnitude of the output gap is a key determinant of the strength of deflationary pressures. Yet this difference has more to do with the underlying assessment of potential output, how lasting the shock's impact on potential would be, and the rightness of monetary ease in dealing with adjustment—that is, the degree to which a demand-dominated versus a supply-dominated view of monetary policy's role prevails—than with the outlook per se. Figure 2.7 shows comparable core inflation rates for the United States, United Kingdom, and euro area. While the United Kingdom has seen a spike in inflation passed through from sterling weakness and a value-added-tax increase, in both the euro area and the United States core inflation is coming down to historical lows. In all three economies, the best single predictor of future inflation is lagged core inflation, so inflation would be well below target in both the United States and euro area (and coming back toward target in the United Kingdom).

The second main difference between, on the one hand, the Fed and the BoE and, on the other hand, the ECB, has to do with their relationship with government. Where this relationship was unproblematic—in the United States and the United Kingdom—the central bank was much freer to go beyond its usual mission than where it was problematic—in the euro area. This relationship with government is likely to continue influencing the willingness to embrace nonconventional policies in continental Europe, even if the ECB is expanding its mandate on the financial stability side.

Fiscal Policy

Institutional Settings and Constraints

Institutional constraints matter considerably in the field of budgetary policy. Three are especially relevant to the transatlantic comparison.

To start with, US budgetary policy is carried out by the federal government, while in the European Union it is only the states whose budgets have a macroeconomic role. The traditional Musgravian allocation of responsibilities, which assigns stabilization to the central level, therefore does not apply to Europe, where the EU budget plays no macroeconomic role whatsoever.

A second relevant institutional constraint involves the role of automatic stabilizers. As indicated in table 2.4, the share of (general) government outlays in GDP is significantly larger in Europe than in the United States, which mechanically increases the impact of automatic stabilizers. Furthermore, more than 40 percent of current public expenditures in the United States are carried out by state and local governments, most of which are subject to some sort of balanced-budget rules and therefore cannot let automatic stabilizers play in full. The upshot is that subfederal budgets tend to behave procyclically and that as a consequence automatic stabilizers are markedly weaker in the United States than in the European Union on net, even more than the relative size of the public sector would indicate.

Finally, euro area national governments are subject to common rules within the framework of the Stability and Growth Pact (SGP).[16] Whereas the SGP does not preclude discretionary countercyclical policies, in practice it creates obstacles to them in countries whose initial budgetary situation is not strong, and it can therefore induce procyclical behavior. These constraints, which tend to make European discretionary budgetary policy less countercyclical than in the United States, matter considerably because of the diversity of situations within the European Union. In fact, although the precrisis *aggregate* budgetary situation was roughly similar on the two sides of the Atlantic

---

16. The prevention of excessive deficits that is enshrined in the treaty nominally applies to all member countries irrespective of their monetary status, but sanctions can be applied only to euro area members. In practice common budgetary rules have a stronger bearing on the euro area member countries' budgetary behavior.

Table 2.4   Precrisis budgetary indicators, 2007 (percent of GDP)

Indicator	United States	Euro area	United Kingdom
Gross public debt	61.9	71.0	47.4
Net public debt	42.2	42.6	28.8
Budgetary balance	−2.8	−0.6	−2.7
Total outlays	36.8	46.0	44.2

Source: Organization for Economic Cooperation and Development, *Economic Outlook* database, www.oecd.org.

(table 2.4), the disaggregated picture was strikingly different, with public debt ratios in 2007 ranging from 25 to 40 percent of GDP in Ireland and Finland (and even less in some non–euro area countries) to more than 100 percent in Greece and Italy.

Taken together, institutional constraints imply stronger automatic stabilizers in Europe and a stronger discretionary role for the US federal budget because the latter has responsibility for overall stabilization and must offset the procyclical behavior of state governments, while EU member governments start from uneven positions and may be forced to consolidate either by the newly aggressive demands for enforcement of the SGP or by market pressures.

Fiscal Stance

As indicated by the discrepancy between traditional ex post measurements based on the change of structural budget balance indicators and ex ante measurements based on the evaluation of actual discretionary decisions, evaluating the fiscal stance in normal times is less easy than it looks. But it is even more challenging in times of financial and economic stress. Indeed, the usual structural balance indicators produced by international organizations such as the IMF, the OECD, and the European Commission are affected by assumptions made about the supply-side impact of the crisis and the timing of its effects. Changes in the structural balance are therefore not reliable indicators of the actual fiscal stance any longer.

For 2009, the IMF (2009) produced estimates of the discretionary stimulus delivered by the G-20 countries, which are broadly consistent with estimates produced independently.[17] They indicate that consistent with what could be expected from institutional constraints and past record, the United States delivered more discretionary stimulus than the United Kingdom and euro area countries, but that the broad gist of policies was similar (figure 2.8). This was in stark contrast with certain past episodes when attempts to coordinate policy responses resulted in failures.

In most countries, 2010 has been a broadly neutral year as far as the fiscal stance is concerned, but debates have been taking place as regards the appro-

---

17. See, for example, von Weizsäcker and Saha (2009).

Figure 2.8   Discretionary stimulus in G-20 countries, 2009

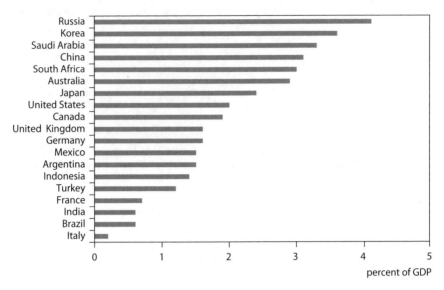

G-20 = Group of Twenty

Sources: Horton, Kumar, and Mauro (2009); Bruegel calculations.

priate stance for the years ahead. The transatlantic difference in attitude became more and more apparent during spring and even resulted in an open rift in the run-up to the June 2010 G-20 summit, where plans for 2011 and beyond were compared. Discussions had already been held by European ministers in autumn 2009 on a coordinated "exit strategy" with the aim of reversing the stance of budgetary policy in 2011 at the latest. The actual pace of exit was accelerated by bond market tensions affecting Southern Europe and Ireland in spring 2010, which led to a series of policy U-turns in Greece, Spain, and Portugal and to policy adjustments in Italy. Consolidation plans in Southern Europe have already affected the 2010 stance. In other euro area countries (especially Germany and France), moderate consolidation measures are on the agenda for 2011. Overall, a fiscal contraction amounting to one percentage point of GDP is expected in the euro area in both 2011 and 2012. In the United Kingdom, Prime Minister David Cameron's government announced in June a major consolidation program over four years, the consequence of which is a reduction of the cyclically adjusted net borrowing by more than two percentage points per year in the next two years.

In the United States, however, the debate is still about the continuation of stimulus, and the Obama administration agreed only reluctantly to the G-20 June commitment to halve budget deficits between 2010 and 2013 and to stabilize public debts by 2016. Plans released by the Office of Management and Budget in summer 2010 envisaged phasing out of the fiscal stimulus over two years and stabilizing the federal deficit at about 4 percent of GDP in the years to come, without attempting to reduce the debt ratio. There are talks of medium-term consolidation but no concrete program at this stage.

Several explanations can be given for this difference in attitudes:

1. Economic situations—and the perception of them—were different, as previously discussed, though as indicated the difference in supply impact across the Atlantic is exaggerated.

2. There are differences in the fiscal space governments enjoy. Clearly, many smaller European countries felt the heat sooner and more distinctly than the United States because of the fragmentation of national budgets and the privileged status of US government securities. More generally, concerns over public finance sustainability are pervasive in Europe, whereas they appear to be much less salient in the United States.

3. Policy doctrines may differ. Confidence in the Keynesian effects of countercyclical fiscal policy is far from universal in the United States but it is more widely accepted than in Europe, where many policymakers are closer to the Ricardian or to classical views of the limited effectiveness of fiscal policy. This is related in part to supply-side pessimism but also to a fragmentation argument: For small, open economies, the countercyclical effects of a stimulus are necessarily smaller, and the balance between Keynesian and Ricardian effects different, than for a large continental economy like the United States, whose financial assets are in global demand. Europe does not see fiscal policy in the aggregate but through the eyes of the national policymakers (thereby often from a small-country perspective).

4. Political economy matters. Disagreements over the distribution of the budgetary adjustment burden are probably more significant in the United States than they are in the typical European countries, and the preference for tax cuts is markedly more pronounced. In Europe, sustainability concerns are not overshadowed by disputes over taxation and spending as they are in the United States.

Fiscal Space and Sustainability

As we indicate above, a potential motive for differing views on the urgency of fiscal retrenchment is that countries do not have the same fiscal space. Where sustainability is more remote a concern, adjustment can be more easily postponed, even if another economy might not be able to similarly increase its debt burden. Cross-country assessments of debt sustainability are generally based on rather crude instruments such as medium-term projections of public debt ratios. These projections are based on necessarily unreliable policy assumptions, and sometimes arbitrary criteria. Furthermore, they give no indication as to what is the sustainable debt level.

A more satisfactory approach has recently been proposed by Jonathan Ostry et al. (2010) on the basis of earlier work by Henning Bohn (1998) and

Olivier Blanchard (1984). The idea is that each country faces a debt limit that depends on the (nonlinear) reaction of the primary balance to the debt-to-GDP ratio and on the (nonlinear) response of market interest rates to the debt level. If this debt limit is exceeded, the debt becomes unsustainable because, barring an exceptional adjustment effort, normal budgetary responses are not sufficient to prevent the debt from expanding beyond market willingness to fund it. Debt limits differ somewhat from one country to another depending in part on past responses of the primary surplus to debt developments, which often reflect political institutions. The available fiscal space can then be defined as the distance of the current or projected debt level to the debt limit.

Figure 2.9 plots the fiscal space calculated by Ostry et al. (2010) for the United States, the United Kingdom, and selected euro area countries. (We do not aggregate the euro area here because countries are separately liable for their debt. Averaging over euro area countries would amount to minimizing potential problems.)

According to this indicator, the United States is not better placed than countries like Ireland and Spain that are under the threat of losing access to capital markets.[18] If anything, it should move toward consolidation faster and more aggressively than a country like Spain, which enjoys significantly more fiscal space—whatever the immediate market concerns or lack thereof. Of course, this indicator does not quantify the value of the dollar's special status, and the additional fiscal space it gives to the United States, but that is subject to change, and could even allow the overextension by the US government that in turn erodes that status.

This indicator, however, depends on past behavior only and does not take into account longer-term, mainly demographic, factors that weigh on a country's fiscal perspectives and may reduce its fiscal space further. It therefore needs to be complemented by a forward-looking approach like the one adopted by the European Commission (2009) in its annual sustainability report. The approach there relies on tax gaps à la Blanchard (1990) computed on the basis of the long-term projections carried out by the European Union's Working Group on Ageing Populations and Sustainability. It results in two tax gap indicators called S1 and S2, which give the permanent adjustment to the primary balance necessary to reach a 60 percent debt-to-GDP ratio by 2060 (S1) or to meet the intertemporal budget constraint over an infinite time horizon (S2).

Equivalent indicators can be computed for the United States on the basis of the Congressional Budget Office's long-term budget projections. This requires making a number of adjustments to ensure that assessments made for the EU countries and the United States are based on sufficiently comparable assumptions. As observed by Carlo Cottarelli and Andrea Schaechter (2010), available projections in fact do not meet this require-

---

18. Calculations do not include the effect of the bank recapitalization announced in Ireland in end-September 2010.

Figure 2.9   Fiscal space in the United States, United Kingdom, and selected euro area countries

percent of GDP

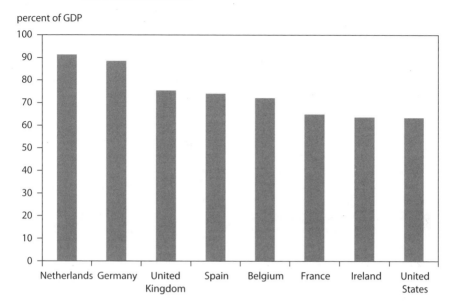

Sources: Ostry et al. (2010); authors' calculations.

Table 2.5   Impact of age-related expenditures on the tax gap

Country/economy	Age-related component of S2 indicator (percent)
United States	2.1
Euro area	3.5
United Kingdom	3.6

Sources: European Commission (2009); Bruegel calculations.

ment. Specifically and importantly, the Congressional Budget Office projections extrapolate trend changes in the relative price of health care services (called excess cost growth), whereas baseline EU projections are based on constant relative prices. Stripping out this relative price change and adapting to the EU framework results in considerable improvement to the relative US fiscal outlook. As indicated in table 2.5, expected aging and its consequences for public finances result in only a 2.1 percent of GDP tax gap for the United States, against 3.5 percent for the euro area, 3.6 percent for the United Kingdom, and 5.7 percent for Spain.

The upshot is that even assuming a similar relative health care price evolution in the United States and the European Union, the more favorable US demographic outlook results in a lower age component of the tax gap. The 1.5 percent of GDP difference, however, is not large enough to qualitatively change the conclusions of the previous analysis, indicating that in view of its current deficit and debt level, the United States has less fiscal room than apparently presumed when assessed on a comparable long-term basis.

Events, Politics, Doctrines, or Institutions?
Summary of Findings

Before turning to international implications and discussing the coordination issue, we here summarize our main findings. We started by asking why postcrisis policy responses have started to diverge while the crisis response was remarkably symmetric. We have identified four nonexclusive explanations.

First, economic developments in the United States are in some respects more worrying than those in Europe, and warrant more aggressive policy action. While GDP has rebounded faster, the sustainability of that recovery is now in question, and employment has declined significantly more, both in absolute terms and in comparison to previous experiences. Furthermore, the extent of deleveraging that remains to be completed in the nonfinancial sector is without doubt more important in the United States, which implies that the drag on domestic demand will remain in place longer. True, euro area aggregates are of limited relevance, as Southern Europe needs to deleverage and as it is not clear that Northern Europe, especially Germany, will compensate through expanding domestic demand. Our assessment is nevertheless that the same policymakers approaching the situation with the same preferences would conclude that the US economy is in need of more support.

Second, political economy factors add to this objective assessment. For reasons that have to do both with its history and with its limited institutions for social protection, the US polity clearly has a lower tolerance for unemployment than European polities, including the United Kingdom. So the pressure to stimulate is bound to be more significant.

Third, an important source of divergence could be laid to fundamentally different beliefs about the nature of the recovery from the common shock. The US government believes that the American growth trend and potential output have not been lastingly damaged by the shock, consistent with their postwar recessionary experience; the EU governments (including the United Kingdom) believe that their economies' growth trends and aggregate supply have been severely damaged by the shock, consistent with their own past recessionary experiences.

As a result, the US government and Federal Reserve officials are far more inclined to maintain aggressively expansionary macroeconomic policies than their counterparts in Brussels, the ECB, and most European capitals. The difference in initial rebounds from the common crisis, with a sharper recovery and higher productivity growth in the United States than in Western Europe, seems to confirm the validity of these opposing views. We believe that the actual degree of lasting damage to the US economy is higher, and to the euro area and UK economies lower, than officials on each side of the Atlantic currently maintain. We therefore argue below that policymakers should be forced to reconsider before their divergent policies become self-fulfilling.[19]

Fourth, institutional factors play a major role as well. The absence of a central fiscal authority, the dispersion of national situations, and the lack of global currency status make the euro area economies much more vulnerable to market attack for their fiscal situation than the US economy. This has contributed to a race to consolidation that would not have happened had the euro area relied for stabilization on a federal budget in the same way the United States does. Similarly (though to a lesser extent), the more limited institutional remit of the ECB relative to that of the Federal Reserve contributed to the sense of reaching an end on unconventional monetary policies. The uneasy relationship between the fiscal and monetary authorities, where testing the limits has reaffirmed mutual suspicions, has also contributed to limiting the euro area central banks' margin of maneuver.

It should finally be added that the financial system rescue and restructuring policies also began to diverge as distance from the initial shock was felt. The false perception among policymakers in the euro area seemed to be that since the Anglo-Saxon type of finance was the source of crisis (a valid claim to a substantial degree), European banks were not going to suffer as much or require as much restructuring as banks in the United Kingdom or United States (a false hope). Again, institutional structures within the euro area that limited coordination of banking standards or fiscal expenditures, as well as a greater number of semipublic or fully public banks before the crisis, reinforced this tendency to be less aggressive than the United States or United Kingdom in cleaning up banks on the continent. The Spanish government's June 2010 initiative to start publishing real stress test results has led to a welcome increase in transparency. That was insufficient, however, to bridge the gap at the G-20 level between US-UK and euro area desires for implementation of capital and liquidity standards (with delays admittedly abetted by other G-20 economies). While not strictly a macroeconomic policy issue, this difference reinforces the divergence politically and economically.

---

19. We do not take the recent US economic performance at face value. We are, however, at least doubtful of the idea of an immediate sharp fall in productive capacity of the major EU economies. If the global financial crisis were to have persistent effects on growth, these should cumulate over time if the recession persists, by depreciating human capital and cutting off investment opportunities. They should not be seen as an immediate excuse for inaction, nor as having had a significant negative effect within the four to six quarters of outright recession in most major EU economies. Claims that structural unemployment rates doubled or potential growth rates halved overnight are hard to substantiate.

How Transatlantic Divergence Matters

If the major EU economies are in a genuinely different situation than the US economy (in terms of demand growth, unemployment, adverse supply shocks, and fiscal space), it is not only likely that macroeconomic policies in Europe and the United States will differ but also desirable that they should. The same to a large extent applies to the consequences of institutional constraints such as central bank mandates or budgetary frameworks, though these cannot be considered entirely given. National interests would be expected to predominate among policymakers, and arguably should. In broad terms, this is why international policy coordination has been rare. This is also why the bulk of analyses of policy coordination in normal times conclude that beyond trying to achieve agreement on the nature of the economic challenges, policy may in the end be best served by each government doing what it thinks is best for its own economy. So why worry about divergence between the European Union and United States following the initial joint crisis response?

There are four reasons why macroeconomic policy divergence may still matter in the current phase more than usually. First, and most importantly, spillover effects between countries' policies, particularly through capital flows, are still not what they are in normal times. Second, there is the possibility of international commercial strife coming out of divergence during a period of austerity—that is, a spiral of protectionism or competitive depreciation. Third, transatlantic divergence could exacerbate imbalances globally, not just bilaterally across the Atlantic. Fourth, there remains the risk of a self-fulfilling low-growth or even deflationary scenario that may arise through premature withdrawal of policy stimulus, which coordination could diminish.

International Spillovers in Postcrisis Times

One surprising aspect of the crisis was the extreme degree to which all asset prices and all indices of real activity moved together. Unlike the 1930s, when the transmission of the depression across countries was low, 2008–09 saw all firms react almost synchronously and identically. Trade and investment collapsed simultaneously around the Western world, and there was little to choose between equities or bonds across countries. The lack of benefits from diversification across the Atlantic (as opposed to the decoupling of large emerging markets) revealed the far deeper integration of Western financial systems and multinational production than seen in the trade data. This had the benefit that when the recovery came in any major economy, it was in large part shared. As policy rates remained at, or close to, the zero bound, and bond rates at historically low levels, positive spillovers through product markets were not hampered by negative spillovers through capital markets. This meant that the impact of any given country's policy measures was felt less at home and more abroad than in the past. That reality constituted a critical argument for a common stance on fiscal and monetary expansion when the crisis hit:

Policies moving together would have offsetting leakage abroad, and on net be far more effective.

The situation nowadays is less symmetric, but demand in all advanced countries still significantly falls short of potential output, inflation is in most cases below target, policy rates are still close to zero, and risk-adjusted bond rates are even lower than two years ago. These conditions imply that product market spillovers continue dominating capital market spillovers. So what might happen in such a world when macroeconomic policies diverge? Large economies that tighten fiscal policy would have less macroeconomic multiplier from their action, as part of it spills over to trade partners; and those doing fiscal stimulus would get less bang for their policy buck. Those tightening governments, however, would previously have expected to gain on net exports by relatively constraining demand in comparison to their trading partners, and that effect would be diminished, too; the tightening country's drag on demand in the other countries would increase, while the relative contraction on demand at home would decrease. The net effect would depend on any given economy's particular attributes and trade patterns. The degree to which governments pulling in opposite directions offset each other's desired policy paths, however, definitely increases. For governments that see a need for significant additional stimulus, this could lead to a greater uphill effort to get the same effect.

Furthermore, capital flows might well amplify rather than offset asymmetric policy moves. In normal times the flow of capital is from tightening countries to stimulating countries as long-term interest rates respond to fiscal policy. But against a background of widespread rising sustainability concerns, governments that loosen fiscal policy risk aggravating sustainability concerns, leading to speculations over a possible sharp depreciation of the currency as a consequence. While depreciation would usually aid in expansion, potential inflation pressures from depreciation and the likely monetary policy reaction could well swamp those benefits in the medium term if not immediately. Meanwhile, those economies that stick to fiscal tightening could find themselves facing additional capital inflows. Under the present circumstances, when investment demand is low and financial intermediation is impeded, the likely further decline in bond rates, let alone investment expansion, is limited; so the drag from currency appreciation is likely to dominate for the relatively austere. Thus, there is a likely asymmetry whereby diverging fiscal policies will frustrate both sides of the situation: The austere governments will be put upon by competitive depreciation, while the stimulating governments will see less benefit from their efforts.

Monetary divergence will have somewhat similar effects, though they will be more in line with the standard experience than for fiscal policy. In the situation where some central banks would undertake additional ease—almost certainly in the form of large-scale asset purchases—while others would be exiting monetary accommodation through interest rate increases, capital would again be expected to flow from the stimulating to the tightening currency areas.

This would abet the desired impact of policy on each side, so long as monetary ease did not lead to rising long-term interest rates. Such increases would be highly unlikely so long as the easing central banks were easing policy in the face of a low-inflation or deflationary forecast. The issues arising from the divergence would be the extent to which such movements led to overshooting when monetary control is limited at best, and again the likelihood that the trade effects on currency would dominate the interest rate effects on investment under present circumstances.

Risks of Protectionism

This scenario leads to the second concern about transatlantic divergence in macroeconomic policy: political reaction to perceived or actual competitive depreciation, and the potential for protectionism as a result. It must be noted that far fewer than expected protectionist policies were undertaken as a result of the crisis, particularly between the European Union and United States. The G-20 agreements to prevent such actions and the role of the World Trade Organization in ensuring discipline merit praise for this success. At the time we write this chapter, however, protectionist risks seem to be rising. So far, they have been more acute across the Pacific than the Atlantic (not that such a geography makes them more welcome), but the bilateral surpluses of Germany with other euro area countries and with the United States are also gaining political salience.

If macroeconomic policy divergence meant that the major European economies would engage in budget cuts while the United States embarked on another round of fiscal stimulus, or that the ECB withdrew accommodation while the Fed and BoE extended quantitative or credit easing, we could expect capital flows into the euro area, particularly into those large members whose budget situations were seen as most sustainable. Already some signs that this is happening are noticeable. Such capital flows could be seen as constructive, reducing imbalances and abetting the respective desired policy stances. Whether the actual impact and political response would be taken that way is another matter.

Impact on the Global Adjustment

As noted, the question of current account imbalances is global, not solely or even primarily transatlantic. The third consideration for the international effects of transatlantic macroeconomic policy differences, then, is the impact this might have on global adjustment. This is primarily a question of currency and trade relationships with China and the economies closely tied to it. For some years, the lack of decisive Chinese action to end the undervaluation of the renminbi has benefited from divisions between the United States and European Union. Whether offering contracts for Airbus and Boeing, power plants, or construction materials, or granting preferred access to domestic

Chinese markets, the Chinese government has played commercial interests in the West against each other. This strategy has made it more difficult to get a common front on the currency issue, on which Europe was slow to come to a common stance and to voice concerns to China. EU-US differences have also persisted on such matters as protection of intellectual property rights for technology, even though the transatlantic economies have largely common interests in these areas.

On the pure economics, the impact on trade balances of transatlantic macroeconomic policy divergence is unclear, depending as it does upon how the relative slowdown of the tightening countries affects trade flows versus the net export impact of the likely associated relative appreciation. Divergence in macroeconomic policies, however, is likely to worsen this political division for China to exploit, as the pressure will increase for elected governments to pursue bilateral trade deals (or to wink at Chinese encroachment on property rights) and to seek direct adjustment of the bilateral exchange rate.

Self-Fulfilling Prophecies

The final international concern arising from divergent macroeconomic policies is of a different nature. As we discussed in earlier sections, there is genuine reason to pursue different monetary and fiscal approaches in the major economies of the euro area and the United States, given the differences in economic pressures (arising from differences in household balance sheets and unemployment) and in policy approaches (arising from fiscal room and central bank mandates). These differences should not be exaggerated—the impact of the crisis on fiscal room and on potential supply lies somewhere between the stated positions on opposite sides of the Atlantic, and the deflationary pressures on both sides are not dissimilar. Yet there remains the real possibility that past recovery patterns from noncrisis recessions or less severe shocks are a poor predictor for what is to come now. In fact, there is arguably a risk that premature tightening or even insufficient macroeconomic stimulus could lock in subpotential growth for an extended period. This move could be self-fulfilling in perpetuating deflationary pressures and eroding potential growth (see Posen 2010a and references therein).

If such a risk is real, a transatlantic divergence that increases competitive pressures for near-term fiscal austerity, or ratifies underestimates of potential rates of growth and current output gaps, could be corrosive to long-term performance—and thus to both price stability and fiscal sustainability. Obvious transatlantic divisions in, if not public disputes over, the economic outlook and the rightness of other countries' policies could erode confidence and limit the effectiveness of the policies taken, particularly in their impact on investment. In essence, the policymakers in the European Union and United States have to make a judgment as to the relevance of the Great Depression, of Japan's lost decade, and of the previous experience of post–financial crisis periods to today (see Abiad et al. 2009, Meier 2010, Posen 2010b, and Reinhart and

Reinhart 2010, among others). The current policy discussion, particularly in the euro area, seems to underestimate the relevance of this parallel, and thus incurs risks from pursuing policy settings as though facing a normal recovery. The lesser degree of leverage and unemployment in the major euro area economies compared to the United States is undeniable (though the differences in financial sector fragility are not so great), but it is not clear that this situation constitutes a free pass from historical precedent, especially if other economies within the euro area and across the Atlantic are at risk.

A Quantum of Ongoing Coordination

Given our assessment of the reasons for transatlantic divergence in macroeconomic policies since the initial crisis response, we would suggest a few measures to maintain what could be termed a critical quantum of policy coordination. The point of a convoy is to get all the ships in the flotilla to their destinations safely, and our economies are not yet fully out of the dangerous open waters. Moreover, the respective destinations of the euro area, UK, and US economies are not as far apart as they are sometimes claimed to be at present, so the convoy keeping us together for a little while longer is at little cost.

- The euro area, United Kingdom, and United States should agree not to intervene unilaterally against one another's currencies, making explicit what is already understood, and avoid other policies geared toward large-scale depreciation of their own currencies. This agreement could be extended to the other major economies. The monitoring of the consistency of actual policies with this commitment should be delegated to the IMF, while the G-20 should serve as the venue for coordination.

- Comparative assessment of the fiscal room—including of potential growth—should be assigned to an independent multilateral assessor, like the IMF. Some framework akin to that we offered above should be the basis for the assessments.

- All countries should adopt and submit to their parliament medium-term fiscal consolidation objectives and guidelines that ensure the sustainability of public finances under prudent economic assumptions. In practice, this would imply adjustment mostly on the US side.

- The European Union and United States should agree that the Chinese undervaluation problem has to be dealt with in a multilateral framework but commit to undertaking joint action under the terms of such a framework, and thereby limit the ability of the Chinese government to play countries against one another for commercial gain.

We have little illusion, however, that these measures will be adopted in the near term. We rather fear that the longer policies diverge across the Atlantic, the more justified each policy stance will seem to its originators.

References

Abiad, A., R. Balakrishnan, P. Koeva Brooks, D. Leigh, and I. Tytell. 2009. *What's the Damage? Medium-Term Output Dynamics After Banking Crises*. IMF Working Paper WP/09/245 (November). Washington: International Monetary Fund.

BCBS (Basel Committee on Banking Supervision). 2010. *An Assessment of the Long-Term Economic Impact of Stronger Capital and Liquidity Requirements* (August). Basel.

Belke, Ansgar, and Thorsten Polleit. 2007. How the ECB and the US Fed Set Interest Rates. *Applied Economics* 39, no. 17 (September): 2197–209.

Bénassy-Quéré, Agnès, Benoît Coeuré, Pierre Jacquet, and Jean Pisani-Ferry. 2010. *Economic Policy: Theory and Practice*. Oxford University Press.

Blanchard, Olivier. 1984. Current and Anticipated Deficits, Interest Rates and Economic Activity. *European Economic Review* 25: 7–27.

Blanchard, Olivier. 1990. *Suggestions for a New Set of Fiscal Indicators*. OECD Economics Department Working Paper 79. Paris: Organization for Economic Cooperation and Development.

Bohn, Henning. 1998. The Behavior of U.S. Public Debt and Deficits. *Quarterly Journal of Economics* (August): 949–63.

CBO (Congressional Budget Office). 2010. *Economic and Budget Outlook* (August). Washington.

Cerra, Valerie, and Sweta Saxena. 2008. Growth Dynamics: The Myth of Economic Recovery. *American Economic Review* 98, no. 1: 439–57.

Cohen, Elie, and Jean Pisani-Ferry. 2007. Economic Institutions and Policies in the US and the EU: Convergence or Divergence? In *The European Economy in an American Mirror*, ed. B. Eichengreen, M. Landesmann, and D. Stiefel. London: Routledge.

Cottarelli, Carlo, and Andrea Schaechter. 2010. *Long-Term Trends in Public Finances in the G-7 Economies*. IMF Staff Position Note 10/13 (September). Washington: International Monetary Fund.

Darvas, Zsolt. 2009. *The EU's Role in Supporting Crisis-Hit Countries in Central and Eastern Europe*. Bruegel Policy Contribution 2009/17 (December). Brussels: Bruegel.

ECB (European Central Bank). 2010. Reinforcing Economic Governance in the Euro Area. Frankfurt. Photocopy (June 10).

European Commission. 2009. *Sustainability Report*. Brussels.

European Commission. 2010. *European Economic Forecast—Autumn 2010*. Brussels.

Gagnon, J., M. Raskin, J. Remache, and B. Sack. 2010. *Large-Scale Asset Purchases by the Federal Reserve: Did They Work?* Federal Reserve Bank of New York Staff Report 441. New York: Federal Reserve Bank of New York.

Horton, Mark, Manmohan Kumar, and Paolo Mauro. 2009. *The State of Public Finances: A Cross-Country Fiscal Monitor*. IMF Staff Position Note SPN/09/21 (July). Washington: International Monetary Fund.

IMF (International Monetary Fund). 2009. *The State of Public Finances Cross-Country Fiscal Monitor: November 2009*. IMF Staff Position Note SPN/09/25. Washington: International Monetary Fund.

IMF (International Monetary Fund). 2010. Unemployment Dynamics During Recessions and Recoveries: Okun's Law and Beyond. In *World Economic Outlook* (April). Washington.

Joyce, M., A. Lasaosa, I. Stevens, and M. Tong. 2010. *The Financial Market Impact of Quantitative Easing*. Bank of England Working Paper 393 (May). London: Bank of England.

Kuttner, Kenneth, and Adam Posen. 2009. Central Bank Independence: Conservative, Yes, but Causal? Paper presented at the ASSA Annual Meeting, San Francisco, January.

Meier, Andre. 2010. *Still Minding the Gap—Inflation Dynamics during Episodes of Persistent Large Output Gaps.* IMF Working Paper WP/10/189 (August). Washington: International Monetary Fund.

OECD (Organization for Economic Cooperation and Development). 2010. *The Impact of the Economic Crisis on Potential Output.* WP1 working document (February). Paris.

Ostry, Jonathan, Atish Gosh, Jun Kim, and Mahvash Qureshi. 2010. *Fiscal Space.* IMF Staff Position Note SPN/10/11 (September). Washington: International Monetary Fund.

Pisani-Ferry, Jean, and Adam Posen, eds. 2009. *The Euro at Ten: The Next Global Currency?* Washington and Brussels: Peterson Institute for International Economics and Bruegel.

Pisani-Ferry, Jean, and André Sapir. 2009. Euro Area: Ready for the Storm? In *The Euro at Ten: The Next Global Currency?* ed. Jean Pisani-Ferry and Adam S. Posen. Washington: Peterson Institute for International Economics and Bruegel.

Posen, Adam. 2010a. The Case for Doing More. Speech given to the Hull and Humber Chamber of Commerce, Industry, and Shipping, Hull, September 28.

Posen, Adam. 2010b. When Central Banks Buy Bonds: Independence and the Power to Say No. Speech given to Barclays Capital 14th Annual Global Inflation-Linked Conference, New York, June 14.

Reinhart, Carmen, and Vincent Reinhart. 2010. After the Fall. Paper presented at the conference "Macroeconomic Challenges: The Decade Ahead," Federal Reserve Bank of Kansas City, Jackson Hole, WY, August 26–28.

von Hagen, Jürgen. 2009. *Monetary Policy on the Way Out of the Crisis.* Bruegel Policy Contribution 2009/15 (December). Brussels: Bruegel.

von Weizsäcker, Jakob, and David Saha. 2009. *Estimating the Size of the European Stimulus Packages.* Bruegel Policy Contribution 2009/02 (April). Brussels: Bruegel.

Wilson, Daniel. 2010. *Is the Recent Productivity Boom Over?* FRBSF Economic Letter No. 2010/28 (September). San Francisco: Federal Reserve Bank of San Francisco.

Woodford, Michael. 2001. Fiscal Requirements for Price Stability. *Journal of Money, Credit and Banking* 33, no. 3 (August): 669–728.

3

US Climate Change Policy
Implementing the Copenhagen Accord and Beyond

WILLIAM R. CLINE

At the 15th Conference of Parties of the United Nations Framework Convention on Climate Change (UNFCCC), held in Copenhagen in December 2009, the United States and other major nations undertook a political commitment to meet certain targets for reducing greenhouse gas emissions by 2020. Although this Copenhagen Accord was not a legally binding treaty like the Kyoto Protocol, it arguably provides an important basis for moving forward on curbing global warming. Crucially, for the first time the accord incorporated action pledges by major emerging-market economies likely to be the largest sources of future increases in emissions.

The first section of this chapter reviews the Copenhagen Accord pledges of the United States and other major nations. It discusses findings of my recent analysis of costs of an international abatement strategy that meets 2020 Copenhagen targets and that then follows a path through 2050 consistent with limiting atmospheric concentrations of carbon dioxide to 450 parts per million (ppm) and limiting the amount of warming to two degrees Celsius. Alternative leading cost models are applied to calculate abatement costs of such a strategy. The second section then considers whether political gridlock in the United States is likely to derail fulfillment of the US Copenhagen Accord pledge, and in particular whether a second-best strategy based on Environmental Protection Agency (EPA) enforcement and regional climate initiatives can provide a strong initial substitute for climate legislation. The third section

William R. Cline has been a senior fellow at the Peterson Institute for International Economics since its inception in 1981. He thanks Yimei Zou for research assistance.

compares the EU and US Copenhagen pledges and considers mechanisms through which transatlantic cooperation can improve the effectiveness of abatement commitments.

Copenhagen Pledges and Abatement Costs

Table 3.1 reports the Copenhagen Accord pledges of 19 major economies.[1] Together, their total carbon dioxide emissions of 24.5 billion metric tons ($GtCO_2$) in 2007 constituted approximately 83 percent of the world total. The table highlights the importance of incorporating the major emerging-market economies into international abatement efforts. By 2007 carbon dioxide emissions (not counting those from deforestation) from 10 major emerging-market economies already were about 80 percent as large as those of 9 major Annex I economies; in the business as usual (bau) baseline paths, these emerging-market economies' emissions would far surpass those of the Annex I countries. So the Copenhagen Accord lays at least the initial groundwork for overcoming the single largest problem of the Kyoto Protocol: its omission of developing countries from any abatement efforts. This being said, it should be noted that typically the submissions of the emerging-market economies to the Copenhagen Accord were couched in language that made reference to prior UNFCCC clauses pertaining to finance and technological transfer to facilitate abatement.

Based primarily on projections by the Energy Information Agency of the US Department of Energy (EIA 2009), I have estimated bau global emissions of carbon dioxide in 2020 at 35.9 $GtCO_2$, or 22 percent above the 2007 level. If the Copenhagen Accord goals of the 19 economies listed in table 3.1 are achieved, the result would be to cut global emissions to 32.7 $GtCO_2$ in 2020, a reduction of 9.1 percent from the bau level but still an increase of 11 percent above the 2007 level. Clearly this reduction would be far from sufficient to limit eventual atmospheric concentrations to 450 ppm or warming to two degrees Celsius, but this outcome would "bend the curve" of increases and could provide a key turning point for subsequent global reductions.

It is important to emphasize, nonetheless, that the pledges of the emerging-market economies are more ambiguous than those of the industrial countries. It turns out that China and India in particular have made pledges that essentially amount to no departure from business as usual. In China, the energy efficiency of output (units of real GDP per unit of energy) grew at 4.8 percent per year in 1990–2006; the carbon efficiency of energy (units of energy per unit of carbon dioxide emissions) deteriorated with a growth rate of –0.9 percent per year; so the carbon efficiency of output (units of GDP per unit of carbon dioxide) grew at the combined impact of 3.9 percent per year. In its bau baseline, the Energy Information Agency projects that for 2010–20 China's energy efficiency of output would grow at 3.6 percent and its carbon efficiency of energy at 0.5 percent,

---

1. Unless otherwise specified, all estimates and calculations in this section are from Cline (2011).

Table 3.1   Copenhagen Accord pledges for reductions in CO_2 emissions

Country	2007 level[a] (million tons of CO_2)	Reduction by 2020[b]
Annex I	13,721	
United States	5,812	17 percent from 2005; 83 percent by 2050
European Union	4,050	20 percent from 1990 (30 percent contingent); 80 percent by 2050
Russia	1,585	15 to 25 percent from 1990
Japan	1,236	25 percent from 1990 (contingent)
Canada	530	Same as the United States
Australia	377	5 percent (15 or 25 percent contingent) from 2000
New Zealand, Norway, and Switzerland	131	10 to 20 percent, 30 to 40 percent, 20 to 30 percent from 1990, respectively
Non-Annex I	10,816	
China	6,603	40 to 45 percent cut in carbon intensity of GDP from 2005 level
India	1,574	20 to 25 percent cut in carbon intensity of GDP from 2005 level
Korea	477	30 percent cut from bau
Mexico	445	30 percent cut from bau
South Africa	434	34 percent cut from bau
Indonesia	416	26 percent cut from bau
Brazil	352	36 to 39 percent cut from bau
Kazakhstan	195	15 percent from 1992
Argentina	172	No specific target; energy efficiency measures, support for renewable energy
Singapore	148	16 percent cut from bau
Total	24,537	

bau = business as usual

a. Excludes deforestation.
b. bau refers to business as usual baseline level by 2020.

Source: Cline (2011).

once again leaving the carbon efficiency of GDP to grow at about 4 percent, even though there is a modest shift toward less ambitious growth in energy efficiency, with some shift toward favorable rather than unfavorable carbon composition of energy. At an annual rise in carbon efficiency of output of 4.1 percent, over the 15 years from 2005 to 2020 the bau baseline would reduce the carbon emissions per unit of GDP by 45 percent. This is just what China pledged in the Copenhagen Accord, suggesting that its effort is not a departure from business as usual. A similar calculation for India yields a similar conclusion. Perhaps the most important implication of the pledges by China and India, then, is not that they will contribute to a substantial cutback in their own emissions from business as usual, but rather that their commitments will place limits on any "carbon leakage" that might otherwise occur through increased production of carbon-intensive products following the curbing of these products in Annex I countries (and other emerging-market economies) that have pledged more aggressive cuts.

In principle, the pledges of several other major emerging-market economies are more ambitious than those of China and India. Brazil, Korea, Indonesia, Mexico, and South Africa have all pledged cutbacks from the bau baseline of about 30 percent or more by 2020. Even so, the ambiguity about what the bau baseline would have been implies future uncertainty about whether the pledge has been fulfilled.

For a meaningful path of global abatement consistent with eventual avoidance of greater than 450 ppm carbon dioxide concentration or warming by more than two degrees Celsius, after 2020 there would need to be aggressive, steady reductions in emissions by both industrial countries and most developing countries. I have calculated that subsequent to 2020, a straight-line reduction in emissions to reach a per capita ceiling of 1.43 tons of CO_2 (tCO_2) by 2050 would be necessary to meet these goals. The current levels are about 20 metric tons per capita (i.e., more than 10 times the eventual ceiling) in the United States, 8 tons in the European Union, 10 in Japan, and 5 in China (but only 1.4 in India). A uniform per capita target by 2050 following achievement of the 2020 pledges, in what can be called a "Copenhagen Convergence" strategy, would have the moral strength of appealing to equity. The industrial countries will be in a much better position to ask China in particular to cut its emissions per capita by about three-fourths from its prospective 2020 peak of 6.7 tons if they themselves commit to future emissions that are no greater per capita than those of China, India, and other emerging-market economies.

For the 13 largest emitting economies, table 3.2 reports the proportionate cutbacks from bau baselines that would be required to meet the Copenhagen Convergence, or CopCon, policy path for carbon dioxide abatement. The table also shows global emissions in the bau baseline, under CopCon, and the depth of corresponding cutbacks.

Globally, emissions cuts from the bau baseline would need to reach 75 percent by 2050. The depth of cutbacks is not only large but also, for some key emerging-market economies, surprisingly similar to that required of industrial countries. Thus, by 2050, cutbacks from baseline are about 85 to 90 percent not only for the United States, the European Union, Russia, Japan, Canada, and Australia, but also for China, Korea, and South Africa. India starts from such low per capita emissions that its proportionate cutbacks by 2050 are only about one-fourth. Other emerging-market economies are intermediate, with cutbacks of about 60 to 70 percent for Indonesia, Brazil, and Mexico.

For China, the absence of any cutbacks from baseline by 2020 means a more abrupt cutback from baseline by 2030 (a jump from zero to 39 percent). This suggests that Chinese planners might consider the merits of advancing cutbacks more aggressively than currently implied by the Copenhagen Accord pledge.

In Cline (2011) I estimate synthesis abatement cost functions for major economies using the results of the Energy Modeling Forum (EMF) survey

Table 3.2   Carbon dioxide abatement under Copenhagen Convergence scenario (percent cutback from bau baseline)

Country	2020	2030	2040	2050
United States	17	40	65	91
European Union	17	41	63	84
Russia	7	40	68	92
Japan	30	50	69	87
Canada	23	47	70	92
Australia	26	48	69	91
China	0	39	68	88
India	0	10	19	27
Korea	30	54	74	91
Mexico	30	46	60	72
South Africa	34	57	76	91
Indonesia	26	38	49	57
Brazil	24	39	51	61
Memorandum: World				
bau emissions ($GtCO_2$)	35.9	41.4	47.1	53.2
Copenhagen Convergence ($GtCO_2$)	32.7	26.8	20.3	13.3
Cut from bau (percent)	9.1	35.2	57.0	75.0

bau = business as usual
$GtCO_2$ = billion tons of CO_2

Source: Cline (2011).

of integrated assessment model results (Clarke et al. 2009). Alternative cost functions are available from the Nordhaus (2010) RICE model (Regional Integrated Model of Climate and the Economy), and for 2030, from cost functions based on McKinsey (2009) estimates.[2] Table 3.3 shows the abatement cost estimates for major economies in 2020 and 2030 that these three cost models arrive at when applied to the CopCon abatement scenario. The table also shows the corresponding marginal abatement costs per ton of CO_2 for two of the three models.

The most important overall implication of table 3.3 is that abatement costs should be manageable for the key emitting economies, certainly through the 2020 Copenhagen targets but also even by 2030, as aggressive cuts are implemented in the convergence path. The lowest costs are those from the McKinsey-based model, which for example indicates that the 40 percent cut from baseline in both the United States and the European Union in 2030 would cost only about 0.1 percent of GDP. An intermediate estimate of 0.23 percent of GDP is obtained in the RICE model. The synthesis models estimated from the EMF survey show considerably higher costs, but these are still only about 0.5 percent of GDP in 2020 for the industrial countries and about 1.5 percent for emerging-market economies (excluding China and India). The higher costs for five emerging-market economies reflect the fact that their Copenhagen

---

2. However, the initial negative-cost section of the McKinsey cost curves is suppressed to zero cost.

Table 3.3 Abatement costs for the Copenhagen Convergence scenario, 2020 and 2030 (percent of GDP and 2005 dollars per tCO_2)

| Country | Abatement cost (percent of GDP) | | | | | Marginal cost (2005 dollars per tCO_2) | | | |
| | RICE | | EMF | | McKinsey | RICE | | EMF | |
	2020	2030	2020	2030	2030	2020	2030	2020	2030
United States	0.02	0.23	0.29	1.18	0.07	12	58	83	166
European Union	0.03	0.23	0.27	0.80	0.12	17	76	81	121
Russia	0.00	0.27	0.17	2.44	0.07	2	44	70	221
Japan	0.17	0.55	0.55	1.14	0.17	55	118	95	127
Canada	0.08	0.46	0.36	1.04	0.28	24	83	60	97
Australia	0.11	0.48	0.44	1.06	0.26	31	92	64	106
China	0	0.36	0	2.42	0.12	0	57	0	188
India	0	0.01	0	0.25	0	0	9	0	159
Korea	0.16	0.70	1.69	3.9	0.09	52	147	272	414
Mexico	0.13	0.37	1.69	3.11	0.08	59	128	378	543
South Africa	0.20	0.69	2.01	4.19	1.08	19	39	96	119
Indonesia	0.16	0.39	1.38	2.39	0.08	54	98	232	306
Brazil	0.07	0.22	1.14	2.36	0.09	47	105	410	603

tCO_2 = tons of CO_2
RICE = Regional Integrated Model of Climate and the Economy
EMF = Energy Modeling Forum

Source: Cline (2011), based on Clarke et al. (2009), Nordhaus (2010), and McKinsey (2009).

pledges amount to greater proportional cutbacks from baseline emissions than those of the industrial countries (except for Japan; see table 3.2).[3]

Table 3.3 also reports the marginal abatement costs for the RICE and EMF-based models. Somewhat surprisingly these tend to be higher for the emerging-market economies than for the industrial countries, again reflecting the more ambitious pledges for 2020. The surge in marginal cost from 2020 to 2030 especially for China (and particularly in the EMF-based estimates) suggests scope for gains from reallocating cutbacks to earlier in the horizon, with cuts already in 2020. An implication of the pattern of marginal abatement costs is that there may be less scope than popularly believed for reducing abatement costs in industrial countries through purchase of offsets from developing countries.[4]

3. Note, however, that the EMF-based estimates probably overstate the abatement costs for these economies, especially by 2030. An alternative estimate also based on a synthesis of the EMF results, but allowing for trading at the international carbon price, places the CopCon abatement costs by 2030 at 1.22 percent of GDP for China, 1.07 percent for Korea, 0.67 percent for Mexico, 2.79 percent for South Africa, 0.85 percent for Indonesia, and 0.50 percent for Brazil, much lower than the EMF-based estimates reported in table 3.3.

4. Purchase of offsets involves purchase of emissions rights from developing countries that otherwise they would use themselves, or arrangements that seek to accomplish this effect in the absence of a formal international emissions rights regime.

Prospects for Action in the United States

The passage of the Waxman-Markey energy and climate bill in the US House of Representatives in June 2009 turns out to have been the likely high-water mark for US climate action for at least some time. The bill sought to reduce greenhouse gas emissions by 17 percent from 2005 levels by 2020 (equivalent to a reduction back to the 1990 level), 42 percent by 2030, and 83 percent by 2050 (equivalent to an 80 percent cut from 1990 levels). A cap-and-trade regime was initially to allocate 85 percent of emissions permits without cost to existing electricity distribution companies, energy-intensive industries, and other emitting sectors, with the portion of permits auctioned rising from the initial 15 percent to 70 percent by 2030. Auction revenues were to be used to offset additional costs for low-income households, and eventually to be used for funding of international aid, forestation, and technology related to climate change action. The bill set a minimum carbon price for permits at $10 per ton of CO_2; the Environmental Protection Agency projected a range of $11 to $15 by 2012 and $22 to $28 by 2025 (in 2005 dollars). The bill provided that 20 percent of electricity would be from renewable sources by 2020 and that new coal-fired plants would capture 50 percent of emissions with carbon capture and sequestration by 2025; it also called for building standards that required a 50 percent increase in efficiency by 2016 and included other regulatory measures. By 2022, the president was authorized to require emissions allowances on imports.

The Congressional Budget Office (CBO) estimated that the bill would reduce US GDP from baseline by 0.2 to 0.6 percent of GDP by 2020, 0.3 to 1.2 percent by 2030, and 1 to 3.5 percent by 2050. It placed the price of emissions allowances at $19 per metric ton of CO_2 in 2015, $25 in 2020, $40 in 2030, and $120 by 2050 (in 2009 dollars). The CBO emphasized that a key factor in curbing abatement costs was the flexibility in the bill to achieve up to 2 $GtCO_2$-equivalent of annual reductions through the use of offsets, amounting to about half of the reductions planned through 2030 (CBO 2009).

Two principal attempts were made toward parallel action in the Senate. The Kerry-Boxer bill, a cap-and-trade proposal similar to Waxman-Markey, passed a key committee in November 2009 despite a Republican boycott, but was subsequently abandoned. Senator John Kerry then sought to develop a bill with Senators Lindsay Graham and Joseph Lieberman that applied less comprehensive and less stringent caps, combined with a carbon tax for some sectors (oil, gasoline) (Tutwiler 2010). But in July 2010, Senate Majority Leader Harry Reid announced he would not bring a compromise bill to the floor. In effect, the concentration of legislative effort on health care reform and then on financial sector regulation, combined with increasing partisan gridlock in especially the Senate, doomed the prospects for legislation on climate action, at least in 2010.

All of the legislative proposals had included a strong incentive to persuade opponents that cooperation would be advisable: The legislation would preempt regulatory controls on greenhouse gases that otherwise might be imposed by the Environmental Protection Agency. In 2007 the US Supreme Court ruled that greenhouse gases constituted "air pollutants" that were subject to regulation by the EPA. In late 2009 the EPA formally made a finding of "endangerment," meaning that greenhouse gases were understood to threaten public health and welfare, a condition for action.[5] Now that legislative initiatives on climate have stalled, the role of the EPA shifts at least potentially from being the club in the closet to becoming the front-line mechanism for implementing the Copenhagen pledge. Ideally the legislative track would regain momentum following the November 2010 midterm elections, and something like the Waxman-Markey bill would become law within the next year or two. However, few observers seem to be optimistic about legislative action within this time frame.

"Plan B" for US climate action does not depend solely on the EPA. There are three regional initiatives at the state level that seek to limit greenhouse gas emissions (see appendix 3A). Researchers at the World Resources Institute have compiled estimates of emissions reductions that might be attained under low, medium, and high levels of intensity of action at the federal and state levels, considering both EPA enforcement and the regional initiatives at the state level (Bianco and Litz 2010).[6] In the area of electric power, which accounts for 28 percent of US emissions in the case of coal-fired plants and another 5 percent for natural gas–fired, the EPA has scope for action under the New Source Performance Standards and preconstruction permits, ash disposal regulations, and traditional air regulations (also subject to state action). The Department of Energy and states can act under energy efficiency standards. For emissions from vehicles, with light-duty vehicles accounting for 16 percent of total US greenhouse gas emissions and medium- and heavy-duty vehicles another 8 percent, regulations apply under the Corporate Average Fuel Efficiency (CAFE) standards of the Department of Transportation, emissions standards under the Clean Air Act (EPA), renewable or low-carbon standards (EPA), and miles traveled policies (states and cities). For light vehicles, the World Resources Institute study assumes CAFE standards of 40 miles per gallon by 2030 in the low case, ranging to 51 mpg in the high case.

At the state level, the study considers existing legislation, additional action under existing gubernatorial executive orders on emissions reduction targets, and additional cap-and-trade action within the regional programs as the three levels of intensity of action. Regarding the regional programs, there are three existing initiatives: the Regional Greenhouse Gas Initiative (RGGI) of 10 northeastern states; the Western Climate Initiative (WCI), encompassing California and 6 other states as well as 4 Canadian provinces; and the Midwestern Greenhouse Gas Reduction Accord (MGGRA), with 6 member states.

---

5. Environmental Protection Agency, "EPA: Greenhouse Gases Threaten Public Health and the Environment," press release, Washington, December 7, 2009.

6. The three scenarios are "lackluster," "middle-of-the-road," and "go-getter," in their terminology.

Together the three initiatives include states that account for about 40 percent of US emissions (Bianco and Litz 2010, 18).[7]

Overall, the study judges that for the low level of ambition, federal and state action would reduce greenhouse gas emissions by 6 percent below 2005 levels by 2020 (and by 5 percent below by 2030); the corresponding intermediate action cuts would reduce emissions by 9 percent by 2020 (18 percent by 2030); the high-intensity level of action would achieve cuts of 14 percent by 2020 (and 27 percent by 2030). About 80 percent or more of the reductions would be attributable to action at the federal level, with the rest occurring from additional state-level action. The upper end of the cutbacks is reasonably close to the US Copenhagen target of a 17 percent cutback from 2005 levels by 2020. A key issue, however, is whether the political obstacles that have hindered federal legislation would impede aggressive action using existing regulatory authority. Some senators have already proposed legislation that would limit or postpone the EPA's authority to regulate emissions of greenhouse gases.

Implications for US-EU Cooperation

The European Union has long taken the lead on international action to limit global warming. Until recent months it seemed that the United States had finally joined in this effort in earnest. Public attitudes had shifted in favor of action, perhaps in part because of Hurricane Katrina.[8] In the 2008 presidential election, both candidates called for action to curb global warming. Despite the financial crisis and Great Recession, as recently as May 2009 a survey commissioned by Pew Charitable Trusts (2009) found that 77 percent of voters favored action to reduce greenhouse gas emissions.[9]

A major political challenge for moving ahead in the United States will be to reengage the climate issue on a bipartisan basis. The dynamics of massive legislative change in 2010, marked by health care reform and financial regulatory reform, became heavily partisan, turning on the ability to muster the 60 votes in the Senate needed to stop a filibuster. Addressing climate change is such a central and long-term issue that it will likely need to marshal wide

---

7. In Canada, the four provinces constitute almost 80 percent of population and GDP (WCI 2010).

8. A global poll in the fall of 2004 found that 58 percent of Americans surveyed considered violent storms, flooding, and drought to be "part of a natural pattern"; the same question asked in 2006 found only 39 percent giving the same response, and 59 percent viewing them as unusual—a change that boosted the US response to the global average (World Public Opinion 2006).

9. Even so, another Pew survey found that out of 20 issues viewed by Americans as "top priorities," such as the economy, terrorism, immigration, and so forth, dealing with global warming slipped from being a top priority for 38 percent in January 2007 to being a top priority for 30 percent in January 2009, whereas strengthening the economy rose from 68 percent to 85 percent (Pew Research Center 2009).

congressional support rather than being forced through with one party heavily in opposition. This could be especially so because several senators from the majority party represent coal and industrial states and might not support a closure vote.

Even before the recent setbacks to climate action by the United States, many in Europe had thought that the US goals in the Waxman-Markey legislation were inadequate and not comparable to the efforts the European Union had made in the past and planned to make in the future. Such doubts were based primarily on the grounds that whereas the European Union sought a goal of reducing emissions 20 percent below the 1990 level by 2020 (and possibly 30 percent if other nations were ambitious in their goals), the US goal of 17 percent below 2005 levels only amounted to a reduction back to the 1990 level. EU carbon dioxide emissions (excluding those from deforestation) were 4.20 $GtCO_2$ in 1990; US emissions were 4.87 $GtCO_2$. By 2007, EU emissions had fallen by 3.6 percent to 4.05 $GtCO_2$, whereas US emissions had risen by 19.3 percent to 5.81 $GtCO_2$.[10]

A major difference in population growth accounts for part of this difference in past performance. From 1990 to 2007, EU population rose only 3.8 percent; US population rose 20.4 percent. In terms of percentage change, then, the per capita comparison shows the United States in a less unfavorable light than the change for total emissions, as the decline of 0.9 percent in US per capita emissions from 1990 to 2007 was considerably closer to the EU performance of a 7 percent per capita decline (a gap of six percentage points) than the 23 percentage point gap in the change in total emissions.

A second consideration is that the abatement performance of the European Union was to some extent exaggerated by developments peculiar to Eastern European members, which experienced sharp reductions in emissions associated with economic reform and the phasing out of highly inefficient energy production facilities. Thus, for the core 15 countries that were initial EU members, carbon dioxide emissions rose by 4.7 percent from 1990 to 2006; it was for the 12 countries that subsequently joined the European Union that emissions declined, by 24.4 percent.[11]

Perceptions about mutual performance are also affected by a popular if misleading impression in the United States that the European Union's Emissions Trading System (ETS) had been a failure—because overissuance of permits led to a collapse of the carbon price to zero in 2007 (CCC 2008). On the other side, a reasonable impression for EU citizens would be that the United States has been a serious laggard on climate change, not only because it failed to join the Kyoto Protocol but also because its emissions are so much higher per capita than those in Europe. In 2007, per capita emissions in the United States amounted to 19.3 tCO_2, more than twice the 8.3 tCO_2 per capita in the European Union (Cline 2011). However, it turns out that the difference

---

10. Unless otherwise specified, data cited in this section once again are from Cline (2011).

11. Calculations are from Carbon Analysis Indicators Tool, 2010, http://cait.wri.org.

Figure 3.1 CO_2 emissions per capita and purchasing power parity GDP per capita, 2007

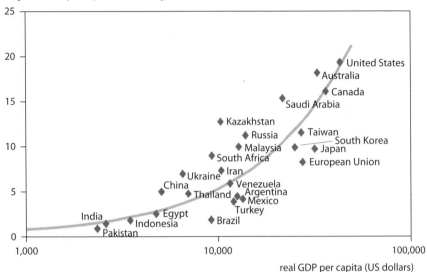

CO_2 emissions per capita (tons of CO_2)

Source: Cline (2011).

between the two is partly explained by per capita income, considering that for the European Union as a whole per capita income (in purchasing power parity [PPP] terms) is considerably lower than in the United States because the European Union includes several Eastern European economies. Average per capita income was approximately $27,500 for the European Union in 2007 versus $43,100 for the United States, in 2005 PPP dollars). Thus, whereas per capita GDP in the EU-15 core of original members at about $32,000 is considerably closer to US per capita income, for the EU-12 group of new members per capita GDP is only about half as high.[12]

For the 25 largest emitting economies, for 2007, a simple regression of the logarithm of emissions per capita on the logarithm of PPP GDP per capita yields a relationship that places the United States almost exactly on the cross-country curve but shows the European Union considerably below it (figure 3.1).[13] The divergence of US and EU emissions per capita can then be decom-

---

12. Comparisons are calculated from World Bank, *World Development Indicators* Database, 2010, http://databank.worldbank.org.

13. For 25 major economies, a regression of the natural logarithm of emissions per capita (EPC), metric tons CO_2 per year on the natural logarithm of PPP per capita income (y, 2005 dollars) yields the following results, for 2007: ln (EPC) = –6.3069 (–5.8) + 0.8664 (7.5) ln y, adjusted R^2 = 0.70, t-statistics in parentheses. Data are from Cline (2011).

posed into two parts: the amount that can be attributed to the fact that the US has higher per capita GDP, and the amount that can be explained by the departure of each economy from the cross-country line. US emissions per capita would be expected to be 48 percent higher than those of the European Union because of higher per capita income. In addition, it turns out that the US emissions per capita were 2.1 percent above the cross-country curve, whereas EU emissions per capita were 36 percent below it. The European Union does have well-above-average efficiency of emissions performance, then, but its superiority to the United States for this measure is much more moderate than would be suspected by a raw comparison of the absolute levels of emissions per capita for the two economies.

Of the other economies shown in the figure, notable departures from the cross-country curve occur in the case of China's high emissions per capita, and Brazil's low emissions (but excluding deforestation). Notably, India's low emissions are explained by low per capita GDP rather than a departure from the cross-country line.

To recapitulate, despite the various qualifications concerning the extent to which the European Union has led and the United States lagged in the international effort to curb global warming, there is little doubt that to at least some degree the European Union has been ahead in this effort. Even so, the US commitment in the Copenhagen Accord marks a major advance over what the United States has done in the past, and it is in both economies' interest to maximize the chances that the United States, the European Union, and other economies actually deliver on the accord pledges going forward. What steps could the European Union and United States take to help ensure this outcome?

One area for possible US-EU cooperation would be in the harmonization of their cap-and-trade systems to allow for trading emissions permits between the two economies. It would be extremely helpful for international progress on abatement if there were a predominant world price on carbon dioxide. Such a price would not only help ensure least-cost abatement but would also be a spur to technological change by sending a strong signal about the likelihood of the future opportunity cost of carbon-based energy. If the United States were to adopt legislation similar to the Waxman-Markey bill, then there is no reason that the trading of emissions allowances could not be made available to potential purchasers from within the European Union's ETS, and vice versa. Mutual eligibility for trading in the two economies' cap-and-trade regimes would go a long way toward establishing *the* world price on carbon dioxide emissions.

The marginal cost estimates in table 3.3 suggest that in principle carbon prices could be broadly comparable in the European Union and the United States in 2020 and 2030. The RICE model is more nonlinear than the synthesis used in the EMF model survey, and the RICE marginal costs are only about $15 per metric ton of CO_2 in 2020 versus about $80 in the EMF models. But in both models the two regions show relatively similar marginal costs. In part this outcome reflects the fact that the European Union and United States have the same estimated cutback from baseline in 2020 (17 percent), as the RICE and EMF-based models both calibrate cost as a function of the depth of emissions cut from baseline.

A similar marginal cost in the European Union and United States could be interpreted as having two alternative implications for trading. The first might be that trading would not accomplish much because neither economy would benefit much from buying or selling permits to the other. The second, which I prefer, is that trading could be allowed without much fear on either side that there would be a severe dislocation domestically as a consequence of large trading operations, yet the availability of trading would strongly enhance the market perception that there was a single world price for carbon. Moreover, there has been sufficient experience with sharply fluctuating prices within the ETS that a much broader market—one that included the United States—would seem desirable to smooth out prices.

At present it might be feared by some in Europe that the US efforts would be so meager, and overallowances so great, that permit trading would simply weaken the overall abatement effort that otherwise would be accomplished under the European Union's leadership. If those in the United States (for example, in regional trading initiatives) shared this expectation, they might similarly be concerned for the opposite reason: that openness to trading would drive up the cost of local abatement. Indeed, if one were to look at today's spot prices for the only relevant trading information, one would conclude that a large price divergence would be likely to realize such fears. Thus, as of early September the ETS trading price for December 2010 was €15 per ton of CO_2, whereas the price in the RGGI auctions was $1.86, only about one-tenth as much.[14] However, in the relevant time period—that is, the third trading period for the ETS beginning in 2013 (the first was 2005-07; the second covers 2008-12)—and a comparable period in the United States, it seems highly likely that the EU price level will be at least modestly higher than presently and the US price will be much higher than the current RGGI level.[15] That would be especially true if either the EPA were to move forcefully ahead and were to use trading mechanisms, as it has done in past abatement initiatives (especially for sulfur dioxide), or, preferably, if Congress were to pass a comprehensive climate bill that implemented either cap and trade (as in Waxman-Markey) or adopted a carbon tax of some form. In principle the regional initiatives could also make their trading regimes open to trading with the European Union's ETS, as was envisioned in mid-2006 in a letter-of-intent agreement between UK Prime Minister Tony Blair and California Governor Arnold Schwarzenegger.[16] However, the EPA would probably need to cooperate, rather than op-

---

14. See www.pointcarbon.com and www.rggi.org/home.

15. As noted above, the CBO estimates the carbon allowance price under Waxman-Markey at $19 per ton of CO_2 by 2015.

16. Patrick Wintour, "Blair Signs Climate Pact with Schwarzenegger," *Guardian*, August 1, 2006.

posing such initiatives on grounds that any such arrangements should be controlled at the federal level.

Besides integrating their cap-and-trade regimes through permitting mutual carbon trading, and first and foremost meeting their own 2020 goals pledged at Copenhagen, perhaps the other most important action the United States and the European Union could take to help ensure successful international action on climate change would be to develop concrete plans for implementing the target for financing of developing-country climate action on something like the Copenhagen Accord's scale of $100 billion per year by 2020. China's huge holdings of foreign exchange reserves (about $2.5 trillion) mean that it should be able to act without external finance. For other developing countries, in Cline (2011), I estimate that annual investments in developing countries needed to meet Copenhagen Convergence abatement goals would amount to about $40 billion annually in 2020 and $120 billion in 2030 (in 2005 dollars). Adaptation costs in developing countries (excluding not only China but also Korea, Malaysia, and Taiwan by virtue of their by-then high income levels) could require financing of about $40 billion in 2020 and $50 billion in 2030. Even with only moderate global financial flows associated with the purchase of offsets from developing countries, by 2020 and especially 2030 the financing needs could easily meet the $100 billion benchmark incorporated in the Copenhagen Accord language. Presumably such financing could be at market-related rates for emerging-market economies but on concessional terms for low-income countries.

Appendix 3A
US Regional Climate Initiatives[17]

Currently there are three regional climate initiatives at the interstate level encompassing a total of 23 US states and 4 Canadian provinces. All three initiatives have announced goals for the next decade of reducing greenhouse gas emissions and intend to implement regional cap-and-trade programs to achieve these goals. Among the three initiatives, the Regional Greenhouse Gas Initiative is the only one that has already begun operating its regional cap-and-trade program. The Western Climate Initiative has completed the design of its cap-and-trade program, which is scheduled to start in January 2012. The Midwest Greenhouse Gas Reduction Accord, the newest initiative, is still in the stage of designing its cap-and-trade program.

Regional Greenhouse Gas Initiative

The member states of RGGI include Connecticut, Delaware, Maine, Maryland, Massachusetts, New Hampshire, New Jersey, New York, Rhode Island, and Vermont. In addition, Pennsylvania has observer status. In January 2009, RGGI launched its regional carbon dioxide cap-and-trade program, which became the nation's first mandatory market-based program to curb emissions of greenhouse gases.[18] The program currently covers 209 fossil fuel–fired power plants of 25 megawatts or greater in capacity in the 10 participating states, accounting for 95 percent of the carbon dioxide emissions from the electric power generation sector in the area.

Total carbon dioxide emissions from RGGI member states are capped by the sum of carbon dioxide allowances issued by the 10 states, which is initially set at 188 million short tons per year.[19] This ceiling applies from 2009 through 2014. From 2015 through 2018, the cap will decline at an annual rate of 2.5 percent, achieving a total four-year reduction of 10 percent.

Carbon dioxide allowances are traded through quarterly regional auctions.[20] According to the 2009 *Annual Report on the Market for RGGI CO₂ Allowances,* by the end of 2009, 172 million allowances had been sold in total, which yielded auction proceeds of $494 million (Potomac Economics 2010). RGGI states are investing approximately 70 percent of auction proceeds in programs that improve energy efficiency and promote renewable energy.

---

17. The appendix was prepared by Yimei Zou.

18. For an overview of the program, see the organization's website, www.rggi.org.

19. A short ton equals 907.2 kg.

20. Detailed auction data and carbon dioxide allowance prices are available on the RGGI website, www.rggi.org.

Western Climate Initiative

Member states of the WCI include Arizona, California, Montana, New Mexico, Oregon, Utah, and Washington, as well as four Canadian provinces: British Columbia, Manitoba, Ontario, and Quebec. Observer states include Colorado, Idaho, Kansas, Nevada, and Wyoming.

The WCI released the design of its regional greenhouse gases cap-and-trade program in July 2010.[21] The program is scheduled to start in January 2012, although not all members will implement the program when it begins. The goal of the program is to cut regional greenhouse gas emissions to 15 percent below 2005 levels by 2020. When fully implemented, the program is projected to cover a broad range of emitters jointly responsible for approximately 90 percent of greenhouse gas emissions in the WCI participating region.

Each state is to issue limited amounts of tradable "emission allowances" that are to follow these guidelines: Starting in 2012, allowances will apply only to the electricity sector and large industrial sources. Each state's allowance ceiling is to be the best estimate of actual emissions anticipated from the covered emitters for that year. In 2015, allowance ceilings are to rise to provide for expansion of coverage to transportation, residential, and commercial fuels. For 2020, allowance ceilings are to be set for each state such that, together with emissions from uncapped sources, they will amount to the state's 2020 economywide emissions target. The allowance budgets are to follow a linear decline from 2012 to 2015, and again from 2015 to 2020.

Midwestern Greenhouse Gas Reduction Accord

Member states of the MGGRA include Illinois, Iowa, Kansas, Michigan, Minnesota, and Wisconsin. States with observer status include Indiana, Ohio, and South Dakota.

The MGGRA, established in November 2007, calls for the development of targets for greenhouse gas emissions and a regional cap-and-trade program to help achieve these targets. The cap-and-trade recommendations were completed in May 2010 and are now under review by the member states.[22] The recommended emissions reduction targets for individual states were set at 18 to 20 percent below 2005 levels by 2020, and 80 percent below 2005 levels by 2050.

---

21. For the design of the program, see the WCI website, www.westernclimateinitiative.org.

22. Full recommendations are available on the organization's website, www.midwesternaccord. org.

References

Bianco, Nicholas M., and Franz T. Litz. 2010. *Reducing Greenhouse Gas Emissions in the United States Using Existing Federal Authorities and State Action.* Washington: World Resources Institute. Available at www.wri.org (accessed on January 15, 2012).

CBO (Congressional Budget Office). 2009. *The Costs of Reducing Greenhouse-Gas Emissions.* Washington.

CCC (Committee on Climate Change). 2008. *Building a Low Carbon Economy: The U.K.'s Contribution to Tackling Climate Change.* London.

Clarke, Leon, Jae Edmonds, Volker Krey, Richard Richels, Steven Rose, and Massimo Tavoni. 2009. International Climate Policy Architectures: Overview of the EMF 22 International Scenarios. *Energy Economics* 31: S64–S81.

Cline, William R. 2011. *Carbon Abatement Costs and Climate Change Finance.* Policy Analyses in International Economics 96. Washington: Peterson Institute for International Economics.

EIA (Energy Information Administration). 2009. *International Energy Outlook 2009.* DOE/EIA-0484(2009). Washington.

McKinsey. 2009. *Pathways to a Low-Carbon Economy: Version 2 of the Global Greenhouse Gas Abatement Cost Curve.* New York: McKinsey & Company. Available at https://solutions.mckinsey.com. (accessed on March 19, 2012).

Nordhaus, William. 2010. RICE-2010 Model (May). Yale University, New Haven, CT. Available at http://nordhaus.econ.yale.edu/RICEmodels.htm (accessed on January 15, 2012).

Pew Charitable Trusts. 2009. Voters Support Congressional Action on Comprehensive Energy and Global Warming Legislation (May 14). Available at www.pewtrusts.org (accessed on January 15, 2012).

Pew Research Center. 2009. Economy, Jobs Trump All Other Policy Priorities in 2009 (January 22). Available at http://people-press.org (accessed on January 15, 2012).

Potomac Economics. 2010. *Annual Report on the Market for RGGI CO$_2$ Allowances: 2009.* Regional Greenhouse Gas Initiative. Available at www.rggi.org (accessed on January 16, 2012).

Tutwiler, Patrick. 2010. *Climate Change Legislation: Where Does It Stand?* (April 27). Available at www.tmacog.org (accessed on March 19, 2012).

WCI (Western Climate Initiative). 2010. Updated Economic Analysis of the WCI Regional Cap-and-Trade Program (July). Available at www.westernclimateinitiative.org (accessed on January 16, 2012).

World Public Opinion. 2006. 30-Country Poll Finds Worldwide Consensus that Climate Change Is a Serious Problem (April 25). Available at www.worldpublicopinion.org (accessed on January 16, 2012).

4

EU Climate Change Policy
Can It Mobilize Innovations for Clean Energy Technologies?

REINHILDE VEUGELERS

In early 2008 the European Union adopted its Climate and Energy Package (CEP), designed to reduce EU greenhouse gas (GHG) emissions by 80 to 95 percent by 2050. The package includes a 20 percent renewables target and a 20 percent GHG reduction target by 2020, with the option to increase to 30 percent. A mix of policy instruments was put together to reach these targets, including the Emissions Trading System (ETS) and a set of regulatory measures on automobile emissions of carbon dioxide and energy efficiency (non-ETS).

Since the adoption of the CEP in 2008, the European Union has experienced important changes, most notably the impact of the global economic crisis. The full force of the economic crisis in 2009 significantly affected emissions in the short term, with estimates putting emissions reduction in 2009 at around –14 percent compared with 1990 levels (Delbeke 2010). Carbon prices fell in early 2009, from €25 to €8, and then slightly recovered. Furthermore, the levels of allowances banked in the ETS unexpectedly increased, offering little incentive to further reduce emissions after 2012. The amount of unused international credits and banked allowances in the system will remain high up to 2020.

Emissions are expected to rebound when GDP growth rates recover, but overall GDP levels by 2020 are projected to remain lower than expected before the crisis. The approximate cost of full implementation of the CEP in the

Reinhilde Veugelers is a senior fellow at Bruegel and a professor at KU Leuven (Belgium) in the Faculty of Economics and Business.

context of the new 2009 baseline framework is estimated to be €48 billion in 2020, or 0.3 percent of GDP. This is a reduction of costs per GDP between 30 and 50 percent (European Commission 2010). Under 2010 projections for 2020, GHG emissions are estimated to be 19 percent below 2005 (compared with –13 percent below 2008 projections). In the 2010 projections for 2020, the ETS price estimate has been reduced to €16.5/allowance (in 2008 prices), down from €30/allowance (in 2005 prices) in the 2008 projections for 2020 (Delbeke 2010).

In the reference scenario with policies in line with the commitments under the CEP, the European Union is now estimated to reach the –20 percent GHG reduction targets of CEP internally, without a need for significant amounts in international credits for either ETS or non-ETS measures.

At the same time, the crisis has spurred governments to kick-start efforts toward a greener economy through their economic recovery packages. But no overall official estimate for the green share or volume of all recovery programs is available. In some countries, the crisis has forced the governments to cut back on green subsidies (e.g., Germany and Spain). Nevertheless, a United Nations Environment Program study estimates the combined stimulus programs related to sustainable energy in five major EU countries at $26 billion in total (UNEP and NEF 2009).

At the EU level, €4 billion is being spent as part of the European Economic Recovery Plan on energy infrastructure projects, including offshore wind electricity generation and demonstration of carbon capture and storage.

From the start, the European Union recognized the importance of research, technology development, innovation, and diffusion of technologies for meeting its targets. In October 2009, it launched the technology pillar of the CEP, called the Strategic Energy Technology Plan (SET Plan). The SET Plan is the European Union's all-encompassing technology roadmap for creating a low-carbon and renewable energy–based economy (see box 4.1). The goal is to coordinate fragmented policies and programs and organize energy research efforts across Europe in a coherent and efficient manner behind a clear set of technology targets in partnership with the private sector. The SET Plan envisions raising the total public and private investment in low-carbon energy technologies from the current €3 billion per year to around €8 billion per year. This would represent an additional investment, public and private, of €50 billion over the next 10 years.

EU Climate Change Policy Beyond 20 Percent

As part of the CEP, the European Union has committed itself to move to a 30 percent emissions reduction target by 2020 if the conditions are right (this is the "high-end" pledge). The European Commission is currently preparing an analysis of the practical policies required to implement such a reduction.

Box 4.1   Europe's Strategic Energy Technology Plan

In October 2009, the European Commission launched its Strategic Energy Technology Plan (SET Plan). The plan's priority is to accelerate the development of low-carbon energy sources in six sectors: wind, solar (both concentrated solar and photovoltaic), smart grids, biofuels, nuclear fission, and carbon capture and storage.

The plan calls for setting up a European Industrial Initiative in each sector. These initiatives, to be led by industry, are large-scale programs that bring together companies, the research community, member states, and the European Commission in risk-sharing public-private partnerships. The plan also establishes the Smart Cities Initiatives and the European Energy Research Alliance, which are designed to coordinate and accelerate research and development of new generations of low-carbon technologies.

The motivation for investigating the 30 percent target does not come primarily from more-active emissions reduction plans by other international players. The main motivation is mostly internal: Stepping up to a 30 percent target would now be less costly to realize than before, thanks to the crisis. Preliminary European Commission estimates suggest that the extra cost would be 0.22 percent of GDP in 2020, lower than estimated before (European Commission 2010). In addition, it is hoped that efforts to meet the target would restore higher carbon prices and in turn would support innovations and technology deployment and thus invigorate the recently launched SET Plan.

Non-ETS measures to accelerate emissions reduction include first and foremost technological options (e.g., product standards and energy efficiency measures) but also energy taxes and the leverage of Cohesion and Common Agricultural Policy funds. Options in the ETS include tightening of targets by auctioning fewer allowances. This would lead to higher carbon prices, which are expected to stimulate innovation.

In any case, in order to keep the costs of reaching targets affordable—both for the 20 percent target and *a fortiori* the 30 percent target—scenarios rely heavily on new technologies coming to market and being smoothly deployed; this approach should prominently feature the SET Plan in future EU clean energy policymaking. Preferably, this faster innovation and deployment should also create a competitive edge for European companies in key sectors, promoting growth and jobs postcrisis in the European Union.

But will the European Union be able to harness its innovation potential for green growth? The next sections examine the performance on green innovations in more detail.

Assessing the Current Performance of Private Green Innovations

To assess the capacity of the private sector to generate new green technologies, I use mostly information on applications for green patents,[1] specifically a recently developed and published categorization of green patents provided by the United Nations Environment Program, European Patent Office, and International Center for Trade and Sustainable Development (UNEP, EPO, and ICTSD 2010). This chapter examines six main categories of clean energy technologies that are either already commercially available or have strong prospects of commercialization in the near to medium term. The categories are solar (both thermal and photovoltaic), wind, carbon capture and storage (CCS), hydro, geothermal, biofuels, fossil and nuclear energy, and integrated gasification combined cycle (IGCC). These technologies are labeled as clean energy technologies (figure 4.1).

Trends in Green Patenting

Overall, clean energy technologies (CET) represent a very small share of total patents, less than 1 percent over the period 1988–2007. But CET patents are growing rapidly (figure 4.1), albeit from a small base.

Until the mid-1990s, CET patents had stagnated and even declined, certainly in relative terms, as overall patenting activities continued to grow. But since the late 1990s, CET patents too have trended upward. This upward trend holds particularly when compared with traditional energy fields (fossil fuels and nuclear), which have trended down since 2000. When looking at individual CET areas, patenting rates in solar photovoltaics, wind, and CCS have shown the most activity. Biofuels are a more recent growth story. IGCC, solar, and geothermal have not yet taken off, probably reflecting their still-premature stage of development.

One cannot ignore the correlation between political decisions and the takeoff of CET, as the upward trend started around 1997, when the Kyoto Protocol was signed.

---

1. With regard to technologies, a multitude of labels exists, including "environment friendly," "green," "clean energy," and "eco-friendly." I try to stick as closely as possible to the labels used by the sources reported; otherwise I use the label "green." With regard to the numbers, here are a couple of caveats: First, not all inventions may be patented; in particular, inventions still far from the market may not yet show up in patent statistics. Second, there is as yet no international standard to classify patents as "green," and the European Patent Office, World Intellectual Property Organization, and Organization for Economic Cooperation and Development each uses its own classification. With regard to the early stages of technology development, data on research and development (R&D) expenditures would be a good measure of activities in the early stage of technology development. Unfortunately, R&D statistics are not collected by area of technology. Green R&D expenditures therefore cannot be assessed easily.

Figure 4.1 Growth rates of patents for selected clean energy technologies

index, 1978 = 100

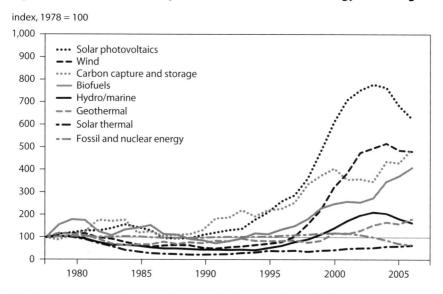

Note: Patents are counted on the basis of claimed priorities (patent applications filed in other countries based on the first filed patent for a particular invention).

Source: UNEP, EPO, and ICTSD (2010).

Who's Who in Green Patenting: Toward a Multipolar Clean Technology Space?

If one looks at which countries are active in green patenting, Japan is the clearest positive outlier (table 4.1). Japan holds about 30 percent of all CET patents, but it is not particularly specialized in CET—meaning it holds many other types of patents as well. It is heavily concentrated in a particular CET technology, namely solar photovoltaics. Korea is another important player in CET patenting; it is specialized in CET and heavily concentrated in solar photovoltaic.

The United States, despite its 16 percent share of world green patents, is not specialized in clean energy technologies. Its CET patents are dispersed across various technologies. In Europe, Germany is by far the largest country for CET patents. It is somewhat specialized in clean energy technologies, and like the United States its CET patents are dispersed across various technologies.[2] If the European Union is counted as a homogeneous block, it has the largest share of CET patents, with a slight specialization in such patents and a relatively dispersed portfolio across CET areas.

---

2. Some other EU countries are specialized in environmental technologies (revealed technological advantage [RTA] greater than 1) but are small players (less than 2 percent of CET patent share). In order of size, they are the Netherlands (RTA of 1.19), Denmark (RTA of 13.46), Spain (RTA of 1.14), Austria (RTA of 1.05), Portugal (RTA of 4.93), and Hungary (RTA of 1.11).

Table 4.1 Who's who in clean energy technology (CET) patenting

Country	Size (percent share in world CET patents)	Specialization (RTA in CET patents)	Concentration (Herfindahl ratio across CETs)
Top 6 plus European Union			
Japan	29.7	0.99	0.72
United States	15.9	0.87	0.33
Germany	15.2	1.05	0.28
Korea	5.6	1.21	0.82
France	3.9	0.70	0.26
United Kingdom	3.6	0.98	0.28
European Union	32.0	1.01	0.25
BRICs			
China	0.9	1.11	0.36
India	0.3	1.44	0.45
Russia	0.2	1.11	0.27
Brazil	0.2	1.51	0.41

Note: Patents are counted on the basis of claimed priorities (patent applications filed in other countries based on the first filed patent for a particular invention). A top 6 country has at least 2 percent of world CET; together the top 6 represent 74 percent of world CET patents. Revealed technological advantage (RTA) represents a country's share in world CET patents relative to its share in total world patents. Thus RTA > 1 measures specialization in CET patents. The Herfindahl ratio is the weighted sum of the share of each CET in the country's CET patents, with the weights being the share. It varies between 0 (maximal dispersion) and 1 (perfect concentration).

Source: Author's calculations based on UNEP, EPO, and ICTSD (2010).

Overall, the BRIC countries (Brazil, Russia, India, and China) are still dwarfs in CET patenting compared with the Big Three (Japan, the United States, and Germany). Of the BRIC countries, China is the most important in terms of CET patents. It has particularly improved its position in recent years. It also specializes in clean energy patents but is less concentrated in solar photovoltaics than are Japan and Korea. Although China has leading manufacturers in solar photovoltaic and wind technologies, these companies are less active in patenting than some others. They may be heavily reliant on technology transfer to develop their products or are largely manufacturing based.

The other BRIC countries are less important in terms of total CET patenting, although they do specialize in clean energy technologies. India and Brazil are concentrated in a few technologies. Patentees from India show the highest activity in solar photovoltaics. The main patenting activity for Brazil lies in hydro/marine and biofuels, though compared with other countries its patenting activity in these areas is limited. For example, China has more patents for biofuels than and as many patents in the area of hydro/marine as Brazil. This suggests that Brazilian companies are focused more on the production process than on developing technologies.

Table 4.2 focuses on which of the clean energy technologies are dominant. By far the most important CET in terms of patents is solar photovoltaics, which

Table 4.2   A multipolar clean technology space? Clean energy technology patenting, by technology type, 1988–2007

Technology	Share of technology in total clean energy technology patents (percent)	Share of largest country (percent)	Share of top 3 countries[a] (percent)	Concentration (Herfindahl ratio)	Countries with specialization technology[b]
Solar photovoltaics	57	44.0 (Japan)	69	24	Japan, Korea, and Taiwan
Wind	14	29.0 (Germany)	52	12	Germany, United Kingdom, Netherlands, Canada, Denmark, Spain, Norway, Sweden, and European Union
Hydro	12	20.0 (United States)	44	9	United States, United Kingdom, Italy, Canada, Switzerland, Spain, Austria, Sweden, Norway, Australia, and European Union
Solar thermal	10	27.0 (Germany)	47	10	Germany, Italy, Netherlands, Canada, Switzerland, Spain, Austria, Australia, Israel, and European Union
Biofuels	5	18.5 (United States)	52	10	Germany, France, United Kingdom, Italy, Netherlands, Canada, Switzerland, China, Austria, Finland, Belgium, and European Union
Carbon capture and storage	4	32.5 (United States)	61	16	United States, France, United Kingdom, Netherlands, Canada, Norway, and European Union

(table continues next page)

Table 4.2   A multipolar clean technology space? Clean energy technology patenting, by technology type, 1988–2007 *(continued)*

Technology	Share of technology in total clean energy technology patents (percent)	Share of largest country (percent)	Share of top 3 countries[a] (percent)	Concentration (Herfindahl ratio)	Countries with specialization technology[b]
Geothermal	2	18.0 (United States)	44	8	Germany, Italy, Netherlands, Canada, Switzerland, China, Austria, Sweden, Norway, Finland, Israel, Hungary, and European Union
All clean energy technologies	100	30.0 (Japan)	61	14	Germany, Korea, Netherlands, Taiwan, Denmark, Spain, China, and European Union

a. Although relative positions vary across technologies, the top three countries are always Japan, the United States, and Germany.
b. This category includes countries with at least 1 percent of world patents in technology; specialization is considered to exist if revealed technological advantage (RTA) > 1.

Source: Author's calculations based on UNEP, EPO, and ICTSD (2010).

represented 57 percent of all CET patents over the period 1988–2007. Solar photovoltaics is a technology that is concentrated in a few countries; Japan in particular is a dominant and specialized player in solar photovoltaic patents.

Wind is the second-largest CET in terms of patents. But in this sector concentration tends to be much lower. Germany holds the largest position and is specialized in wind, but many other European countries specialize in wind technology as well. The strong patenting activities in solar photovoltaic and wind suggest that these technologies are extensively used in the market and can therefore be considered the more mature clean energy technologies.

Geothermal and solar thermal, hydro, and biofuels all have lower dominant positions than the big players, with many countries active and specializing in these technologies.

CCS is a sector with a high level of concentration. In this sector the United States is a strong and specialized player, although several European countries also specialize in CCS, including France and the United Kingdom. The share of CCS patents in total CET patents is low, reflecting the technology's still-early stage of development.

Taken as an integrated unit, the European Union holds a specialized position in all CET but solar photovoltaics. It is particularly specialized in geothermal and solar thermal and to a lesser extent in biofuels, hydro/marine, and wind. It specializes only marginally in CCS.[3] The United States is specialized only in CCS and hydro/marine.

Table 4.2 shows that the pattern of countries active in patenting CET (with the exception of solar photovoltaics and CCS) is quite geographically dispersed and multipolar. Different countries tend to specialize in different clean energy technologies. Particularly in the newer, emerging technologies, like biofuels, hydro, and geothermal, the concentration is still low. In contrast, in the more mature clean technologies, especially solar photovoltaics, concentration is high, with Asia holding a dominant position in this technology.

Government Intervention for Green Innovations

In view of the pervasive environmental and knowledge externalities characterizing green innovations, the private green-innovation machine cannot be expected to be effective on its own. It needs government intervention to start. The patterns in patenting clearly suggest the importance of government intervention. The growth in clean energy patenting, for example, began in earnest only after the Kyoto Protocol came into force. Moreover, which countries are strong in which technologies is significantly related to government policies. Econometric analysis in Johnstone, Hascic, and Popp (2010) shows that policies indeed have a significant impact on a country's green patenting. Policies such as feed-in tariffs, renewable energy credits, carbon taxes, and subsidies for research and development (R&D) are found to significantly affect innovators in a country, although the strength of the effects varies over technologies, instruments, and countries. For example, Germany has seen a dip in wind patenting despite the existence of feed-in tariffs. Policies therefore are no straightforward mechanism for stimulating green innovations.

Philippe Aghion, David Hemous, and I (2009) have discussed how government intervention should be designed in order to effectively turn on the private green-innovation machine. In particular, the analysis strongly supports the case for a portfolio of instruments that includes carbon prices, R&D subsidies, and regulation. With a sufficiently and consistently high carbon price, R&D support for clean technologies is needed. Public R&D support is especially crucial for clean technologies that are still in the early stages of development because it will help to neutralize the installed base advantage of the older, dirtier technologies.

So are governments deploying the right policies for stimulating private green innovations? In Aghion, Veugelers, and Serre (2009), we examined in detail the record of government policies for green innovation, we still are a long way from ideal policy support. On carbon prices, the evidence showed not

---

3. The values for the RTA index showing the European Union's specialization pattern are 1.80 (geothermal), 1.70 (solar thermal), 1.39 (biofuels), 1.35 (hydro/marine), 1.23 (wind), 1.05 (CCS), and 0.62 (solar photovoltaics).

only a low level of carbon taxes in most countries but also a high dispersion in carbon taxes across countries, leaving a worldwide carbon price a distant reality. At the EU level, the first phase of the ETS established a carbon market but with prices at low and volatile levels. Beyond the question of whether taxes and cap-and-trade systems currently in place generate a sufficiently high carbon price to induce green innovations, there is the issue of the carbon price being far from predictable over the long term. If carbon prices are to serve as an incentive for green innovations, they must be predictable.

The evidence on subsidies to green R&D showed the poor performance of major policy actors. Public R&D spending on environment and energy efficiency remains a very minor share of total public R&D spending.[4] In keeping with its leading position in CET patents, Japan is clearly the front-runner with respect to public funding for energy R&D, spending 0.11 percent of GDP on this category in 2006. Compared with Japan, the aggregated EU figure (0.02 percent of GDP in 2007) is low and almost unchanged since 2006. The share of energy R&D in the total public R&D budget was 2.9 percent in 2007 for the European Union, compared with a share of 15.2 percent for Japan. The United States, with a mere 1.1 percent share for energy in the total public R&D budget in 2007, is worse than the European Union.

For the technologies included in the European Union's SET Plan, the European Commission Joint Research Center (ECJRC) has tried to assess the amounts currently being invested in these technologies in the European Union, both by the public sector (including EU member governments and the European Union as a whole) and by the private sector (table 4.3).

At the EU level, 25 percent of the total public R&D budget is spent on CET, indicating the importance of public funding for clean technology. Most of the public budget goes to nuclear energy, an area that also has the highest ratio of public to private investment. For nonnuclear energy, hydrogen and fuel cells along with photovoltaics are the largest recipients of public R&D funds in the European Union, and they also have the highest ratio of public to private investment. CCS, closely followed by biofuels, smart grids, and wind, has the lowest ratio of public to private investment. The relative position of the European Union among public financiers is the highest in CCS and hydrogen and fuel cells. These also happen to be the two CET areas where the European Union is the weakest in terms of patenting, as indicated above. As photovoltaic technology is among the most mature CET area, its still-high share of public funding is somewhat surprising. Equally surprising is the high share of private funding in CCS, which is still an early-stage technology.

---

4. Unfortunately, data available on public spending tend not to be comparable across countries. For discussion of R&D subsidies, Aghion, Veugelers, and Serre (2009) use Eurostat data on government budget appropriations or outlays on R&D (GBAORD).

Table 4.3 R&D funding for clean energy technologies in the European Union, 2007 (percent)

Technology area	Share of technology area in total public R&D funding[a]	Share of the European Union in total public R&D funding	Share of private investment in total R&D funding
Hydrogen and fuel cells	13	29	61.0
Solar photovoltaics	9	17	58.0
Wind	5	12	76.0
Biofuels	4	17	77.5
Carbon capture and storage	3	30	81.0
Smart grids	3	23	77.7
Solar	2	13	58.0
Nuclear fission	37	16	43.0
Nuclear fusion[b]	25	42	0
Total	100	25	53.0

a. Total public R&D funding = €476 million.
b. Nuclear fusion, although a technology closely related to technologies in the Strategic Energy Technology Plan, is not included in the plan.

Source: ECJRC (2010).

A New Momentum for Europe in Clean Energy Technologies?

Although EU countries have started becoming active patentees in specific clean energy technologies, the European Union, lacking integration, is overall not a leader in this area. Asian countries—Japan, Korea, and increasingly also China—are active patentees, particularly of the more mature technologies. Low, uncoordinated, and volatile carbon prices, as well as public funding for CET investments, help to explain why the European Union's innovative capacity in CET is below potential.

Through its Europe 2020 strategy and the Innovation Union program, the European Union is seeking to encourage innovation with the goal of creating sustainable growth and jobs. Green innovation, crystallized in the SET Plan, has never been higher on the agenda of EU policymakers. Is there a new momentum for the private green-innovation machine in Europe?

The ECJRC (2010) estimated the total amount in R&D investments that would be needed to match the roadmaps designed by the various European industrial initiatives that are part of the SET Plan. The total amount of yearly investments in CET is estimated to be €5.8 billion. CCS and solar technologies will soak up most of the money—28 and 22 percent, respectively. For CCS, 2007 investment levels cover only 13 percent of the needed yearly investment; for solar, the figure is 18 percent.

Where will the money come from? To launch the first industry initiative in CCS in 2009, the European Commission tapped €1.05 billion in EU crisis funds. To bolster resources for the other five industrial initiatives, which did not receive EU crisis funds, the commission is lobbying individual member states to take the financial lead so that projects can get rolling. But the major battle will be over the 2014–20 budgets.

Starting in 2013, the new European ETS will make it possible for auction revenues to be reinvested at the national level to fund the development of more efficient and lower-cost clean technologies. The use of these revenues is determined by the member states, but at least 50 percent is to be used for climate change–related activities, including in developing countries. A total of 300 million EU allowances set aside from the New Entrants Reserve of the ETS will be used to support CCS and innovative renewables. These allowances will be made available via member states to fund demonstration projects selected on the basis of criteria defined at the community level.

But it is clear that public funding will not be sufficient and that private funding needs to be leveraged. Will the private sector and its financiers be willing to initiate and cofund clean technology projects?

As indicated above, an important incentive for private innovation is a sufficiently high and predictable carbon price. The current carbon price is not likely to create strong incentives, so the ETS move to a 30 percent target is an improvement, although it is still unclear whether a 30 percent target, if implemented, would be sufficient.

A signal that the EU private sector is still not convinced of the public sector's long-term commitment to developing clean energy technologies comes from the venture capital market (see figures 4.2 and 4.3). Venture capital funding for renewable energy, which was trending up in 2007–08, has been hard hit by the global crisis. But while it seems to have recently recovered in the United States, it continues to trend downward in Europe (figure 4.2). This situation is all the more remarkable as the downward trend seems to have stopped for overall venture capital funding in Europe (figure 4.3). For the United States, the strong upward trend in 2010 in venture capital for renewable energy (stronger than the upward trend in overall venture capital funding in the United States) suggests that despite the lack of strong government impetus, the US private (venture capital) market has some confidence in the US clean energy innovation market.

Toward a Global Clean Energy Technology Market

If governments want to leverage the needed private innovations for clean energy technologies, they will have to provide a well-designed and timely policy and reduce commercial and financial risk via a combination of consistent carbon pricing, regulations, and public funding. With current public budgets heavily constrained, it is all the more important that this public funding be allocated as cost-effectively as possible. This implies that public funding will have to be able to leverage private funding.

Beyond efficiently targeting and timing public budgets to support CET, particularly early-stage or high-risk projects, governments should first and

Figure 4.2   Funding per semester in renewable energy by venture capital companies in the European Union and United States, 2003–10

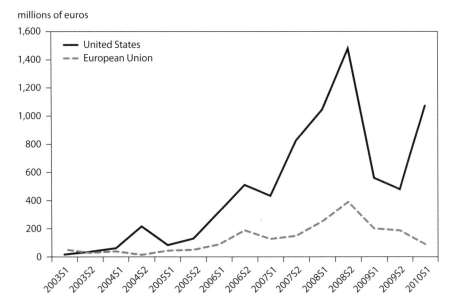

millions of euros

Sources: European Central Bank (for exchange rates on a quarterly basis); DowJones VentureSource, www.venturesource.com.

foremost establish a sufficiently high and predictable carbon price. A well-functioning carbon market is essential for driving low-carbon investments and achieving global mitigation objectives in a cost-efficient manner, particularly for investments in development, demonstration, and deployment of later-stage technologies.

For the European Union, the biggest threat to its SET Plan may be the lack of a sufficiently high carbon price. To address this problem, a larger effort should be made to integrate carbon taxes among the EU member states. At the same time, the ETS and emissions allowances should be designed to leverage innovation. A move to a 30 percent target, which would involve fewer allowances being auctioned, could reinforce innovation incentives.

Patent data have shown that the world of green technologies is becoming a global, multipolar one, with many geographically dispersed sources in the various clean energy technologies. Coordination of green policies internationally among the major players should therefore be high on the policy agenda.

The development of green technologies would benefit most from an international carbon price established on a globally integrated carbon market, or at least internationally linked domestic cap-and-trade systems. Any segmentation would reduce the incentives for clean energy innovations.

Figure 4.3   Total funding per semester by venture capital companies in the European Union and United States, 2003–10

millions of euros

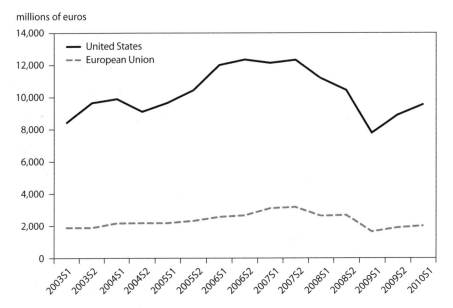

Sources: European Central Bank (for exchange rates on a quarterly basis); DowJones VentureSource, www.venturesource.com.

In addition, global coordination of public R&D programs for clean energy innovations would help to pool resources and know-how, avoid duplication, and speed up the diffusion of results. While a certain level of competition between countries could be healthy for nurturing a larger set of potential technology trajectories, eventually, the best technologies that emerge from this competition should be diffused as broadly and quickly as possible. This goal implies well-functioning global markets for clean energy technologies where private actors have the incentive to transact their clean technologies. Well-functioning green technology markets require clear intellectual property rights systems. For developing countries that lack the finance and the technological capacities to be active in green innovations, specific financial support and support for deployment of the best technologies available need to be in place.

References

Aghion, Philippe, David Hemous, and Reinhilde Veugelers. 2009. *No Green Growth Without Innovation.* Bruegel Policy Brief 2009/07. Brussels: Bruegel.

Aghion, Philippe, Reinhilde Veugelers, and Clement Serre. 2009. *Cold Start for the Green Innovation Machine.* Bruegel Policy Contribution 2009/12. Brussels: Bruegel.

Delbeke, J. 2010. Moving Beyond a –20% Greenhouse Gas Target: Costs, Benefits and Policy Options. Paper presented at Bruegel, Brussels, June 8.

ECJRC (European Commission Joint Research Center). 2010. *Effective Research and Innovation Agendas to Tackle Societal Challenges: The Case of the SET-Plan.* Seville.

European Commission. 2010. *Analysis of Options to Move Beyond 20% Greenhouse Gas Emission Reductions and Assessing the Risk of Carbon Leakage.* Commission Staff Working Document. Brussels.

Johnstone, N., I. Hascic, and D. Popp. 2010. Renewable Energy Policies and Technological Innovation: Evidence Based on Patent Counts. *Environmental and Resource Economics* 45, no. 1: 133–55.

UNEP, EPO, and ICTSD (United Nations Environment Program, European Patent Office, and International Center for Trade and Sustainable Development). 2010. *Patents and Clean Energy: Bridging the Gap Between Evidence and Policy: Final Report.* Available at www.unep.ch (accessed on January 18, 2012).

UNEP and NEF (United Nations Environment Program and New Energy Finance). 2009. *Global Trends in Sustainable Energy Investment.* Available at www.unep.org (accessed on January 18, 2012).

5

The Transatlantic Relationship in an Era of Growing Economic Multipolarity

MARIO DRAGHI

Keynote address at the PIIE-Bruegel conference in Washington, DC, October 8, 2010

Achieving a more stable and resilient global financial system requires coordinated action at the global level. The United States and Europe have strong joint interests in this goal, and each is critical to its progress. But so are countries beyond these continents, and they have come to play an increasingly important role in shaping global outcomes. I review below what we have achieved so far in terms of financial reforms. I then turn to important challenges still ahead of us. I conclude with some thoughts on international policy coordination and the role of the Financial Stability Board (FSB).

Achievements So Far

We have come a long way toward strengthening the financial system since the financial crisis began, and these gains reflect an unprecedented amount of international coordination in achieving consistent reforms. While issues remain to be resolved in Europe, in the United States, and elsewhere, we are, collectively, fundamentally reshaping the framework for systemic financial oversight.

Mario Draghi has been the president of the European Central Bank since November 2011. Before taking up this position, he had been the governor of the Bank of Italy since December 2005 and the head of the Financial Stability Board, formerly the Financial Stability Forum, since 2006. This speech was delivered when he was the governor of the Bank of Italy. It is available at www.bancaditalia.it/interventi/integov/2010/081010/draghi_081010.pdf (accessed on April 3, 2012).

Let me note some examples:

- First, top-down, systemwide oversight arrangements are being put in place at national, regional, and international levels. These arrangements are designed to deliver more-encompassing surveillance, with broadened macroprudential perspectives, and better mechanisms for triggering action on identified risks. Examples are the European Systemic Risk Board and related arrangements, the US Financial Services Oversight Council, the International Monetary Fund (IMF)-FSB Early Warning Exercise, and the establishment of the FSB itself.

- Second, major jurisdictions have overhauled their regulatory and supervisory structures to strengthen responsiveness to risks, improve coordination, and close gaps. The FSB is in many ways the international manifestation of these efforts.

- Third, the regulatory perimeter is being expanded. Major jurisdictions have finalized or will shortly finalize legislation that establishes regulation and oversight of the over-the-counter (OTC) derivatives markets, hedge funds, and credit rating agencies. In each of these areas, principles for what regulation should achieve have been internationally agreed upon, and implementing regulation is being closely coordinated.

- Fourth, we have put in place cross-border oversight and contingency planning for the largest and most complex global financial institutions, each of which now have functioning core supervisory colleges and crisis management groups.

At the level of the essential regulatory policies to buttress financial stability, the following achievements are noteworthy:

- First, with Basel III, we have a fundamentally revised global bank capital framework that will establish stronger protection through improved risk coverage, more and higher-quality capital, a countercyclical buffer, and a constraint on the buildup of banking sector leverage.

- Second, as part of Basel III, we have a global liquidity standard for banks that will promote higher liquidity buffers and constrain the maturity mismatching that created the conditions for this crisis.

- Third, as I describe below, we are making progress in developing a policy framework and tools to roll back the moral hazard risks posed by institutions that are too big to fail.

- Fourth, through changes to accounting standards and regulatory and prudential rules, we have eliminated the perverse incentives that pervaded securitization, including the scope for leverage to develop in opaque off-balance sheet vehicles.

- Fifth, we are establishing central clearing of standardized contracts in the OTC derivatives markets, and an OTC global trade repository is now in operation.

- Finally, we have developed a series of supervisory tools to raise standards of governance, risk management, and capital conservation at financial institutions. In this context, let me note that we are making good progress with accounting standard setters toward an expected-loss provisioning regime for credit losses, which will dampen procyclicality and align accounting and prudential objectives in this key area. Moreover, principles and standards have been issued to better align compensation systems with prudent risk taking. The standards give supervisors powers to restrain compensation structures and the level of payout to conserve capital in the firm. As we move to raise capital levels, we will encourage supervisors to use these powers.

I have been selective in my enumeration. But my point is that we should not underestimate what has been accomplished. Each of the above areas is difficult in its own right. We have never before been able to make progress on global policy development and implementation on such a broad front, while at the same time fighting a very serious financial crisis.

So the direction in which we are moving internationally is encouraging. But important issues remain. And it is political resolve that will determine whether we accomplish the credible and robust reforms that our citizens rightly demand, yet preserve the enormous advantages of an internationally integrated financial system.

Addressing "Too Big to Fail"

Addressing the "too big to fail" problem is perhaps the most challenging remaining legacy of the crisis. Basel III will greatly strengthen banking system resilience, but it does not address this problem.

The FSB has assessed a broad range of policy options in this area and will present its recommendations to the Group of 20 (G-20) in November 2010.

It is important to recognize that systemically important financial institutions (SIFIs) vary widely in structures and activities and that the nature and degree of the risks they pose also differ. Some are large, complex, highly integrated global financial institutions with activities spanning a range of sectors. Others may have a global customer base but are simpler commercial banking operations. Yet a third category is entities that are large at a domestic or regional level but nonetheless globally interconnected through wholesale funding markets.

Whatever their nature, SIFIs have two things in common: their uncontrolled failure would cause significant systemic disruption; and such failure cannot at present be resolved in an orderly fashion without use of public funds. The framework we have agreed on to address SIFIs is therefore based on four necessary pillars.

First, we must radically improve our capacity to resolve SIFIs without disruptions to the financial system and without taxpayers' support. Effective resolution regimes must advance the goals of both financial stability and market discipline. This means they need to be able to impose losses on shareholders as well as creditors while ensuring continuity of essential financial functions. All countries should have a Dodd-Frank-style regime in place, and we need to acquire additional resolution tools as well. The "bail-in" of debt holders holds significant attractions from the perspective of correcting creditor incentives and protecting taxpayers. But the legal issues associated with the bail-in—specifically in group structures and in a cross-border context—are nontrivial.

Moreover, to be effective backstops in dealing with global firms, national resolution regimes need to converge toward common standards. And these need to be supplemented by cross-border cooperation arrangements underpinned by national law that provides both mandate and capacity for resolution authorities to cooperate. Legislative changes will be needed in many countries to enable this cooperation. Lastly, "living wills" will need to be mandatory for major firms. These will include assessments of firm resolvability. Supervisors will have the power to require changes to a firm's structure to improve its resolvability.

Second, the loss absorption capacity of systemically important firms should reflect their role in the global financial system and their potential contribution to systemic risk. Even with the best possible resolution tools, the failure of a major global firm would cause significant damage—hence the importance of strengthening the resilience of major global firms. Higher loss-absorption capacity for SIFIs than the minimum agreed Basel III standards, especially for the largest globally operating SIFIs, therefore is at the core of our recommendations. A credible process of peer review will be established to challenge the policy choices made within each jurisdiction and to ensure that measures applied on a country-by-country and SIFI-by-SIFI basis are consistent and mutually supportive.

Third, strengthened oversight and supervision are needed. Senior line supervisors have drawn a frank assessment of weakness leading up to this crisis. These weaknesses were not present to the same degree everywhere, but there is scope for improvement all around. Our recommendations in this area have been developed with the IMF. One set is focused on the mandates, independence, and resourcing of supervisors. Another is on improved methods and practices to proactively identify and address risks.

Fourth, we will be setting out higher robustness standards for core financial infrastructure. This infrastructure—including for central counterparties—is itself a source of systemic risk were it to malfunction or fail. This is a complex project that will unfold over a number of years. It will need to be consistently implemented in all major countries to maintain a level playing field, avoid regulatory arbitrage, and effectively address the risks to the overall system. The already established FSB framework for country and thematic peer review will address improved resolution frameworks and more intensive supervision In addition, for SIFIs with the potential to create damages at a global level, we will establish a mutual policy review process that will assess and challenge the national policies governing major global SIFIs.

Other issues still require attention in the future. So far, most of our attention has been on strengthening the resilience of the banking system, and rightly so. Yet the shadow banking sector remains a large part of our financial system, less regulated than other parts of the system but nonetheless significant in credit intermediation and maturity transformation, and subject to runs in damaging ways.

We need to make frameworks for macroprudential policies and system-wide oversight operational. We will be sharing approaches for surveillance, powers to obtain information, and modalities for action on identified risks. The FSB will coordinate approaches where an international regulatory response is needed. We will be working with the Bank for International Settlements and the IMF to build principles for effective macroprudential policies.

Lastly, the FSB is developing arrangements to broaden the involvement of nonmembers in its work at early stages of policy development. We will be setting up regional arms of the FSB. Each regional group will be cochaired by an FSB member and a regional nonmember who will attend FSB plenary meetings.

Conclusion

Three things have been important in enabling us to make progress on reforms: first, the sheer seriousness of the crisis and the recognition that, in a globally integrated system, we all sit in the same boat; second, the readiness in the official community to agree on objectives and timelines for substantial reform, including through the G-20 process; and third, the establishment of mechanisms, such as the FSB, to hasten the policy development needed to meet these objectives.

I am quite confident that with these mechanisms, we will be able to achieve globally consistent rules that will lastingly increase the resilience of the financial system and the real economy, and that will deliver the level playing field that a global system needs.

6

Too Big to Fail
The Transatlantic Debate

MORRIS GOLDSTEIN and NICOLAS VÉRON

The problem of dealing with "too big to fail" (TBTF) financial institutions is not a new one in financial policy,[1] but the severity of the global economic and financial crisis that started in 2007 has put a spotlight on it as never before, and has also made more noticeable the size and scope of the measures taken by the official sector to prevent the failure of a host of large and complex financial institutions. This chapter aims at reviewing the key dimensions of the policy debate on the TBTF problem, as distinct from other dimensions of discussions aimed at strengthening financial stability, in the

Morris Goldstein, senior fellow at the Peterson Institute for International Economics, has held several senior staff positions at the International Monetary Fund (1970–94), including deputy director of its Research Department (1987–94). From 1994 to 2010, he was the Dennis Weatherstone Senior Fellow at the Peterson Institute. Nicolas Véron is a senior fellow at Bruegel and a visiting fellow at the Peterson Institute for International Economics. The authors are indebted to Victor Zhikai Gao, Anil Kashyap, and Paul Tucker for their comments; to Gonzalo Caprirolo, Gerry Cross, Douglas Elliott, Wilson Ervin, Wim Fonteyne, Mojmír Hampl, Nicolas Jabko, Micol Levi, Sergio Lugaresi, Christian Mouillon, Philippe Peuch-Lestrade, Elliot Posner, Nikhil Rathi, Barbara Ridpath, Jörg Rocholl, and David Westbrook for subsequent feedback; to Philip Turner of the Bank for International Settlements (BIS) for sharing with the authors BIS data on concentration ratios in banking; and to Allie Bagnall for excellent research assistance.

1. We use the TBTF shorthand in full awareness of its shortcomings, especially the fact that the systemic importance of financial firms is not dependent on size alone, as we discuss later in this chapter. Other shorthand characterizations have been proposed; for example, "too important to fail (TITF)" has become standard at the International Monetary Fund. However, TBTF has acquired sufficiently wide acceptance to be considered a standard way to refer to our subject.

two major jurisdictions directly affected by the financial crisis, namely the United States and the European Union.[2]

The TBTF problem gained particular prominence in March 2008 with the controversial rescue of Bear Stearns, when the US Federal Reserve backed JPMorgan Chase's purchase of that ailing investment bank, and then again symmetrically in September 2008 when the US authorities' decision to let Lehman Brothers fail ushered in a sequence of major market disruptions. On October 10, 2008, a few weeks after the Lehman collapse, the finance ministers and central bank governors of Group of Seven (G-7) countries met in Washington, DC, and "agreed to take decisive action and use all available tools to support systemically important financial institutions and prevent their failure,"[3] thus providing official confirmation that the TBTF label was more than just an allegation. A few days later, EU leaders clarified at the October 15–16, 2008, European Council meeting their "commitment that in all circumstances the necessary measures will be taken to preserve the stability of the financial system, to support the major financial institutions, to avoid bankruptcies, and to protect savers' deposits,"[4] while adding that "measures to support financial institutions in difficulty should go hand in hand with measures to protect taxpayers, to secure accountability on the part of executives and shareholders, and to protect the legitimate interests of other market players." Given such pledges, it is no wonder that policymakers and analysts alike are seeking to understand how to avoid a future situation where authorities would once again be faced with an unpalatable choice between massive bailouts and market chaos.

The existence of TBTF financial institutions represents a threefold policy challenge, which we refer to throughout this chapter as the "TBTF problem."

First, such institutions exacerbate systemic risk by removing incentives to prudently manage risks and by creating a massive contingent liability for governments that, in extreme cases, can threaten their own financial sustainability. Iceland in 2008–09 and Ireland in 2010 serve as dramatic, recent cases in point. Larger and more diversified banks have shown greater write-downs of assets than smaller and less diversified ones,[5] lending support to the proposition put forward by Gary Stern and Ron Feldman (2004) that large banks "spend" any diversification cost saving on greater risk taking.

Second, TBTF institutions distort competition. According to Moody's, the 50 largest banks in 2009 benefited from an average three-notch advantage

---

2. Our geographic focus means that we do not take up some elements of the wider global debate on TBTF, such as the impact of dominant state ownership of large banks in countries such as China, India, or Russia.

3. Final declaration of the meeting of the Group of Seven Finance Ministers, October 10, 2008, www.g8.utoronto.ca/finance/fm081010.htm.

4. Conclusion of the European Council of October 15-16, 2008, www.consilium.europa.eu/ueDocs/cms_Data/docs/pressData/en/ec/103441.pdf.

5. Andrew Haldane, The $100 Billion Question, speech given to the Institute of Regulation and Risk, Hong Kong, March 2010.

in their credit ratings, which has been understood to be at least partly related to official support.[6] US banks with assets of more than $100 billion can fund themselves by more than 70 basis points more cheaply than smaller banks. The largest banks have received the lion's share of state intervention: Andrew Haldane reports that 145 global banks with assets over $100 billion each accounted for more than 90 percent of the government support since the start of the crisis.[7]

Third, the treatment of TBTF institutions lowers public trust in the fairness of the system and undermines the framework of responsibility and accountability that is supposed to characterize capitalist economies if and indeed when it boils down to the privatization of gains and socialization of losses. Simon Johnson and James Kwak (2010), among others, regard TBTF institutions as a threat not only to financial stability but to the political fabric as well.

Leading policymakers have often emphasized the importance of TBTF in the context of the financial crisis. Mervyn King, governor of the Bank of England, said in June 2009 that "if some banks are thought to be too big to fail, then . . . they are too big. . . . Privately owned and managed institutions that are too big to fail sit oddly with a market economy."[8] US Federal Deposit Insurance Corporation (FDIC) chairman Sheila Bair opined in mid-2009 that the TBTF problem "is at the top of the list of things that need to be fixed. . . . It fed the crisis, and it has gotten worse because of the crisis."[9] US Federal Reserve chairman Ben Bernanke, testifying before the US Financial Crisis Inquiry Commission, concluded that "if the crisis has a single lesson, it is that the too big to fail problem must be solved."[10] The Irish crisis of November 2010, which led to an official rescue package of €85 billion, more than 40 percent of which is to be used for immediate bank recapitalization and contingent support for the banking system, should further increase the prominence of the TBTF problem in European policy debates.

The TBTF problem is reflected in recent trends in concentration of the banking industry. Piergiorgio Alessandri and Andrew Haldane (2009) indicate that the share of the five largest global banks in global banking assets has doubled over the past decade, from 8 percent in 1998 to 16 percent in 2008. Drawing on The Banker database, International Financial Services London (IFSL 2010) reports that this increase in concentration has been particularly

---

6. Bank for International Settlements, 80th Annual Report, June 2010, Basel.

7. Haldane, The $100 Billion Question, speech given to the Institute of Regulation and Risk, Hong Kong, March 2010.

8. Mervyn King, speech given at the Lord Mayor's Banquet for Bankers and Merchants of the City of London at the Mansion House, London, June 17, 2009.

9. Bair is quoted in David Cho, "Banks 'Too Big to Fail' Have Grown Even Bigger," *Washington Post*, August 28, 2009.

10. Benjamin Bernanke, testimony before the US Financial Crisis Inquiry Commission, Washington, September 2, 2010, available at www.federalreserve.gov (accessed on January 21, 2012).

pronounced during the crisis, with the share of the 10 largest global banks (in the assets of the largest 1,000) rising from 14 percent in 1999 to 19 percent in 2007 and to 26 percent in 2009. This trend toward higher concentration also seems to be strongest among the very top banks: the changes in asset share for the next 10 and next 30 largest banks are more modest and different in sign, respectively. The next 10 largest saw their share increase only modestly, from 12 percent in 1999 to 15 percent in 2009, with essentially no change between 2007 and 2009. The next 30 saw their share decrease modestly between 1999 and 2009 and more sharply between 2007 and 2009. Using Bank for International Settlements (BIS) data on the ratio of top-three bank assets to home-country GDP, we find that the level of concentration was higher in 2009 than in 2006 in 10 out of 14 large advanced economies.[11] Whatever the causality, concentration figures suggest that the recent crisis has exacerbated the TBTF problem.

Some policy initiatives have been taken since the start of the crisis to address the TBTF problem, especially through the introduction or reform of special resolution regimes that would provide an alternative to normal insolvency procedures for financial institutions (Goldstein 2011). However, there is no consensus that decisions made so far will be sufficient to defang the TBTF problem, and this issue is likely to provoke policy debates for years to come. Both the difficulty of the problem and its continuing relevance are underlined by the report recently delivered to the Group of 20 (G-20) summit in Seoul by the Financial Stability Board (FSB) following difficult international discussions.[12] Specifically, the Basel III agreement on minimum global capital standards was announced in September 2010 without a consensus on whether to impose a capital surcharge on what the Basel-located bodies call "systemically important financial institutions" (SIFIs)—i.e., financial firms whose disorderly failure would be likely to create systemwide instability.[13]

This chapter is organized as follows. The following two sections look, respectively, at how history and structural differences (in the financial sector) can help to explain current differences between the United States and the European Union on policy orientations related to the TBTF issue. The two sections following those break up the TBTF debate into its two components: the debate on the "bigness" (size, interconnectedness, and systemic importance) of financial institutions on the one hand, and the debate on how to make the "failure" of these institutions less costly or disorderly, and ultimately a more credible prospect, on the other. Finally, the last section offers some brief concluding remarks.

---

11. The findings are qualitatively similar if one substitutes top-five bank assets for top-three bank assets.

12. For an account of the discussions, see for example Brooke Masters, " 'Too Big to Fail' Debate Still Muddled," *Financial Times*, September 17, 2010. For the report itself, see FSB (2010).

13. Basel Committee on Banking Supervision, "Group of Governors and Heads of Supervision Announces Higher Global Minimum Capital Standards," press release, September 12, 2010.

Historical Background, Before and During the Crisis

The United States and European Union have different starting points for the TBTF debate, in part for reasons linked to their respective histories, including the experience of the recent crisis. These legacies form a crucial backdrop for any forward-looking policy discussion.

Precrisis History

The United States has a long tradition of suspicion and concern about large banks, which goes as far back as the controversy between Alexander Hamilton and Thomas Jefferson about the establishment of the First Bank of the United States in 1791. For a long time, the growth of a "national" financial system was kept in check by initiatives to restrain banking. The 1927 McFadden Act prohibited national banks from opening new branches across state lines. During the Great Depression, the Glass-Steagall Act (1933) forced a strict separation of investment banking activities from depositary banks, leading to the breakup of major institutions, such as the 1935 spinoff of Morgan Stanley from JP Morgan & Co. However, much of this framework was repealed in the 1980s and 1990s. The 1982 Garn–St. Germain Act allowed out-of-state bank holding companies to acquire failed banks and thrifts, regardless of state law. The Riegle-Neal Act of 1994, which took effect in 1997, largely did away with restrictions on interstate branching for domestic bank holding companies and foreign banks. The Gramm-Leach-Bliley Act of 1999 repealed much of Glass-Steagall and lifted restrictions on the formation of diversified financial conglomerates.

The banking crisis of the 1980s provided a rehearsal for some of the current arguments about the TBTF problem. In 1984, the Continental Illinois National Bank and Trust Company, then the seventh-largest US bank by deposits, ran into severe difficulties and had to be rescued with liquidity support from the Federal Reserve, and with guarantees from the FDIC under a provision of the 1950 Federal Deposit Insurance Act, which had been seldom used until then. In subsequent hearings, the US Comptroller of the Currency admitted that regulators would not let the largest 11 US banks fail.[14] The expression "too big to fail," at least as applied to banks, is said to date from this episode.[15] Partly as a result, the 1991 Federal Deposit Insurance Corporation Improvement Act established a special resolution regime for commercial banks and gave the FDIC a mandate to administer it. However, until 2008 this regime was applied only to relatively small institutions and was therefore not tested on a TBTF institution.

---

14. Charles Conover, testimony before US House Committee on Banking, Finance and Urban Affairs, Subcommittee on Financial Institutions Supervision, Regulation and Insurance, Inquiry into Continental Illinois Corporation and Continental Illinois National Bank, 98th Congress, 2nd Session, September 18–19 and October 4, 1984.

15. Eric Dash, "If It's Too Big to Fail, Is It Too Big to Exist?" *New York Times*, June 20, 2009.

The crisis surrounding Long-Term Capital Management (LTCM), a hedge fund that suffered heavy losses and liquidity tensions as a result of the Asian and Russian financial crises in 1997–98 and had to be bailed out by major banks under the auspices of the Federal Reserve Bank of New York in September 1998, illustrated a new dimension of the TBTF problem—sometimes referred to as "too interconnected to fail." With assets in excess of $100 billion, LTCM was not huge, but it was felt that its bankruptcy would cause a chain reaction throughout the financial system that could have catastrophic consequences, as assets would have to be liquidated at fire-sale prices.

In the European Union, the historical and political underpinnings of the TBTF problem are very different. Because the continent is composed of independent, generally centralized nation states with strong cross-border financial linkages, national governments have been encouraged to favor the emergence of a strong and autonomous national financial sector that could successfully compete with its neighbors. Thus, the inclination is generally to protect and foster "national banking champions." When these run into difficulties the inclination is to prevent their disappearance or foreign takeover, either by forcing domestic consolidation or (if this option is not available) by nationalization.

An early example of such "financial nationalism" is the creation of Deutsche Bank in 1870 in Berlin, partly to counteract the dominance of British banks in international transactions, in the context of the formation and rise of the German Empire. As a consequence of the Great Depression and Second World War, large swaths of the financial system were nationalized in several countries, including Italy in 1933 and France in 1946. Since then, privatizations and financial crises (such as those in Spain in the 1980s, or the difficulties of France's Crédit Lyonnais in the 1990s) have spurred considerable intracountry consolidation. Somewhat paradoxically, the introduction of the euro as a single currency in much of the European Union first resulted in further intracountry consolidation rather than the cross-border variety, as governments wanted stronger national champions to be ready for what they saw as a forthcoming increase in cross-border competition—the main exceptions being within groupings of small like-oriented countries (such as the Benelux or Scandinavia), and in central and eastern European countries, where the banking sectors were privatized.

Since the 1990s, the European Commission has intervened more assertively in the consolidation process than in previous decades. Its Directorate General for Competition (known as DG COMP) has not generally objected to mergers among financial institutions with a cross-border market impact, as the creation of pan-European financial groups was generally seen positively from the perspective of integration of the single European market.[16] On the

---

16. DG COMP's mandate is only about competition and not about assessing the financial stability impact of mergers and acquisitions, at either the national or the European level. However, EU legislation allows prudential considerations to be invoked by national authorities to defend a combination that might otherwise be rejected on competition grounds.

contrary, the European Commission has tended to intervene to unblock cross-border combinations that were opposed by national prudential authorities supervising the target firm, particularly since the landmark case of Santander's attempted acquisition of Portugal's Champalimaud Group in 1999. This intervention, combined with the limits reached by intracountry consolidation as some national banking systems became extremely concentrated, encouraged a wave of cross-border banking mergers and acquisitions in the 2000s, which led to the emergence of a handful of truly "pan-European" groups (such as BNP Paribas, Santander, and UniCredit). In terms of deal size, the high point of this wave was the ill-fated hostile takeover of ABN AMRO in 2007 by a consortium of Royal Bank of Scotland (RBS), Fortis, and Santander, which in turn contributed to the downfall of the former two.

Overall, this history has produced a wide diversity of banking structures within the European Union, with the larger continental economies (France, Germany, Italy, the Netherlands, and Spain) still relying predominantly on domestically headquartered banks, and most smaller countries (Belgium, Finland, all former communist countries) dominated by local affiliates of foreign banks. The United Kingdom is a category of its own with, inter alia, one large foreign-owned retail bank (Santander UK), along with very large wholesale activities of nondomestic, European, and non-European financial institutions in the City of London, now the undisputed financial hub of Europe, as the continent's capital markets have gradually integrated over the past two decades (a development that has mostly happened independently from banking consolidation).

Apart from the "domestic champions" mindset, a second major difference between the United States and European Union is the attitude toward bank failures. It is often asserted that the United States is more tolerant of corporate insolvency than most European cultures, and that the US bankruptcy code, at least when applied to nonfinancial companies, is comparatively more protective of corporate executives and employees than most European counterparts. In the case of banking, this difference is compounded in the European (and especially the German) psyche by the memories of the last significant wave of bank defaults in Europe, which in 1931 played a prominent role in enabling the subsequent rise to power of Adolf Hitler's National Socialists. Thus, it is common among European policymakers to see bank failures as politically ominous disasters to be avoided at all costs, even in the case of relatively small banks. The head of Germany's financial supervisory authority, BaFin, commented in early August 2007, in the very first stages of the financial crisis, that the bailout of IKB, a second-tier specialized bank that most observers would have thought far smaller than any reasonable TBTF threshold, was necessary to avoid "the worst financial crisis since 1931."[17]

By "failure" we mean here the case where a financial institution fails to meet its contractual obligations to third parties. In the corporate world, the

---

17. Wolfgang Reuter, "German State-Owned Banks on Verge of Collapse," *Der Spiegel*, February 20, 2008, www.spiegel.de/international/business/0,1518,536635-2,00.html.

default process for handling failures is bankruptcy. In banking, and finance more generally, the existence of systemic risk means that bankruptcy can be disruptive much beyond the individual institution that fails. There are essentially three alternatives to bankruptcy when a financial institution reaches the point of insolvency. The first is a specific "resolution regime" involving the transfer of the institution's assets and economic rights into receivership by a public entity, such as the FDIC in the United States, which can then decide which obligations will be honored. The second, nontechnically known as a "bailout," is government intervention to repay creditors, which in certain cases is accompanied by nationalization, i.e., a voluntary or forced transfer of ownership to the state without interrupting business continuity. The third, sometimes euphemistically referred to as "regulatory forbearance," is a temporary (sometimes extended) denial by the authorities that the institution is indeed insolvent, if necessary involving the softening or outright exemption of public disclosure requirements. (Of course, this cannot be considered "crisis resolution" but only a dilatory measure in the hope that the crisis will disappear or become less acute with the passing of time.) In our use of the word, failure is a possibility under the first of these alternatives to bankruptcy, but not under the latter two.

Using this definition, we are not aware of any single major EU-headquartered bank failing in the first three years of the crisis.[18] Several banks, such as Northern Rock and Bradford & Bingley in the United Kingdom and Hypo Real Estate in Germany, have been nationalized (using newly introduced legislation) and subsequently dismantled, but they have honored all contractual obligations throughout the process, as have Spanish savings banks taken over by the Bank of Spain, such as Caja Castilla–La Mancha and CajaSur (using legislation dating from the 1980s). There were some actual bank failures but only of fairly small institutions, such as Weserbank in Germany, which was declared insolvent in April 2008; Dunfermline Building Society in Scotland in March 2009; and DSB Bank in the Netherlands in October 2009. This stands in contrast to the United States, where failures included Lehman Brothers, Washington Mutual (a major US savings bank placed in receivership in late September 2008 whose banking subsidiaries were subsequently acquired by JPMorgan Chase), CIT Group (a mid-sized commercial finance company that entered bankruptcy in November 2009), and scores of smaller US depositary institutions found insolvent and taken into receivership by the FDIC. Only the funding difficulties of some EU member states may bring significant change. In November 2010, the Irish government decided to impose losses on junior bondholders of Anglo Irish Banks, which had been nationalized in January 2009, and at the time of writing there was expectation of other cases to follow.

---

18. Iceland, which is part of the European Economic Area but not of the European Union, is obviously not included here.

A third specific "European" feature is linked to Europe's welfare and/or social-democrat heritage, namely the importance of cooperatives and savings banks in several EU countries. The United States had a rough equivalent with the savings and loan (S&L) institutions and credit unions, but their importance and specificity have decreased in the last two decades, not least as a consequence of the S&L crisis of the 1980s. Many demutualizations and transformations into commercial bank entities have taken place in Italy, Sweden (with the formation of Swedbank), and the United Kingdom, but the cooperative and savings bank segment remains prominent in Austria (Erste, Raiffeisen), Denmark (savings banks), Finland (OP-Pohjola), France (Banques Populaires–Caisses d'Épargne Groupe, Crédit Agricole, Crédit Mutuel), Germany (savings banks and *Volksbanken*), the Netherlands (Rabobank), and Spain (savings banks). In general, cooperative and savings banks have proved fairly resilient in financial crises, except when they diversified beyond their core retail business, in which case they have often run into major difficulties (Fonteyne 2007). As they are not publicly listed, they typically disclose less financial information than listed peers; this in turn can be a contributing factor to market distrust, as has recently been the case, arguably, in both Germany and Spain.

Outright government ownership of banks used to be widespread, but it largely disappeared from the European Union with the large-scale privatizations of the 1980s and 1990s. The main exceptions are Germany's seven *Landesbanken*, generally jointly owned by local governments (*Länder*) and local savings banks in varying proportions;[19] a few remaining state-owned banks in formerly communist countries, most prominently Poland's largest bank, PKO-BP (51 percent owned by the Polish state as of mid-2009); and specialized national financial institutions with public service mandates, such as France's Caisse des Dépôts et Consignations, Italy's Cassa Depositi Prestiti, Germany's Kreditanstalt für Wiederaufbau, or Spain's Instituto de Crédito Oficial, which, on most activities, do not compete directly with private sector financial firms (in the United States, Fannie Mae and Freddie Mac would arguably form a similar category). In addition, of course, there are legacies of government interventions in financial crises, such as the Swedish state's stake in Nordea (19.9 percent as of mid-2009); or more recently the controlling stakes of the UK government in Northern Rock, RBS, and Lloyds Banking Group; and the government ownership of virtually the entire banking sector in Ireland. But in these cases, the respective governments proclaim their intent to sell their shares as soon as market conditions are favorable.

---

19. For example, BayernLB is 94 percent owned by the state of Bavaria, while Helaba is 85 percent owned by savings banks in the state of Hesse, and Landesbank Berlin is 99 percent owned by the German national association of savings banks (DSGV).

Developments Since 2007

In the United States, the July 2010 Dodd-Frank Wall Street Reform and Consumer Protection Act (Dodd-Frank Act 2010) contains a host of provisions targeted at the regulation and supervision of SIFIs (Davis Polk 2010), including, inter alia, the following stipulations:

- Bank holding companies with $50 billion or more in assets are automatically subject to enhanced prudential standards.

- Once designated, systemically important nonbank financial companies must register with the Federal Reserve within 180 days.

- The Federal Reserve is required to establish enhanced risk-based capital, leverage, and liquidity requirements as well as overall risk management requirements, resolution plans, credit exposure reporting, concentration limits, and prompt corrective action to apply to systemically important bank and nonbank financial firms.

- The enhanced prudential standards will also apply to US operations of foreign bank holding companies, although it is not yet known whether such provisions will apply extraterritorially to the foreign parent.

- Subject to some exceptions and a transition period, any "banking entity" will be prohibited from engaging in proprietary trading or sponsoring and investing in a hedge fund or private equity fund; systemically important nonbank financial companies, while not prohibited from engaging in such activities, will be required to carry additional capital and comply with certain other quantitative limits on such activities (part 1 of the so-called Volcker Rule).[20]

- Any insured depository institution or systemically important nonbank financial company will be prohibited from merging with, or acquiring substantially all the assets or control of, another company if the resulting company's total consolidated liabilities would exceed 10 percent of the aggregate consolidated liabilities of all financial companies at the end of the prior calendar year (part 2 of the Volcker Rule).

- Systemically important nonbank financial companies and large, interconnected bank companies will be required to prepare and maintain extensive rapid and orderly resolution plans, which must be approved by the Federal Reserve and the FDIC.

Many of these provisions require regulations to be issued by federal agencies, and these were still in the works at the time of writing this chapter. In a speech in August 2010, the US Treasury secretary continued to underscore the priority attached to making progress on TBTF when he emphasized that "the final area of reform . . . is perhaps the most important, establishing new

---

20. While the Volcker Rule applies to all banks and is therefore not exclusively targeted at SIFIs, it was partly motivated by considerations of systemic risk.

rules to constrain risk-taking by—and leverage in—the largest global financial institutions."[21]

By contrast, in the European Union there have so far been no legislative or regulatory initiatives to establish size caps, mandatory capital, or liquidity standards applicable specifically to SIFIs, nor anything resembling the Volcker Rule. The only item in the Dodd-Frank "menu" that has already been met with some action in the European Union is the last one in the list, as various EU member states are asking leading banks to produce proposals to facilitate their possible recovery and/or resolution in a crisis, whether formally as specifically defined "living wills" or as part of the ongoing supervisory dialogue. In Belgium, recent legislation has created a national systemic risk board that will publish and regularly update an official list of SIFIs requiring special attention: a first version of this list was published in October 2010 and includes 15 legal entities belonging to nine different financial groups.[22] In the United Kingdom, the coalition government elected in May 2010 has established the Independent Commission on Banking, which is expected to propose a policy strategy to address the TBTF issue. Its conclusions are expected in June 2011, and an active public debate will certainly take place before then.

At the European Union level, the legislative response to the crisis has been generally slower than in the United States for four main reasons. First, legislative proceedings are structurally slow in the European Union because of the complex interaction between the EU level and 27 sovereign states. The lawmaking framework combines the exclusive right of initiative for the European Commission and the need to reach agreement both with the Council of Ministers, which represents the 27 member states voting (in most financial services matters) under a qualified-majority rule, and with the European Parliament. Second, at the time of the Lehman Brothers collapse, the European Commission was already in lame duck mode awaiting its planned renewal in 2009, and this renewal was then further delayed for procedural reasons involving the adoption of the Lisbon Treaty. The new team, including Michel Barnier, the new commissioner for Internal Market and Services (who oversees most financial services issues), took the reins only in early 2010. Third, priority was initially given to the necessary overhaul of the European Union's supervisory architecture. This is an innovative policy endeavor that in 2011 will establish three supranational European supervisory authorities, with respective mandates over banks (European Banking Authority), securities and markets (European Securities and Markets Authority), and insurance (European Insurance and Occupational Pensions

---

21. Timothy Geithner, Rebuilding the American Financial System, speech given at NYU Stern School of Business, New York, August 2, 2010.

22. Of the nine, five are headquartered in Belgium (Ageas, Dexia, Ethias, Euroclear, and KBC) and four are foreign headquartered (AXA, Bank of New York Mellon, BNP Paribas Fortis, and ING). Belgian Committee for Systemic Risks and System-Relevant Financial Institutions (CSRSFI), Circulaire CREFS 2010-01, Brussels, October 2010.

Authority), as well as a European Systemic Risk Board to oversee macropru-dential issues. The corresponding legislation, based on a report published in February 2009 (de Larosière 2009), was finalized in September 2010. This rather long delay is unsurprising given the political significance of the changes: the US equivalent is not the limited reorganization of federal agencies included in the Dodd-Frank Act, but rather the establishment of federal financial au-thorities such as the Securities and Exchange Commission and the Federal Deposit Insurance Corporation in the 1930s, even though the European agen-cies will start with a more limited mandate that does not supersede all existing competencies of national supervisors at the level of EU member states. Fourth, and not least, the European Union remains in the midst of an unresolved major banking crisis, while in the United States the "stress tests" of spring 2009 and subsequent recapitalization managed to restore a sense of normalcy at the core of the national banking system, even though many smaller banks have failed since.

Now that a new commission is in charge and a suitable supervisory in-frastructure is being put in place, new policy initiatives are to be expected. The indications so far, however, are that the EU institutions are reluctant to envisage specific policies to address the TBTF problem. Two European Com-mission communications (nonbinding statements of policy principle) were published in 2010, the first on bank resolution funds in May and the second on crisis management and resolution in October (European Commission 2010a, 2010b). Both contain essentially no reference to a possible differential treatment of SIFIs compared to smaller financial institutions, and suggest that the commission at this point remains markedly more cautious on the TBTF problem than the United States has been with the adoption of the Dodd-Frank Act. The same applies to a more recent consultation on "tech-nical details of a possible EU framework" for bank recovery and resolution (European Commission 2011).

Such caution reflects a more structural challenge for the European Com-mission as a direct result of the financial crisis. In the preceding decade, the European Union relied on an implicit agreement within both the commission and the European Parliament to foster financial market integration through the dismantling of national regulatory barriers that hindered it, and thus de facto aligned itself with an international deregulatory agenda (Posner and Véron 2010). Now that reregulation is the order of the day, this alignment is no longer relevant, and the European Commission finds itself with the need to define a new strategic orientation that must still be compatible with the be-guiling diversity of national positions and regulatory cultures within the Eu-ropean Union. One option may be to replicate US choices under the guise of transatlantic convergence, as Commissioner Barnier seems to have chosen in the important issue of moving over the counter derivatives toward centralized clearing. However, it is doubtful that the same can be achieved in the highly politically charged area of bank regulation. Thus, it is to be expected that some time will pass before a clear orientation emerges at the EU level in this area.

Structural Differences Between the United States and European Union

In this section, we examine the differences in financial and political structures that result from the contrasting historical paths of the United States and European Union. We would argue that such structural differences are influential in shaping the policy arguments on issues such as TBTF.

Financial Industry Structures

In the European Union banks play a much bigger role in financial intermediation than in the United States. This contributes to different attitudes toward regulatory reform. The Institute of International Finance (IIF 2010b) calculates that, as of end-2009, US banks accounted for only 24 percent of credit intermediation in the country, versus 53 percent in Japan and as much as 74 percent in the euro area. Many financial services that in the United States are provided by nonbank financial firms, such as asset management, broker dealing, and specialized credit functions, are mostly delivered by banking conglomerates in the European Union. To give an illustration: In the Financial Times Global 500 ranking of the world's 500 largest listed companies (by market value as of end-June 2010, the latest data available), all 18 noninsurance financial firms with headquarters in Europe that were listed were referred to as banks, compared with only 7 out of 18 such firms based in the United States (representing 65 percent of the corresponding aggregated market capitalization).[23]

One consequence is that for all the consolidation that has taken place in the United States in recent years, EU-headquartered banks are comparatively larger than their US counterparts, especially when measured by assets. IFSL (2010) research reports that of the worldwide assets of the 1,000 largest banks in 2008–09, EU banks had the largest share at 56 percent, versus 13 percent for US banks and 14 percent for Asian banks. Table 6.1 shows that of the top 25 banks worldwide, ranked by assets at end-2009, 10 of the top 15, including the 6 largest, were in the European Union.

Another consequence is that measured by the ratio of assets to home-country GDP, the largest EU banks are much larger, and thus even more likely to be considered TBTF, than their largest US counterparts. As shown in table 6.2, ratios of top-three or top-five bank assets to GDP show a considerable increase in the size of the largest banks since 1990 (earliest available year) in all nine of the large advanced economies included in the sample. As noted earlier, for more than two-thirds of the cases, this increase in the size of the largest banks relative to the size of the economy also continued during the

---

23. See www.ft.com. The *Financial Times* list does not refer to Goldman Sachs, Morgan Stanley, and American Express as "banks," even though they converted to bank holding company status at the height of the crisis in late 2008. If these were considered banks, the share of nonbanks in the sample's aggregate market value would decrease from 35 to 19.5 percent.

Table 6.1 Top 25 banks worldwide, by assets, 1990 and 2009 (millions of US dollars)

Rank	1990 Institution	1990 Assets	2009 Institution	2009 Assets
1	Dai-ichi Kangyo Bank Limited, Tokyo	428,167	The Royal Bank of Scotland Group PLC, Edinburgh	3,500,950
2	Sumitomo Bank Limited, Osaka	409,161	Deutsche Bank AG, Frankfurt	3,065,307
3	Mitsui Taiyo Kobe Bank Limited, Tokyo	408,754	Barclays Bank PLC, London	2,992,682
4	Sanwa Bank Limited, Osaka	402,699	BNP Paribas SA, Paris	2,888,728
5	Fuji Bank Limited, Tokyo	399,545	HSBC Holdings, London	2,418,033
6	Mitsubishi Bank Limited, Tokyo	391,528	Crédit Agricole SA, Paris	2,239,370
7	Crédit Agricole Mutuel, Paris	305,206	JPMorgan Chase, New York	2,175,052
8	Banque Nationale de Paris	291,873	The Bank of Tokyo-Mitsubishi UFJ Limited, Tokyo	2,025,830
9	Industrial Bank of Japan Limited, Tokyo	289,067	Citigroup, New York	1,938,470
10	Crédit Lyonnais, Paris	287,331	UBS AG, Zürich	1,894,423
11	Deutsche Bank AG, Frankfurt	266,286	ING Bank NV, Amsterdam	1,853,393
12	Barclays Bank PLC, London	258,983	Bank of America, Charlotte	1,817,943
13	Tokai Bank Limited, Nagoya	249,751	Société Générale, Paris la Défense	1,572,721
14	Norinchukin Bank, Tokyo	249,667	Banco Santander SA, Madrid	1,460,866
15	Mitsubishi Trust & Banking Corporation, Tokyo	237,696	UniCredit SpA, Milan	1,455,270
16	National Westminster Bank PLC, London	232,512	Industrial & Commercial Bank of China, Beijing	1,427,685
17	Bank of Tokyo Limited	223,185	Sumitomo Mitsui Banking Corporation, Tokyo	1,219,544
18	Société Générale, Paris	219,983	China Construction Bank Corporation, Beijing	1,105,471
19	Sumitomo Trust and Banking Company Limited, Osaka	218,916	Crédit Suisse Group, Zürich	1,100,263
20	Mitsui Trust and Banking Company Limited, Osaka	210,935	Agricultural Bank of China Limited, Beijing	1,026,300
21	Long-Term Credit Bank of Japan Limited, Tokyo	200,679	Bank of China Limited, Beijing	1,017,718
22	Dresdner Bank, Frankfurt	186,936	Mizuho Financial Group, Tokyo	1,494,960
23	Union Bank of Switzerland, Zurich	183,443	Wells Fargo, San Francisco	1,309,639
24	Yasuda Trust & Banking Company Limited, Tokyo	175,552	Bank of Scotland PLC, Edinburgh	1,005,710
25	Daiwa Bank Limited, Osaka	171,239	Dexia, Brussels	906,063
	Total top 25	6,819,094	Total top 25	44,912,391

Sources: Jason Goldberg; American Banker; The Banker, *Top 1000 World Banks*; and Barclays Capital, *Large-Cap/Mid-Cap Banks 2010 Outlook.*

Table 6.2   Combined assets of the three or five largest banks relative to GDP, 1990, 2006, and 2009 (percent)

Country	Top 3 banks			Top 5 banks		
	1990	2006	2009	1990	2006	2009
Germany	38	117	118	55	161	151
United Kingdom	68	226	336	87	301	466
France	70	212	250	95	277	344
Italy	29	110	121	44	127	138
Spain	45	155	189	66	179	220
Netherlands	154	538	406	159	594	464
Sweden	89	254	334	120	312	409
Japan	36	76	92	59	96	115
United States	8	35	43	11	45	58

Source: Bank for International Settlements, www.bis.org.

recent crisis (where 2006 represents the precrisis observation and 2009 the latest observation).

Just as important for our purposes, table 6.2 shows that large banks have considerably more systemic importance in all major EU economies than they do in the United States—at least if systemic importance is proxied by the size of the balance sheet, which probably underestimates the importance of banks in the United States given the broader development there of the shadow banking system (Pozsar et al. 2010). Our interpretation is that the TBTF problem is actually much more pressing in the European Union than the United States, and also much more difficult to address. Some might argue that since the European Union has a policy to create a single financial market, bank assets should be compared to the EU GDP rather than the national GDP of the country of headquarters, in which case the EU and US figures would be of a comparable order of magnitude. However, such a comparison of aggregates is less relevant from a policy perspective: As the recent crisis brought home forcefully, de facto public guarantees for most banks come from the home country and only from there, a reality aptly summarized by the quip, often attributed to Mervyn King, that "international banks are global in life, but national in death."

In truth, the European reality is somewhat blurred by some banks' multiple national allegiances. Thus Dexia was jointly rescued by France and Belgium (and their respective taxpayers) in late September 2008, and it is likely that some burden sharing would be sought in the case of a public intervention to help, say, Nordea (in this case involving Denmark, Finland, and Norway in addition to Sweden, the country where the group is formally headquartered). Standard Chartered, while headquartered in the United Kingdom, has much of its activity and also many of its central decision-making functions located in Asia, and it is therefore unclear that the UK government would support it even in the event of very serious difficulties. However, even after much cross-border integration, these are exceptional cases, and most European banking groups have an unambiguous "home country" that the current policy framework designates by default as the one whose national government is likely to intervene in a crisis. The same applies to all significant US banks.

It should be noted that European banks are less globally dominant when ranked by other measures of size or strength. By absolute value of Tier 1 capital (also in 2008–09), US banks dominate the top-10 list: Four of this group are US banks (including the top three), four are EU banks (two from the United Kingdom and one each from Spain and France), one is Japanese, and one is Chinese (IFSL 2010). Rankings by market capitalization have been dominated since late 2007 by leading Chinese banks, with ICBC consistently at the top and China Construction Bank more often than not number two.[24] By end-September 2010, HSBC (ranked third) was the only "European" bank in the top five, notwithstanding the fact that much of its activity is in Asia and its chief executive is based in Hong Kong. Santander was the only other European bank in the global top 10, and is the smallest of that group, which otherwise includes two other Chinese institutions (Agricultural Bank of China and Bank of China) and four American ones (JPMorgan Chase, Bank of America, Wells Fargo, and Citigroup).

Another major structural difference between the United States and the European Union is the higher degree of internationalization of European banks, most of which takes place within the European Union. Table 6.3 illustrates the degree to which European banks have internationalized from their home base to the rest of Europe, less so in the rest of the world. The typical large European bank has less than half its activity in its home country; the corresponding proportion for US banks sampled is above three-fourths.

This difference in the degree of internationalization implies that cross-border linkages, especially intra–European Union ones, are typically much more important in policy discussions within the European Union than they are in the United States. In a way, one might even say that discussion of the cross-border dimensions of financial stability policy has largely crowded out discussion of the TBTF issue in (continental) Europe, at least for the time being.

Political Systems

A more intangible but no less important factor of transatlantic policy differences is the difference in political systems, which leads to strikingly different decision-making processes and to different allocations of priorities. In most EU countries, the parliamentary nature of the regime means that the executive and legislative branches are closely aligned, while in the United States, divergence between Congress and the executive branch is not unusual. EU countries also vary widely in the respective strengths of the executive and legislative branches, with a rule of thumb that parliaments are generally stronger in Northern than Southern Europe. The United States mainly relies on federal regulation of

---

24. Based on quarterly Financial Times Global 500 rankings, available at www.ft.com.

Table 6.3 International versus national sources of bank revenue, large global banks, 2009

EU bank	Assets, 2009 (billions of US dollars)	Estimated share of total 2009 revenue (percent)			
		Home country	Rest of Europe	Americas	Rest of world
BNP Paribas SA	2,952	34	42	14	9
The Royal Bank of Scotland Group PLC	2,728	48	27	18	6
HSBC Holdings PLC	2,356	25	11	34	31
Crédit Agricole SA	2,227	49	38	4	8
Barclays Bank PLC	2,223	44	15	19	22
Deutsche Bank AG	2,151	26	41	22	11
ING Bank NV	1,668	26	24	32	18
Lloyds	1,651	94	0	0	6
Société Générale	1,469	43	39	9	9
UniCredit SpA	1,439	49	41	0	10
Banco Santander SA	1,439	23	27	50	0
Commerzbank	1,203	84	14	1	0
Intesa Sanpaolo	878	79	19	0	2
Dexia	829	47	43	7	3
BBVA	760	41	0	59	0
Nordea	729	19	81	0	0
Danske Bank	597	54	40	0	6
Standard Chartered	436	6	3	3	88
Average	1,541	44	28	15	13

US bank		Home country (United States)	Rest of Americas	Europe	Rest of world
Bank of America Corporation	2,223	82	1	8	9
JPMorgan Chase & Company	2,032	75	2	17	6
Citigroup	1,857	32	20	25	23
Wells Fargo	1,244	100	0	0	0
Goldman Sachs Group, Inc.	849	56	0	26	18
Morgan Stanley	771	81	0	11	9
US Bancorp	281	100	0	0	0
PNC Financial	270	100	0	0	0
Bank of New York	212	47	0	37	16
BB&T	166	100	0	0	0
Average	991	77	2	12	8

Sources: Forbes Global 2000, April 2010, available at www.forbes.com; annual reports and websites of individual companies listed; authors' calculations. Mauricio Nakahodo's research assistance is gratefully acknowledged.

finance (with some exceptions such as insurance), whereas in Europe competencies in financial and banking regulation are shared between the national and EU levels. Some important matters, such as bankruptcy and tax legislation, are entirely or almost entirely national; others, such as accounting standards for listed companies' consolidated financial statements and oversight of rating agencies, are entirely set at the EU level; and many others are a combination of EU directives (EU-level legislation that requires "transposition" into national law) and additional national requirements, sometimes referred to in EU jargon as "gold plating."

Less well documented is the way the respective political and financial systems interact with and depend on each other, a factor that an abundant political science and journalistic literature suggests can be an important driver of policy. In the United States, the attempts of private sector actors to influence public policy decisions are typically measured in terms of election campaign contributions and lobbying expenses, for which there is a comparatively high degree of public transparency in spite of continuous (and often successful) attempts by private donors to circumvent existing disclosure requirements. For example, Johnson and Kwak (2010) calculate that campaign contributions from the US financial sector have grown from $61 million in 1990 to $260 million in 2006, a more than fourfold increase. In Europe, no equivalent benchmarks are available. In most EU countries, election campaigns are largely (though not entirely) funded by the public purse, and the granularity of available data on private campaign contributions is inferior to the US equivalent. Lobbying activities tend to be of a more informal nature than in America, and typically go entirely unreported.

That said, numerous examples and anecdotes support the proposition that the financial industry is at least as influential in shaping policy in many parts of Europe as it is in the United States. In Spain and Germany, local politicians sit on savings banks' boards, and regions have direct equity ownership in the *Landesbanken*. In France, most senior executives in the banking industry have a civil service background, and conversely many prominent civil servants expect to move to banks in their later working years, which may influence their behavior and priorities. In Italy and Belgium, local communities play a significant role in the governance of key financial institutions. In the United Kingdom, city financiers actively engage political leaders in various informal venues. At the EU level, international financial institutions have built considerable influence in recent years, helped by an alignment between their own aims of winning international business and the EU institutions' commitment to cross-border financial integration (Posner and Véron 2010). It remains to be seen how this relationship is to be affected by the European Commission's change of emphasis since 2008 toward more intrusive regulation, as a consequence of the financial crisis. The assertive competition policy developed by the European Union since the 1990s illustrates that when no such alignment of aims exists, the European Commission can display a level of imperviousness to corporate influence that is rarely matched by national governments.

Yet another significant dimension is the fact that not all political leaders involved in financial regulation face the same kind of constituencies. In the United States, congressional representatives from states with major financial centers commonly take more favorable views of the financial industry than those without, but no such differences exist within the executive branch, as it has a nationwide mandate. In the European Union, however, much of the decision making results from the interaction of member states. Some countries, such as the United Kingdom, host global financial centers; in others, such as Cyprus, Ireland, or Luxembourg, the financial industry is a major contributor to the local economy, while in others still it is not seen as a significant contributor to national competitiveness. Some countries, such as France or Spain, have very limited penetration by foreign banks in their domestic banking markets, but have strong "national champions" that have dynamically expanded abroad in recent years. Not surprisingly, countries of this type have repeatedly displayed a strong inclination for home-country regulation, especially in comparison with countries (such as Finland and most Central and Eastern European member states) where most banks are in foreign hands, and where more emphasis tends to be placed on host-country control.

Differences are especially prominent in matters relative to wholesale financial intermediation, especially those segments that are concentrated in the United Kingdom as a result of several decades of (largely successful) EU financial integration. In such matters, an overwhelming majority of the EU Council of Ministers has no direct political stake in the outcome, as those market participants potentially affected are not among its constituents. The discussion of the Alternative Investment Fund Managers directive has been a prominent example of such dynamics. Conversely, the United Kingdom, partly because it hosts the continent's major financial center and its banks have comparatively little activity on the continent, tends to downplay the need for consistent and binding policy frameworks at the EU level. All these specificities tend to make financial policy decision making at the EU level generally more complex, and often less fact based, than it can be in a single, coherent political entity.

The "Bigness" Debate: Size, Interconnectedness, and Systemic Importance

In a report to G-20 finance ministers and governors, the International Monetary Fund (IMF), BIS, and FSB (2009, 2) define systemic risk as "a disruption to financial services that (1) is caused by an impairment to all parts of the financial system, and (2) has the potential to have serious negative consequences for the real economy." SIFIs—be they banks or nonbanks—can then be seen as institutions whose impending failure, inability to operate, and disorderly wind-down could produce such systemic effects.[25] The key criteria most

---

25. Thomson (2009, 1) argues that a firm is systemically important "if its failure would have economically significant spillover effects [that], if left unchecked, could destabilize the financial system and have a negative impact on the real economy." The ECB (2006, 132) argues similarly that large and complex banking groups are those "whose size and nature of business are such that their failure and inability to operate would most likely spread and have adverse implications for the smooth functioning of financial markets or other financial institutions operating within the system."

often listed for identifying such SIFIs include size, concentration (sometimes employed as a proxy for substitutability), interconnectedness, performance of systemically important functions, and complexity (which some argue is proxied by the number of majority-owned subsidiaries or affiliates, or by the number of regulatory agencies or courts that would be involved in a resolution of the group). Many analysts also throw in leverage and liquidity as helping to define SIFIs, although these can be regarded as characteristics of vulnerability that apply to all financial institutions. Most analysts also recognize that TBTF has a time-dependent or context-dependent dimension—that is, thresholds for TBTF can be much lower if impending failure occurs at a time when and/or in a context in which the economy is fragile and/or other financial institution failures have recently taken place.

To address the challenge posed by TBTF institutions, the first set of proposals concentrates roughly on the notion of "too big." This section accordingly explores the options and prospects for regulation of bank size, and their respective implications in the United States and European Union.

Defining Bigness

As suggested above, there is no single measure or single firm characteristic that could provide a simple and straightforward gauge of systemic importance. A flavor of what has been done to gauge which financial institutions are and are not "systemically important" can be gleaned from the following examples.

The European Central Bank (ECB 2006, 2007) has published a framework for identifying what it calls large and complex banking groups (LCBGs). It argues that the size of the balance sheet alone may fail to capture important interconnections, especially given the growing importance of off–balance sheet activities. It therefore proposed a multi-indicator approach that incorporates the following 13 variables: assets under custody, contingent liabilities, interbank assets, interbank liabilities, net interest revenue, proceeds from equity issuance, deposits, customer loans, net noninterest revenue, proceeds from syndicated loan issuance, other assets, proceeds from bond issuance, and mortgages (ECB 2006). In ECB (2007), six more indicators were added to cover cross-border assets, overnight lending contributions, market capitalization, number of recorded subsidiaries, subordinated debt issuance, and trading income. The indicators were applied to a 2006 sample of 415 euro area and non–euro area banks, and cluster analysis was employed to demarcate the LCBGs from the others. In the end, the ECB (2007) wound up with 36 banking groups that were "large and complex." Of these, 21 were headquartered in the euro area and 15 outside. A composite size measure, based on the 19 indicators, was also constructed for each of these 36 institutions, and tests were conducted to see how that measure correlated with total assets (the traditional size measure). Despite the ECB's (2006) a priori argument that asset size alone was not likely to be a sufficient indicator for indentifying LCBGs, it turned out that the R^2 between total assets and the composite size measure was about 0.93, indicating that asset size alone conveys a good deal of useful information.

A second example comes from James Thomson (2009), who aimed to establish a set of criteria for designating US financial firms as "systemically important." He did not base these criteria on empirical studies but instead used his judgment to suggest measures of size, contagion, correlation, concentration, and conditions and/or context. A sampling from Thomson's criteria conveys the basic idea. His size threshold would be any of the following: 10 percent or more of nationwide banking assets; 5 percent of nationwide banking assets paired with 15 percent or more of nationwide loans; 10 percent of the total number or total value of life insurance products nationwide; and (for nonbank financial firms that were not traditional insurance companies) either total asset holdings large enough to rank it as one of the 10 largest banks in the country or accounting for more than 20 percent of securities underwritten over the past five years. On contagion, a firm would merit designation as systemically important if its failure could result in substantial capital impairment of other institutions accounting for a combined 30 percent of the assets of the financial system or the locking up or material impairment of essential payments systems. Turning to concentration, Thomson (2009) would regard any financial firm as systemically important if it cleared and settled more than 25 percent of trades in a key financial market, processed more than 25 percent of the daily volume of an essential payments system, or was responsible for more than 30 percent of an important credit activity. However, it is not clear from the article how these thresholds were decided.

Example number three derives from chapter 2 of the April 2009 IMF *Global Financial Stability Report* (IMF 2009). The IMF explores four approaches for measuring interconnectedness: (1) network simulations that draw on BIS data on cross-border interbank exposures and that track the reverberation of a credit event or liquidity squeeze via direct linkages in the interbank market; (2) a default intensity model that uses data from Moody's Default Risk Service and that measures the probability of failures of a large fraction of financial institutions due to both direct and indirect linkages; (3) a corisk model that utilizes five-year credit default swap (CDS) spreads of financial institutions and that assesses systemic linkages among financial institutions under extreme duress; and (4) a stress-dependence matrix that incorporates individual CDS and probability of default data, along with stock prices, to examine pairs of institutions' probabilities of distress.

Among other findings, the IMF (2009) reports the following: (1) simulations with the network model confirm that the US and UK banking systems are the most systemic systems in terms of triggering the largest number of contagion rounds and highest capital losses; (2) the Belgian, Dutch, Swedish, and Swiss banking systems are relatively highly vulnerable to banking distress in other economies; (3) if Citigroup's CDS spread were at a very high level (the 95th percentile), this would lead (in a March 2008 simulation) to an increase of 390 percent in AIG's CDS spread but only a 13 percent increase in the

CDS spread of Wells Fargo; similarly, if Goldman Sachs's CDS spread were at the 95th percentile level during that period, the induced increase in the CDS spread would have been much higher for Bear Stearns than for HSBC or JPMorgan Chase; (4) in March 2008, extreme stress in CDS markets would have had greater spillover effects for 10 other large financial institutions if the stress occurred at HSBC or Commerzbank than if it took place at Wachovia or Bear Stearns; (5) the probability of default of any other bank conditional on Lehman falling into distress went up from 22 percent on July 1, 2007, to 37 percent on September 12, 2008; and (6) drawing on simulations from the default intensity model, the likelihood of the failure of a relatively large number of financial institutions increased sharply during 2008 to exceed the levels seen during the Internet bubble.

Our fourth example deals specifically with complexity. Richard Herring and Jacopo Carmassi (2010) use the number of majority-owned subsidiaries as a rough proxy for the complexity of a large and complex financial institution (LCFI). They note that the 16 LCFIs identified by the Bank of England (2007) and IMF have 2.5 times as many majority-owned subsidiaries as the 16 largest multinational manufacturing firms. As shown in table 6.4, taken from Herring and Carmassi (2010, table 8.1, 199), such financial conglomerates typically have hundreds of majority-owned subsidiaries; 8 of the 16 LCFIs in table 6.4 have more than 1,000 subsidiaries each, and one (Citigroup) has nearly 2,500—half of which are chartered abroad. Lehman Brothers had 433 subsidiaries in 20 countries at the time of its failure. Herring and Carmassi (2010) note that as well as having roughly $700 billion in assets, Lehman was the sixth-largest counterparty in the over-the-counter derivatives market, was a major player in the repo market, and had among its unsecured creditors the US federal government's Pension Benefit Guarantee Corporation, the German government's deposit insurance arm, and money market mutual funds, including the Reserve Primary Fund, which eventually "broke the buck." On top of this, the Fed and Treasury claimed they lacked the tools and/or authority to take over Lehman. Carmassi, Elisabetta Luchetti, and Stefano Micossi (2010) note that subsidiaries constitute the principal legal form of European cross-border banks, holding assets of almost €4.6 trillion; subsidiaries of third countries' credit institutions in Europe hold assets of almost €1.3 trillion. With such complexity for almost all financial conglomerates, it is very difficult to map lines of business into legal entities. Unwinding such complex financial institutions can be a nightmare because SIFIs have operations in many countries, because resolution regimes differ (and often conflict) across countries in many respects, because there is no agreement on a cross-border resolution plan, and because the recent crisis demonstrated that national "ring-fencing" of assets is likely to be the default plan when an international bank fails without an agreed-on burden-sharing formula—an outcome that led some host-country supervisors to press for either an insistence on adequately capitalized subsidiaries or greater say in supervision over foreign banks operating in their backyard (FSA 2009).

Table 6.4 Large and complex financial institutions

Institution	Total assets, year end 2006 (billions of US dollars)[a]	Total subsidiaries[a]	Percent of foreign subsidiaries	Percent of net foreign income before taxes, 2006[b]	HHI business line revenues, 2006[c]	Number of countries[d]	Subsidiaries in OFCs[e]	
							Number	Percent
UBS AG	1,964	417	96	62	2,903	41	38	9
Barclays PLC	1,957	1,003	43	44	2,179	73	145	14
BNP Paribas SA	1,897	1,170	61	51	1,843	58	62	5
Citigroup	1,884	2,435	50	44	4,122	84	309	13
HSBC Holdings PLC	1,861	1,234	61	78	3,945	47	161	13
The Royal Bank of Scotland Group PLC	1,711	1,161	11	34	1,966	16	73	6
Deutsche Bank AG	1,483	1,954	77	80	3,931	56	391	20
Bank of America Corporation	1,460	1,407	28	12	4,256	29	118	8
JPMorgan Chase & Company	1,352	804	51	26	2,086	36	54	7
ABN AMRO Holding NV[f]	1,300	670	63	77	1,381	43	37	6
Société Générale	1,260	844	56	46	4,128	60	64	8
Morgan Stanley	1,121	1,052	47	42	4,476	46	203	19
Credit Suisse Group	1,029	290	93	71	3,868	31	53	18
Merrill Lynch & Company, Inc.	841	267	64	35	4,089	25	23	9
Goldman Sachs Group, Inc.	838	371	51	48	5,391	21	29	8
Lehman Brothers Holdings, Inc.	504	433	45	37	7,807	20	41	9

a. Bankscope. Data on subsidiaries refer to majority-owned subsidiaries for which the large and complex financial institution (LCFI) is the ultimate owner with a minimum control path of 50.01 percent.

b. Annual reports for each LCFI. Net income before taxes with five exceptions: net income after taxes for Citi and net revenues for Barclays PLC, BNP Paribas, Lehman Brothers Holdings, Inc., Merrill Lynch & Company, Inc.

c. Oliver Wyman. The Herfindahl-Hirschman Index (HHI) ranges from 0 to 10,000 and is calculated on the percentage of revenues per business line. Higher values indicate a higher degree of specialization. Lower values imply a higher degree of diversification.

d. Number of countries in which the LCFI has at least one majority-owned subsidiary.

e. Offshore financial centers (OFCs) identified by the Financial Stability Board (2000). We exclude Swiss subsidiaries for Credit Suisse and UBS and Hong Kong subsidiaries for HSBC. Four subsidiaries were allocated to OFCs on the basis of locations designated in their names even though Bankscope did not specify a home country.

f. After the most recent list of LCFIs (Bank of England 2007) was published, a consortium of three banks (RBS, Fortis, and Santander) acquired ABN AMRO.

Source: Herring and Carmassi (2010) and sources therein.

Our fifth and last example refers to attempts to gather a list of SIFIs—presumably based on the kind of criteria outlined above. One such attempt, reported in the *Financial Times*, referred to a list of 24 global banks and 6 global insurance companies that were earmarked for cross-border supervision by regulators.[26] The list included six US banks (Goldman Sachs, JPMorgan Chase, Morgan Stanley, Bank of America, Merrill Lynch, and Citigroup), four UK banks (HSBC, Barclays, RBS, and Standard Chartered), one Canadian bank (Royal Bank of Canada), two Swiss banks (Credit Suisse and UBS), two French banks (Société Générale and BNP Paribas), two Spanish banks (Santander and BBVA), four Japanese banks (Mizuho, Sumitomo Mitsui, Nomura, and Mitsubishi UFJ), two Italian banks (UniCredit and Intesa), one German bank (Deutsche Bank), one Dutch bank (ING), and six European insurance groups (AXA, Aegon, Allianz, Aviva, Zurich, and Swiss Re).

Irrespective of the specific yardstick used to identify SIFIs, one nontrivial policy question is the following: If financial institutions deemed systemically significant are subject to a specific regulatory regime, should the list of such institutions be made public? Some have argued that making it public would undesirably confer official TBTF status on such institutions, thus reinforcing moral hazard. However, it appears unlikely that the identity of firms subject to a specific regulatory treatment can in fact be kept private, especially since such firms would likely be able to challenge their designation as SIFIs, including before the fact. Indeed, such a challenge is part of the Dodd-Frank Act of 2010 in the new US financial reform legislation, and similar concerns are likely to arise in other countries. Also, as argued above, most large and complex financial institutions already receive in the market a funding discount and credit rating upgrade (relative to smaller financial institutions) that can be at least partly linked to the formers' perceived higher probability of obtaining government support should they get into trouble. Thus, it is not as if the absence of a public SIFI list will eliminate perceptions of unequal bailout treatment. Most importantly, designation as a SIFI is not identical to deeming that institution TBTF; a SIFI can fail if other elements of the regulatory and/or supervisory regime (discussed in the next section) make resolution credible and orderly and do not make liquidation too expensive for the taxpayer.

Conversely, the cases of LTCM in 1998 and of IKB and Northern Rock in 2007 suggest that even institutions unlikely to be included in an official list of SIFIs can be considered too important to be allowed to fail. Indeed, as previously mentioned, Belgium has already proceeded with public disclosure of those firms deemed systemically significant there, including some local affiliates of nondomestic groups, and has done so even before the formal establishment of the public body that will determine which specific regulatory regime such firms should be subject to.

---

26. Patrick Jenkins and Paul Davies, "Thirty Financial Groups on Systemic Risk List," *Financial Times*, November 29, 2009.

Discouraging Bigness Through Curbs and Incentives

A first set of policy options is to discourage TBTF and to internalize the externalities associated with bigness and complexity through curbs and incentives (as opposed to absolute size limits, which are discussed in the next subsection). We identify three main such options: capital and liquidity surcharges; size-related taxes or levies; and competition policy.

The Basel Committee on Banking Supervision, which prepares capital and liquidity standards, has discussed for some time the idea of imposing higher capital (and perhaps also liquidity) requirements on financial institutions deemed systemically important relative to those not so designated. In its September 12, 2010, communication announcing what is commonly known as the Basel III agreement, the Basel Committee referred to this possibility as work in progress, to be decided in coherence with other FSB initiatives, but stated expressly that "systemically important banks should have loss-absorbing capacity beyond the standards announced today."[27]

Here again, one objection to a TBTF capital surcharge is that the financial firms paying such a surcharge will have their TBTF status further enhanced (from de facto to de jure) and that this official designation will provide them with a further unwarranted funding subsidy, thereby exacerbating the misallocation of resources. However, one can doubt how the list of surcharge payers could be very different from the market's existing perceptions of who is and who is not systemically important. Moreover, there is no reason why the surcharge needs to be zero-one; it can be graduated depending on the official sector's evaluation of the size, interconnectivity, and complexity of the individual institution, in which case there is no threshold between non-SIFIs and SIFIs, and no need for a list of SIFIs, public or otherwise. The IMF (2010) has explored various alternative approaches to estimating capital surcharges for large and complex financial institutions, which present conceptual similarities to risk-based deposit insurance.

A second approach would be to create disincentives to bigness through tax or taxlike instruments. This would be especially relevant in countries that envisage setting up a new contribution, tax, or levy on financial institutions as a form of compensation for the public support they receive in the event of crises. However, considerations of tax fairness could play a role, at least in some legal environments, and limit the margin for governments to modulate the burden according to size or systemic importance. Those EU countries that have introduced a contribution from the banking industry so far, such as Sweden in 2009, have not decided to include a surcharge for systemic significance. In the United States a financial contribution from the financial industry was proposed by the Obama administration in January 2010 and

---

27. Basel Committee on Banking Supervision, "Group of Governors and Heads of Supervision Announces Higher Global Minimum Capital Standards," press release, September 12, 2010.

debated by Congress, but was not included in the final version of the Dodd-Frank Act and remains an open option at this time.

Yet a third approach in this category is to use competition policy to curb the size of the largest financial firms. In the European Union, the European Commission has extensively used its powers since the beginning of the crisis to keep a check on state rescues and on the size of rescued firms. Specifically, it has required firms that received significant support from member states under the cover of safeguarding financial stability, such as RBS, WestLB in Germany, KBC in Belgium, or ING in the Netherlands, to trim the size of their balance sheets and divest important parts of their business portfolios. However, the commission has acted only in cases when the government guarantee has been made explicit, i.e., in a corrective not preventive mode. Nor is it entirely clear at this stage to what extent TBTF concerns could also be applied to EU merger control and perhaps block the acquisitions or mergers that would exacerbate the TBTF problem, even as applicable EU regulations recognize the legitimacy of prudential and financial stability considerations in this area. In the United States, it is also unclear how much the domestic competition policy framework would allow similar approaches, especially as, unlike the comparable EU framework, it does not explicitly include control of state aid. As a substitute, the Dodd-Frank Act empowers financial regulators to force a systemically important financial institution to sell activities deemed to contribute to excessive systemic risk. The extent to which this provision will be used in practice remains to be seen.

Prohibiting Bigness Through Size Caps and Breakups

A more radical approach than curbing the size of financial institutions is to prohibit them from growing beyond a maximum size. The Dodd-Frank Act of 2010 specifies that any insured depository or systemically important nonbank could be prohibited from merging or acquiring substantially all the assets or control of another company if the resulting company's total consolidated liabilities would exceed 10 percent of the aggregate consolidated liabilities of all financial companies. This liability size cap would not require existing US financial institutions to shrink, though, and does not prohibit their organic growth in the future. It parallels and complements a preexisting cap of 10 percent of total domestic deposits that cannot be exceeded by some forms of external growth, introduced by the Riegle-Neal Interstate Banking and Branching Efficiency Act of 1994.

Some observers have suggested going further, by imposing size limits on systemically important financial institutions relative to GDP. Johnson and Kwak (2010) propose that the size cap for US commercial banks be set at 4 percent of GDP and that the cap for investment banks be set at 2 percent of GDP. Applied to the present US financial industry structure, this would require the six largest institutions—namely JPMorgan Chase, Bank of America, Citigroup, Wells Fargo, Goldman Sachs, and Morgan Stanley—to shrink or split into separate entities. In Goldstein (2010) one of us has favored size caps for US banks along Johnson-Kwak (2010) lines, although he could live with somewhat higher caps.

While the size cap proposal is certainly controversial in the US context, it becomes even more so when viewed in an international environment. As emphasized in the previous section, many European countries have higher levels of banking sector concentration than the United States, and their banks carry comparatively more assets on their balance sheets. As a consequence, a consistent cap set at a few percentage points of GDP would require them to split their prominent banks into myriads of tiny entities. It would also explicitly prohibit small countries from hosting the headquarters of large banks, a proposition that might well generate political and diplomatic tensions.

Conversely, an international uniform size cap that would not depend on national GDP, say a maximum total of assets that banks should not exceed, would be questionable in terms of TBTF avoidance. A cap of $100 billion of assets, say, would force many banks in large countries to restructure and splinter drastically. Based on IIF (2010a) calculations, it would require 410 banks to replace the top 20 and 750 banks to replace the top 100. But it would still be too high to affect TBTF dynamics in most small and mid-sized countries.

At a more fundamental level, substantial disagreement presently exists on the economic costs and benefits that such a size limit would entail.

On the one hand, a long-standing strand of economic literature argues that significant economies of scale exist in banking (Diamond 1984, Allen 1990). More recently, studies such as Wheelock and Wilson (2009) find empirical evidence of economies of scale in the US banking sector. Large banks may also play a specifically important role in an internationally integrated financial system. Charles Calomiris argues that large and complex financial institutions are needed to service large and global nonfinancial businesses.[28] In this view, we would not have the degree of global integration of stock, bond, and foreign exchange markets that we enjoy today without large, global financial firms; nor would the flow of finance to emerging economies be what it is with the assorted economic benefits (as discussed, for example, in Cline 2010). Accordingly, so the argument goes, to deny the links between large, global corporations and large, global banks is to ignore both important supply-chain links that have transformed the way global firms do business and the globalization of professional services more broadly, including, for example, law firms and accounting firms. Banks with less than, say, $100 billion of assets tend to be mostly domestic in their focus and would not be able to substitute for the cross-border activities of the very large banks.

Moreover, some relatively highly concentrated banking systems in the advanced world (e.g., those in Canada and Australia) escaped relatively unscathed from this crisis, while some less concentrated ones (like that in the

---

28. Charles Calomiris, "In the World of Banks, Bigger Can Be Better," *Wall Street Journal*, October 19, 2009.

United States) incurred relatively high costs. More generally, there is no empirical evidence that banking concentration is positively related to the incidence of banking crises; if anything, the evidence goes the other way (Beck, Demirgüç-Kunt, and Levine 2003). Also, foreign bank participation in national banking systems, which often involves comparatively larger financial institutions (Focarelli and Pozzolo 2001), can be associated with higher financial stability. Avinash Persaud argues that contagion in a systemic financial crisis is an effect more of investor psychology (if firm A has a problem and firm B apparently carries the same type of risk, investors go short on firm B) than actual financial interconnections.[29] Adair Turner, the chairman of the UK Financial Services Authority, has similarly argued recently that "there is a danger that an exclusive focus on institutions that are too big to fail could divert us from more fundamental issues" of precarious credit supply and corresponding macroeconomic volatility (Turner 2010).

On the other hand, some analysts—such as Johnson and Kwak (2010), Stern and Feldman (2004), Group of Thirty (2009), and Goldstein (2011)—stress that other empirical studies on the economies of scale in banking find such economies only for small banks and certainly not beyond $100 billion in asset size—to say nothing of the trillion-dollar-plus balance sheets of the world's largest banks (Berger and Mester 1997, Amel et al. 2004, Herring 2010). As banks become very large, diseconomies of scale can set in, particularly regarding ability to manage prudently and to implement effective risk-management systems. While the main motive for consolidation is usually described as maximization of shareholder value, there is also evidence of other motives behind the trend toward larger, more complex financial institutions—such as the desire to avoid taxes and financial regulations, the drive for market power, and the link between firm size and executive compensation—which typically subtract from, rather than add to, social value. In this strand of thought, the defense of universal banks on grounds of diversification and "economies of scope" across bank products and activities is a false hope. Research finds that markets impose a "discount" on banks when they become more complex—not a diversification premium (Laeven and Levine 2005). As noted earlier in this chapter, measures of bank size and bank diversification were *positively* (not negatively) correlated with income volatility during the 2006–08 period. Haldane finds that larger and more diversified banks have also shown greater write-downs of assets than smaller and less diversified ones.[30] Some authors holding this view also argue that—contrary to industry claims—large, complex financial institutions are not needed to service large, global nonfinancial businesses, and that the needs of those businesses can just as well be met by consortia of medium-sized banks without the excess

---

29. Avinash Persaud, "Too Big to Fail Is No Redemption Song," VoxEU, February 10, 2010, www.voxeu.org (accessed on January 22, 2012).

30. Haldane, The $100 Billion Question, speech given to the Institute of Regulation and Risk, Hong Kong, March 2010.

baggage that TBTF institutions bring with them (Goldstein 2011, Johnson and Kwak 2010).

An alternative perspective is to focus not on financial institutions' overall size but on the way critical market functions can become overwhelmingly reliant on a limited number of actors. For example, Gillian Tett notes that the triparty repurchase (or "repo") market is predominantly cleared by only two large firms, JPMorgan Chase and Bank of New York Mellon.[31] The systemic importance of that market is such that, as Tett notes, it is impossible to avoid massive moral hazard without a radical change of market structure. More broadly, Alberto Giovannini (2010) advocates a separation of all "infrastructure" functions into separate entities as a way to reduce systemic risk. Such focus on functions that may be deemed incompatible within the same financial group underpins the Volcker Rule, as it did the Glass-Steagall Act in a different era. However, as this category of approaches does not in principle differentiate institutions according to size, it may not address the TBTF question in a comprehensive way.

Altogether, it is unlikely at this point—for better or worse—that international agreement can be reached on hard size caps for banks. In the United States, aside from the hard size cap on the share of systemwide liabilities that is already in the Dodd-Frank Act and the older cap on deposits, regulators will rely on other types of incentives to limit the "bigness" of financial institutions. Meanwhile, it looks like EU countries will be reluctant to envisage the somewhat disruptive prospect of a mandatory breakup of large banks, given the already mentioned heterogeneity of country preferences linked to diverse structures of national banking markets, and to the perception that prevails there that no sufficiently strong analytical basis exists for assessing both the costs and benefits of such an option. Softer curbs on the size of financial conglomerates, through a targeted adjustment of prudential, tax, and competition policy, will be insufficient to put an end to the TBTF problem but can at least help to somewhat correct the competitive distortions it creates. In Europe, more cross-border banking integration and centralization of the supervision of the largest institutions at the EU level would allay the current competitive tensions, and would make the TBTF issue less intractable than it currently is in individual EU member states.

The "Failability" Debate: Allowing Banks to Go Under?

The second class of proposals to address TBTF relates not to the size of institutions but to the possibility of their failure—what might be called for lack of a better term their "failability." If even huge financial conglomerates can fail without creating major market instability, then their bigness becomes less of an inherent problem. The financial crisis, and especially the successive deci-

---

31. Gillian Tett, "Repo Needs a Backstop to Avoid Future Crises," *Financial Times*, September 24, 2010.

sions taken by the US authorities on Bear Stearns, Lehman Brothers, and AIG, have illustrated both the difficulties of applying a consistent policy framework to all crisis situations without creating massive moral hazard, and the disadvantages of taking different stances in different cases.

Failure and Competition

It is difficult to separate the debate about the possibility of financial institution failure from a more general conversation about competition in the financial industry, which is made more complex by its multifaceted links with financial stability. Competition simultaneously imposes discipline on financial firms and can foster excessive risk taking. A bank failure can increase concentration or, on the contrary, provide opportunities for new entrants, depending on how open and competitive the banking system is. In a system where all or most of the financial industry is in government hands, an actual bank failure is virtually impossible and a government bailout is almost guaranteed.[32]

In many EU countries, the financial sector has long been sheltered from competition policy (Carletti and Vives 2007), and the more assertive stance of the European Commission's Directorate General for Competition (the EU competition authority) since the late 1990s is too recent to have had structural impact in all the European Union's financial systems. Many specific features, even when considered compliant with EU competition policy, restrict the competitive field. For example, German savings banks are generally considered autonomous (see for example the ECB's 2010 statistics on banking concentration in the euro area), but the so-called regional principle prevents each of them from proposing or supplying services on another savings bank's territory (they also rely on mutual guarantee schemes at regional and national levels). In other countries such as France, Belgium, or Austria, successive waves of consolidation have led to the almost complete disappearance of independent local banks. There are almost no new entrants in many (Western) European banking markets, in stark contrast to the almost continuous flow of "de novo" banks being created at the local level in the United States.

A large sector enquiry carried out by the European Commission between 2005 and 2007 found major competition barriers in many countries in several areas, including payment cards and payment systems, credit registers, product tying, and obstacles to customer mobility.[33] Competition issues are also present in US retail financial services, but the large size and relative openness of the national market, near-continuous emergence of new entrants, and

---

32. It is not absolutely guaranteed, though, especially at times of major shifts in government policy. Thus Guangdong International Trust and Investment Company, a large state-owned Chinese bank, declared bankruptcy in January 1999. See Mark Landler, "Bankruptcy the Chinese Way: Foreign Bankers Are Shown to the End of the Line," *New York Times*, January 22, 1999.

33. European Commission, "Competition: Commission Sector Inquiry Finds Major Competition Barriers in Retail Banking," press release, Brussels, January 31, 2007.

provision of many financial services by nonbanks contribute to a generally more competitive playing field than in most EU countries.[34] In wholesale financial services, the difference is less apparent, as indeed many of the most prominent actors are the same on both sides of the Atlantic.

Special Resolution Regimes

As mentioned above, special resolution regimes administered by an out-of-court resolution authority appear better adapted to the conditions of financial firms than ordinary corporate bankruptcy processes. As analyzed in Cohen and Goldstein (2009), this is primarily because bankruptcy processes pay little attention to third-party effects that are the essence of systemic risk; because creditor stays, and their potential adverse systemic effects, are part and parcel of the bankruptcy process; because bankruptcy proceedings move too slowly to protect the franchise value of the firm; and because bankruptcy does not permit pre-insolvency intervention. However, resolution authority should not be seen as a panacea, if only because it may sometimes be difficult to implement in a way that simultaneously supports market discipline and avoids the contagion effects that financial stability policy is intended to minimize. Supporting market discipline usually is interpreted to mean wiping out shareholders, changing management, and paying off creditors (promptly) at estimated recovery cost (not at par). It may also entail not selling the failing firm to one of the larger players in the field. And it is also increasingly seen as meaning that the resolution authority should be funded in part with ex ante and/or ex post fees on other financial institutions so that the financial sector, rather than the general government budget, pays the lion's share of the costs. However, in some crisis scenarios, policymakers may stray from following through on some of these measures (for example, imposing haircuts to senior bondholders) out of concern that they may precipitate "runs" on similar instruments in other firms. This appears to have been the case when the EU authorities insisted that the Irish rescue package of November 2010 should not include the imposition of losses on the holders of senior debt issues by Ireland's failed banks. Ultimately, the proof of the pudding will be in the eating.

The US Dodd-Frank Act introduces a new procedure that in effect allows US authorities to apply a special resolution procedure to systemically important nonbank financial institutions, on the initiative of the secretary of the treasury and subject to approval of the systemically significant status by a special panel of bankruptcy judges (and of the newly formed Financial

---

34. In fact, in the US case, one of the most common concerns about tougher new financial regulations—be they size related or otherwise—is that they will prompt a large (and undesirable) migration of financial activities to the shadow banking system. Indeed, for that very reason, some analysts (e.g., Hanson, Kashyap, and Stein 2011) have proposed that such regulations be defined on a "product" basis so that they bite equally across the banking and nonbanking sectors.

System Oversight Council). Once agreed to, the resolution procedure would be administered by the FDIC.

In the European Union, the situation varies widely from one country to another, but new resolution regimes for either banks or systemically important financial institutions (or both) have been introduced recently or are being introduced through new legislation in Sweden, the United Kingdom, Belgium, and Germany. It is likely that other countries will follow suit in the near future. The idea of an integrated EU bank resolution framework has recently been forcefully endorsed by the IMF[35] and by the European Parliament's Committee on Economic and Monetary Affairs, including the specific proposal of a common "European Bank Company Law, to be designed by the end of 2011" (European Parliament 2010). However, the European Commission has not attempted to harmonize national resolution initiatives so far, let alone create an integrated framework. Even its limited, nonbinding suggestions about the funding of national resolution schemes (European Commission 2010a) have not been taken on board by several member states. Its latest proposals on crisis management essentially amount to delaying any harmonization of bank resolution frameworks to after 2012, and any discussion of an EU-level resolution framework to 2014 at the earliest (European Commission 2010b).

That said, the European Union is playing a role in bank resolution through another channel, namely control of national state aid as part of its competition policy framework. Mathias Dewatripont et al. (2010) note that under this mandate, the European Commission has effectively contributed to the objectives of mitigating moral hazard and correcting competitive distortions resulting from national bank bailouts. They advocate a reinforcement of this function, as a complement to or substitute for a still-to-be-decided European resolution framework.

Orderly Dismantling of Complex Groups

The availability of a resolution regime and resolution authority is a necessary condition for the orderly resolution of large financial institutions, but it is not sufficient. The resolution authority does not only need the legal powers to intervene, it must also have the operational capability to do so, which can prove to be a significant challenge in itself. The failure of a large financial conglomerate can be a hugely complex affair, especially as corporate structures in the financial sector have become ever more complex, partly as a result of continuous regulatory and tax arbitrage (Herring and Carmassi 2010).

Since the idea was floated in the UK Turner Review (FSA 2009), regulators have pinned hopes on the notion that the financial institutions themselves could meaningfully contribute to accomplishing this herculean task.

---

35. Fonteyne et al. (2010); Dominique Strauss-Kahn, Building a Crisis Management Framework for the Single Market, keynote speech at the European Commission conference, Brussels, March 19, 2010.

One option is to require each systemically important institution to prepare and maintain a "living will" or "wind-down plan" (or, if it also includes provisions aimed at preventing failure in a crisis, a "recovery and resolution plan") that would guide regulators through the maze of subsidiaries, commitments, and contingent liabilities.

In the United States, the Dodd-Frank Act of 2010 stipulates that all systemically important nonbank financial companies and large, interconnected bank companies will be required to prepare and maintain extensive rapid and orderly resolution plans, which must be approved by the Federal Reserve and the FDIC. In cases where the institution is too large and complex to be wound down in a nonsystemic way, the supervisor would have the authority to require the institution to shrink and to become less complex. In several EU countries, the authorities have initiated a dialogue with key financial institutions on resolution options, even if this effort may not always be reflected in a formalized, self-standing plan.

According to Herring (2010), the orderly resolution plans must

- map lines of business into the corporate entities that would be taken through the resolution process;
- describe the resolution procedures for each entity, along with an estimate of how long each will take;
- identify key interconnections across affiliates (such as cross guarantees, standby lines of credit, etc.), along with operational interdependencies (such as information technology systems);
- provide for developing and maintaining a virtual data room with information that the resolution authority would need to expeditiously resolve the entity;
- identify key information systems, their location, and the essential personnel to operate them;
- identify any activities or units deemed systemically relevant and demonstrate how they operate during a wind-down;
- consider how its actions may affect exchanges, clearing houses, custodians, and other important elements of the infrastructure; and
- be updated annually, or more often if a substantial merger or acquisition or restructuring adds extra complexity.

As this list illustrates, the credible maintenance of living wills could represent a significant administrative burden for financial institutions, and there will be tradeoffs as to how the requirements will be implemented. The fundamental difficulty is that the resolution strategy depends, in many aspects, on the actual features of the crisis in which it would take place. For example, selling certain assets early in the resolution process may depend on whether the markets for these assets remain liquid, which itself depends on the specific crisis scenario. As 19th-century Prussian general Helmuth von Moltke famously quipped, "no campaign plan survives first contact with the enemy." If orderly resolution plans are very detailed, they might not withstand the first contact with a real crisis. If they stay general and do not provide detail, they might not be able to serve their purpose.

The magnitude of the challenges is compounded by international complexity, which is a common feature of many SIFIs. The Lehman Brothers bankruptcy has illustrated the potential for difficulties to arise from the international interdependencies that must be unwound in the resolution process. While there may be exceptions, this difficulty is in general vastly more pronounced in investment banking than in retail services. As retail operations are local in nature, it can be relatively easy to ring-fence them in a resolution process even if some functions, such as information technology and some aspects of risk management, are provided on a cross-border basis. Global banks with significant retail operations, such as Citi, HSBC, or Santander, often claim that they would be fairly easy to wind up on a country-by-country basis in the event of major financial difficulties—even though this claim is ultimately unverifiable, at least for outside observers, as long as no such process has been tested in real conditions. For investment banks, however, the ability to manage complex and fast-moving cross-border linkages is a core part of the business model and of the value proposition to customers, and for that reason their orderly resolution on a transnational basis is almost by definition a highly problematic endeavor. In effect, there is no relevant precedent. Cross-border banking resolutions have been extremely rare, and generally horribly messy, as in the case of Herstatt Bank in 1974, Bank of Commerce and Credit International in 1991, or indeed Lehman Brothers. Conversely, resolutions that have happened in a relatively orderly way, such as that of Washington Mutual or CajaSur, have generally been largely managed within a single country.

One probably inevitable consequence of the emphasis on resolvability is growing host-country insistence on autonomous capitalization and funding of local operations for international banks, certainly in retail activities but also, perhaps increasingly, for wholesale business as well. In some cases this can take the form of conversion of branches into subsidiaries—especially since the Icelandic crisis brought home the importance of host-country control and protection of local depositors. This will rightly worry advocates of cross-border financial integration, as it may hamper the international intermediation role of financial firms, but the importance of protecting local stakeholders will, in most cases, weigh heavier than concerns about financial fragmentation.

It remains to be seen whether this same concern will be applicable to intra–European Union (or perhaps intra–European Economic Area) activity. On the positive side, there is at the supranational level a higher degree of commitment to cross-border financial integration and the creation of a single financial market, and there is also more of a legal, regulatory, and (to some extent) political infrastructure to credibly oversee the financial sector. From this perspective, the creation of the European Banking Authority is probably a step toward a more integrated future supervisory and crisis management framework. In such a framework, we would see a clearer division between financial institutions with a national or local reach, for which supervision shall remain at national level, and "pan-European" ones, which would be at least partly supervised at the EU level—even as fiscal resources are likely to stay managed by member states for the foreseeable future (Véron 2007). However, as emphasized above, there is not yet a consensus in EU policy circles on such a proposal, and therefore the European Union is bound to retain for an undetermined period of time its current unstable mix of centralized rule making, commitment to a single market, and absence of an integrated crisis management and resolution framework.

Making Creditors Pay: Contingent Capital and Bail-Ins

Another proposal that has caught momentum in the past few months would require SIFIs to convert a portion of their debts into common equity under prespecified stress conditions (Squam Lake Working Group on Financial Regulation 2009, Goldman Sachs 2009, Herring 2010). At the time of writing, two concepts are widely debated: "contingent capital" or "CoCos" (for "contingent convertible instruments"), which have been endorsed in a proposal of the Swiss authorities for additional requirements to Basel III for Swiss-headquartered SIFIs; and "bail-ins," which have been actively discussed within the Basel Committee and FSB (BCBS 2010).[36] These ideas have received support from significant financial industry bodies such as the Institute of International Finance (IIF 2010b) and the Association for Financial Markets in Europe (AFME 2010). Some have also argued (Goldstein 2011) that the minimum global capital standards recently agreed to under Basel III are too low and that this will increase the need for some type of contingent capital.

In "bail-ins," regulators would call for the conversion of specific tranches of debt (in the Association for Financial Markets in Europe proposal, preferred stock or unsecured debt) to equity, as an alternative to resolution; this approach would require new enabling legislation. By contrast, in the case of contingent capital, the debt instruments would be automatically converted into equity in the application of preexisting contractual arrangements whenever a predefined trigger was reached. (Somewhat comparable instruments have existed for some time in the insurance industry.) Both notions, contingent capital and bail-ins, are seductive as they hold the promise of bringing loss-absorbing equity to financial firms exactly when they need it most, in the midst of a crisis. However, both are also essentially untested. Contingent convertible bonds were issued by Lloyds Banking Group and somewhat similar instruments were issued by the Netherlands' Rabobank, but these precedents are widely seen by market participants as not sufficient to establish the commercial viability of the concept, let alone its effectiveness in crisis conditions.

---

36. Bail-ins are explained by Paul Calello and Wilson Ervin, "From Bail-Out to Bail-In," *Economist*, January 30, 2010.

Thus, caution is warranted as to whether these concepts are potentially a way of "ending too big to fail" (Goldman Sachs 2009) or merely another hybrid structured finance product that may not succeed when tested under stress.

At this stage, it seems prudent to see contingent capital and bail-ins as possible complements to other TBTF antidotes such as capital surcharges for SIFIs, special resolution regimes, and orderly wind-down planning, rather than substitutes—provided they stand the test of the marketplace, which is too soon to assess at the time of writing, especially given the lack of consensus about them in the supervisory community.[37]

Concluding Remarks

In its report for the Seoul summit in November 2010 (FSB 2010), the FSB acknowledged the difficulty of addressing the TBTF problem on a transnational basis and recommended that international discussions focus on what it termed "global SIFIs" or "G-SIFIs," which exclude institutions that are systemically important in a domestic context but have limited international activity (say, Japan Post or the large Chinese banks). This limited agenda underlines the prospect for divergence of practice and implementation in the years ahead, including between the United States and European Union, and to some extent also among EU member states. This need not necessarily be a fatal problem. A global level playing field in finance is a worthy ideal, but it remains a vision rather than a reality and will remain so for some time. The IMF (2010) notes that tax rates on the financial sector in advanced economies differ markedly from one another, without provoking massive moves by financial institutions in response to these differences. Within the European Union, there is a need for a higher degree of harmonization, and leaders have committed to the notion of a "single rulebook," even if this is unlikely to include tax and bankruptcy arrangements for some time. Elsewhere, regulatory constraints will continue to vary widely, including between both sides of the Atlantic. In a politically heterogeneous world, such variations have to be accepted as a necessary evil.

The adoption of binding "bigness" caps that would cut SIFIs down to a more limited size do not seem likely on either side of the Atlantic, at least in the next few years. In the United States, where hard size caps are viewed perhaps the most favorably, it appears improbable that officials will go beyond the market-share funding caps that are in the Dodd-Frank Act—at least until the more comprehensive approach to deterring TBTF in that legislation has had enough time to be tested. In the European Union, size caps are highly unlikely if measured in terms of assets (or another yardstick) to national GDP. It may be more promising over the longer term to envisage caps defined by size to EU GDP, even though they would not correspond to the current patterns of bank

---

37. See, for example, Huw Jones, "Regulators Sound Caution on Bank Bail-In Proposal," Reuters, October 18, 2010.

rescues. If this happens, it is likely that such caps would at least initially be set at a relatively high level, comparable to the existing limits applicable to American financial institutions in terms of share of total US deposits and liabilities (10 percent in each case).

There are somewhat higher prospects for change regarding other forms of constraints on the structure of financial conglomerates, namely incompatibilities between certain lines of business corresponding to different types of risk exposures within the same group, akin to the Volcker Rule now adopted in the United States. Giovannini (2010) makes a strong argument for this category of curbs, and we believe an active debate will develop on this issue, not only in the United Kingdom (which has put it on the agenda of its Independent Commission on Banking) but possibly to some extent in the rest of Europe as well, in spite of the dominance of the universal banking model. That said, such functional separation is not about TBTF in a strict sense and is therefore beyond the scope of this chapter.

We also regard the arguments for a comprehensive approach toward discouraging TBTF as compelling enough to expect several initiatives to be adopted in the United States and in several, perhaps all, EU member states. These may include capital surcharges as floated by the Basel Committee, even though they are now fiercely resisted in several parts of the European Union; more-than-proportional levies on large banks, in those countries that would introduce such mandatory contributions; and an assertive conduct of competition policy, at least at the EU level, to put a check on excessive intracountry bank concentration (while still favoring cross-border integration). A transparent designation of SIFIs in Europe would have the additional advantage of raising public awareness of the disturbing number of European banks that are indeed systemically important, including most household brand names. This may, in an optimistic view, create incentives for more competition in the European banking sector, a more favorable environment for new entrants, and more effective cross-border regulatory integration, which would be a way to raise the SIFI threshold (if systemic importance is assessed vis-à-vis the EU financial system as a whole, as opposed to national ones).

We underlined why making orderly failure of SIFIs a credible prospect is even more difficult in the European Union than it is in the United States; in this connection, it is desirable that all EU countries adopt special resolution regimes and correspondingly empower their financial authorities, which will have the desirable effect of broadening the range of options available to policymakers in future crises. In the medium term, we expect a resolution authority to be introduced at the EU level, broadly along the lines suggested by the IMF (Fonteyne et al. 2010). In the meantime, resolution authorities should be established or reinforced at the national level, and should assertively obtain knowledge on how to unwind the complex structures of SIFIs they oversee, in spite of predictable resistance from the financial industry. The most recent working document from the commission at the time of writing (European

Commission 2011) suggests cautious hope that some progress may be made along these lines in 2011–12.

We would, of course, be happier if we could say with a straight face that the TBTF problem was well on its way to being solved on a comprehensive G-20 basis. We cannot say that. But we can say that current policy approaches toward SIFIs have taken into account some of the lessons from this global economic and financial crisis, that serious efforts to address the TBTF issue have made their way into legislation in some major economies (so far more in the United States than in the European Union), that there does seem to be a healthy willingness to experiment with different approaches, and that much will depend on whether regulators are willing to exercise their newly acquired authority to curb the excesses that turned out to be so costly in the past. Even if these measures do not bring a final solution to the TBTF problem, they are well worth the continued attention of policymakers in the years to come.

References

AFME (Association for Financial Markets in Europe). 2010. *Contingent Capital and Bail-In*. London.

Alessandri, Piergiorgio, and Andrew Haldane. 2009. *Banking on the State* (November). London: Bank of England.

Allen, Franklin. 1990. The Market for Information and the Origin of Financial Intermediation. *Journal of Financial Intermediation* 1, no. 1: 3–30.

Amel, Dean, Colleen Barnes, Fabio Panetta, and Carmelo Salleo. 2004. Consolidation and Efficiency in the Financial Sector: A Review of the International Evidence. *Journal of Banking and Finance* 28, no. 10 (October): 2493–519.

Bank of England. 2007. *Financial Stability Report*. London.

BCBS (Basel Committee on Banking Supervision). 2010. *Proposal to Ensure the Loss Absorbency of Regulatory Capital at the Point of Non-Viability*. Consultative Document (August). Basel.

Beck, Thorsten, Asli Demirgüç-Kunt, and Ross Levine. 2003. *Bank Concentration and Crises*. NBER Working Paper 9921 (August). Cambridge, MA: National Bureau of Economic Research.

Berger, Allen, and Loretta Mester. 1997. *Efficiency and Productivity Change in the US Commercial Banking Industry: A Comparison of the 1980s and 1990s*. Federal Reserve Bank of Philadelphia Working Paper 97-5. Philadelphia: Federal Reserve Bank of Philadelphia.

Buehler, Kevin, Hamid Samandari, and Christopher Mazingo. 2009. *Capital Ratios and Financial Distress: Lessons from the Crisis*. Working Paper 15. McKinsey & Company.

Carletti, Elena, and Xavier Vives. 2007. Regulation and Competition Policy in the Banking Sector. Paper prepared for the IESE Business School conference Fifty Years of the Treaty: Assessment and Perspectives of Competition Policy in Europe, Barcelona, November 19–20, 2007. Available at http://blog.iese.edu.

Carmassi, Jacopo, Elisabetta Luchetti, and Stefano Micossi. 2010. *Overcoming Too-Big-To-Fail: A Regulatory Framework to Limit Moral Hazard and Free-Riding in the Financial Sector*. Brussels: Center for European Policy Studies.

Cline, William. 2010. *Financial Globalization, Economic Growth, and the Crisis of 2007–09*. Washington: Peterson Institute for International Economics.

Cohen, Rodgin, and Morris Goldstein. 2009. *The Case for an Orderly Resolution Regime for Systemically-Important Financial Institutions*. Briefing Paper 13. Washington: Pew Financial Reform Project, Pew Charitable Trusts.

Davis Polk. 2010. *Summary of the Dodd-Frank Wall Street Reform and Consumer Protection Act, Passed by the House of Representatives on June 30, 2010.* Washington.

de Larosière, Jacques. 2009. *Report of the High-Level Group on Financial Supervision in the EU.* Brussels: European Commission. Available at www.ec.europa.eu (accessed on January 21, 2012).

Dewatripont, Mathias, Gregory Nguyen, Peter Praet, and André Sapir. 2010. *The Role of State Aid Control in Improving Bank Resolution in Europe.* Bruegel Policy Contribution 2010/04 (May). Brussels: Bruegel.

Diamond, D. W. 1984. Financial Intermediation and Delegated Monitoring. *Review of Economic Studies* 51, no. 3 (July): 393–414.

ECB (European Central Bank). 2006. Identifying Large and Complex Banking Groups. In *Financial Stability Review* (December). Frankfurt.

ECB (European Central Bank). 2007. Financial Conditions of Large and Complex Banking Groups. In *Financial Stability Review* (December). Frankfurt.

ECB (European Central Bank). 2010. *EU Banking Structures—September 2010.* Frankfurt.

European Commission. 2010a. *Bank Resolution Funds.* COM (2010) 254 (May). Brussels.

European Commission. 2010b. *An EU Framework for Crisis Management in the Financial Sector.* COM (2010) 579 (October). Brussels.

European Commission. 2011. *DG Internal Market Services Working Document on "Technical Details of a Possible EU Framework for Bank Recovery and Resolution"* (January). Brussels.

European Parliament. 2010. *Report with Recommendations to the Commission on Cross-Border Crisis Management in the Banking Sector.* ECON 2010/2006(INI) (June 28). Brussels.

Focarelli, D., and A. F. Pozzolo. 2001. The Patterns of Cross-Border Bank Mergers and Shareholdings in the OECD Countries. *Journal of Banking and Finance* 25: 2305–37.

Fonteyne, Wim. 2007. *Cooperative Banks in Europe—Policy Issues.* IMF Working Paper 07/159 (July). Washington: International Monetary Fund.

Fonteyne, Wim, Wouter Bossu, Luis Cortavarria-Checkley, Alessandro Giustiniani, Alessandro Gullo, Daniel Hardy, and Sean Kerr. 2010. *Crisis Management and Resolution for a European Banking System.* IMF Working Paper WP/10/70. Washington: International Monetary Fund.

FSA (Financial Services Authority). 2009. *The Turner Review: A Regulatory Response to the Global Banking Crisis* (March). London.

FSB (Financial Stability Board). 2010. *Reducing the Moral Hazard Posed by Systemically Important Financial Institutions—FSB Recommendations and Time Lines.* Basel. Available at www.financial stabilityboard.org/publications/r_101111a.pdf.

Giovannini, Alberto. 2010. *Financial System Reform Proposals from First Principles.* Center for Economic and Policy Research Policy Insight 45 (January). Washington: Center for Economic and Policy Research.

Goldman Sachs. 2009. *Ending Too Big to Fail. Effective Regulation: Part 5* (January). New York: Goldman Sachs Global Markets Institute. Available at www.gs.com (accessed in October 2010).

Goldstein, Morris. 2010. *Confronting Asset Bubbles, Too Big to Fail, and Beggar-Thy-Neighbor Exchange Rate Policies.* Policy Briefs in International Economics 10-3 (February). Washington: Peterson Institute for International Economics.

Goldstein, Morris. 2011. *Integrating Reform of Financial Regulation with Reform of the International Monetary System.* Working Paper 11-5 (February). Washington: Peterson Institute for International Economics.

Group of Thirty. 2009. *A Framework for Financial Stability.* New York.

Hanson, Samuel, Anil Kashyap, and Jeremy Stein. 2011. A Macroprudential Approach to Financial Regulation. *Journal of Economic Perspectives* 25, no. 1 (winter): 3–28.

Herring, Richard. J. 2010. *Wind-Down Plans as an Alternative to Bailouts*. Briefing Paper. Washington: Pew Financial Reform Project, Pew Charitable Trusts.

Herring, Richard J., and Jacopo Carmassi. 2010. The Corporate Structure of International Financial Conglomerates: Complexity and Its Implications for Safety and Soundness. In *The Oxford Handbook of Banking*, ed. Allen Berger, Philip Molyneux, and John Wilson. Oxford: Oxford University Press.

IFSL (International Financial Services London). 2010. *Banking 2010* (February). London.

IIF (Institute of International Finance). 2010a. *Systemic Risk and Systemically Important Firms: An Integrated Approach* (May). Washington. Available at www.iif.com (accessed on January 22, 2012).

IIF (Institute of International Finance). 2010b. *A Global Approach to Resolving Failing Financial Firms: An Industry Perspective* (May). Washington. Available at www.iif.com (accessed on January 22, 2012).

IMF (International Monetary Fund). 2009. *Global Financial Stability Report: Responding to the Financial Crisis and Measuring Systemic Risk* (April). Washington.

IMF (International Monetary Fund). 2010. *A Fair and Substantial Contribution by the Financial Sector, Interim Report for the G-20* (April). Washington.

IMF, BIS, and FSB (International Monetary Fund, Bank for International Settlements, and Financial Stability Board). 2009. *Guidance to Assess the Systemic Importance of Financial Institutions, Markets, and Instruments: Initial Considerations*. Report to the G-20 Finance Ministers and Governors (November). Available at www.financialstabilityboard.org (accessed on January 22, 2012).

Johnson, Simon, and James Kwak. 2010. *13 Bankers: The Wall Street Takeover and the Next Financial Meltdown*. New York: Pantheon.

Laeven, Luc, and Ross Levine. 2005. *Is There a Diversification Discount in Financial Conglomerates?* (June). Washington: World Bank.

Posner, Elliott, and Nicolas Véron. 2010. The EU and Financial Regulation: Power Without Purpose? *Journal of European Public Policy* 17, no. 3: 400–415.

Pozsar, Zoltan, Tobias Adrian, Adam Ashcraft, and Hayley Boesky. 2010. *Shadow Banking* (July). Federal Reserve Bank of New York Staff Report 458. New York: Federal Reserve Bank of NY.

Squam Lake Working Group on Financial Regulation. 2009. *An Expedited Resolution Mechanism for Distressed Financial Firms: Regulatory Hybrid Securities*. Council on Foreign Relations (April). Available at www.cfr.org (accessed on January 22, 2012).

Stern, Gary, and Ron Feldman. 2004. *Too Big To Fail: The Hazards of Bank Bailouts*. Washington: Brookings Institution.

Thomson, James. 2009. *On Systemically Important Financial Institutions and Progressive Systemic Risk Migration*. Policy Discussion Paper 27 (August). Cleveland: Federal Reserve Bank of Cleveland.

Turner, Adair. 2010. *Too Much "Too Big to Fail?"* Project Syndicate, September 2. Available at www.project-syndicate.org (accessed on January 22, 2012).

Véron, Nicolas. 2007. *Is Europe Ready for a Major Banking Crisis?* Bruegel Policy Brief 2007/03 (August). Brussels: Bruegel.

Wheelock, David, and Paul Wilson. 2009. *Are US Banks Too Large?* Federal Reserve Bank of St. Louis Working Paper 2009-054B (December). St. Louis, MO: Federal Reserve Bank of St. Louis.

7

Reform of the Global Financial Architecture

GARRY J. SCHINASI and EDWIN M. TRUMAN

It is now more than three years since the onset of the global financial and economic crisis and two years since the global market dysfunctioning that occurred in the aftermath of the public bankruptcy of Lehman Brothers and the US government takeover of AIG. Although some progress has been made in reforming financial sector policies and the International Monetary Fund (IMF) and Financial Stability Board (FSB), the bulk of reforms required to improve the ability to safeguard global financial stability and resolve global crises have yet to be agreed on much less fully legislated and implemented.[1]

Against this background, this chapter examines the implications of the global crisis for reform of the global financial architecture, focusing in particular on areas where further reforms of the IMF and FSB could help to improve the functioning and governance of the global financial system. The chapter is organized as follows: The next section examines the precrisis framework for safeguarding global financial stability and identifies six key areas where

Garry J. Schinasi joined the International Monetary Fund (IMF) in 1990, where he has focused on global finance and financial stability issues. He is currently on sabbatical from the IMF and is working as an independent researcher and consultant on global financial stability issues. Edwin M. Truman, senior fellow at the Peterson Institute for International Economics since 2001, served as assistant secretary of the US Treasury for International Affairs from December 1998 to January 2001 and returned as counselor to the secretary March–May 2009. They thank Morris Goldstein and Larry Promisel for comments on an earlier draft. The views expressed in this chapter are their own.

1. For some of the many reform recommendations, see UK Treasury (2009), US Treasury Department (2009), European Commission (2009), de Larosière (2009), G-30 (2009), UK Financial Services Authority (2009), Committee on Capital Markets Regulation (2009), FSB (2008), G-20 (2009), Issing Committee (2009), and IMF (2009).

financial system reforms are necessary. The following section focuses on the IMF and the FSB (the successor to the Financial Stability Forum [FSF]) and their recent and prospective reforms. The penultimate section addresses how the IMF and FSB can effectively address the six principal issues facing the global financial architecture. The last section provides our key conclusions and recommendations.

In summary, we conclude that the IMF and FSB are distinct and not fully comparable institutions, but they must cooperate more closely than in the past on the reform and performance of the global financial system. No other global financial architecture is up to the task and is politically feasible at this time. To that end, we outline the key tasks that the IMF and FSB should address.

We make recommendations for substantive and institutional governance reforms of both the IMF and FSB; reorientation of central banks vis-à-vis the IMF and vice versa and vis-à-vis macroprudential policies; and use of the FSB-IMF collaborative structure to help address the troubling issue of global capital flows.

We also recommend a number of institutional reforms: adding expert staff resources to both the IMF and FSB, formalizing the reporting by the FSB to the International Monetary and Financial Committee (IMFC), adopting an inclusive policy agenda, and seeking more direct engagement by the IMF in the work of the FSB.

Before proceeding to our analysis, the remainder of this introduction provides some definitions and sets the stage.

The main focus of our analysis is the global financial system and its supporting global financial architecture. The global financial system consists of the global (international) monetary system with its official understandings, agreements, conventions, and institutions as well as the private and official processes, institutions, and conventions associated with private financial activities.[2] For completeness, we refer to Joseph Gold's (1981) definition of the international (global) monetary system, which consists of the rules governing the relations of countries through their balance of payments and the monetary authorities that manage them (treasuries, central banks, stabilization funds, and other country-specific institutions).

The global financial system has three components: private sector institutions, the nations that have supervisory jurisdiction over the private institutions, and the international institutions through which the national authorities coordinate and cooperate. The global financial architecture is the collective governance arrangements at the global level for safeguarding the effective functioning (or the stability) of the global financial system.[3] It is governed first and foremost by the countries that have agreed to be part of it, for example, through their IMF membership, their participation in other

---

2. This definition is a slight modification of the definition in Truman (2003).

3. Here we have adapted Elson's (2010) definition to suit our purposes.

institutions and agreements, and their adherence to various codes, standards, and understandings. Accordingly, accountability for its successes and failures rests squarely with its member countries, in particular those that strongly influence it. These same countries are accountable to their own constituencies for the performance of the global financial architecture and any implications its performance may have on national, regional, continental, and global economic and financial outcomes.

The global financial and economic crisis of 2007–10 revealed that the pre-crisis global financial architecture was flawed both in its implementation and in its structure. With the benefit of hindsight, it is apparent that there were warning signs and policy mistakes and misjudgments. But as structured and implemented, the global financial architecture was not effective in encouraging or persuading remedial actions at the national, regional, continental, or global level until a full-scale global systemic crisis was a reality to be dealt with. As Stanley Fischer wisely observed, warnings are one thing, but they are worth little unless they lead to meaningful actions.[4]

The global financial architecture was revealed to be structurally flawed. Its coordination mechanisms failed to resolve cross-border problems without the resort to national ring-fencing, unprecedented volumes of liquidity provided by central banks to markets, and volumes of credit guarantees and recapitalizations provided by national treasuries to individual financial institutions not previously witnessed on a global scale. In light of the need for unprecedented massive interventions, one important and perhaps overriding lesson for global governance emerging from the crisis is that the international community lacks a body of international law, or at least official agreements and conventions, and—importantly ex ante—lacks burden-sharing mechanisms (or balance sheets) for resolving the weaknesses or insolvencies of large, complex, interconnected financial conglomerates.

Table 7.1 summarizes the IMF's and FSB's policy mandates, tools, and governance structures. As discussed in more detail in the body of this chapter, the FSB is the successor body to the FSF. It has a broader membership and remit, but its basic structure remains the same as that of the FSF.

As the table demonstrates, the IMF has concrete policy instruments and substantial resources: It lends, engages in bilateral and multilateral surveillance (evaluations), and it provides technical assistance for improving macroeconomic and financial sector policymaking in member countries. By contrast, the FSF was, and the FSB is, primarily a coordinating body. The FSF's advanced country membership, before the crisis, used the FSF to try to form consensus about best practices in microprudential regulation and supervision for all countries as well as to identify vulnerabilities in the global financial system and supervisory gaps. Neither the IMF nor the FSF had the policy

4. Stanley Fischer, Preparing for Future Crises, speech given at the Federal Reserve Bank of Kansas City symposium "Financial Stability and Macroeconomic Policy," Jackson Hole, WY, August 21, 2009, www.kansascityfed.org (accessed on January 27, 2012).

Table 7.1   Policy focus, tools, and governance: International Monetary Fund and Financial Stability Board

	International Monetary Fund	Financial Stability Board
Policy focus	• Exchange rate system and balance-of-payments equilibrium • Member country macroeconomic and financial stability • Global economic and financial stability	• International standards and best practices for financial regulation and supervision • Global financial stability
Tools	• Financing facilities for balance-of-payments needs • Bilateral and multilateral surveillance • Technical assistance	• Identification/assessment of sources of global financial vulnerabilities • Development of remedial policies to safeguard/restore stability • Coordination of member country financial system policies
Internal governance structures	• Board of governors consisting of one governor and alternate for each of the 187 member countries (usually the finance minister or central bank governor) • Executive board in continuous session • Management and staff • International Monetary and Financial Committee • Development Committee	• Plenary comprises G-20 central bank governors or deputies, heads or deputies of main supervisory/regulatory agency, and deputy finance ministers; and high-level representatives of standard-setting bodies, central bank committees, International Monetary Fund, World Bank, Bank for International Settlements, and Organization for Economic Cooperation and Development • Steering Committee selected by plenary • Chairperson • Secretariat drawn from members
Accountability	• Member country governments	• G-20 heads of state

G-20 = Group of 20

Sources: IMF website, www.imf.org; FSB website, www.financialstabilityboard.org.

instruments to prevent or resolve financial crises involving private financial institutions and markets. They can hardly be held fully accountable for not preventing or resolving the global crisis of 2007–10. But, as institutions, the IMF and FSF (including their managements and staffs) can and should be held accountable for failing to deliver what was expected—such as candid assessments of the impending financial system imbalances and more effective pressure on their membership and constituencies to adopt remedial measures to safeguard stability.

Although the IMF and the FSB, and the FSF before it, have been tasked to cooperate on assessing systemic risks and vulnerabilities and share a common purpose in providing financial stability–enhancing global public goods, they are very different types of organizations.

As is clear from its Articles of Agreement, the IMF was established by a formal international agreement that was ratified by governments. It was organized to promote international monetary cooperation and stability as well as to provide other public goods. As such, it should be viewed as an organization that has an identity separate from and in some respects transcending its country membership. In addition, the IMF is constituted with a management and staff structure separate from its governing or executive boards but with the mandate to pursue the objectives of the IMF. In addition to speaking on behalf of the organization, staff are also free, subject to quality controls, to publicize their professional research, analyses, and policy judgments on matters of concern to the Fund and its membership, of course with the appropriate disclaimers. Both management and staff do so frequently and at times forcefully. For example, the two leading publications of the IMF—the *World Economic Outlook* and the *Global Financial Stability Report*—express the views of the IMF staff and not those of the IMF as an organization.

Like the IMF, the FSF and FSB charters also make clear that their mandates entail the provision of global public goods that transcend the membership: developing and promoting effective global regulatory, supervisory, and financial sector policies and assessing financial system vulnerabilities that threaten the global financial system. However, the roles of the FSB chair and secretariat are to represent the FSB and its views, not to express views independent of its members.

Global Financial Systemic Issues Revealed by the Crisis

The global crisis revealed fundamental weaknesses in the precrisis global financial architecture for preventing, managing, and resolving crises in the global financial system. This section concludes, not surprisingly, that all lines of defense against a systemic crisis were breached during the crisis. This section highlights the principal areas where reforms are necessary.

Precrisis Framework for Safeguarding Global Financial Stability

The precrisis framework for safeguarding financial stability and encouraging economic and financial efficiency can be seen as lines of defense against systemic problems that could threaten stability. It was put in place over time by both private and public stakeholders in the major financial centers.[5] This architecture evolved over time as events occurred. It is the result of neither a grand design nor an underlying "genetic" code that predisposed the evolution of the system to emerge in the way it has. It is more akin to an evolving

---

5. This subsection is adapted from the framework in Schinasi (2009a) and earlier work in Schinasi (2006).

patchwork quilt of consensus decisions by stakeholders in the major financial centers to deal with problems as they emerged and as an organic collection of private and public international agreements and conventions.

A simplified framework of potential threats to stability and of the lines of defense against them is summarized in table 7.2. The columns of the table represent four important sources of global systemic financial risk: (1) global financial institutions—primarily large, international banks/groups but also including global investment banks and insurance/reinsurance companies; (2) global financial markets—foreign exchange, bond, and over-the-counter (OTC) derivatives markets; (3) unregulated financial market activities of institutional investors such as the capital markets activities of insurance and reinsurance companies and of mutual, pension, and hedge funds; and (4) economic and financial stability policy mistakes.

Financial infrastructures could be added as another source of systemic risk but they are excluded for simplicity. By and large, clearance, settlement, and payments systems performed reasonably and comparatively well during the crisis. There are some notable exceptions, such as the repo market, but problems there were related to the weaknesses that surfaced in the financial institutions that are the major counterparties in the repo markets. More generally, the large global banks typically are the major participants in national and international clearance, settlement, and payments infrastructures—both public and private—as well as the major trading exchanges. Many of these financial institutions co-own parts of the national and international infrastructures and have a natural interest in their performance, stability, and viability. Incentives are to some extent aligned to achieve both private and collective net benefits.

Increasingly, however, internationally active banks have been more heavily involved in OTC transactions, which do not pass through these infrastructures. This poses systemic risk challenges, many of which surfaced dramatically during the global financial crisis and earlier during the Long-Term Capital Management (LTCM) crisis. In addition, broader aspects of finance can also be considered as part of the infrastructure and pose systemic risks—such as the frameworks for risk management (grounded heavily in value-at-risk or VAR models), the very notion and practical meaning of risk diversification, important market segments that provide essential "utility" and "liquidity" services to the broader market place (such as the repo market and swaps markets), accounting rules and practices, corporate governance and compensation practices, and supervisory and regulatory standards and practices (Garber 2009).

The rows of table 7.2 represent what can be characterized as lines of defense against systemic problems: (1) market discipline—including private risk management and governance, along with adequate disclosure via financial reporting and market transparency; (2) financial regulations—which define the rules of the game for transactions and relationships; (3) microprudential supervision of financial institutions and products; (4) macroprudential supervision of markets and the financial system as a whole; and (5) crisis management and resolution.

Table 7.2   Precrisis framework for safeguarding global financial stability

Line of defense	Sources of cross-border systemic risk			
	Global financial institutions	Global financial markets	Unregulated financial activities	Economic and financial stability policy mistakes
Market discipline and transparency	Partially influential	Primarily influential	Exclusively influential	Committee structures; peer pressure; lack of clarity and transparency
Financial regulation	National orientation with international cooperation on capital requirements	No formal regulation	No regulation	No explicit framework and ineffective coordination and cooperation
Microprudential supervision	National orientation with cooperation on best practices via Basel process	Not applicable	No supervision	International cooperation proved inadequate to supervise systemically important financial institutions
Macroprudential supervision	If systemically important	National market surveillance; International Monetary Fund multilateral surveillance; Financial Stability Forum vulnerabilities discussions	Some via surveillance of national markets and financial institutions	National authorities and international cooperation failed to adjust macroeconomic and supervisory policies in advance of systemic pressures
Crises management and resolution	National legislation and orientation	National orientation with some central bank cooperation and coordination	No framework	No framework and ineffective cooperation and coordination

Source: Adapted from Schinasi (2007, 2009a).

As indicated in the first column of table 7.2 ("global financial institutions"), large cross-border banking groups are within the perimeter of all five lines of defense. As such, these financial institutions are the most closely regulated and supervised commercial organizations on the planet, and for good reasons. These institutions pose financial risks for depositors, investors, markets, and even unrelated financial stakeholders because of their size, scope, complexity, and of course their risk management systems, which may permit excessive, often highly leveraged, risk taking. Some of them are intermediaries, investors, brokers, dealers, insurers, reinsurers, and infrastructure owners and participants; and in some cases many of these roles exist within a single complex institution. They are systemically important: all of them nationally, many of them regionally, and about 20 or so of them globally. Protection, safety net, and systemic risk issues are key public policy challenges. Oversight of these institutions occurred at the national level, through both market discipline and official involvement, with a degree of indirect surveillance carried out at the international level through the IMF, the Organization for Economic Cooperation and Development (OECD), and the Bank for International Settlements (BIS), and committees and groups, including the Basel Committee on Banking Supervision and Financial Stability Forum prior to the crisis.

At the other extreme of regulation and supervision are unregulated financial activities (and entities), as can be seen in the third column of table 7.2. These financial activities and entities are neither regulated nor supervised. Many of the financial instruments—OTC derivatives for example, used strategically and tactically by these unregulated entities—are not subject to formal securities regulation.[6] Moreover, the markets in which they transact are by and large the least regulated and supervised. This lack of regulation, supervision, and surveillance is often the basis for their investment strategies and it defines the scope of their profit making. Unregulated entities (such as hedge funds and certain kinds of special investment vehicles) are forbidden in some national jurisdictions. In jurisdictions where they are partially regulated, this is tantamount to being forbidden—given the global nature and fungibility of their business models. Some market activities of unregulated entities are subject to market surveillance just like other institutions, but this feature does not make transparent who is doing what, how they are doing it, and with whom they are doing it. Investor protection is not an issue for many individual unregulated entities to the extent that they restrict their investor base to institutions (pension funds, insurance companies, hedge funds) and wealthy individuals willing to invest with relatively high minimum amounts.

Starting with the collapse of the European exchange rate mechanism in 1992–93, intensified during the Asian crises and the financial market disruptions associated with the Russian sovereign default and the collapse of LTCM,

---

6. These activities are subject to laws against fraud and the general provisions of commercial codes.

and in light of their tremendous growth over the past several years, hedge funds came to be seen by many, correctly or incorrectly, as potentially giving rise to systemic risk concerns. Others believed that the attention paid to hedge funds as posing systemic risks was misplaced and instead should have been focused on the OTC derivatives markets (Schinasi et al. 2000). As the recent global crisis demonstrated, hedge funds did not play a (major) role in the virulent market dynamics and dysfunctioning whereas the OTC markets did play a major role.

Global financial markets—a third source of systemic risk identified in the second column of table 7.2—fall between being and not being regulated and supervised. What is meant by global markets? Examples are the foreign exchange markets and their associated derivatives markets (both exchange traded and over the counter) and the G-3 (dollar, euro, and yen) fixed-income markets as well as others associated with international financial centers (pound, Swiss franc, etc.) and their associated derivatives markets. Dollar, euro, and yen government bonds are traded more or less in a continuous global market and the associated derivatives activities are also global. The primary line of defense is market discipline.

Global markets are only indirectly regulated. They are subject to surveillance of one form or another through private international networks and business cooperation agreements; information sharing by central banks and supervisory and regulatory authorities; official channels, committees, and working groups; and less directly through IMF multilateral surveillance of global markets. Parts of these markets are linked to national clearance, settlement, and payments infrastructures, so they are also subject to surveillance through these channels. The risks they potentially pose are less of a concern to the extent that the major players in them—the large internationally active banks—are supervised and market disciplined by financial stakeholders. Nevertheless, if there is poor oversight of the major institutions, then these global markets are subject to considerable risks, including a greater likelihood of systemic risk. One obvious example is the global over-the-counter derivatives markets, which are unregulated and which were prior to the crisis (and still now are) subject to little formal oversight except through the regulation and supervision of the institutions that engage in the bulk of these markets' activities.

The fourth and final source of systemic risks identified in table 7.2 is the policy framework itself, which includes both macroeconomic policies as well as the financial stability architecture. As will be discussed later, we believe there were mistakes made in many policy areas which either encouraged the behavior that led to systemic risks or directly posed systemic risks, as with some aspects of the financial stability architecture itself.

As noted in row five of table 7.2, an additional aspect of the policy framework is crisis management and resolution of financial problems once they become systemic. This part of the policy framework entails the following key components: deposit insurance protection to prevent bank runs; appropriate liquidity provision by central banks to keep markets smoothly functioning; lender of last resort operations to prevent market dysfunctioning and illiquid but viable financial institutions from failing; and recapitalization, restructuring, and resolution mechanisms (private preferred to public) to maintain orderly transitions for institutions that are not viable. As the global crisis revealed, an important missing element of this policy architecture was an effective framework for resolving potential systemic problems experienced by systemically important financial institutions.

What We Know from the Crisis

Although the global financial crisis has been characterized by some as caused by the US subprime mortgage crisis, the continuing crises in the euro area, and in Europe more generally, suggest that the earlier and ongoing US problems should be seen as symptomatic of an economic and financial environment that encouraged imprudent risk taking, excessive leverage, a worldwide credit boom, and the accumulation of an unsustainable amount of private and public debt. As has been widely discussed, including in the press, many economic and financial factors contributed to the crisis, and we do not need to repeat the long list here.[7]

The relevant observation for the purposes of this chapter (and for reforming the global financial architecture) is that the precrisis policy framework and architecture described above failed to prevent and resolve in a cost-effective manner the kind of financial imbalances that ultimately created systemic risks and events that threatened to create a worldwide depression. This framework—created over time primarily by US and European policy architects—relied heavily on achieving and maintaining a balance between market discipline and official oversight, with the objective of providing checks and balances to prevent systemic threats to financial and economic instability.

The balance was wrong. Neither market discipline nor official oversight by national authorities and international institutions such as the IMF and FSF performed its function as intended. Regarding the balance, it was tilted too heavily toward ex ante market discipline, which proved to be elusive until it was too late—at which point the ex post exercise of market disciplining behavior created panic and market dysfunctioning. It also relied too little on official oversight, which failed to foresee the buildup of systemically significant imbalances and weaknesses; it also failed to deal as effectively as it might (in a least cost manner) with the crisis once it was upon us. For example, in

---

7. There is a wide range of papers expressing a diversity of views. See, for example, Carmassi, Gros, and Micossi (2009); Caprio, Demirgüç-Kunt, and Kane (2009); de Larosière (2009); Gorton (2008, 2009); Lane and Milesi-Ferretti (2010); Levine (2009); Obstfeld and Rogoff (2009); Truman (2009); and Visco (2009).

the United States, if Lehman Brothers had been subject to regulation that included a Federal Deposit Insurance Corporation (FDIC)–type procedure for prompt corrective action, it is arguable that Lehman's bankruptcy could have been avoided. In addition, even if prevention failed, Lehman's ultimate bankruptcy and resolution would have occurred in a less disruptive manner and at lower taxpayer cost. The same arguments apply to the resolution of Fortis in Europe. As these examples suggest, national frameworks for crisis management and resolution also proved to be inadequate for managing and resolving cross-border problems and even some national stability problems.

In summary, the precrisis lines of defense against threats to systemic stability proved to be inadequate and were breached most visibly in the European Union and the United States:

- Private risk management and market discipline failed and markets dysfunctioned, the result of a combination of imperfect information, opaque instruments and exposures, poor incentive structures, insufficient capital and liquidity buffers and excessive leverage, inadequate governance/control by top management, insufficient ex ante market discipline, and loss of trust.

- Official supervision failed to promote safety and soundness of systemically important financial institutions (SIFIs).

- Macroeconomic policies contributed to conditions conducive to financial crisis.

- National and global market surveillance failed to identify the buildup of institutional, market, and systemwide financial imbalances with sufficient clarity and rigor to persuade policymakers to take remedial action.

- Precrisis central bank and finance ministry tools for addressing liquidity/solvency issues and for restoring market trust and confidence proved to be inadequate and were out of date and out of tune with the fast-paced nature and global reach of 21st century finance.

In line with this assessment—which broadly is conventional wisdom despite important differences of emphasis—reforms are necessary and being considered in a broad range of areas where the global crisis revealed important weaknesses. Many of these areas have been discussed extensively since the onset of the crisis three years ago, and officials in the major financial centers and other Group of 20 (G-20) countries are actively debating and crafting solutions aimed at dealing with these weaknesses.

Principal Areas Where Reforms Are Necessary

Six broad and closely related and overlapping areas can be identified that are particularly relevant for considering reforms of the global financial architecture as it impacts the stability of the global financial system.

Regulatory Requirements for Capital, Liquidity, and Leverage and the Potential Benefits/Costs of "Systemic Risk" Taxes

The global crisis revealed that regulatory requirements for ensuring the safety and soundness of individual financial institutions (or microprudential bank regulations) were inadequate. Many facets of these requirements contributed to the buildup of imbalances and risks: (1) Basel II methodologies were flawed in determining capital requirements for both on- and off-balance sheet credit exposures; (2) liquidity risks were misunderstood, as were private risk management and regulations; (3) leverage limits were either inadequate or unbinding, or in Europe completely absent; and (4) other aspects of national supervisory frameworks and day-to-day practices were ineffectively applied.

The Basel Committee on Banking Supervision and the Financial Stability Board are considering reforms to deal with the four above-mentioned revealed flaws in the approaches taken to ensure the safety and soundness of institutions. Significant increases in capital, liquidity, and leverage requirements were originally envisioned in a Basel Committee proposal sent out for comment in December 2009.

On July 26, 2010, the Group of Governors and Heads of Supervision—the oversight body of the Basel Committee on Banking Supervision—met to review the Basel Committee's capital and liquidity reform package. Its announcement expressed a deep commitment to increasing the quality, quantity, and international consistency of capital, strengthening liquidity standards, discouraging excessive leverage and risk taking, and reducing procyclicality. They also announced they had reached broad agreement on the overall design of the capital and liquidity reform package, including the definition of capital, the treatment of counterparty credit risk, the leverage ratio, and the global liquidity standard. Unfortunately, compared to the revisions to Basel II put forward in the December 2009 proposals, the agreement reached in July 2010 provided many concessions favorable to the banking industry, including a less demanding definition of Tier 1 capital, less stringent liquidity requirements, and a lower leverage limit (only 3 percent) phased in over a longer period ending in 2017.

The Group of Governors and Heads of Supervision announced on September 12, 2010, a strengthening of capital requirements (Basel III), and it fully endorsed the agreements it reached in July 2010. The Basel Committee agreed on a package of reforms that raises the minimum common equity requirement from 2 percent to 4.5 percent and requires banks to hold a capital conservation buffer of 2.5 percent to withstand future periods of stress. This brings the total common equity requirements to 7 percent. The minimum common equity and Tier 1 requirements will be phased in between January 1, 2013, and January 1, 2015, whereas the capital conservation buffer will be phased in between January 1, 2016, and December 31, 2018, becoming fully effective on January 1, 2019. Other more detailed but no less important elements, such as the treatment of noncore equity assets and recapitalizations, will be phased in by January 1, 2018.

The Basel Committee is planning on supplementing these higher capital requirements with liquidity requirements and leverage restrictions, but they also will be phased in over time. The former comprise a new liquidity coverage ratio (effective 2015) and a revised net stable funding ratio (effective 2018) and the latter a leverage ratio of 3 percent (to be phased in by 2018). The Group of Governors and Heads of Supervision also noted in the September 12 press release that systemically important banks should have loss-absorbing capacity beyond the standards announced and that this issue will continue to be addressed as part of the work streams of the FSB and the Basel Committee.

Although the agreement announced in September 2010 constitutes progress, it is clear that the committee could not reach a consensus on earlier implementation of important elements of reform. Capital requirements are raised significantly as agreed by G-20 leaders (in 2009), but they are not introduced until 2013 and are not completely phased in until 2015. This carries the risk that some banks will continue to be "undercapitalized" until 2015. Moreover, the committee could not reach a consensus on implementing other important aspects of the reforms agreed on by G-20 leaders until 2018—notably, an increase in liquidity requirements to improve liquidity-risk management and a leverage ratio of 3 percent to reduce the propensity for excessive leverage. That a consensus could not be reached is disappointing: excessive leverage and poor liquidity-risk management by the major global banks played an important role in creating the conditions for the global crisis. They also contributed importantly to the virulent market dynamics and market dysfunctioning that prevailed throughout 2008–09. This mixed record to date by the regulators and supervisors is not reassuring for the prospects to agree on the difficult reform tradeoffs and decisions that are yet to be taken and implemented on both sides of the Atlantic, including those pertaining to SIFIs, OTC derivatives markets, and resolution mechanisms for cross-border banking problems.

Authorities in the major financial centers have also been grappling with ways of addressing the systemic nature of nonbank financial institutions after learning that even a relatively small but highly interconnected financial firm like Lehman Brothers could pose a systemic risk to the global financial system and economy. Various taxes, surcharges, and levies on individual SIFIs are being considered to meet a variety of objectives: to pay for past costs of recapitalization; to set aside "insurance" funds to pay for future problems; and to alter incentives so that excessive risk taking is reduced. A part of the challenge is to develop microprudential measures that can be imposed on those institutions that are deemed to pose systemic risks regardless of their legal and regulatory organizational structure. Earlier the G-20 considered the possibility of a systemic risk capital surcharge with the aim of imposing a microlevel tax on SIFIs to add protection to capture systemic externalities posed by individual institutions. It is not clear whether this idea is still under active consideration.

The US regulatory reform legislation, the Dodd-Frank Act, did not impose an ex ante tax even though at various points in the process the draft legislation anticipated doing so. US financial institutions may be required ex post to repay the FDIC and US Treasury for the fiscal costs of orderly liquidation of a US financial company. The United Kingdom is considering an internationally coordinated systemic risk tax on financial institutions that could help to reduce the risks and impact of future financial crises, and other countries within Europe are also considering levies to deal with future problems. Because finance is fungible and global—as are the relevant institutions—systemic risk capital charges or taxes are likely to have limited impact on reducing systemic risk if they are imposed unilaterally. Global coordination would enhance the effectiveness of a systemic risk charge, but the playing field for SIFIs is not level today and is unlikely to be level in the future. It is an unfortunate political reality that international agreements tend at best to produce common minimum standards even when obvious collective solutions can be envisioned and implemented.[8]

Perimeters or Boundaries of Financial Regulation, Supervision, and Infrastructures

The "perimeter" or "boundary" of financial regulations, supervision, and infrastructures proved to be too narrow or ill defined to prevent systemic problems from arising and worsening. For example, US authorities in charge of managing crises and resolving bank failures had no legal authority or standing in resolving the problems of Bear Stearns and Lehman Brothers. The Federal Reserve was able to help to facilitate an acquisition of Bear Stearns but was unable or unwilling to do so with Lehman Brothers. That was all about firefighting ex post not ex ante. Ex ante, the perimeter problem and challenges are particularly acute for nonbank financial institutions with significant cross-border exposures and businesses.

The boundary or perimeter challenge is multidimensional. The most obvious sources of perimeter or boundary problems are: (1) off-balance sheet activities conducted through over-the-counter derivatives markets and embodied in unregulated special purpose vehicles; (2) the national orientation of prudential oversight despite the existence of systemic cross-border institutions operating in multiple jurisdictions; (3) the banking orientation

---

8. The G-20 in Toronto (2010, annex II, paragraphs 21–23) endorsed five principles to promote financial sector responsibility via a financial levy. It remains to be seen whether the application of these principles satisfies the fifth, which is to "help provide a level playing field." Testifying on July 20, 2010, before the Subcommittee on Security and International Trade and Finance of the US Senate Committee on Banking, Housing, and Urban Affairs, US Treasury Undersecretary Lael Brainard and Federal Reserve Board Governor Daniel Tarullo both acknowledged that global convergence may require different approaches across nations and identified aspects of the Dodd-Frank Act that are not likely to be embraced outside the United States, including restrictions on proprietary trading, participation in derivatives transactions, and any limits on the size of financial institutions.

of supervisory oversight to the exclusion of other systemically important nonbank financial institutions (AIG, Lehman, GE Capital, hedge funds); and (4) many sources of regulatory arbitrage within national financial systems (for example, Basel-related off-balance sheet arbitrage of capital requirements) and across geographical as well as legal boundaries.

Key unresolved questions include the following. Can the existing national frameworks be reformed so that they can better anticipate and prevent problems in cross-border institutions? In the transatlantic or global spheres, for example, can international groupings and committee structures be reformed to provide sufficient early warnings? In this regard, are supervisory colleges for cross-border supervision a promising avenue? If not, what steps are necessary to improve global coordination so that more-effective prevention and resolution mechanisms are established to deal with problems emanating from any systemic financial institution regardless of its core franchise?[9] Can differences in the legal treatment of country bankruptcy be managed short of adopting a uniform approach? How should differences in accounting practices be treated if not harmonized? It is far from clear that the evolving US and EU approaches to these areas are consistent.

Regulation and Surveillance of Global Money and Financial Markets

Although authorities in all of the major financial centers agree that global money and financial markets, in particular the OTC derivatives markets, need to be effectively regulated and subject to surveillance, creating an effective regulatory framework is likely to pose significant operational and politically contentious challenges. OTC derivatives markets constitute a global network of counterparty relationships among and between primarily SIFIs—a network in which these institutions act as dealers and market makers, manage financial risks, and trade on their own account (capital). In effect, this network is an extension of the global interbank money market. It is at the core of the global financial system, and it provides "utility" financial services that affect indirectly many aspects of company and household finance. As the global crisis demonstrated, a single credit event or weak link in this network can quickly lead to a systemic problem as SIFIs rebalance and reprice their portfolios to minimize exposure and preserve their own liquidity. When this happens, the network shrinks, becomes fragile, and (as we saw in autumn 2008) can ultimately dysfunction.

The autumn of 2008 was not the first time this network threatened to melt down. Ten years before, in September 1998, the market turbulence surrounding

---

9. Giovannini (2010) examines the "boundary problem"—the problem with the boundary between the financial functions (services) society desires and the set of financial institutions that actually try to deliver them. He observes that the global crisis revealed a "boundary" or "perimeter" mismatch between functions and institutions. He concludes that reforms are necessary to realign financial functions (or services) with the institutions that deliver them so they can be more effectively privately risk managed as well as officially regulated and supervised to prevent systemic problems.

the collapse of LTCM occurred in this same network; it was a wake-up call indicating that this market was subject to considerable systemic risk.[10] In the event, as the crisis revealed, many of the counterparty risk and liquidity risk problems that surfaced during the LTCM crisis surfaced again in more dramatic fashion in 2007–10 and without hedge funds playing a major role. It is at least a reasonable hypothesis that sufficient reforms to procedures and practices for managing counterparty and liquidity risk were not effectively implemented, even though the private and official community gathered many times and wrote many reports about what needed to be reformed and how to accomplish it.

Effective and enduring reform efforts in this area will require changes in many dimensions: legal, process, architecture, and cross-border cooperation. Reform proposals across the Atlantic differ, and fierce competition between the major financial centers is active, but there is also much common ground. The OTC money and derivatives markets are truly global and systemic. Uncoordinated solutions risk exacerbating problems, for example a massive shift of these activities to the least regulated and/or weakest oversight jurisdiction with the potential consequence of even greater excessive risk taking, risk concentrations, and excessive leverage. More generally, anything short of a global solution could lead to the persistence of regulatory arbitrage, complexity, opacity, and systemically threatening counterparty relationships. For these reasons, leadership at the head-of-state level may be required to force a consensus that a global regulatory framework and platform is necessary to regulate the activities in these markets and conduct continuous effective surveillance over them.

Systemically Important Financial Institutions, or the "Too Big to Fail" Problem[11]

As touched upon above in the discussion of systemic risk charges and taxes, the global crisis revealed a fundamental flaw in the precrisis architecture for preventing global financial systemic problems in systemically important financial institutions. Over the years, several reports were written that identified and examined sources of systemic risk, including financial institutions, specific markets, and financial infrastructures (see, for example, G-10 1992, 2001; and Schinasi et al. 2000). Because of the strong adverse economic impact of the global financial crisis, greater attention is now being paid to these sources of systemic risk—including by the G-20 leaders and the general public at large (taxpayers). Thus, it is now more widely understood that some financial institutions pose risks to the stability of the entire global financial system because of their size, complexity, and interconnectedness.

One way of interpreting this heightened recognition is that, prior to the crisis, there was a widespread misunderstanding—an intellectual deficit and even a lack of imagination—about how systemic financial risks and, ultimately,

---

10. For an extensive discussion of the potential for systemic risk in over-the-counter derivatives markets, see Schinasi et al. (2000).

11. Chapter 6 by Morris Goldstein and Nicolas Véron focuses primarily on the TBTF issue.

economic instability can be caused by the activities of a single financial institution (a complex financial conglomerate). As Fischer observed, there is a clear distinction to be made between the *recognition* of a source of risk, a *warning* that the risk is growing and becoming systemic, and actually taking *action* to prevent the risk from being realized.[12] Over the years prior to the crisis, there was much recognition of risks, fewer serious and credible warnings, and very few instances in which strong actions were taken to reduce or avoid the kind of imbalances that led to systemic events.

In this regard, the precrisis architecture for safeguarding global financial stability can be judged to have failed to assess, monitor, and manage the wider implications of financial imbalances and weaknesses that can emerge within individual financial institutions. Simply put, the authorities in charge of safeguarding financial stability fell behind the curve in understanding how to manage the changed nature of systemic risk in a financial system comprising global institutions and market-oriented securitized finance. For lack of a better label, the relevant financial institutions have become known as too big to fail (TBTF).[13] A more neutral and appropriate phrase—systemically important financial institutions—focuses on systemic importance and downplays the role of any one of the often-mentioned characteristics, such as large, complex, interconnected, unique, etc.

According to a recent report to G-20 ministers of finance and central bank governors (FSB, IMF, and BIS 2009):

> In practice, G-20 members consider an institution, market or instrument as systemic if its failure or malfunction causes widespread distress, either as a direct impact or as a trigger for broader contagion. The interpretation, however, is nuanced in that some authorities focus on the impact on the financial system, while others consider the ultimate impact on the real economy as key.

This specific language reflects the difficulty both of defining systemic importance and of reaching a consensus among G-20 finance ministers and central bank governors.[14]

Nevertheless, other authors have been less shy and reserved in trying to define SIFI (Federal Reserve Bank of Cleveland 2009; Thomson 2009; US

---

12. Fischer, Preparing for Future Crises, speech given at the Federal Reserve Bank of Kansas City symposium, 2009.

13. In normal circumstances, a financial institution like Northern Rock would not be considered a systemically important financial institution. It became systemic because of the way specific circumstances and situations evolved in the United Kingdom. Thus, as is discussed later, systemic importance is not just a matter of size, complexity, or interconnectedness; it is also situational, state dependent, and time varying.

14. The FSF identified 30 or so large complex financial institutions that were considered to merit, and now have, core supervisory colleges and standing cross-border crisis management groups. For the presumptive list of these entities—which has not been made available to the public at large—see Patrick Jenkins and Paul J. Davies, "Thirty Financial Groups on Systemic Risk List," *Financial Times*, November 29, 2009.

Treasury 2009; Brunnermeier et al. 2009; ECB 2006, 2007, 2008). Drawing on their suggestions, we list the following as factors that either alone or in combination could render individual financial institutions systemically important:

- size relative to the economy, key markets, or other like institutions;
- scope of activities;
- complexity of business model, organization, and risk-taking activities;
- opacity of the nature and magnitude of risk exposures;
- interconnectedness of activities with other financial institutions, markets, and infrastructures;
- similarity of (or correlation with) activities and risk exposures to other institutions; and/or
- nonsubstitutable, systemically important activity.

Other factors could be relevant as well, including the macroeconomic and macrofinancial environment. Thus, whether an institution is a SIFI depends in part on its structure as well as economic and financial conditions beyond its control. In other words, the definition itself is "state contingent" and "time varying" to some degree.

Regardless of the nomenclature, several global financial conglomerates were both the cause and consequence of the systemic risks and events they collectively helped to create. In the event, the activities of Bear Stearns, Lehman, and AIG (to name a few) helped to create the complex network of counterparty relationships that ultimately became unsustainable, unraveled, and caused repeated episodes of market panic and the dysfunctioning of the global financial system. Many other large, global financial institutions that were not merged or did not fail also contributed to the buildup of excessive risk taking and leverage prior to the crisis, but they too required unprecedented remedial actions individually and collectively. The remaining global institutions now compose a more highly concentrated network of counterparty relationships within the core of the global financial system than before the crisis. In other words, the restructurings and bankruptcies of several global financial institutions have created a more highly concentrated global financial system. It is not unreasonable to think that the systemic risks associated with the activities of the remaining global institutions have gone up because of this restructuring and the manner of its financing.

It is reasonable to conclude from the crisis that precrisis banking regulations, supervisory frameworks/practices, and market surveillance did not just fail but were in fact incapable of assessing, monitoring, and supervising the risk profiles of global institutions and the implications for global financial systemic stability both prior to and during the early stages of the crisis. The inadequacy of the global financial architecture for dealing with these institutions and their roles in global markets shaped importantly the policy responses. Responses entailed unprecedented public credit guarantees, unprecedented recapitalizations, forced restructurings with public guarantees and ownership, and perhaps unprecedented and still extant moral hazard.

An additional problem revealed by the crisis is that government efforts to recapitalize cross-border institutions (for example, Lehman Brothers) reverted immediately to national ring-fencing and solutions—which exacerbated market panic and systemic problems. Even in the case of Fortis in Europe, for which it can be argued that excellent preconditions for coordinating a rescue existed between Belgium, Luxembourg, and the Netherlands, the financial resolution ultimately devolved to each country ring-fencing and recapitalizing the domestic pieces of the pan-European institution.

Our takeaway is that reforms are necessary in many related areas pertaining to SIFIs if systemic risk management is to be improved significantly in the future. These areas include regulation, supervision, market surveillance, crisis management, rescue, and resolution. Some reformers have advocated breaking up these institutions into more transparent, focused, and specialized institutions that are easier to regulate, supervise, rescue, or resolve. But, whatever its merits, the political will does not exist to consider this approach seriously. Short of this more surgical approach, reforms will have at least to recalibrate the balance between the private benefits and potential social costs of SIFIs in providing financial services in our modern financial system and the best way to risk-manage their delivery (FSB, IMF, and BIS 2009; FSB 2010).

Crisis Management, Rescue, and Resolution

Much of the reform agenda has focused appropriately on improving the architecture's ability to prevent the next crisis. For example, the creation of a US Financial Stability Oversight Council and a European Systemic Risk Board are necessary and worthwhile efforts aimed at improving the ability to assess the potential for systemic risk in the absence of market pressures and adequate supervision and regulation. Early detection of financial imbalances is necessary to avoid systemic problems through the implementation of risk-mitigating measures that could reduce the potential for financial imbalances becoming systemic and threatening financial stability. Authorities on both sides of the Atlantic are proposing to devote considerable resources and political capital to improving early warning systems to the point where they become more reliable.

However, authorities should have realistic expectations about whether these early warning systems will be effective. The reality is that crises will occur again. The crucial question is whether warnings will lead to action.

The costly and ad hoc rescue and resolution efforts of authorities during the global crisis provide clear evidence that countries generally lack effective mechanisms for managing, rescuing, and resolving weak or insolvent financial institutions with significant cross-border exposures, including SIFIs, in a cost-effective manner. These widespread challenges were apparent in dealing with national, continental, and global financial institutions and markets.

The challenge for all of the major financial centers is to establish legally robust, operationally practical, and compatible frameworks designed for the orderly resolution of systemically important financial institutions in a timely manner and with the capacity to minimize both the systemic consequences and taxpayer costs of resolution. Solutions are being pursued on both sides of the Atlantic, but the outcomes are likely to be less coordinated and compatible than is desirable for resolving cross-border institutions operating in several legal jurisdictions.

In addition to rescue and resolution, the crisis also revealed weaknesses in the ability to manage and to resolve liquidity problems associated with financial distress and instability. Notably the European Central Bank, the Bank of England, and the US Federal Reserve all lacked established instruments to resolve liquidity problems and needed to innovate and introduce new ways of operating in the markets with financial institutions to maintain monetary stability in the presence of financial instability. In effect, prior to the crisis, the major central banks all fell behind the curve in understanding the liquidity-hungry nature of securitized markets and the changed nature and greater market orientation of systemic risk, including their global scope (Schinasi 2009c). Many policy issues need to be addressed to improve the ability of central banks to manage future crises. In the area of prudential oversight, two particular issues stand out.

- Central bank mandates for prudential supervision in all of the transatlantic financial centers fell short of what was required to prevent financial problems from becoming systemic and for dealing with the crisis once it was systemic. In the United States, the Federal Reserve did not have oversight responsibilities for all of the SIFIs operating in US markets, as some of them were investment banks and insurance companies. In the United Kingdom, the Bank of England had responsibility for financial market stability but did not have responsibility for banking supervision and had to rely on cooperation with the UK Financial Services Authority, an arrangement that proved to be ineffective. In the euro area, while some national central banks within the European System of Central Banks have supervisory powers, the European Central Bank itself had no formal responsibility for supervision.

- The relevant authorities had neither the comprehensive power to obtain relevant timely information from all SIFIs and other unregulated financial institutions nor the authority to intervene (place in administration, liquidate, resolve) SIFIs when it was necessary.

Effective Management of Volatile Capital Flows

The epicenter of the global crisis of 2007–10 was the US financial system and economy, and the principal locus of secondary eruptions was Western Europe. But the crisis became global, encompassing Central and Eastern Europe,

Latin America, Asia, and Africa before running its course. A major transmission mechanism was the global financial system and associated capital flows, which dried up, first, for Iceland and Eastern Europe and ultimately for many of the major emerging-market economies, for example Korea. A second transmission mechanism was the recession in the advanced countries that led to a collapse in global trade that was unprecedented in the post–World War II era (IMF 2010b, Herrmann and Mihaljek 2010, McGuire and von Peter 2009).

As is documented by Olivier Blanchard and Gian Maria Milesi-Ferretti (2009), the major portion of the precrisis gross capital flows involved the advanced countries, primarily of the North Atlantic. The emerging-market economies were the source of net capital flows. In the case of the Eastern European countries, net and gross capital flows financed large current account deficits. However, the emerging-market economies of Asia and Latin America, in particular, were also recipients of substantial gross capital flows. Korea is exhibit number 1.

Korea had the fifth-largest foreign exchange reserves as of February 2008 and ran substantial cumulative current account surpluses during the years in advance of the crisis (Truman 2009). Nevertheless, it was hit hard by a reversal of the gross inflows of capital to Korea that were a feature of the immediately preceding years. One consequence was that the Bank of Korea took advantage of the Federal Reserve's offer to open a $30 billion swap line for use in support of financial institutions needing to repay US dollar borrowings. The Federal Reserve opened similar lines with the central banks of Brazil, Mexico, and Singapore.[15] Mexico along with Colombia and Poland also took advantage of the flexible credit line put in place by the IMF in March of 2009.

In the aftermath of the global crisis, many emerging-market countries have recovered more rapidly than the advanced countries, causing some of their central banks to raise their official interest rates; as a result, global capital flows have reemerged as a problem for some countries. A few have instituted controls to curtail the inflow of capital.

Unwanted capital flows are generally a problem both in the management of macroeconomic policies and in safeguarding the stability of domestic financial systems, which are the normal, but not necessarily the only, conduit for such flows.[16] Moreover, with the globalization of the financial system, capital flows are likely to continue to be a source of concern even without crises on the scale of that of 2007–10. Thus, the effective management of such flows is a key challenge in ensuring financial stability and for macroeconomic policies. Reasonable responses to such flows require cooperation both by source and recipient countries and involve both prudential and macroprudential policies (Truman 2010a).

---

15. In addition to the Bank of Korea, the Bank of Mexico drew on its line, but the Central Bank of Brazil and the Monetary Authority of Singapore did not.

16. Roberto Zahler (2010) emphasizes that short-term capital inflows can go directly to equity markets or to nonfinancial borrowers, bypassing domestic financial institutions.

This is an area where representatives of both the European Union and the United States have reservations. The United States appears to be more receptive to expanding the IMF's lending facilities, and the Europeans appear to be less so, even though a number of countries in the European Union (and now the euro area) have taken advantage of the increased flexibility of the IMF's lending operations. As of this writing, Europeans are resisting a substantial increase in the IMF's quota resources, which would be necessary if the IMF were to play an expanded role as a lender of last resort. The US position remains one of skepticism. The views of both on the use of controls on capital inflows appear to have mellowed since the late 1990s. A reasonable guess, however, is that neither is prepared openly to embrace the view that its own macroeconomic, in particular monetary, policies should or might need be altered in light of trends in capital movements.

The IMF and FSB Today

Against the background of the previous section outlining the principal areas where reforms are necessary, this section examines the IMF and the FSB, the principal international institutions responsible for the global financial system in the postcrisis environment. We examine five aspects of those institutions: membership and representation; tools and instruments; compliance and leverage; macroprudential orientation; and accountability and transparency.

The International Monetary Fund

The IMF commenced operations in 1945—67 years ago. Its objectives were then, and remain today, to promote growth and financial stability via its lending and surveillance activities and a variety of mechanisms in support of international cooperation. At the start, the IMF's role was focused on exchange rate stability and the removal of restrictions on payments that limited the expansion of international trade.

The IMF's primary focus was on the international monetary system and the Bretton Woods regime of fixed, but occasionally adjustable, exchange rates. Indeed, the purposes of the IMF stated in Article I of the Articles of Agreement as they stand today focus on the promotion of "international monetary cooperation . . . [and] the machinery for consultation and collaboration on international monetary problems." In the period immediately after World War II and continuing into the 1960s, when the Bretton Woods exchange rate regime came under pressure, the private sector's role in the global financial system was largely ignored. The international monetary system was the entire global financial system as we defined that term earlier. Even today, Article VII limits the use of the IMF's resources to make capital transfers. The only limitation on the use of capital controls is that they should not be used to impede trade and current account transactions.

The expansion of private capital flows in the 1960s was one of the many contributing factors to the demise of the Bretton Woods system. Some thought that with the passing of fixed exchange rates among the currencies of the major countries, which were then the currencies of the G-10 countries,[17] the IMF would and should go out of business. These hopes or fears did not materialize. The members of the IMF supported the evolution of the institution in the context of the oil shocks and inflationary chaos of the 1970s, the global debt crisis of the 1980s, the challenges of transition economies in the 1990s, the debt crises of the middle and late 1990s, and more recently the global economic and financial crisis of 2007–10 (Truman 2006b, 2008, 2010b).

As time passed the attention of the IMF and its members turned increasingly away from the structure and functioning of the international monetary system and arrangements among governments toward the global financial system. This was most vividly illustrated by the IMF's involvement in capital account financial crises of the 1990s. Since 2001, the IMF has published its *Global Financial Stability Report*, first as a quarterly publication and subsequently as a semiannual publication updated quarterly. The *Global Financial Stability Report* was preceded in the 1980s and 1990s by the annual *International Capital Markets* reports, which focused on sources of vulnerabilities in international capital markets, and evolved in response to the global debt crises in the earlier decade and in response to subsequent periods of turbulence and crisis throughout the 1990s. Thus IMF staff, management, and membership have engaged in one or another systematic form of assessments or surveillance of global financial system vulnerability for more than three decades.

Nevertheless, the IMF (management and staff) did not warn about the impending global economic and financial crisis, although some of its various papers and reports identified some red flags. In that sense, its value added to the assessment of the emerging global financial crisis was limited.

In the remainder of this subsection, we discuss various aspects of the IMF's evolving role in the global financial system.

Membership and Representation

The IMF with its 187 member countries is essentially a universal international organization. In principle, it is fully representative because each member country is directly or indirectly represented on its board of governors (see table 7.1).

However, the Fund departs from the principle of one nation, one vote because the preponderance of its formal decisions are taken by weighted majorities, based largely on IMF quotas, in which each country's voting power rests broadly on its economic importance. Currently, those weights are considered by many observers to be unrepresentative (Bryant 2010).

---

17. The 11 G-10 countries are Belgium, Canada, France, Germany, Italy, Japan, the Netherlands, Sweden, Switzerland, the United Kingdom, and the United States.

In addition, and partly as a consequence, representation on the 24-person IMF executive board, its day-to-day decision-making body, is heavily influenced by the 8 to 10 chairs held by European countries as well as by the United States.[18] With a very few exceptions, the executive directors and their alternates, their advisors, and their staffs are drawn from finance ministries, rather than central banks, and only by coincidence would they include anyone with supervisory or regulatory experience.

Thus, the IMF, in principle, is representative, but the structure of its current representation in terms of both voting shares and talking chairs has undercut its legitimacy (as Locke understood that concept) in the sense that all countries are members and have representatives in Washington.[19] In the view of some, IMF representation is deficient, and consent of the governed is incomplete or blunted. It remains to be seen whether this situation will be substantially changed as the result of agreements reached at the Seoul G-20 summit in November 2010.

Tools and Instruments

The IMF has a range of tools and instruments that it can employ to help it achieve its objectives: lending, surveillance, analytical studies, and technical assistance.

Although IMF lending operations normally absorb less than one-quarter of IMF administrative expenses, they attract a disproportionate share of attention. The IMF directly impacts the policies of its members primarily via its lending programs, imposing conditions designed to get out of current crises and to reduce the probability of future crises.

IMF lending, built up to more than $100 billion in credit and commitments outstanding in the early 2000s, was back down to about $10 billion in September 2008, at the end of the first year of the financial crisis, and subsequently expanded to more than $200 billion. This was accompanied by a substantial addition to the IMF's resources, principally via ad hoc borrowing from individual members and, potentially, from an expansion of the

---

18. The countries with the five largest IMF quotas are each entitled to appoint an executive director. The remaining 19 executive directors are elected by constituencies; currently three are one-country constituencies (China, Russia, and Saudi Arabia). The countries in the European Union are spread across 10 appointed executive directors and elected directors of constituencies, which include nonmembers of the European Union; in principle each of those chairs could be occupied by an EU representative. Switzerland is one of those constituencies and heads its own constituency. In addition, the European Central Bank may be separately represented at some meetings of the executive board (Truman 2006a). This European dominance is likely to be reduced somewhat with the election of a new executive board that is scheduled to take over on November 1, 2010.

19. We use the word "legitimacy" as it is used in the literature on political theory. For example, according to John Locke (see Ashcraft 1991, 524), "The argument of the [Second] Treatise is that the government is not legitimate unless it is carried on with the consent of the governed."

New Arrangements to Borrow to $550 billion to supplement its usable quota resources of about $250 billion.[20]

IMF surveillance over members' policies and the global economic and financial environment has increased in importance in recent decades. These activities include bilateral surveillance focused on the economic and increasingly the financial policies of individual countries in the form of mandatory Article IV reviews at 12- to 18-month intervals, and since 1999 its voluntary reviews under the Financial Sector Assessment Program (FSAP).[21] IMF surveillance also has its global component—multilateral surveillance—in the form of executive board discussions and conclusions based on reports on the economic outlook and financial system prepared by the staff. The *World Economic Outlook* was first published semiannually in 1980, and quarterly updates are now issued (Hacche 2009).

In 2006-07, the IMF executive board experimented with a multilateral consultation with China, the euro area, Japan, Saudi Arabia, and the United States on global imbalances. It did not have a great impact because the countries participating did not want to commit to any new policy measures, and the topic of global imbalances was soon overwhelmed by the economic and financial crisis.[22] At the time, it was expected that the next such consultation exercise would involve the global financial system issues, but that intention was displaced by the crisis.

The IMF's analytical multilateral surveillance publications such as the *World Economic Outlook* and *Global Financial Stability Report* and their predecessors, along with an array of working papers, staff position notes, and other documents, are an important tool by which the IMF staff of close to 3,000 with the support, and in some cases instigation, of IMF management (the managing director and the three deputy managing directors) attempt to influence the policies of members and shape debates about current policy issues and challenges.

The IMF's technical assistance programs offer another mechanism through which the IMF can promote and support better policies, including policies of member countries in the financial area. Those policies contribute to financial stability in the financial systems of the individual countries and to the aggregate stability of the system as a whole, but they are not at the core of issues confronting the architecture of the global financial system today as we outlined earlier.

---

20. The allocation of about $280 billion in special drawing rights by the IMF directly augmented the resources of member countries to deal with the consequences of the crisis.

21. The World Bank participates in FSAPs for developing countries. In the case of both institutions, the staff conducting the reviews are largely seconded from national authorities because the Fund and the Bank lack the staff and other resources to do the work in-house.

22. An active minority of observers think that global imbalances played a major role in precipitating the 2007-10 crisis, but that is not our view.

Compliance and Leverage

The IMF is not constituted to be a rigorous international regulator. The formal obligations of members under the IMF Articles of Agreement are few, and many of those obligations are honored in the breach. Based on this reality, one of us (Truman 2010b, 38) has argued that the IMF's regulatory role "is considerably broader in practice than that of a regulator in the national context, but that role is dependent on the mutual consent of governments initially to agree to subject themselves individually to the IMF's oversight and subsequently to adjust their policies in response to that oversight. The oversight or regulatory role to a substantial degree is enforced via the self-application by its members of peer review processes."

The IMF does have considerable leverage over countries that require financial assistance in support of recovery and reform programs, and the Fund has used that leverage effectively. We would submit that the record of increased financial stability in recent years among Latin American, Asian, and African countries owes substantially to reforms encouraged by the IMF in connection with reform programs of those countries that were supported by IMF financial assistance, as well as by the World Bank and other development banks.[23] When assistance is not leveraged by lending operations, the IMF can assist only those countries that want to be assisted.

Finally the IMF, by virtue of the size, range of skills, and relative independence of its professional staff and management, can influence and exert leverage over the policies of member countries via the bully pulpit backed by robust analysis.[24] Many observers note the important role of the IMF staff and management as "trusted advisors." This role sometimes comes in conflict with "name and shame" efforts to pressure members to bring their policies into

---

23. This is the principal conclusion in IMF (2010b, 4): Emerging-market "countries that had improved policy fundamentals and reduced vulnerabilities in the precrisis period reaped the benefits of these reforms during the crisis."

24. We use the phrase *professional staff* to mean a staff whose primary objective is to use its skills, training, experience, and expertise to help the organization achieve its mandate largely free from the political influence or policy preferences of member countries and organizations. By *independence* we mean a staff that is largely free to exercise, express, and publish its professional judgments and opinions without the political and policy influence of member countries and organizations. Article VII, section 4(c) states, "The Managing Director and the staff of the Fund, in the discharge of their functions, shall owe their duty entirely to the Fund and to no other authority. Each member of the Fund shall respect the international character of this duty and shall refrain from all attempts to influence any of the staff in the discharge of these functions." In practice, IMF staff are encouraged to express their professional judgment and personal views in several publications, including IMF working papers, occasional papers, and staff position notes. The *World Economic Outlook* and *Global Financial Stability Report* are documents of the staff in which a disclaimer notes that the views expressed are those of the authors and not those of IMF management or its executive board. A majority of IMF economists are hired directly from graduate schools; some are hired and sometimes seconded for a limited term from national authorities. The IMF website provides disclosures on professional requirements, salaries, benefits, and other staff-related information.

better compliance with global norms and standards. However, the resistant or recalcitrant country is free to ignore the advice and entreaties of the IMF staff, and even to deny information to the IMF, unless the country requires financial support from the IMF or its blessing to receive financial support from the private sector. Moreover, messages from the management and staff of the IMF are often diluted by the softer messages from the more political executive board.

The IMF's representation issues that affect its legitimacy, in turn, weaken its leverage, including via peer review processes. In addition, the extent of leverage the IMF management and staff have over the largest member countries—once the G-7 countries and now a longer list—can be questioned. It depends in part on the governance processes in those countries and the role of the media and interest groups as well.

Macroprudential Orientation

The IMF is the premier international organization when it comes to the analysis and assessment of macroeconomic policies. The IMF does not have a monopoly on these issues among international organizations, but its mandate and near-universal membership guarantee the IMF the widest scope and respect.[25] As noted above, the IMF has engaged in surveillance of capital markets and the global financial system since the 1980s and has published numerous, regular reports since then. It has a large staff focusing on multilateral issues, and its bilateral country surveillance has been refocused toward a more macrofinancial orientation as an additional pillar to supplement bilateral surveillance work on macroeconomics and monetary, fiscal, and exchange rate policies.

On the other hand, since the collapse of the Bretton Woods exchange rate regime, the IMF's governance has become increasingly dominated by finance ministries and increasingly distrusted, partly as a consequence, by central banks. Moreover, the finance ministry representation on the executive board and among the deputies of the IMFC—that is, below the level of the ministers and governors—is by individuals with experience and skills in international affairs but not necessarily macroeconomic affairs. Thus, the expertise of the IMF staff is disconnected from formal interaction with the relevant macroeconomic and also supervisory authorities by virtue of the IMF's governance structure.

The national authorities, in turn, are to varying degrees engaged in systemwide financial surveillance activity as well, in the form of financial stability reports. However, these reports are largely focused on national (or regional) markets and priorities except to the extent that the global environment impinges on them. Many of the financial stability reports set the stage for risk

---

25. Among the competing international organizations are the World Bank (equally universal but with a different mandate), the Organization for Economic Cooperation and Development (more limited membership), and the Bank for International Settlements (more limited membership and a more limited mandate).

assessments by surveying the global financial landscape as it relates to conditions and risks in national markets, financial institutions, and infrastructure. However, they are drafted primarily by central banks with some input from national supervisory authorities, and the IMF itself has limited interactions with these groups.[26]

Accountability and Transparency

The IMF is viewed by many private sector observers as opaque and mysterious, and some see it as conspiratorial if not malevolent. The IMF has a formal anchor in its establishment by an international agreement that was ratified by its member governments, clearly establishing its governance if not its broader governmental processes. Because the IMF is an intergovernmental organization, it can operate above the political processes that affect its member governments. If a substantial majority of them are satisfied with the IMF's work, the institution is largely protected from outside pressures and criticisms.

However, as noted above, some member governments question the IMF's legitimacy. Moreover, the legitimacy of some of the member governments is questioned by the nongovernmental organization (NGO) community, which also criticizes the Fund for a lack of accountability and transparency. Thus, the IMF faces its own issues in this area along with the associated questions concerning access to, and the transparency of, its decision-making processes. As a formal matter, IMF transparency about its official business, for example minutes of executive board discussions, is controlled by its members through the executive board. The management and staff, responding to the increased pressures for accountability and transparency from 21st century public opinion, have carved out some scope to act informally and independently of the board via papers and web postings.

The Financial Stability Board

The Financial Stability Forum—the forerunner to the Financial Stability Board—was established by the G-7 countries in February 1999 in the aftermath of the Asian financial crises, the Russian default, and the financial turmoil that accompanied the demise of the hedge fund Long-Term Capital Management (see box 7.1). It was created and structured to coordinate, not to act.

The FSF's secretariat was small. Aside from those activities directed at identifying vulnerabilities and gaps in policy with associated recommendations to fill the gaps, the bulk of the substantive work was produced by committees composed of and chaired by FSF members. The reports issued were high-quality consensus documents focusing on a few key issues. After the first

---

26. In the future, the United States will be an exception to this generalization. The US Treasury will have responsibility for financial stability reporting on behalf of the Financial Stability Oversight Council.

Box 7.1   A brief history of the Financial Stability Board

The following brief history of the Financial Stability Board (FSB) is derived from the organization's website:

The FSB was established in April 2009 as the successor to the Financial Stability Forum (FSF).

The FSF was founded in 1999 by the G-7 Finance Ministers and Central Bank Governors following recommendations by Hans Tietmeyer, President of the Deutsche Bundesbank. G-7 Ministers and Governors had commissioned Dr. Tietmeyer to recommend new structures for enhancing cooperation among the various national and international supervisory bodies and international financial institutions so as to promote stability in the international financial system. He called for the creation of a Financial Stability Forum.

G-7 Ministers and Governors endorsed the creation of the FSF at a meeting in Bonn in February 1999. The FSF would bring together:

- national authorities responsible for financial stability in significant international financial centers, namely treasuries, central banks, and supervisory agencies;
- sector-specific international groupings of regulators and supervisors engaged in developing standards and codes of good practice;
- international financial institutions charged with surveillance of domestic and international financial systems and monitoring and fostering implementation of standards; and
- committees of central bank experts concerned with market infrastructure and functioning.

The FSF was first convened in April 1999 in Washington.

In November 2008, the leaders of the G-20 countries called for a larger membership of the FSF. A broad consensus emerged in the following months toward placing the FSF on stronger institutional ground with an expanded membership—to strengthen its effectiveness as a mechanism for national authorities, standard-setting bodies, and international financial institutions to address vulnerabilities and to develop and implement strong regulatory, supervisory, and other policies in the interest of financial stability.

As announced in the G-20 Leaders' Summit of April 2009, the expanded FSF was reestablished as the Financial Stability Board with a broadened mandate to promote financial stability.

Source: Financial Stability Board, www.financialstabilityboard.org/about/history.htm (accessed on January 27, 2012).

burst of reports in the 2000–2002 period, the FSF largely settled into a role of trying to identify incipient national and international financial vulnerabilities and of reviewing reports from other bodies.[27]

During its tenure, the FSF coordinated work in developing and disseminating standards, codes, and best practices in regulation and supervision of finance in concert with the international standard setters, the IMF, and World Bank. It served as a useful forum for member countries, international financial institutions, and standard-setting bodies (SSBs) to share information and analyses and learn from each other, which was one of its principal purposes. It created opportunities to address many of the externalities that exist in finance (information asymmetries, for example, within the context of the vulnerabilities discussions) and that posed risks to the global financial system. Public-good benefits were captured as a result of the work of the FSF and the resulting learning by its members, with implications for the work under their own remits.

The FSF, as a collective of countries and organizations, identified some risks that were later proved to be central to the global economic and financial crisis. In particular, the FSF starting in 2003 encouraged the Joint Forum in its work on the issue of credit risk transfer activities.[28] However, insufficient action was taken by member countries in light of the Joint Forum's work. More broadly, the FSF membership included all of the suspect jurisdictions with respect to the global crisis, and they did not act sufficiently forcefully, either independently or collectively in advance of the crisis.

It is therefore reasonable to question the value added of the FSF's work during the period prior to the global crisis, when systemic risks and vulnerabilities were accumulating. Notably, the FSF (as a collective organization) can reasonably be viewed as having been unsuccessful both in terms of developing and implementing supervisory and regulatory standards to prevent global systemic risks and in terms of developing a collective process accurately to identify and assess sources of global systemic risks and vulnerabilities. In addition, it is notable that the political authorities of nonmembers were critical of the FSF's limited size and coverage of issues prior to the crisis.

By contrast, once the crisis broke, the FSF produced what many observers regard as an excellent report in early April 2008 (FSB 2008) on enhancing market and institutional resilience. This report laid much of the groundwork for subsequent reforms endorsed and instigated by the G-20 leaders, who did not assemble until November that year.

---

27. In an initial burst of activity in its first two years, the FSF sponsored working groups on highly leveraged institutions (hedge funds), capital flows, and offshore financial centers. However, responding to the wishes of the United States and other G-7 countries, it subsequently took fewer such initiatives (Griffith-Jones, Helleiner, and Woods 2010; Helleiner 2010).

28. The Joint Forum includes the Basel Committee on Banking Supervision, the International Organization of Securities Commissions, and the International Association of Insurance Supervisors.

Partly as a consequence, in the heat of the global crisis, the leaders of the G-20 countries in November 2008 called for a larger membership of the FSF. A broad consensus emerged in the following months toward placing the FSF on stronger institutional ground with an expanded membership—to strengthen its effectiveness as a mechanism for national authorities, standard-setting bodies, and international financial institutions to address vulnerabilities and to develop and implement strong regulatory, supervisory and other policies in the interest of financial stability. As announced at the G-20 leaders' London summit on April 2, 2009, the expanded FSF was reestablished as the FSB with a broadened mandate to promote financial stability. The FSB's broadened mandate made mandatory its members' compliance with IMF/World Bank FSAPs and Reports on the Observance of Standards and Codes (ROSCs) and made more explicit and comprehensive its focus on macroprudential work in cooperation with the IMF (see box 7.2 and table 7.3).

US Treasury Secretary Timothy Geithner has argued that the enlarged FSB with expanded powers is now the fourth pillar of global economic governance along with the IMF, World Bank, and World Trade Organization.[29] The discussion of the FSB that immediately follows, and implicitly this chapter as a whole, examine that proposition. We conclude that this characterization of the FSF is not useful.

Article I of the FSB's charter (FSB 2009) spells out the objectives envisioned by the heads of state of the G-20 countries: "The Financial Stability Board (FSB) is established to coordinate at the international level the work of national financial authorities and international standard-setting bodies (SSBs) in order to develop and promote the implementation of effective regulatory, supervisory and other financial sector policies. In collaboration with the international financial institutions, the FSB will address vulnerabilities affecting financial systems in the interest of global financial stability."

As envisioned in the FSB's charter, the FSB plenary is the FSB's governing and decision-making body; a steering committee is its co-coordinating body; and there are three operational standing committees addressing vulnerabilities assessment, supervisory and regulatory policies and coordination, and standards implementation. The FSB has an explicit mandate to assess and act on vulnerabilities. It is in a position to draw on the best analysis available globally, and it has a highly professional staff running the secretariat.

The FSB chairman and secretariat acting together are coordinators. Box 7.3 summarizes the role of the FSB chairman. The FSB has neither an explicit policy mandate nor the critical mass of professional staff that would be necessary to engage in analytical studies and independent assessments of

---

29. Timothy F. Geithner, press briefing on the G-20 Meeting, September 24, 2009, www.ustreas. gov (accessed on March 8, 2012).

Box 7.2   Mandate of the Financial Stability Board

The following account of the Financial Stability Board's (FSB) mandate is derived from the organization's website:

The mandate of the FSB is to:

- assess vulnerabilities affecting the financial system and identify and oversee action needed to address them;
- promote coordination and information exchange among authorities responsible for financial stability;
- monitor and advise on market developments and their implications for regulatory policy;
- advise on and monitor best practice in meeting regulatory standards;
- undertake joint strategic reviews of the policy development work of the international standard-setting bodies to ensure their work is timely, coordinated, focused on priorities, and addressing gaps;
- set guidelines for and support the establishment of supervisory colleges;
- support contingency planning for cross-border crisis management, particularly with respect to systemically important firms; and
- collaborate with the IMF to conduct early warning exercises.

As obligations of membership, members of the FSB commit to pursue the maintenance of financial stability, maintain the openness and transparency of the financial sector, implement international financial standards (including the 12 key International Standards and Codes), and agree to undergo periodic peer reviews, using among other evidence IMF/World Bank public Financial Sector Assessment Program reports.

The FSB, working through its members, seeks to give momentum to a broad-based multilateral agenda for strengthening financial systems and the stability of international financial markets. The necessary changes are enacted by the relevant national financial authorities.

The FSB plenary meets two times per year and has calls as needed. To broaden the circle of countries engaged in work to promote international financial stability, the FSB also holds regional outreach meetings with nonmember financial authorities.

Source: Financial Stability Board, www.financialstabilityboard.org/about/mandate.htm (accessed on January 27, 2012).

Table 7.3   Evolution of membership and representation in the Financial Stability Forum and its successor the Financial Stability Board

Member	Representation	
	Financial Stability Forum	Financial Stability Board
Initial membership		
Canada	3	3
France	3	3
Germany	3	3
Italy	3	3
Japan	3	3
United Kingdom	3	3
United States	3	3
International Monetary Fund	2	2
World Bank	2	2
Bank for International Settlements	1	1
Organization for Economic Cooperation and Development	1	1
Basel Committee on Banking Supervision	2	2
International Organization of Securities Commissions	2	2
International Association of Insurance Supervisors	2	2
Committee on the Global Financial System	1	1
Committee on Payment and Settlement Systems	1	1
European Central Bank	1	1
Added to FSF in 1999		
Australia	1	2
Hong Kong	1	1
Netherlands	1	2
Singapore	1	1
Added to FSF in 2002		
International Accounting Standards Board	1	1
Added to FSF in 2007		
Switzerland	1	2
Added to FSB in 2009		
Argentina	n.a.	1
Brazil	n.a.	3
China	n.a.	3
India	n.a.	3
Indonesia	n.a.	1
Mexico	n.a.	2
Russia	n.a.	3
Saudi Arabia	n.a.	1
South Africa	n.a.	1
South Korea	n.a.	2
Spain	n.a.	2
Turkey	n.a.	1
European Commission	n.a.	1

n.a. = not applicable.

Source: FSB website, www.financialstabilityboard.org.

Box 7.3   Role of the chairman of the Financial Stability Board

According to the language of the Financial Stability Board (FSB) charter, the organization's chair

- is appointed by the plenary from members for a term of three years;
- shall have recognized expertise and standing in the international financial policy arena;
- convenes and chairs the meetings of the plenary and of the Steering Committee;
- oversees the secretariat;
- is the principal spokesperson for the FSB and represents the FSB externally;
- shall be informed of all significant matters that concern the FSB;
- more generally, shall make all decisions and act as necessary to achieve the objectives of the FSB in accordance with the directions given by the plenary; and
- in the discharge of the functions as the chair, shall owe the duty entirely to the FSB and to no other authorities or institutions.

Source: Financial Stability Board, www.financialstabilityboard.org/publications/r_090925d.pdf (accessed on January 27, 2012).

---

global financial vulnerabilities.[30] But it can draw on the work and resources of the international financial institutions to do so. The FSB secretariat very capably convenes meetings, organizes agendas, and manages the processes that produce multinational reports on issues pertaining to its financial stability mandate (see box 7.4). The key exceptions to these generalizations are its work on risks and vulnerabilities in the global financial system, which it does jointly with the IMF, and the commitments of its members to participate in peer review processes within the FSB "framework for strengthening adherence to international standards."[31]

---

30. Article 15 of the FSB's charter spells out the role of the secretariat, but neither the charter nor the FSB website provides information about the professional status or independence of the staff of the secretariat. Our understanding is that except for the secretary general and some secretarial and administrative staff, the "professional" staff of the FSB are seconded from and paid by member organizations.

31. The first such thematic peer review completed in March 2010 focused on the application of standards for sound compensation practices and their implementation. The second will examine implementation of recommendations on risk disclosures in light of the 2008 FSB report on *Enhancing Market and Institutional Resilience*. The FSB is also scheduled in 2010 to conduct country peer reviews of Italy, Mexico, and Spain based on their recent IMF/World Bank FSAPs.

Box 7.4   Role of the Financial Stability Board Secretariat

As stated in Article 15 of the Financial Stability Board's (FSB) charter:

(1) The secretariat shall be directed by the secretary general.

(2) The secretary general shall be appointed by the plenary at the proposal of the chair.

(3) The secretary general shall be under the responsibility, and shall act in accordance with the instructions, of the chair. The chair is responsible for providing general direction to the secretary general, in accordance with any directions given by the plenary.

(4) In appointing the secretariat staff, the secretary general shall, subject to the importance of securing the highest standards of efficiency and of technical competence, pay due regard to the importance of a balanced composition in terms of geographic regions and institutional functions.

(5) The secretary general and the secretariat staff, in the discharge of their functions, shall owe their duty entirely to the FSB and to no other authorities or institutions.

(6) The main responsibilities of the secretariat shall be the following:

 (a) to support the activities of the FSB, including its standing committees and working groups;

 (b) to facilitate cooperation between members and between the FSB and other institutions;

 (c) to ensure efficient communication to members and others;

 (d) to manage the financial, material, and human resources allocated to the FSB (including the appointment of staff who may be seconded by members);

 (e) to maintain the records, administer the website, and deal with the correspondence of the FSB; and

 (f) to carry out all other functions that are assigned by the chair or the plenary.

(7) The secretariat shall be located in Basel at the BIS [Bank for International Settlements].

Source: Financial Stability Board, www.financialstabilityboard.org/publications/r_090925d.pdf (accessed on January 27, 2012).

Membership and Representation

The FSF's initial membership was confined to the G-7 countries, international financial institutions, and the international standard-setting bodies. Later in 1999, the FSF membership was expanded to include representatives of four important financial centers: Australia, Hong Kong, the Netherlands, and

Singapore; Switzerland was invited to join in 2007 (see table 7.3). This limited membership in the FSF and the Basel Committee on Banking Supervision, the principal SSB associated with the FSF, contributed to the perception that there are "rule makers" (the G-7 and the FSF structure) and "rule takers" (the rest of the world).

This perception was ameliorated only in part by the FSF's regional meetings. There were five in 2001–02, but they tapered off to only six over the following four and a half years to mid-2007, before the start of the crisis.[32] The fact that the crisis was a G-7-centered affair that also affected many other countries only strengthened the view of outsiders that the FSF and SSBs had paid too much attention to nonmember jurisdictions and not enough to monitoring internal problems and issues in member jurisdictions. Thus, as with the IMF and considerably more so, the FSF had, and the FSF still has, a legitimacy problem in the sense of John Locke (see footnote 19).

As noted above, partly in response to these criticisms, the FSB's country membership has been expanded to include all of the G-20 countries and the European Commission. This expansion of membership should improve the coverage of issues by giving a potential voice to emerging-market country issues, needs, and concerns. It could also help to improve compliance with international standards, codes, and best practices in financial regulations and supervision. To the extent that continental/regional membership and representation within the FSB has been expanded and improved, this could help to improve the perceived legitimacy of the FSB with respect to standards and best practices for global finance.

Having said this, the membership is still skewed toward the G-7 countries and geographically toward Europe. The G-7 countries still have 21 of the 52 seats in the 67-seat FSB occupied by country representatives, and European countries occupy 20 of the 54 country seats, including the seats of the European Commission and the European Central Bank for this purpose. Although membership has been expanded to include most, if not all, of the systemically important emerging-market countries, it gives the greatest representation, and therefore potential voice, to the larger countries that are aspiring quickly to enter the realm of advanced countries.

One can argue that adding the voice and perspectives of China and the other systemically important emerging-market countries under the umbrella of the FSB is the key innovation. However, looking at the specifics, while the G-7 countries, Brazil, China, India, and Russia each have three representatives within the FSB, Australia, Mexico, the Netherlands, Spain, South Korea, and Switzerland each have two representatives and Argentina, Hong Kong, Indonesia, Singapore, Saudi Arabia, South Africa, and Turkey each have only one representative. The FSB operates by consensus and so the number of voices matters.

---

32. In some sense, the role of the IMF and the World Bank representatives in the FSF was to "represent" nonmembers, but that view has been put forward with respect to the IMF and the G-7 and has not been very convincing.

Thus, the limited and skewed country and geographic membership of the FSB and the country representation within it will most likely continue to have implications for perceptions about the political legitimacy of the FSB. Perceptions often shape outcomes.

Tools and Instruments

The FSB does not have policy tools or instruments beyond its mandate to promote collaboration and coordination among its constituent members and to identify gaps and financial system vulnerabilities.

The FSB has a small professional secretariat largely drawn from its member institutions. The secretariat is not designed or intended to conduct independent studies of key issues (see box 7.4). The FSB relies on its member countries, member organizations, and member international financial institutions with their substantial resources to carry out the mission of the FSB. This institutional arrangement places much of the initiative and analytical firepower with those who have national or organizational priorities and political imperatives with their own constituencies. This poses a risk that the national authorities from the larger countries—which influence the work programs of FSB members that are not countries—will continue to shape the FSB's agenda and consensus to their advantage, which could be detrimental to collective action in the interest of global economic and financial stability.

Compliance and Leverage

FSF member countries' compliance with international standards and best practices was voluntary, which was perceived by some at the start as a weakness. This structure was a compromise. In 1999, there was no appetite as there is none now for a global regulator or supervisor. The FSF structure comprised three related elements targeted on improving global financial stability: voluntary IMF/World Bank financial sector surveillance in the form of FSAPs and ROSCs; market pressure/discipline to encourage adherence to international standards and best practices; and a formal process of name and shame, and possibly sanctions, for offshore financial centers.

The FSB's charter is more prescriptive. It mandates that each member country (1) be subjected to IMF/World Bank FSAPs every five years with published assessments used as a basis for ROSCs; (2) implement international standards; and (3) undergo peer reviews within the FSB as well assessments performed by the IMF. Moreover, the process of name and shame may be extended beyond the offshore financial centers to other nonmember countries (Helleiner 2010).

This mandatory approach would constitute a substantial improvement were it to significantly increase the number of systemically important countries that comply with international standards and IMF/World Bank financial sector surveillance. However, as of September 2008, all but four of the regular members of the G-20 had already participated in the financial sector surveillance process. The exceptions were Argentina, China, Indonesia, and the United States (Truman 2010c). Notably, the United States has just completed its FSAP/ROSC process with the IMF/World Bank, and those for China and Indonesia are also under way.[33]

The more difficult and pressing postcrisis challenge faced by the FSB is to improve further the existing standards and practices that shape financial regulation and accounting, supervisory frameworks, and day-to-day supervisory practices. As we discussed in earlier sections, this challenge is especially pressing in the major financial centers, where the crisis revealed key weaknesses in the supervisory and regulatory architectures. The mandating of FSAPs every five years and the peer review process within the FSB for members may help in this regard while at the same time creating possible conflicts with the work of the IMF and World Bank. But the onus is on the major financial centers, working through and with the FSB, to develop and implement more effective supervisory and regulatory frameworks, standards, codes, and best practices.

The FSF's charter on its face was at best ambiguous about the relationship between the FSF and the international SSBs. The Tietmeyer Report (1999, 6) assigned to the FSF the task of "creating procedures for coordinating the work of national and international regulatory groupings, and for the exchange and pooling of information among them." This formulation raised the question whether the FSF was a "rule maker" or "rule taker." As part of monitoring and coordinating, there may have been a two-way process. But the lack of clear FSF oversight was seen by some as a shortcoming because one of the reasons for creating the FSF was to improve standards and compliance with them.

In this regard, the FSB takes three qualified steps forward for influencing SSBs' work and decisions. In particular, FSB members have agreed to the following:[34]

- SSBs will report to the FSB on their work—with the objective of strengthening support for strong standard setting by providing a broader accountability framework—but without prejudice to the SSBs' independence and existing reporting arrangements.

- The FSB will undertake joint strategic reviews of the policy development work of the SSBs to ensure their work is timely and coordinated, focuses on priorities, and addresses gaps.

- The FSB will promote and help coordinate the alignment of the activities of SSBs to address any overlaps or gaps and clarify demarcations in light of changes in national and regional regulatory structures relating to prudential and systemic risk, market integrity and investor and consumer protection, and infrastructure, as well as accounting and auditing.

33. See the US FSAP documents on the IMF website, www.imf.org.
34. See the FSB's charter (FSB 2009).

While these principles defining the FSB's relationship with the SSBs may be an improvement over the FSF, it is unclear whether the FSB has the clout to influence the agenda and content of the work of the SSBs. One can see the tension in the language used in the FSB's charter. Moreover, arguably the most important of the SSBs is the Basel Committee, which now formally reports to the Group of Governors and Heads of Supervision as its oversight body. That group, now chaired by European Central Bank President Jean-Claude Trichet, consists of the G-20 central bank governors and the supervisors from the G-20 countries. Until 2009, the Group of Governors and Heads of Supervision was an informal body. It was created to resolve the ambiguous situation that came to exist between the G-10 central bank governors, which established the Basel Committee in 1974 and to which the committee previously "reported," and the evolving membership of the committee that increasingly included banking supervisors who were not part of their national central banks because central bank involvement in banking supervision was scaled back or eliminated.

Since 2009, the IMF has had observer status on the Basel Committee and it participates with other international institutions on the Basel Consultative Group involving larger emerging-market countries, such as Chile, Malaysia, and Thailand, which are not represented on the Basel Committee (the committee now includes all the G-20 countries).

Our inference is that, while there is scope for a two-way interaction during the process of standard development, by the time Basel Committee proposals reach the FSB, which also includes representation of 17 finance ministries and international institutions, the decision to support them is essentially a formality. In countries where policy development is well coordinated between finance ministries, central banks, and supervisors, this three-tier structure may not matter with respect to the substance of national positions, but the voices of the other international organizations in the final approval process are absent.

Macroprudential Orientation

As we argued in the previous section, an important failure of the precrisis framework for safeguarding global financial stability was that it was focused too heavily on microprudential regulation and supervision and not enough on assessing, monitoring, and resolving problems at the systemwide level. In our view, the macroprudential orientation of supervision and regulation should have two major focal points: (1) the impact of the aggregation of financial risks on the system as a whole, including externalities and cross-correlations of risks (that is, a focus on systemic risk); and (2) the impacts on the financial system as a whole of macroeconomic policies—monetary, fiscal, and financial.

The first focal point has a regulatory dimension, as well as an ongoing supervisory dimension. The regulatory dimension involves restructuring the regulatory system to improve the ex ante alignment of incentives and to minimize ex post any unwanted consequences such as moral hazard.[35] The supervisory dimension involves the aggregation and calibration of the importance of risks across financial institutions or the financial sector as a whole. The second focal point requires assessing whether macroeconomic policies are encouraging or contributing to financial imbalances and systemic risks.

We would submit that neither when the FSF was established in 1999, nor in the wake of the crisis of 2007–10, has sufficient attention been paid to this second focal point. The boldest evidence of this bias is, first, the lack of consensus on how monetary policy should deal with asset price bubbles, and more broadly on the role of monetary (and more generally macroeconomic) policies in contributing to the conditions that caused and facilitated the recent crisis. Second is the widespread, but not universal, rejection of the view that aggregate quantities are relevant for assessments of systemic risk and financial stability, for example, the growth of aggregate credit (private and public) and off–balance sheet leverage.

Whatever one's view about the role and definition of macroprudential concerns, going into the recent crisis, the global financial architecture was to a considerable degree intellectually and operationally oriented toward ensuring the safety and soundness of individual institutions and toward thinking that this would be sufficient to safeguard systemic financial stability.

This ineffective orientation need not have been so. One reason why the FSF was originally established was to provide a forum for national central bankers, supervisory and regulatory authorities, officials from SSBs, and finance ministry officials to discuss these matters at arm's length—including with the international institutions.[36] As Hans Tietmeyer (1999, 6) indicated in his report to the G-7 finance ministers and central bank governors concerning the establishment of the FSF, one of the four early action areas for the FSF was "improving arrangements for surveillance of global vulnerabilities including the pooling of information available to the IFIs [important financial institutions] and the international regulatory groupings, the development and assessment of macro-early-warning indicators, and the creation of procedures to ensure that information reaches the relevant parties."[37] The FSF did convene a vulnerabilities group—composed of key representatives from a small number of members with expertise in market surveillance and systemic risk

---

35. See the exposition in Hanson, Kashyap, and Stein (2011, 5) in which the authors define the macroprudential approach to capital regulation as an "effort to control the social costs associated with excessive balance-sheet shrinkage on the part of multiple financial institutions hit with a common shock."

36. Central bankers outnumber finance ministry officials on the FSB 27 to 17.

37. The other three action areas were (1) coordinating the work of national and international regulatory groups; (2) assessing the need for the regulation of nonregulated entities (hedge funds and those operating out of offshore financial centers); and (3) encouraging the development and implementation of international best practices and standards.

assessment—in order to identify sources of risks and vulnerabilities so that the FSF could recommend remedial actions when and where necessary.

One possible reason why the FSF itself may have limited its attention to the macroeconomic policy aspects of macroprudential supervision is that central banks with some reasonable justifications tend to be reluctant to discuss or analyze their (monetary and macroprudential) policies in a forum that includes outsiders, including other central banks as well as supervisory authorities, finance ministries, and other organizations. Out of the 36 seats at the FSF table initially, almost a third (11) were occupied by representatives of central banks or central bank institutions, such as the BIS, or central bank committees. The original intent of the FSF was and that of the FSB is to expand these open discussions precisely to fill in gaps of information and analysis between central banks, supervisory authorities, and finance ministries. There is no reason to think that a continuation of this practice will not be self-defeating once again.

The FSF did address in its vulnerability discussions some of the aggregated aspects of macrofinancial imbalances and their implications for macroprudential policies, but with insufficient value added to head off the crisis. Much of the FSF's attention was concentrated on financial institutions for which there was little available data and information (such as highly leveraged institutions and other types of nonbank financial institutions), international standards and codes, and of course the crisis of the day, such as Argentina or Turkey.

The charter of the FSB tries to redress this balance by more explicitly acknowledging a role for the FSB in macroprudential assessments in concert with the IMF. Three of the FSB's assigned tasks can be interpreted as macroprudential in nature: assessment of vulnerabilities affecting the global financial system, monitoring and advising on market developments, and collaborating with the IMF to conduct early warning exercises (FSB 2009).[38] It is unclear at this point whether this new FSB focus on macroprudential issues is oriented toward the aggregation aspects and away from the macroeconomic policy aspects as described above. We suspect that it is. We note that the FSB as initially reconstituted includes among its 69 initial members 27 (more than one-third) from central banks or their institutions.

Accountability and Transparency

As a coordination mechanism, the FSB in principle should be able, at least, to consider how to internalize many of the externalities that exist in global

---

38. The other five identified tasks are promotion of information exchange, promotion of regulatory best practices, reviews of the work of the international standard-setting bodies, guidelines for supervisory colleges, and contingency planning with respect to systemically important firms. (See box 7.2.)

finance. One would hope that it would also be successful in formulating coordinated policy solutions that would actually internalize many of these externalities, for example to manage systemic risks in the global over-the-counter derivatives markets. Internalization of finance-related externalities can occur through information sharing; through the development of international standards, codes, and best practices; and through policy formulation and implementation. This is an essential process for promoting collective action with the objective of improving the ability to safeguard global financial stability.

Because the transparency of the FSB's work is largely confined to the publication of its *consensus* reports and findings, much of what is learned in reaching a consensus cannot find its way into the public domain. The consultation documents of the SSBs do provide a bit more transparency. However, for the severe critics in the NGO and academic communities, the SSBs are the regulators to which the regulated have privileged access, with the result that the accountability and transparency of their processes are inherently suspect, and the FSB layer adds only the central bankers and representatives of finance ministries, which are no better in this regard.

There are three potential problems with this lack of transparency. The first two involve nonmember countries. First, while nonmember countries have direct access to all FSB website-published reports and even some indirect access to FSB documents through their memberships in the institutions that are FSB members, nonmembers, as discussed above, by and large do not see this as sufficient involvement in the formulation of the standards, codes, and best practices to which they are expected to adhere. This is one reason why the FSB was expanded to include the G-20 countries, but this expansion may not be sufficient.

A second potential problem involving nonmembers is that nonmembers only get to see the work of the FSB that the SSBs decide to publicize. This work is likely to continue to be confined to consensus documents. However, the process of reaching a consensus is itself an important part of the information flow; it is a learning process that takes place within committees and between national authorities with varying degrees of experience and through information and analysis sharing. Nonmember countries are excluded from this learning process involving the dialogue, debate, and consensus-building procedures of FSB deliberations, meetings, and report researching and writing.

The third potential problem is with respect to the public at large. The issue is whether the FSB—because it is further removed from the political processes of the member governments—accentuates perceived structural problems at the national level. The insiders are the gatekeepers to influencing the regulatory process, and the capacity of the guardians of the public interest in such matters is severely attenuated. The charter of the FSB does call upon it to "consult widely" not only among its members but also with other stakeholders identified as the private sector and nonmember authorities. Some observers are concerned about too much consultation with the former and too little with the latter. The ultimate governance over the FSB and its deliberations is exercised somewhat removed from governance at the national level by electorates and public interest groupings—including affected industries—and more generally through public perceptions and opinion. It should be acknowledged that some regard this independence as a plus, but in individual societies striking the right balance between independence and accountability is not easy, and across societies it is even more challenging. The most limited standard tends to prevail.

Implications for the Global Financial Architecture

This section examines the implications of the preceding analysis of the institutions of the global financial architecture for the principal issues facing the global financial system. The IMF and FSB are different organizations with separate, but overlapping, mandates. Nevertheless, in the aftermath of the crisis, they have been asked to enhance their cooperation in key global financial architecture reform areas. Thus, we first compare and contrast these two architecture-central institutions, and we then consider the extent to which they are positioned to address the six major issues coming out of the crisis of 2007–10 that we earlier identified.

The Central Global Institutions

The IMF and the FSB are the principal institutions of governance of the global financial architecture. The preceding section reviewed the strengths and weaknesses of each institution individually, but it is useful to summarize that review via comparison.

By virtue of universal membership and representation the IMF is seen as having greater legitimacy (as we have defined that term) than the FSB. But the IMF still falls short of the ideal in the view of many observers. Although universal, the IMF currently faces its own challenges to adjust its representation with respect to voting shares and voices from chairs. European countries have a disproportionate share of the votes and voices at the IMF. They also have a disproportionate share of the voices at the FSB.[39] One difference between the two organizations is that the IMF is dominated by the views of governments as articulated by more politically responsible finance ministries. In the FSB the views of independent central bankers and supervisors have substantially greater influence.

Turning to tools and instruments, the IMF has a limited set of policy tools in its lending, surveillance, research, and technical assistance activities. The FSB is principally a coordinating body with few tools aside from its own nascent peer review processes, which potentially are in conflict with those of the IMF itself.

---

39. Voices may be more important in the FSB given that it reaches decisions entirely via consensus.

On compliance and leverage, the FSB is a voluntary organization, and compliance with its decisions and recommendations depends on the independent actions of member and nonmember countries. As noted, the FSB is experimenting with a peer review process applied to its own members, and has been mandated by the G-20 to conduct a review of the supervisory policies of nonmembers. These could lead to some degree of naming and shaming and subsequent response by both members and nonmembers. Its predecessor, the FSF, took some of these actions; however, the subsequent reliance on IMF assessments of offshore financial centers because of that institution's greater resources and legitimacy failed to generate meaningfully differentiated assessments. The IMF, for its part, has limited leverage, in particular over its largest members. The principal instruments are its lending programs, its surveillance activities, which may be more credible than those of the FSB, and its large professional staff. The IMF, like the World Bank, has an internal governance structure that provides scope for the expression of independent staff views.

The IMF, along with the World Bank for developing countries, disseminates and evaluates compliance with international standards, codes, and best practices in each of its member countries. In principle, it is positioned to assume in the future a greater (still informal) financial regulatory role in both its country and multilateral surveillance work and in joint IMF/World Bank/FSB efforts in financial sector surveillance, not only for the FSB member countries but for the universal membership of the IMF. At present, the IMF has a critical shortage of the relevant staff expertise to conduct this work effectively on its own and must draw on independent experts and at times member countries' government experts.

The macroprudential orientation of the IMF is greater than that of the FSB by dint of its broader remit and more extensive experience on macroeconomic issues. The IMF and the FSB have been called upon by the G-20 countries to enhance their cooperation in conducting early warning exercises. This is a ramping up of the vulnerability exercises that the FSF was asked to coordinate when it was first established. The crisis revealed that neither the IMF nor the FSF individually or collectively was able to provide much value added via its vulnerability, early warning, and surveillance activities. We think this judgment of low value added is justified by the lack of success in providing the kind of consistent and credible risk and vulnerability assessments that would move policymakers to action to prevent or at least lessen the impact of potential systemic events and ultimately the global financial crisis.

Going forward, a key challenge is whether the new early warning systems will be more effective. The G-20 countries—as members of the IMF—already are subject to the IMF's annual bilateral surveillance and its global financial system surveillance conducted twice annually and published in its *Global Financial Stability Report*. In addition, the IMF's *World Economic Outlook* also delves into the risks to the global economy emanating from global financial imbalances and market pressures. The G-20 countries influence the work program of the IMF through their role in the governance of the institution.

What more can the FSB add to the work of the IMF management, staff, and executive board? One answer might be that the FSB has more of a comparative advantage in the aggregation dimension of macroprudential supervision, whereas the IMF's comparative advantage seems to be in the macroeconomic policy dimension. However, that division of labor is complicated by the fact that central banks essentially are not and do not want to be engaged with the Fund, and are more engaged with the FSB even though they may be reluctant in any institutional context to consider the global impact of their monetary policies on financial stability. In the end, it is not appropriate to view the exercise of the traditional tools of monetary policy (interest rates) as separate from the use of other so-called macroprudential tools, because monetary policy affects the financial system and financial system supervision—regulation in particular; and adjustments to that supervision and regulation to achieve financial stability affect the performance of the macroeconomy.[40] As wisely observed by Fischer, coordination is essential.[41]

Finally, with respect to accountability and transparency, neither the IMF nor the FSB is exempt from criticism. Nevertheless, the edge goes to the IMF in part because of the breadth of its membership and the more avenues it has to open up to the general public. The FSB is a more closed club of supervisors, central bankers, and selected finance ministry officials.[42]

The IMF, the FSB, and Principal Global Financial System Issues

In the wake of the 2007–10 crisis, the substance and modalities of IMF collaboration with the FSB and vice versa are not fully established. For the general public the operative framework is contained in a joint letter from IMF Managing Director Dominique Strauss-Kahn and FSB Chairman Mario Draghi dated November 13, 2008, and addressed to the G-20 finance ministers and central bank governors (Strauss-Kahn and Draghi 2008). Note that the letter, quoted directly below, predates the transformation of the FSF into the FSB and specifies the respective roles of the IMF and the FSF:

1. Surveillance of the global financial system is the responsibility of the IMF.

2. Elaboration of international financial sector supervisory and regulatory policies and standards, and coordination across the various standard-setting bodies, is the principal task of the FSF. The IMF participates in this work and provides relevant inputs as a member of the FSF.

3. Implementation of policies in the financial sector is the responsibility of national authorities, who are accountable to national legislatures and governments. The IMF

---

40. On the effects of central bank monetary policy on the stability of the financial system see Giavazzi and Giovannini (2010).

41. Fischer, Preparing for Future Crises, speech given at the Federal Reserve Bank of Kansas City symposium, 2009.

42. An examination of the websites of each organization provides the basis for our evaluation of their relative transparency.

assesses authorities' implementation of such policies through FSAPs, ROSCs and Article IVs.

4. The IMF and the FSF will cooperate in conducting early warning exercises. The IMF assesses macrofinancial risks and systemic vulnerabilities. The FSF assesses financial system vulnerabilities, drawing on the analyses of its member bodies, including the IMF. Where appropriate, the IMF and FSF may provide joint risk assessments and mitigation reports.

The letter concludes, "Our shared goal is to strengthen the international financial system. To that end, the IMF and the FSF stand ready to support the work of the G-20."

A few points are notable about this document. First, the letter is oriented toward the work of the G-20 finance ministers and central bank governors in the precrisis context, rather than toward the G-20 leaders to which the FSB is formally responsible, in the postcrisis environment of a substantially transformed landscape of regulation. Second, the letter acknowledges that, as previously, the IMF has a role to play in the setting of standards, for example by drawing on the analyses and experience of IMF staff to devise certain standards such as with respect to data reporting. Third, although the IMF was assigned responsibility with the World Bank in the late 1990s for assessment of the implementation by national authorities of regulatory policies and standards, the FSB has assumed a portion of that role vis-à-vis the G-20 countries themselves as well as nonmembers. A relevant question is, Although the FSB secretariat has a capable, professional staff, does it have the kind of human capital—in both expertise and scale—to add value to the Fund's and, in the case of FSAPS and ROSCs, the World Bank's resources and efforts in these areas? Notably, neither the IMF nor the Bank has sufficient in-house expertise and resources, and there remains the challenge of ensuring the arm's-length independence of the resources that they hire temporarily from member countries. Some of this risk in making the examined themselves the examiners can be mitigated through the careful selection and allocation of "borrowed" resources, but the risk remains. This is less true of the Fund and Bank reviews of policies. In his criticism of the FSB-IMF relationship on this point, Fischer observed that the collegial nature of the FSB may limit a frank exchange of views, and peer reviews may take the form of nonaggression pacts.[43] In the IMF institutional context, a more independent staff and management increases the probability that sensitive issues at least will be raised.

How might this IMF/FSB framework apply to the six areas we earlier identified as particularly relevant for considering reforms of the global financial architecture?

---

43. Fischer, Preparing for Future Crises, speech given at the Federal Reserve Bank of Kansas City symposium, 2009.

Regulatory Requirements for Capital, Liquidity, and Leverage and the Potential Benefits/Costs of "Systemic Risk" Taxes

The FSB and the SSBs would be expected to take the lead in the area of capital liquidity and leverage requirements, and they have largely done so. But the reality is somewhat more complex given the existing architecture for consensus building.

The current structure has the FSB reporting through the G-20 finance ministers and central bank governors to the G-20 leaders on capital, liquidity, and leverage for banks at their upcoming summit in Seoul, South Korea. Our understanding is that there is a continuous flow between the Basel Committee and the FSB on banking regulations and standards.[44] Finance ministries that have a role in financial regulation and policies also exert direct influence over decisions. As one might expect, ministries tend to reflect the political pressures on reform efforts against the background of still-recovering financial institutions and systems. These pressures tend to call for a delay in implementation, if not the watering down, of capital, liquidity, and leverage requirements. G-20 leaders have also been involved, but as the Toronto summit revealed there are contrasting views on both capital and liquidity requirements, and so a lack of consensus exists at the head-of-state level. Some argue that greater independence from political influences produces better regulations; others would argue that the regulations will be watered down via the influence of banks on finance ministries and regulators.[45] Moreover, this reality may not sit well with the non-G-20 countries that presumably will be expected to apply these new banking standards to their internationally active institutions. Once endorsed by the G-20 leaders, the voluntary nature of such standards is more difficult to maintain. They will be incorporated directly and indirectly into IMF/World Bank reviews of all countries without the consent of most of them. The FSB in effect uses the IMF for leverage.

The G-20 leaders requested the advice of the IMF on the related issue of the costs and benefits of "systemic risk" taxes. As noted earlier, the G-20 leaders appear to have rejected the uniform application of the advice from the management and staff (IMF 2010a), which proposed two taxes: (1) a financial stability contribution to cover the fiscal costs of any future crises; and (2) a financial activities tax on the profits and remuneration of financial institutions, which would flow to the general revenues to cover the wider costs of such crises and limit distortions that favor excessive size and risk taking by financial institutions. This example illustrates that the FSB is not solely

---

44. The IMF is also involved because it has had "observer" status in the Basel Committee since mid-2009.

45. For a perspective on what has already been agreed by the Basel Committee and endorsed by its oversight body, see Megan Murphy and Patrick Jenkins, "Shares Bounce as Rules Are Softened," *Financial Times*, July 28, 2010: "The principles outlined . . . contained far-reaching concessions."

responsible for proposals affecting the financial system and that the IMF has relevant expertise as well.[46]

Another question is the role that the FSB plays in this process as a coordinating body. Member countries are undertaking reform efforts and expending political capital at home while implementing national policies aimed at national objectives. They may not align national efforts with agreements and understandings reached in the FSB. Europeans have criticized the US Dodd-Frank legislation in this regard and the United States has been critical of some European thinking and initiatives. This tends to undermine the FSB's effectiveness.

Perimeters or Boundaries of Financial Regulation, Supervision, and Infrastructures

It would be natural to think that the countries that are members of the FSB should take the lead in setting perimeters and boundaries with respect to financial regulation, supervision, and infrastructures and therefore in the guidance of the FSB itself on these issues. However, even more so than with the area previously discussed, this topic involves primarily only a few key jurisdictions. Even the FSB may be too large a group to reach agreement, for example, on the appropriate degree of regulation and surveillance of hedge funds. On the other hand, when it comes to infrastructures, the interests of a very broad group of countries are potentially involved, and the FSB may be too small a group to command full acceptance and compliance. This suggests a potentially important role for the IMF.

Regulation and Surveillance of Global Money and Financial Markets

When it comes to the regulation and surveillance of global money and financial markets, in particular OTC derivatives markets, the arguments advanced with respect to the regulatory and supervisory perimeter hold with even greater force. While it is natural to think that representatives from the major markets serving on the FSB should take the lead in this area, they also have their own axes to grind and turf to defend. It is not clear that their interests coincide with those of all participants in the global financial system. Thus, there is a role for the IMF in representing those less parochial and global interests as well as in providing a perspective from outside a closed circle to help to align incentives and help to internalize externalities.

---

46. In April 2009, the G-20 leaders requested a joint IMF/FSB/Basel Committee report to the G-20 ministers and governors on the identification of SIFIs (FSB 2010).

Systemically Important Financial Institutions or the TBTF Problem

This area is one that involves the interests of the global financial system to a greater degree even than the two previous areas. Although it is natural that agreements would first be reached in the context of the FSB and the SSBs about how to treat SIFIs in life, near death, or in death, the consequences of countries' mistreatment or their clumsy treatment, as witnessed in the case of the Lehman and Fortis bankruptcies, can affect many jurisdictions and creditors. In particular, if the global financial system is not to degenerate into one in which most financial institutions are heavily ring-fenced (an outcome favored by many), or in which the authorities try, and more likely fail, to ring-fence them, global standards are needed.[47]

Crisis Management, Rescue, and Resolution

The IMF is the preeminent international organization for country crisis management and country economic and financial rescues. That status has been enhanced in the crisis of 2007–10 by the fact that European countries that many thought were not or should not be in need of such rescue operations ended up needing the Fund's not-so-tender ministrations.

On the other hand, crisis management blends into crisis prevention both in anticipating crises and in learning lessons from them. It follows that the IMF alone cannot be held responsible for insuring that the right mechanisms are in place. In particular, where frameworks need to be put in place to facilitate the rescue of institutions or their resolution, the IMF can prod the individual national authorities, but those authorities must collaborate in advance to set up the appropriate procedures. A forum such as the FSB is broadly appropriate to help to establish such understandings.

Effective Management of Volatile Capital Flows

As with crisis management, the IMF is the natural locus of decision making with respect to establishing a framework for the more effective management of volatile capital flows. If as a consequence of lessons learned from the crisis of 2007–10 the IMF is to become more of an international lender of last resort than it has been in the past—as some have proposed, a kind of global financial safety net—should the Fund have a more enhanced role in regulation? One of the arguments for such a role is that it would help to address the moral hazard

---

47. The question is whether the FSB acting alone can deliver those standards or whether a more representative group should be involved. It should be noted that the IMF staff have opined on this topic (IMF 2010c, Kodres and Narain 2010). Rottier and Véron (2010) emphasize the growing risk of fragmentation in the global financial system.

issues associated with lender-of-last-resort activities by linking the availability of financing more directly to prior supervision or surveillance.[48]

Alternatively, is it sufficient for the Fund to play a role in other international bodies, such as the FSB, that have the mandate to reach agreements on the principles and standards to be applied in supervision and regulation? Similarly, is it sufficient for the IMF to share responsibility with respect to early warning systems? Whether responsibility for early warning systems is shared or not, the relevant concern is not with who issues the warnings, but with whether the authorities take action in response to those warnings.[49]

From another perspective, how can the FSB best add value to work in this area without duplicating the efforts of the IMF or perhaps even affecting perceptions of the IMF's legitimacy? For example, with the new enhanced role of the FSB (as a creature of the more political G-20) in rule making and the associated closer scrutiny of the IMF's work in this area, non-G-20 members of the IMF may come to question the IMF's role and importantly its capacity to serve the interests of its non-G-20 as well as G-20 members.

Conclusions and Recommendations

Our broad conclusion is that the structural financial weaknesses revealed by the global crisis require further reforms of the global financial architecture if future crises are to be managed and resolved more cost effectively, both in terms of preserving the efficiency gains of global modern finance and in terms of taxpayer monies. First and foremost, reforms are required at national levels. However, to maximize the probability that these reforms contribute to greater stability of the global financial system and are implemented consistently, the financial stability roles of the relevant international institutions, the IMF and FSB in particular, should be enhanced individually and collectively. More specifically, the IMF and the FSB must cooperate and collaborate as closely as possible on the reform and operation of the global financial system in order to achieve their mandated objectives that overlap in many areas.

Our assessment is that the global financial architecture will not soon include a global financial regulator that is empowered to replace or even substantially influence sovereign supervision and regulatory decisions. In particular, as currently constituted and situated, the FSB is not positioned to become the fourth pillar of global economic governance as was suggested by US Treasury Secretary Geithner. It has been called upon to cooperate with the IMF and vice versa, and the collaboration should be mutually reinforcing, drawing on the respective strengths of the two institutions. By cooperating with the IMF, the FSB may enhance its accountability and transparency to stakeholders in the global financial system. By cooperating with the FSB, the IMF may gain greater

---

48. For more on this line of argumentation see Truman (2010b).

49. Fischer, Preparing for Future Crises, speech given at the Federal Reserve Bank of Kansas City symposium, 2009; Schinasi (2009b).

trust from central bankers and supervisory and regulatory authorities and in the process enhance its leverage with these policymaking organizations.

Is there a case to be made for greater separation between the IMF and the FSB because they have different, if overlapping, mandates? Is there a concern that forcing more collaboration between the two institutions will reduce accountability? The answer is yes to both questions. However, our view is that the crisis has increased the pressure on both institutions to add more value in the financial stability sphere both individually and collectively, as mandated by the G-20. Moreover, the business-as-usual model with its associated jealousies and turf battles will not meet the needs of the global financial system going forward.

The IMF and the FSB are different institutions, but their financial sector stability operations and activities should be more closely aligned. The overall objective should be to tie the IMF and the FSB closer together rather than to allow them to compete, to remain distant, and to engage in turf wars.

Given the global financial system reform challenges, the IMF must focus on macroeconomic and macrofinancial stability, the linkages between them, and the implications of macroeconomic policies for the stability of the global financial system. For its part, the FSB must focus its efforts on sponsoring the adoption of new international supervisory and regulatory standards that improve the ability to assess, monitor, and hopefully maintain systemic financial stability in addition to the safety and soundness of financial institutions. As noted earlier, this challenge is especially pressing in the major financial centers, where the crisis revealed key weaknesses in the supervisory and regulatory architectures. Accordingly, the major onus is on the major financial centers, working through and with the FSB, to develop and implement more effective supervisory and regulatory frameworks, standards, codes, and best practices. In addition, it is an important responsibility of the FSB—even if it is not explicitly mandated—to facilitate the coordination of reforms among the country membership to the benefit of global stability in areas where unilateral actions are unlikely to be effective in safeguarding global stability.

In this regard, international standards and best practices that are likely to have the highest payoff are in the following areas:

- capital, liquidity, and leverage standards of financial institutions;
- resolution of complex cross-border financial institutions;
- rescues of such financial institutions short of their resolution; and
- determination of whether a financial institution, market, or instrument is systemically important.

However, these focal points clearly interact and overlap. In both institutions, the need is to try to affect national policies and priorities. In general, reform efforts should be aimed at improving the ability to foresee and prevent future crises and to resolve the next one when it occurs.

To mitigate the dominance of national priorities in the FSB's work, we recommend that the international organizations that are members of the FSB—the IMF in particular—should be empowered and emboldened to facilitate the dialogue between member countries so that national reform efforts and policies focus on global externalities and priorities. This was the original intent of the IMF's multilateral consultation exercise on global imbalances in 2007–10 involving China and the United States along with the euro area, Japan, and Saudi Arabia. Perhaps the IMF can play this role in the financial stability sphere within the context of the FSB's discussions.[50]

The challenge of managing volatile capital flows, including the macroeconomic, regulatory, and financing aspects of this challenge, provides the scope and opportunity for a bargain between historically dominant countries and the emerging-market countries for the greater involvement of the latter. As is now better understood, both micro- and macroprudential policies can help to manage the risks associated with volatile capital flows and in so doing allow countries to rely less on costly self-insurance in the form of high levels of international reserves. This topic should be on the agenda of the FSB—initially it was on the agenda of the FSF—as well as that of the IMF.

In this regard, both the IMF and FSB need to address institutional representation issues per se. For example, prior to the crisis and the recent reform efforts, Europe (including Switzerland) and the United States played dominant roles relative to all other country groups. With the emergence of volatile capital flows and new major players (among them several emerging-market countries and smaller financial centers, such as Hong Kong and Singapore), there is a need to rebalance the influence structure toward more inclusiveness and representation on relevant issues and policy challenges without compromising standards.

The need for such institutional governance reform is overwhelming in the case of the IMF, which, as an older institution, has ossified for a longer period. In the case of the FSB, its governance structure should in due course be streamlined, for example, by dramatically consolidating European representation, building on a consolidation of European representation on the IMF executive board and in other governance bodies such as the IMFC. That desirable step within the FSB also will require greater consolidation of the European financial regulatory and supervisory structure than is likely to result immediately from the recent crisis—notwithstanding the European progress that has already been achieved.

It may ultimately be desirable to move within the FSB to a constituency system, but that would have to wait for the adoption of such a system among

---

50. This kind of arrangement need not apply in all cases; for example, the key players on some issues may include only a small set of countries, and it is not clear that the presence or active engagement of a mediator or facilitator would advance the process. Recall that the Basel I capital standard was built on a bilateral agreement between the US and UK authorities after the Basel Committee on Banking Supervision demonstrated its inability to come to grips with the issue.

the G-20 leaders and finance ministers and central bank governors groups. We do not think that this is the most urgent issue facing the G-20 groups today.

Short of expanding its membership, a key issue for the FSB is to engage effectively the large number of nonmember countries and persuade them to adopt the standards the SSBs develop and the FSB proselytizes. To open its doors more, deliberations of the FSB should be routinely publicized, including those on the issues where it cannot reach a consensus and why. As we understand is intended, the FSB should resume regional meetings with regulators from nonmember countries and routinely provide them with information on the agenda for FSB meetings, papers, and outcomes. This would improve the ability of nonmember countries to learn and benefit from the work of the FSB that does not get published because it is in areas where consensus cannot be attained.

The IMF, similarly, is less open about deliberations of its executive board than it can and should be. The internal debates at the executive board level are obscured, for example, by incomplete concluding-remarks references to country positions of "a few," "some," or "many" directors, and many documents are not released until decisions have been made, for example, on quota realignments.

The balance of roles for the authorities of their respective memberships within the IMF and FSB should be addressed. Within the IMF, the global crisis has had implications for the roles of central banks vis-à-vis finance ministries. The IMF, in particular, must engage more with central banks and vice versa because of the now more widely acknowledged close interlinkages and policy challenges in simultaneously achieving and safeguarding both macroeconomic and financial stability. As the global crisis demonstrated, a slavish defense of central bank independence in the narrow pursuit of (for example) price stability, or of macroeconomic stability, can become inconsistent analytically and institutionally with the need to rely on macroeconomic tools to restore or to pursue financial stability. Naturally, the extent of inconsistencies will depend on the specific mandate(s) of a particular central bank, but they are most likely to become critical soon enough for central banks with mandates focused exclusively, or overridingly, on price stability. Contrary to its past practice, the IMF management and staff should exploit the FSB to engage with central bankers collectively on these issues because it has no other regular forum in which to do so.

To tie the FSB and IMF closer together in recognition of their overlapping missions and mandates, we recommend a formalization of the current de facto practice of the FSB reporting to the IMF's International Monetary and Financial Committee in addition to the G-20 ministers and governors and G-20 leaders.[51] This would help defuse concerns about FSB legitimacy. We also recommend that strong consideration be given to providing the IMF with the

---

51. We join de Larosière (2009) in this recommendation with respect to the FSB's predecessor the FSF.

"authority" to call on the FSB, perhaps through the IMFC, to consider certain issues and to report back—just as the G-20, and implicitly the FSB, now call on the IMF to consider and deliver results on certain issues.

To enable the IMF to provide more effective surveillance over national financial systems and the global system, the Fund needs more in-house expertise and resources in relevant areas. We also favor increasing the resources available to the FSB secretariat to fortify its own permanent professional staff. Short of this, resources should be added to the secretariat on the current seconded basis so that it has the capability to contribute to the FSB's efforts with its own analytical work in core areas. We think the risk of duplicating the IMF's staff work is worth taking. Consideration should also be given by both the IMF and the FSB to the active, continuous use of panels of independent experts to review the work of the institutions as it evolves in the period ahead. This would help to address the perceived problem of capture of regulatory and supervisory authorities and institutions.

A longer-term option is to consider placing the FSB secretariat under the auspices of the IMF. This would require a clear set of understandings, for example about how the G-20, IMF executive board, and G-20 FSB representatives interact and are governed. In addition, there would also need to be guidance and understandings on the extent to which the FSB could draw upon the Fund's human capital for FSB work beyond the Fund's own contributions to FSB work as an FSB member.[52]

The FSB should adopt the practice of dual chairs for its standing committees and working groups, including one chair from one of the advanced countries and one chair from other members. Care should be taken not to perpetuate such a system indefinitely because it cuts against broader globalization trends in which all countries are treated the same, but for the next 5 to 10 years it would be desirable.

Within the institutions and country groups that make up the global financial architecture, substantive policy challenges often condition international policymaking, coordination, and governance. For example, the European Union and United States both desire reforms in areas that require international or global consensus and agreement to be effective and to achieve a level playing field, such as the cross-border supervision and resolution of systemically important financial institutions and the OTC derivatives markets. At the same time, because of financial globalization, without greater global coordination facilitated by the IMF and FSB working together, it is unlikely the European Union and the United States will be able to achieve desired reforms in many areas.

The only way to achieve the potential benefits of collective action is to establish the conditions for closely coordinated policy development and

---

52. The IMF's new income model, relying less on charges on loans because of the availability of income from investments on the profits from gold sales, should lessen these concerns somewhat. The Fund will be better positioned to produce a wider array of public goods.

implementation. This may require significantly more give and take among countries than is now extant as well as strengthened roles for both the IMF and the FSB within the global financial architecture. Such a reorientation would endeavor collectively and equitably to create, manage, and capture the benefits of global public goods for the global financial system. International and global collective action to safeguard financial stability has to flow from a shared interest in the objective of financial stability.

References

Ashcraft, Richard, ed. 1991. *John Locke: Critical Assessments*. London: Routledge.

Blanchard, Olivier, and Gian Maria Milesi-Ferretti. 2009. *Global Imbalances: In Midstream?* IMF Staff Position Note 09/29. Washington: International Monetary Fund (December). Available at www.imf.org (accessed on July 24, 2010).

Brunnermeier, Markus, Andrew Crockett, Charles A. Goodhart, Avinash Persaud, and Myun Song Shin. 2009. *The Fundamental Principles of Financial Regulation*. Geneva Reports on the World Economy 11. London: Center for Economic Policy Research.

Bryant, Ralph C. 2010. *Governance Shares for the International Monetary Fund: Principles, Guidelines, Current Status*. Washington: Brookings Institution. Available at www.brookings.edu (accessed on July 22, 2010).

Caprio, Gerard Jr., Asli Demirgüç-Kunt, and Edward J. Kane. 2009. *The 2007 Meltdown in Structured Securitization: Searching for Lessons Not Scapegoats*. Paolo Baffi Center Research Paper Series No. 2009-49. Milan: Paolo Baffi Center.

Carmassi, Jacopo, Daniel Gros, and Stefano Micossi. 2009. The Global Financial Crisis: Causes and Cures. *Journal of Common Market Studies* 47, no. 5: 977–96.

Committee on Capital Markets Regulation. 2009. *The Global Financial Crisis: A Plan for Regulatory Reform* (May). Available at www.capmktsreg.org (accessed on January 27, 2012).

de Larosière, Jacques. 2009. *Report of the High-Level Group on Financial Supervision in the EU* (February 25). Brussels: European Commission. Available at http://ec.europa.eu (accessed on January 21, 2012).

ECB (European Central Bank). 2006. Special Feature A: Identifying Large and Complex Banking Groups for Financial Stability Assessment. In *Financial Stability Review* (December). Frankfurt.

ECB (European Central Bank). 2007. Box 10: Special Feature A: Identifying Large and Complex Banking Groups for Financial Stability Assessment—An Update. In *Financial Stability Review* (December). Frankfurt.

ECB (European Central Bank). 2008. *Financial Stability Review* (December). Frankfurt.

Elson, Anthony. 2010. The Current Financial Crisis and Reform of the Global Financial Architecture. *International Spectator* 45, no. 1 (March): 17–36.

European Commission. 2009. *The Presidency Conclusions of the Council of the European Union* (June 19). Brussels.

Federal Reserve Bank of Cleveland. 2009. *What to Do About Systemically Important Financial Institutions*. Cleveland. Available at www.clevelandfed.org (accessed on January 27, 2012).

FSB (Financial Stability Board). 2008. *Enhancing Market and Institutional Resilience*. Available at www.financialstabilityboard.org (accessed on March 8, 2012).

FSB (Financial Stability Board). 2009. *Financial Stability Board Charter*. Available at www.financialstabilityboard.org (accessed on January 27, 2012).

FSB (Financial Stability Board). 2010. *Reducing the Moral Hazard Posed by Systemically Important Financial Institutions: Interim Report to G-20 Leaders.* Available at www.financialstabilityboard. org (accessed on March 8, 2012).

FSB, IMF, and BIS (Financial Stability Board, International Monetary Fund, and Bank for International Settlements). 2009. *Guidance to Assess the Systemic Importance of Financial Institutions, Markets and Instruments: Initial Considerations.* Report to G-20 Finance Ministers and Governors by the staffs of the IMF and BIS, and the Secretariat of the Financial Stability Board (October). Available at www.financialstabilityboard.org (accessed on January 27, 2012).

G-10 (Group of Ten). 1992. *Recent Developments in International Interbank Relations (Promisel Report).* Basel: Bank for International Settlements.

G-10 (Group of Ten). 2001. *Report on Consolidation in the Financial Sector (Ferguson Report).* Available at www.imf.org (accessed on January 27, 2012).

G-20 (Group of Twenty). 2009. *Declaration on Strengthening the Financial System* (April). Available at www.g20.utoronto.ca (accessed on January 27, 2012).

G-20 (Group of Twenty). 2010. *The G-20 Toronto Summit Declaration* (June 27). Available at www. g20.utoronto.ca (accessed on January 27, 2012).

G-30 (Group of Thirty). 2009. *Financial Reform: A Framework for Financial Stability* (January). Washington.

Garber, Peter. 2009. Comments on US and EU Reform Efforts in Improving the Management of Systemic Financial Risk by Garry Schinasi, presented at the conference "An Ocean Apart? Comparing Transatlantic Responses to the Financial Crisis," Bank of Italy, Rome, September 10–11.

Giavazzi, Francesco, and Alberto Giovannini. 2010. *Central Banks and the Financial System.* NBER Working Paper 16228 (July). Cambridge, MA: National Bureau of Economic Research. Available at www.nber.org (accessed on January 27, 2012).

Giovannini, Alberto. 2010. *Financial System Reform from First Principles.* CEPR Policy Insight 45 (January). London: Center for Economic Policy Research.

Gold, Joseph. 1981. *Legal and Institutional Aspects of the International Monetary Fund.* Washington: International Monetary Fund.

Gorton, Gary B. 2008. *The Panic of 2007.* NBER Working Paper 14358 (September). Cambridge, MA: National Bureau of Economic Research.

Gorton, Gary. 2009. Slapped in the Face by the Invisible Hand: Banking and the Financial Panic of 2007. Paper presented at the Federal Reserve Bank of Atlanta's Financial Market Conference (May). Available at www.frbatlanta.org (accessed on March 8, 2012).

Griffith-Jones, Stephany, Eric Helleiner, and Ngaire Woods. 2010. *The Financial Stability Board: An Effective Fourth Pillar of Global Economic Governance?* Waterloo, Canada: Center for International Governance Innovation. Available at www.cigionline.org (accessed on July 26, 2010).

Hacche, Graham. 2009. The IMF Staff's View of the World: The World Economic Outlook. In *Successes of the International Monetary Fund: Untold Stories of Cooperation at Work,* ed. Eduard Brau and Ian McDonald. London: Palgrave Macmillan.

Hanson, Samuel, Anil K. Kashyap, and Jeremy C. Stein. 2011. A Macroprudential Approach to Financial Regulation. *Journal of Economic Perspectives* 25, no. 1 (Winter): 3–28.

Helleiner, Eric. 2010. *The Financial Stability Board and International Standards.* Center for International Governance Innovation G-20 Paper 1 (June). Waterloo, Canada: Center for International Governance Innovation. Available at www.cigionline.org (accessed on March 8, 2012).

Herrmann, Sabine, and Dubravko Mihaljek. 2010. *The Determinants of Cross-Border Bank Flows to Emerging Markets: New Empirical Evidence on the Spread of Financial Crises.* BIS Working Paper

315 (July). Basel: Bank for International Settlements. Available at www.bis.org (accessed on January 27, 2012).

IMF (International Monetary Fund). 2009. *Lessons of the Financial Crisis for Future Regulation of Financial Institutions and Markets and for Liquidity Management.* Available at www.imf.org (accessed on January 27, 2012).

IMF (International Monetary Fund). 2010a. *A Fair and Substantial Contribution by the Financial Sector.* Final report by the IMF staff to G-20 (June). Available at www.imf.org (accessed on January 27, 2012).

IMF (International Monetary Fund). 2010b. *How Did Emerging Markets Cope in the Crisis?* Paper prepared by the Strategy, Policy, and Review Department (June 15). Available at www.imf.org (accessed on January 27, 2012).

IMF (International Monetary Fund). 2010c. *Resolution of Cross-Border Banks: A Proposed Framework for Enhanced Coordination.* Paper prepared by the Legal and Monetary and Capital Markets Department (June 11). Available at www.imf.org (accessed January 27, 2012).

Issing Committee. 2009. *New Financial Order.* Center for Financial Studies. White Paper No. 1 (February). Available at www.ifk-crs.de (accessed on March 8, 2012).

Kodres, Laura, and Aditya Narain. 2010. *Redesigning the Contours of the Future Financial System.* IMF Staff Position Note 10/10 (August 16). Available at www.imf.org (accessed on January 27, 2012).

Lane, Philip R., and Gian Maria Milesi-Ferretti. 2010. *The Cross-Country Incidence of the Global Crisis.* IMF Working Paper 10/171 (July). Available at www.imf.org (accessed on January 27, 2012).

Levine, Ross. 2009. The Sentinel: Improving the Governance of Financial Policies. In *The International Financial Crisis: Have the Rules of Finance Changed?* eds. Asli Demirgüç-Kunt, Douglas D. Evanoff, and George G. Kaufman. Hackensack, NJ: World Scientific Publishing Company.

McGuire, Patrick, and Götz von Peter. 2009. *The US Dollar Shortage in Global Banking and the International Policy Response.* BIS Working Paper 219 (October). Basel: Bank for International Settlements. Available at www.bis.org (accessed on January 27, 2012).

Obstfeld, Maurice, and Kenneth Rogoff. 2009. Global Imbalances and the Financial Crisis: Products of Common Causes. Paper presented at the Federal Reserve Bank of San Francisco Asia Economic Policy Conference, October 18–20. Available at www.frbsf.org (accessed on January 27, 2012).

Rottier, Stéphane, and Nicolas Véron. 2010. *Not All Financial Regulation Is Global.* Bruegel Policy Brief 2101/07 (August). Brussels: Bruegel. Available at www.bruegel.org (accessed on January 27, 2012).

Schinasi, Garry J. 2006. *Safeguarding Financial Stability: Theory and Practice.* Washington: International Monetary Fund.

Schinasi, Garry J. 2007. Causes and Conditions for Cross-Border Threats to Financial Stability. In *Cross-Border Banking and National Regulation,* ed. George G. Kaufman et al. London: World Scientific Publishing Company.

Schinasi, Garry J. 2009a. US and EU Reform Efforts in Improving the Management of Systemic Financial Risk. Paper presented at the conference "An Ocean Apart? Comparing Transatlantic Responses to the Financial Crisis," Bank of Italy, Rome (September 10–11).

Schinasi, Garry J. 2009b. *More Than One Step Necessary to Financial Stability.* Bruegel Policy Brief 2009/06 (October). Brussels: Bruegel.

Schinasi, Garry J. 2009c. The Changing Nature of Systemic Risk. In *Toward a New Framework for Financial Stability,* ed. David Mayes, Robert Pringle, and Michael Taylor. London: Central Banking Publications.

Schinasi, Garry, J., Sean Craig, Burkhard Drees, and Charles Kramer. 2000. *Modern Banking and OTC Derivatives: The Transformation of Global Finance and Its Implications for Systemic Risk.* IMF Occasional Paper 203. Washington: International Monetary Fund.

Strauss-Kahn, Dominique, and Mario Draghi. 2008. Joint Letter Addressed to the G-20 Finance Ministers and Central Bank Governors (November 13). Available at www.financialstability board.org (accessed on January 27, 2012).

Thomson, James B. 2009. *On Systemically Important Financial Institutions and Progressive Systemic Mitigation.* Federal Reserve Bank of Cleveland Policy Discussion Paper 27 (August). Available at www.clevelandfed.org (accessed on January 27, 2012).

Tietmeyer, Hans. 1999. *International Cooperation and Coordination in the Area of Financial Market Supervision and Surveillance.* Tietmeyer Report (February 11). Available at www.financial stabilityboard.org (accessed on July 22, 2010).

Truman, Edwin M. 2003. *Inflation Targeting in the World Economy.* Washington: Institute for International Economics.

Truman, Edwin M. 2006a. Rearranging IMF Chairs and Shares: The Sine Qua Non of IMF Reform. In *Reforming the IMF for the 21st Century,* ed. Edwin M. Truman. Washington: Peterson Institute for International Economics.

Truman, Edwin M. 2006b. *A Strategy for IMF Reform.* Washington: Peterson Institute for International Economics.

Truman, Edwin M. 2008. *On What Terms Is the IMF Worth Funding?* Working Paper 08-11 (December). Washington: Peterson Institute for International Economics.

Truman, Edwin M. 2009. The Global Financial Crisis: Lessons Learned and Challenges for Developing Countries (June). Available at www.piie.com (accessed on January 27, 2012).

Truman, Edwin M. 2010a. Dealing with Volatile Capital Flows: The Case for Collective Action (May). Available at www.piie.com (accessed on January 27, 2012).

Truman, Edwin M. 2010b. *The G-20 and International Financial Institution Governance.* Working Paper 10-13 (September). Washington: Peterson Institute for International Economics.

Truman, Edwin M. 2010c. The IMF and Regulatory Challenges. *The International Spectator* 45, no. 1: 37–58.

UK Financial Services Authority. 2009. *The Turner Review: A Regulatory Response to the Global Banking Crisis* (March). Available at www.fsa.gov.uk (accessed on March 8, 2012).

UK Treasury. 2009. *Reforming Financial Markets* (July). Available at www.hm-treasury.gov.uk (accessed on March 8, 2012).

US Treasury Department. 2009. *Financial Regulatory Reform: A New Foundation.* Available at www.financialstability.gov (accessed on January 27, 2012).

Visco, Ignazio. 2009. *Global Imbalances in the Financial Crisis and the International Monetary System* (December 4). Available at www.bis.org (accessed on March 8, 2012).

Zahler, Roberto. 2010. The FSB: Macroprudential and Counter-Cyclical Regulation. In *The Financial Stability Board: An Effective Fourth Pillar of Global Economic Governance?* ed. Stephany Griffith-Jones, Eric Helleiner, and Ngaire Woods. Waterloo, Canada: Center for International Governance Innovation. Available at www.cigionline.org (accessed on January 27, 2012).

II

2011 POLICY CONFERENCE, BERLIN

8

Transatlantic Relations and Globalization in Time of Crisis?

VÍTOR GASPAR

Opening address at the PIIE-Bruegel conference in Berlin, September 27, 2011

I would like to reflect on likely trends for transatlantic dominance of globalization. I will first comment on some long-term trends leading to shifting patterns of power at the global level. Second, I will argue that the current crisis will likely accelerate these trends. Finally, I will suggest that, in this context, transatlantic cooperation is crucial for a smooth transition at the global level.

It is a long-standing tradition that the leadership of the World Bank is entrusted to an American, while the managing director of the International Monetary Fund (IMF) is European. This state of affairs reflects the balance of world economic power that prevailed in the 1950s, when these multilateral international organizations were starting. In 1950, Europe, the United States, and other "Western Offshoots" (using the expression of Angus Maddison) represented about 57 percent of world GDP; at the time, the 27 member states of the European Union represented 28.2 percent of world GDP and the United States 27.3 percent. The transatlantic dominance was even more pronounced if measured by shares in world trade or finance. In terms of population the shares were much lower, at 14.8 and 6.2 percent, respectively, reflecting the relative patterns of prosperity and deprivation around the world.

It is impressive to compare these indicators with the prospects for 2050. Such a long-term perspective suggests a profound change going forward. In the century from 1950 to 2050, the share of Europe and European offshoots will have fallen from about 57 percent to about 40 percent of world GDP. The

---

Vítor Gaspar has been the finance minister of Portugal since June 2011.

share of Western Europe will have fallen from 26.2 to 17.9 percent and that of the United States from 27.3 to 19.6 percent. In the same period Asia's share will have moved from about 18.4 to 36.5 percent.

To a very large extent these trends reflect the reversal of the Great Divergence that took place from the mid-1700s to the mid-1950s and led to the dominance of world trade and finance by Europe and European offshoots. The shifting patterns of power going forward are clear. Effective cooperation and coordination in the global economy require that governance of multilateral organizations and groups adapts to these changing patterns. The process of transition may be characterized by growing multipolarity as the theme for this conference suggests. There can be no guarantees that the transition will proceed smoothly. A cooperative and multilateral approach (that I am tempted to label the European approach) is only one possible way to conceive of the transition. But, in whatever way it occurs, the transition at the global level will have profound effects on transatlantic political, economic, and financial relations. Global transition is a powerful undercurrent that persistently influences transatlantic relations.

This undercurrent operates today in an environment dominated by the global crisis. The crisis is often referred to as the first crisis of globalization. If that were the case it would be without historical precedent. However, I think it is the case that the current crisis is one of the few crises on record that affects the very core of the international financial system. Dates that the current crisis brings to mind are 1825, 1873, and 1929. In all these cases history bears witness to profound changes in economic and financial regimes. The same can reasonably be expected this time around.

In Washington the sovereign debt crisis in the euro area, together with banking fragility, has been the topic of lively debate and is widely regarded as the single most important risk to the global economy. At the same time, developments in the United States—persistent high budget deficits and increasing debt ratios combined with a weak economy—are also a cause for concern. Risks affecting global developments are identified as centering in the North Atlantic area.

The IMF (2011) identifies two main risks for world economic prospects. The first is "that the euro area debt crisis runs beyond the control of policymakers, notwithstanding the strong political response agreed in the July 21, 2011 EU summit. . . . Leaders must stand by their commitments to do whatever it takes to preserve trust in their national policies and the euro." The second risk is "that activity in the United States, already softening, might suffer further blows—for example, from a political impasse over fiscal consolidation, a weak housing market, rapid increases in household saving rates, or deteriorating financial conditions. Deep political divisions leave the course of U.S. policy highly uncertain." The IMF concludes:

> Either one of these eventualities would have severe repercussions for global growth. The renewed stress could undermine financial markets and institutions in advanced economies, which remain unusually vulnerable. Commodity prices and global trade

and capital flows would likely decline abruptly, dragging down growth in emerging and developing economies. The extent to which this could lower global growth is illustrated in more detail in a downside scenario—the euro area and the United States could fall back into recession, with activity some 3 percentage points lower in 2012 than envisaged in WEO [*World Economic Outlook*] projections. Damage to other economies would also be significant.

It seems to me very likely that the perception of Europe and the United States as the two most important sources of risk for the global economy will accelerate the shifting in patterns of power that would likely occur in any event. Relative positions are changing rapidly and a new paradigm seems to be closer. It is clear that in this context the world governance model will need to change. Europe and the United States should be prepared to work constructively to adapt global governance as required.

The financial crisis has represented a turning point for global governance, both politically and economically. The crisis has spread globally through strong economic and financial linkages. In fact, the interlinkages and the spillover effects across countries are evident as never before. In this context, we have seen a new willingness to engage in multilateral coordination and cooperation.

However, further progress is necessary. Economic and political power will need to be reorganized to include rising powers. This change will inevitably require the involvement of more countries in the center of global decisions. The Group of 20 (G-20) meetings are a clear example of this change and of the growing significance of the concept of multipolarity.

The United States and the European Union have a lot in common. Democracy, human rights, and the market as the predominant resource allocation mechanism are fundamental values for both. A recent survey by the German Marshall Fund (released in July 2011) contains much interesting material and illustrates many important points. Let me give you just a few examples. To the question "How desirable is it that the United States exert strong global leadership?" 85 percent of Americans responded "desirable" and 14 percent "undesirable." Among EU-12 respondents, 54 percent were in favor and 39 percent were opposed. When the question is asked about the European Union exerting strong global leadership, 69 percent of Americans answered "desirable" while 20 percent found it "undesirable." The corresponding proportions for the EU-12 were, respectively, 76 percent in favor and 18 percent opposed. Interestingly, when asked "To what extent do you agree with the following: economic power is more important than military power?" 85 percent of respondents from the EU-12 agreed and an impressive 71 percent of Americans agreed as well.

Clearly there is a lot to build on to deepen transatlantic cooperation. Adam Smith (1754, 239–40) wrote in his *Theory of Moral Sentiments*:

Independent and neighbouring nations, having no common superior to decide their disputes, all live in continual dread and suspicion of one another. Each sovereign, expecting little justice from his neighbours, is disposed to treat them with as little as he expects from them. The regard for the laws of nations, or for those rules which independent states profess or pretend to think themselves bound to observe in their dealings with one another, is often very little more than mere pretence and profession. From the smallest interest, upon the slightest provocation, we see those rules every day, either evaded or directly violated without shame or remorse.

In my view it is of central strategic interest to the parties on both sides of the Atlantic to show that we are well past the pessimistic realism expressed by Smith. In the early days of the crisis, in the autumn of 2008, the United States and the European Union pushed strongly for cooperative solutions at the global level. In current circumstances it is vital to frame transatlantic relations in an inclusive multilateral global framework.

References

IMF (International Monetary Fund). 2011. *World Economic Outlook: Slowing Growth, Rising Risk* (September). Washington.

Smith, Adam. 1754. *The Theory of Moral Sentiments.* Glasgow Edition of the Works and Correspondence of Adam Smith. Volume 1, part 6, chapter 2. Available at http://oll.libertyfund.org (accessed on January 22, 2012).

9

The International Monetary System at a Crossroads
Opportunities and Risks for the Euro

IGNAZIO ANGELONI and ANDRÉ SAPIR

After a pause of 30 years, discussions on the future of the international monetary system (henceforth IMS or "the system") have restarted. An increasing number of observers are arguing that the system has facilitated, or at least not prevented, the economic and financial imbalances that helped generate the recent crisis. Meanwhile, due to market forces and policy action, the system has evolved, and more changes are likely in the near future. The aim of this chapter is to outline some of these developments and to discuss foreseeable implications for Europe.

Before 2007, some had already noted the peculiar configuration that the post–Bretton Woods system had assumed, with China and the United States increasingly unbalanced in their external positions and with each interested in postponing or even avoiding adjustment (Dooley, Folkerts-Landau, and Garber 2004). With the crisis, concerns about this situation have increased. Three things happened. First, analyses of the mechanisms driving the supply and demand for risky assets in the precrisis years have shed light on the links between the expansion of global liquidity and the propensity by wealth holders and banks to take on leverage and risk (see, for example, Adrian and Shin 2008). A connection with the IMS arises because the hegemonic position of the US dollar, in combination with the expansionary stance of US monetary policy, is often recognized as an indirect cause of the rising supply of interna-

Ignazio Angeloni has been a visiting fellow at Bruegel since June 2008 and is an advisor to the European Central Bank's Executive Board. André Sapir is a senior fellow at Bruegel and professor of economics at the Université libre de Bruxelles. The ideas expressed in this chapter are their own. They are grateful to discussants Otmar Issing and Adam Posen and other conference participants for helpful comments.

tional liquidity in the years preceding the outburst of the crisis (as argued, for example, by Pierre-Olivier Gourinchas 2010). Second, the depreciation of the dollar and the ensuing search for portfolio diversification by official reserve holders accelerated a demand-driven evolution toward a "multipolar" IMS (at least if measured at current exchange rates).[1] On the supply side, China is making increasing efforts to encourage the cross-border use of its currency. Finally, the growing evidence that global imbalances are not going to go away, even once the global economy emerges from the crisis, has injected a sense of "quid agendum" among policymakers.

Clearly, the fact that there are discussions does not ipso facto mean that reform will actually happen. It does not even mean that the current market-driven evolution (that we will describe in some detail below) will lead to a discernibly distinct endpoint in a foreseeable future. History is not encouraging in this respect. The extensive debate in the 1960s and 1970s on the weaknesses of the dollar-centered fixed rates system and its possible alternatives did not lead anywhere, except its dissolution (40 years ago as we write) and replacement with what was later dubbed, dismissively, a "nonsystem." By contrast, a monetary order bound to last for decades was delivered in a three-week secluded conference (July 1–22, 1944), with little contribution from outside experts or public opinion. Can this time be different? Perhaps; it is significant that in addition to discussions there are, at present, powerful economic forces at work that should plausibly propel further changes, on top of those we already see today.

In this piece, we first review the main recent developments in the IMS and possible future trends in the medium term, including the role of China and its currency. Here we draw mainly on a recent report by Bruegel and CEPII that we coauthored (Angeloni et al. 2011), in which these trends are examined in depth. Second, we discuss the position of the euro in the context of these developments. Discussing prospects concerning the international role of the euro may seem hazardous at the present time, when some are prophesying its demise. While not underestimating these risks, we contend that the prospects are not necessarily as grim as they appear at present. Our focus is on the fundamental forces that will, assuming the current tensions subside, shape the position of the euro within different possible scenarios for the evolution of the IMS in the foreseeable future.

We make three main points:

1. The international position of the US dollar is going to erode further, though the speed of the process is uncertain. This will create a demand for other currencies to be used internationally as means of payment and store of value.[2] The real question is how this vacuum will be filled.

---

1. Evidence is provided in European Central Bank, *The International Role of the Euro* (Frankfurt, various years).

2. A different view is presented by Peter Kenen (2011), according to whom "There are no alternatives to the present role of the dollar in the international monetary system."

2. Barring a resurgence of monetary multilateralism, leading, for example, to a revival of the special drawing rights (SDR)—an eventuality that, however desirable, we regard as implausible except in case of major crises—the most realistic scenario is one in which other currencies will come to share the privilege, and the burden, of exercising an international role. Both the Chinese renminbi and the euro are partially qualified to play this role, alone or in combination, and are bound to compete for that role. The outcome will depend on a mix of circumstances and policies.

3. The prospects for the euro are challenging but far from hopeless. Like others, we are of the view that the euro crisis will be overcome only with radical steps toward fiscal and financial integration, requiring strong political cohesion and leadership. One should note that, historically, political and economic unifications have typically progressed in times of crisis. Like the IMS, the euro is at a crossroads, but what should be emphasised is that the reforms needed to stabilize it internally—some of which are already in progress—are the same that would promote its international attractiveness. Internal stabilization, if achieved, is likely to be matched by a growing international strength.

IMS and the Crisis

The current system emerged from the ashes of the Bretton Woods regime in the early 1970s. Its emergence was accompanied by major policy reforms at the national level that, taken together, gave rise to the current international financial architecture, which is made of widespread financial liberalization, the almost universal adoption of central bank independence, policy regimes aimed at delivering domestic stability, and the general acceptance of exchange rate fluctuations among currency areas. For many observers and policy players this represents not just the only viable system, but the most desirable one. A system of generalized floating and flexible inflation targeting with full capital mobility, at least in the advanced world, seemed well suited to achieving policymakers' goals of full employment, stable prices, and sustainable current account positions. In this setting, policymakers' main task was to "keep their own house in order" (generally intended as some notion of internal balance: low inflation and near-full resource utilization, along with fiscal sustainability). International coherence should, in this ideal model, result from the consistency of national self-centered policies and appropriate exchange rate fluctuations, helping contain the international spillovers of such policies.

Gradually, however, this hope dissipated as the two assumptions on which it rested became untenable. First, macroeconomic policies by the key players were meant to remain disciplined and consistent with maintaining the system in balance. This was obviously not the case for the United States, whose currency retained a central role in the system and thus gave it the "exorbitant privilege" of easy external deficit financing and seigniorage extraction across borders. Second, countries outside the advanced world, often unable or unwilling to abide by the system of generalized floating and flexible inflation targeting with full capital mobility, went from being a relatively marginal component of the global economy to being major players.

As a result, in recent years the IMS has undergone a transition, the most important one since the end of Bretton Woods. The conditions for change were already in place before the crisis, as a result of a number of factors.

The first is the trend decline in the weight of the United States in the global economy. This movement is clearly under way and will continue, or even accelerate, as we document below. History shows that monetary dominance is persistent: currencies tend to preserve their international role long after the decline of the respective economy (Flandreau and Jobst 2009). Over time, however, economic size and performance become increasingly relevant to the attractiveness of a currency for global investors.

In addition, the position of the US dollar was threatened by the uncertainties connected with the growing external imbalance of the US economy. US deficits contributed to the supply of dollars in the global economy, hence initially supporting the position of the hegemon, but over time they generated doubts about the sustainability of such a position—the time-honored and still valid Triffin (1960) dilemma—and a growing demand for portfolio diversification. The financial crisis has accelerated this evolution. Perceived risks in the US banking system and sovereign debt have fueled the demand for diversification by private and official wealth holders. The weakness of the US dollar has intensified, except for a short-lived "safe haven effect" during the first phases of the turmoil.

Another contributing factor is the transformation of Asia, since the end of the 1990s, from chronically underdeveloped to a thriving, competitive, and highly interconnected economic region. The web of financial and trade linkages across the region has grown exponentially (Kubelec and Sá 2010). Though a regional "monetary pole" has not emerged yet, the conditions for one arising are increasingly present. China, the largest regional economy, while still hesitant on whether such developments should be encouraged, has nonetheless moved some steps toward developing an international role for its currency (Vallée 2011).

Since 2005, and increasingly after 2008, China has adopted a more flexible exchange rate stance, something that is seen by some as another step toward an open monetary and financial system, including more cross-border use of the renminbi within the region. Interestingly, Marcel Fratzscher and Arnaud Mehl (2011) document a sharp increase in the influence exerted by the Chinese currency on other regional exchange rates, starting after the softening of the dollar peg in 2005 and particularly after the financial turmoil of 2008. These authors go as far as suggesting that the renminbi may already have acquired, unnoticed by most, the status of an international currency.

Furthermore, dissatisfaction with capital flows volatility has revived the debate about the costs and benefits of free capital mobility. The general consensus established in the 1990s about the benefits of financial globalization has been undermined, not only because of the crisis but also, and more simply, because many emerging countries have been repeatedly overwhelmed by surges of capital inflows followed by sudden outflows. Also, many of them, including China and India, have demonstrated that they could perform economically while retaining tight capital controls.

The accumulation of very large international reserves by still relatively poor countries raises concerns about the welfare cost of holding reserves and capital allocation at the global level. Foreign exchange reserves are mostly invested in high-quality and low-yielding liquid assets, mainly government bonds issued in advanced economies. Such an investment strategy has welfare costs for countries that accumulate reserves and has implications for international capital flows that are undesirable from an allocative viewpoint. It also has consequences for global financial stability, because it increases the burden of maturity transformation on banking sectors located in the reserve currency countries—mainly the United States. Moreover, there is a growing fear among major official reserves holders that the present system exposes them to the risk of large capital losses, should the dollar depreciate in a disorderly way. In brief, foreign exchange reserves accumulation does, beyond a certain point, offer an unfavorable risk-return tradeoff and may be a source of negative global externalities. Rising concerns in the developing and emerging world were vividly exposed in a widely commented-on post by China's central bank governor in March 2009 (Zhou 2009), in which he unexpectedly called for a reform of the IMS based on a revival of the SDR.

Finally, increasing disputes over the pegging strategies of emerging countries, and monetary policies in the advanced countries, emphasize the increasingly evident need for an emancipation of monetary policies in large emerging countries. The process started before the crisis with the adoption of inflation-targeting strategies by many emerging economies. However, fear of floating and lack of international cooperation led many other countries to maintain the objective of a stable exchange rate and to sterilize the monetary consequences of increased net capital inflows. In the wake of the crisis, the large growth differential between the North and the South has made such a double-target model unworkable without raising barriers to capital flows. These developments have also prompted fears of "currency wars."

The common theme running through these developments is the recognition that current international monetary arrangements seem incapable of delivering not only domestic internal and external stability for each individual country, but also global economic and financial stability. A broadly shared, though not unanimous, opinion among academics (see, for example, Eichengreen 2009, Portes 2009) and policymakers (de Larosière 2009, Turner 2009, King 2010) is that the interplay between external imbalances among the main currency areas and financial market developments was an essential ingredient in the genesis of the crisis. There is also broad (but again not unanimous) recognition that macroimbalances were facilitated by the lack of incentives for policy adjustment and the weakness of multilateral disciplines. Whether the uneasiness about the performance of the system—well articulated by the report of the Palais-Royal Initiative (Camdessus, Lamfalussy, and Padoa-Schioppa 2011)—and the ensuing discussions will lead to reform action soon, or will lose force in the face of the formidable negotiating difficulties that any reform of international monetary relations entails, is difficult to predict. Skeptics point out that agreements on overhauls of the IMS were only reached in exceptional circumstances, typically following major wars.[3]

All in all, there are in our view reasons to believe that the current IMS, in spite of the fact that it proved fairly resilient during the crisis, is bound to evolve through either policy initiatives or market developments, or probably both. The two main factors that have contributed to the preservation of the status quo in the last three decades—the uncontested dominant position of the US economy and the absence of plausible candidates to join the US dollar in its international role—are gradually eroding. What is much less clear at present is what direction this evolution will take, say, over a horizon of 10 to 15 years.

Realistic Options for the Foreseeable Future

To design possible medium-term scenarios for the evolution of the IMS, it is useful to examine the structural factors that shape the global monetary order, their balance, and their likely development over time. Following Angeloni et al. (2011), we distinguish three shaping factors.

The first is the sheer economic size of nations. Throughout the history of the IMS, there has been a link, albeit a complex one, between economic size and monetary leadership, with the complexity coming from the fact that incumbency matters because of "network externalities" associated with the international use of currencies. A similar tension between economic size and incumbency is likely to apply in the decades to come as well, suggesting that the impact of economic size on monetary power, while surely present, is likely to be delayed.

Figure 9.1, borrowed from Angeloni et al. (2011), provides a bird's-eye view of the evolution of the world economy and the distribution of economic power from 1870 to 2050, at 2005 exchange rates. Throughout the 19th and 20th centuries, the share of the largest economy in world GDP remained consistently above 15 percent. In the gold standard period (1879–1913), the sterling area composed of the United Kingdom and its main colonies met this

---

3. The Smithsonian Agreement of 1971, which simply took note of the unilateral decision by the US government to end the Bretton Woods system, is hardly an exception.

Figure 9.1 Share in world GDP, selected countries and economies, 1870–2050 (at 2005 exchange rates)

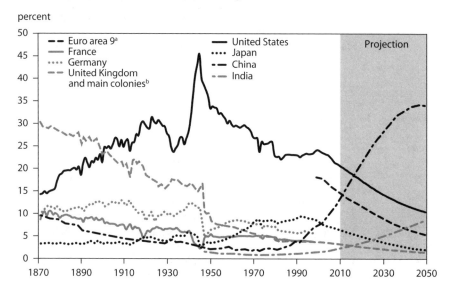

a. Austria, Belgium, Finland, France, Germany, Italy, the Netherlands, Portugal, and Spain.
b. Australia (up to 1900), New Zealand (up to 1939), and India (up to 1946). Canada is not included as it was already granted significant autonomy in 1867.

Sources and methodology: Angeloni et al. (2011), including the sources and notes therein.

criterion, being either the dominant power in terms of GDP or a close second to the United States. Throughout the Bretton Woods period (1945–73), the United States was the undisputed dominant power, with a weight consistently over one-fourth of world GDP.

According to long-term projections elaborated by CEPII,[4] the world economy in the 21st century is likely to see the emergence of two new dominant players: China and India. China should overtake the United States around 2035, at constant relative prices. (See Subramanian 2011 for a comprehensive account of the progress of China). By the middle of the century, US weight should be down to less than 20 percent and, unless significant enlargements take place, the euro area's weight will be down to 10 percent. Even assuming enlargement of the euro area to the current European Union and beyond, the euro's weight is unlikely to reach 15 percent. In contrast, China could account for one-fourth of the global economy at the 2050 horizon, and India almost as much as the euro area. In the meantime—say, in the next 10 to 20 years—there

4. The projections in this paragraph are from Fouré, Bénassy-Quéré, and Fontagné (2010) and are based on assumptions about demography and productivity.

Table 9.1   The incumbent and the challengers: State of play in 2011

Measure	US dollar	Euro	Renminbi
Financial markets and openness	Unrivaled liquidity and depth, full capital mobility	Second after the United States, but bond markets remain fragmented in the absence of unified eurobonds. Full capital mobility	Underdeveloped markets and restricted capital mobility
Legal system	Strong	Strong	Weak
Budgetary and monetary policy	Increasing concerns over the sustainability of budgetary policy and the risks of debt monetization	Strong monetary record and institutional independence. Concerns over solvency of some state borrowers	Strong fiscal position. Good monetary policy track record but at risk, in part because of currency peg
Ability/willingness of policy system to respond to unexpected shocks, lender of last resort function	Strong	Strong for central bank but broader capacity limited by institutional arrangements	Strong
Stance toward international currency role	Incumbent	Officially neutral. Unilateral euroization by nonmember countries actively discouraged	Support for renminbi internationalization
Political cohesion and geopolitical power	Strong	Limited by political fragmentation	Strong and in ascendance

Source: Angeloni et al. (2011).

will be an interregnum during which economic power will be more evenly distributed among a core group of countries.

The second factor has to do with the ability of a country or a group of countries to exercise monetary leadership. Beyond economic size, this ability depends on financial development, on the quality of economic and financial institutions, on the nature and effectiveness of governance, and on an economic power's political might and commitment to global leadership. Table 9.1 summarizes the respective situations of the US dollar, the euro, and the renminbi relative to these elements.

The table indicates that there are several reasons why the dollar is dominant at the moment, including the breadth of its financial sector and the strength of its legal system. Its main, not negligible, weakness arises from concerns over the sustainability of budgetary policy and the possible monetary consequences of debt unsustainability. The dollar faces two potential rivals. The first, the euro, has many of the attributes of an international currency and already a sizeable share in foreign exchange reserves and international bond issuances, but comparatively weak governance and political foundations. The second potential rival, the renminbi, has strong underpinnings in terms of economic potential and coherence in policymaking but is still far from having acquired the characteristics of an international currency. In short, for the time being the euro and the renminbi cannot, for different reasons, rival the US dollar. This is what gives the dollar its still-unrivaled status. But this situation is unlikely to last beyond the 10- to 15-year horizon considered here.

The third factor relates to the likely evolution of global financial conditions. A major question is whether the trend toward global financial integration observed in the last decades will continue and lead to the full inclusion of emerging-market countries in the global financial network. The appetite for unfettered capital market liberalization has significantly diminished in the wake of the 1997–98 Asian crisis and of the more recent global crisis. An increasing number of emerging-market economies have reintroduced capital controls or are contemplating such a move, often with explicit or implicit support from the IMF. The resumption of capital flows after the worst of the global crisis was over nevertheless suggests that these controls were more defensive than offensive; they convey a more cautious approach to liberalization by emerging and developing countries rather than an irreversible U-turn. Meanwhile, Asian financial centers have continued to strengthen, and their openness and integration have increased.

A separate issue concerns the direction of capital flows. A striking characteristic of the last decade is that, in net terms, while private capital has been flowing "downhill," from relatively richer to relatively poorer countries, official reserve hoarding has reversed the direction of total net flows, to "uphill." Although they abated somewhat in the aftermath of the global crisis, South-North capital flows are likely to remain strong, and the world saving-investment balance pattern is unlikely to reverse dramatically over the next 10 to 15 years (IMF 2011).

Based on these observations, there seem to be three scenarios for the IMS in the foreseeable future, say the next 10 to 15 years:

1. A repair-and-improve scenario whereby changes to current arrangements are introduced through incremental reforms. These are inter alia enhanced surveillance; a voluntary reform of exchange rate arrangements, especially in Asia; improved international liquidity facilities; accompanying domestic reforms such as the development of home-currency financial markets; and regional initiatives to complement current IMF facilities. Under this scenario, the international role of key currencies remains broadly constant and the US dollar retains its dominant role, the euro's role remains broadly unchanged, and the role of the Chinese renminbi increases, but remains marginal in comparison to the dollar and the euro.

2. A multipolar scenario in which a system structured around two or three international currencies—the dollar and, presumably, the euro and/or the renminbi—emerges over a 10- to 15-year horizon. Although a move to a multipolar system is generally viewed as a remote prospect, especially in the case of the renminbi, it would be entirely consistent with the long-run evolution of the world economy. Moreover, the Chinese authorities have taken significant steps in this direction through various schemes, and their currency has a strong potential for internationalization. As for the euro, it has already developed as a diversification currency, and in this scenario the euro area overcomes its current difficulties and the euro graduates from a mainly regional to a truly global currency. Yet an alternative bipolar scenario with the dollar and the renminbi could occur if the euro remains handicapped economically and politically.

3. A multilateral scenario in which participants agree to take steps toward a strengthened international monetary order. In contrast with the multipolar scenario, which will largely rely on market forces and national policies, renewed multilateralism would require a fairly intense degree of international coordination and the development of new instruments to help escape the pitfalls of regimes based on the dominant role of one or a few national currencies, to foster macroeconomic discipline, and to provide for international liquidity management. A system of this sort could build on the existing SDR or rely on other, new vehicles.

Compared with the current regime, each of these three scenarios has advantages and disadvantages in terms of efficiency, stability, and equity. Each has also its own specificity in terms of feasibility. Table 9.2 provides an assessment of the three scenarios in terms of these four criteria.

The first scenario is the least demanding in terms of both domestic policies and international coordination, hence is the most likely in the short run. The third one is the most demanding in terms of both domestic policies and international coordination, and therefore the least likely in the foreseeable future, unless serious shocks in the global economy (e.g., a deep and prolonged recession, disorderly exchange rate and asset price movements, financial instability and contagion, or any combinations thereof) force a quantum increase in monetary cooperation. The second scenario relies on market forces, geopolitical trends, and domestic policies rather than international cooperation. Its probability is low in the short run, but significant at the 10- to 15-year horizon.

In terms of efficiency, stability, and equity, all three scenarios offer improvements over the current system. A comparison among them suggests that the desirability of a scenario is negatively correlated to its feasibility, at least in the short run. The multipolar and the multilateral scenarios are both superior to the more modest repair-and-improve scenario, especially on grounds of equity and, to some extent, stability, although their pros and cons vary across the different criteria. But they are also less likely in the short run

Table 9.2 Assessing the three international monetary system scenarios

Criterion	Scenario 1: Repair and improve	Scenario 2: Multipolarity	Scenario 3: Renewed multilateralism
Efficiency			
Economies of scale	0	–	0/–
Savings on reserve accumulation	+	++	+++
Limitation of foreign exchange misalignments	+	++	++
Stability			
Global anchor	0	?	+
Discipline	+	++	+++
Limitation of foreign exchange volatility	0	–	–
Resilience to shocks	+	+	++
Equity			
Adjustment symmetry	+	++	+++
Limitation of exorbitant privilege	0	+	++
Global seigniorage	0	+	+
Limitation of policy spillovers	+	++	+++
Feasibility	+++	++	+

Note: Gains (+) or losses (–) are those implied by moving from the current international monetary system to each of the alternative regimes.

Source: Angeloni et al. (2011).

precisely because they are more demanding in terms of domestic or international policies.

More extreme multilateral scenarios involving the creation of an "outside" international currency in a proper sense (modelled for example on John Maynard Keynes's bancor) rather than simply the SDR—a scenario envisaged recently by Tommaso Padoa-Schioppa[5]—would be preferable in our view, at least theoretically, as they would guarantee a fully symmetric adjustment mechanism and full control of global reserves. Admittedly, however, they are far less realistic than the more modest multilateral scenario considered here.

If feasibility in the medium term is the main guiding principle, then the multipolar scenario is clearly the most interesting to explore, since it best corresponds to the structural changes in the world economy discussed earlier, in particular the role of China. It should be emphasized, though, that the gains from multipolarity can materialize only if key currencies are truly allowed to float (although maybe in a managed way), and if third countries move toward more flexibility or regional pegs. Here the key question concerns the

5. Tommaso Padoa-Schioppa, The Ghost of Bancor: The Economic Crisis and Global Monetary Disorder, Triffin Lecture, Louvain-la-Neuve, 2010, www.notre-europe.eu/en.

internationalization of the renminbi and whether it will make exchange rate flexibility more acceptable for both China and its regional partners.

A Key Question: The Role of China

There are several reasons to assume that the renminbi will become a major international currency. As the second largest economy in the world, China already has the scale necessary to create deep and liquid financial markets. The huge size of its foreign trade and foreign direct investment volume forms the basis for renminbi-denominated transactions. In addition, the People's Bank of China (PBC) and the State Administration of Foreign Exchange have large balance sheets and already actively intervene in onshore and offshore financial markets. Moreover, importantly, as Barry Eichengreen (2010) argues, the rise of the renminbi to a fuller international status will be advantageous to China. Besides the extraction of seigniorage, domestic firms will be able to limit their foreign exchange exposures by transacting internationally in their own currency, the PBC will be able to follow an independent monetary policy, and China's financial sector will become more competitive.

At the moment, however, the internationalization of the renminbi remains very limited, even compared with currencies of other emerging countries. Yin-Wong Cheung, Guonan Ma, and Robert McCauley (2010) show that, in 2007, daily trading of the renminbi barely surpassed the sum of daily imports and exports from China, whereas foreign exchange turnover in relation to foreign trade was around 10 for the Indian rupee or the Korean won and roughly 100 for international currencies such as the Swiss franc or the US dollar.

There are, clearly, formidable obstacles that must be overcome before China's currency gains international status. A key ingredient is likely to be capital account convertibility—the ability to freely convert domestic into foreign financial assets at market-determined exchange rates. Obstacles include the quality of financial regulation and supervision, the degree of the rule of law, an opaque exchange rate peg, and the strong reliance on exports. These obstacles are all interrelated, and overcoming them will amount to a fundamental change in China's economic model. Eichengreen argues that "these kinds of changes are coming. While one can question the timing—whether Shanghai will have become a true international financial center by 2020 [as China's State Council has announced] and whether the renminbi will be a first-rank international currency by that date—one cannot question the direction" (Eichengreen 2010, 6–7).

Indeed, timing is a key factor behind the different scenarios for the evolution of the IMS over the next 10 to 15 years discussed in the previous section. In scenario 1, it is assumed that China gradually aligns its monetary regime with those of other Asian emerging-market countries, which can be characterized by "dirty" float and a limited use of capital controls. Building on its experience with the creation of an offshore market for the renminbi, it continues to foster the international role of its currency, but at a gradual pace.[6]

By contrast, scenario 2 assumes that China moves at a more sustained pace toward the internationalization and liberalization of its currency. Changes are initially gradual (for example, we suppose an extension of the "pilot" project of renminbi internationalization launched in 2009, the promotion of one or several active financial centers, and initiatives toward increased financial account openness), but they create a momentum and trigger enough two-way capital mobility for a degree of internationalization to take place for the renminbi. Relative to the first one, this scenario implies greater capital account liberalization and a freely floating exchange rate.

Whether the 15-year time horizon we envisage here would be sufficient for the renminbi to achieve the full combination of convertibility-floating-capital mobility is difficult to say. Eichengreen (2010) argues that it took only 10 years (1914 to 1924) for the US dollar to go from a situation where, like the renminbi today, it played a negligible role in international trade and payments to one where it became the leading international and reserve currency. It is not clear, however, whether the international circumstances would allow such a rapid rise of the renminbi in the coming 10 years, or even whether the Chinese authorities have the will and the capacity to transform their economy and, indeed, their social and political systems to a sufficient extent to make that possible.

Opportunities for Europe

In the 10-plus years of its existence, the euro has made only limited progress in its international presence. Measured by the usual yardsticks—share in global official reserves, use as currency anchor for exchange arrangements, denomination of foreign trade—it is the second currency after the US dollar. But so it was already shortly after its introduction; the more recent years have seen little progress in this respect.[7] The stability of the euro's position in the rankings of international use over the decade is striking in light of the diverse influences acting in opposite directions—the sharp depreciation in the first two years, the subsequent reappreciation coupled with euro area enlargement, recently the financial crisis, etc. The remarkable stability of the status quo for many years may have been due on the one hand to inertia generated by the long-standing dominance of the US economy and its currency, and on the other to the lack

---

6. At the time of this writing, the Chinese authorities announced a "roadmap" for currency convertibility that is a clear step in this direction, though it does not necessarily remove all uncertainties about the future timing of this complex process (see Nicholas Borst, "Capital Account Liberalization and the Corporate Bond Market," Peterson Institute China Economic Watch, February 12, 2012, www.piie.com/blogs/china/?p=1093).

7. See Dorucci and McKay (2011); European Central Bank, *The International Role of the Euro* (Frankfurt, various years).

of serious contenders from the emerging world. Both conditions are rapidly changing.

The stance of European policymakers toward the phenomenon has been ambivalent. In 1999, the European Central Bank (ECB 1999) formulated a doctrine that can be labelled "watchful neglect." According to it, the internationalization of the euro is a market-driven process that should be monitored, not pursued ("neither fostered nor hampered" is the expression used); it is a by-product of other goals (price stability, financial integration), not a goal in itself. This view arose partly from the consideration of the potential costs and risk of an international currency, in terms of added volatility and vulnerability to external influences (an aspect emphasized in Gourinchas, Govillot, and Rey 2010). Over the years, the ECB has regularly monitored and reported extensively on the euro's usage in international markets. On the other hand, other policymakers in Europe have expressed different nuances. The European Commission has seemed typically more sympathetic toward internationalization,[8] and even at times endorsed it openly.[9] A keen attention to the phenomenon has come from the European Parliament.[10] Among member states, different positions have been expressed, some sharing the "neglect" view, others more openly sympathetic to the euro's promotion.

Looking ahead, two major questions arise. The first is whether the transition of the IMS suggests that the "neglect" doctrine prevailing in Europe in recent years should be reviewed. The second is whether, regardless of the policy stance, those changes imply that a market-driven acceleration of the progress in the euro's international position is likely. Let's consider the two questions in turn.

Historical experience suggests a negative answer to the first question. The British pound and the US dollar—the main global currencies in the last two centuries—acquired their international position not as a result of policy actions deliberately aiming at that goal, but mainly as a consequence of a variety of economic, financial, and geopolitical developments and conditions. Economic policy may well help those conditions materialize, but its effect on whether a currency is accepted across borders as a medium of exchange and used as store of value is mainly indirect. For example, consider the circumstances linking the creation of the US Federal Reserve (1913) to the establishment of the dollar's international position in subsequent years (Eichengreen 2011). The presence of a central bank at the center of the then-developing US financial system, guarding financial stability after the major banking crises of

---

8. Joaquín Almunia, The Second Decade of the Euro: What Role for the Euro in the Global Economy? Speech given at the Peterson Institute for International Economics, Washington, April 11, 2008.

9. See European Commission, Frequently-Asked-Questions on EMU and the Euro, May 7, 2008, available at http://europa.eu (accessed on January 24, 2012).

10. European Parliament, Draft Resolution to the ECB Annual Report, various years; see, for example, the 2005 issue, available at www.europarl.europa.eu.

the earlier years and providing the real economy with an "elastic currency," undoubtedly contributed to the rising cross-border role of the dollar after the Great War (Eichengreen and Flandreau 2009, 2010). But neither was the Fed founded to promote such a role nor was this a prominent consideration in the mind of Benjamin Strong or other early US central bankers.

Different, in our view, is the answer to the second question, namely, whether the present circumstances are more favorable for the euro to expand internationally. The euro has shown, in recent years, a considerable attractiveness at the regional level, especially in Eastern Europe. This process possesses a built-in inertia, which creates favorable conditions for a further spreading in coming years, other things equal. In addition, as we observed, there is now a new and genuine demand for currency diversification in the system. It is unlikely that this demand will go away in the foreseeable future—on the contrary. This should create, ceteris paribus, favorable conditions for the gradual emergence of a multipolar IMS, as we have argued, in which the euro would be a natural candidate for a prominent role.

A major obstacle to such a development at present is clearly the European sovereign debt crisis. As we write, the crisis is far from settled. Whatever the eventual outcome, more market turbulence is likely. While there is no decisive evidence yet that the euro debt crisis has altered the portfolio shares of global private and official asset holders or has affected other indicators measuring the international use of the euro yet, it is clear that the efficiency and integration of the euro area financial sector have been severely damaged.

While caution is warranted, two arguments should be made. The first is that the present crisis is likely to give rise to reforms that would not otherwise have been made and that will, in the end, permanently strengthen the institutional foundation of the euro. The recent euro area treaties on fiscal coordination and the European Stability Mechanism are of this nature. There are several relevant historical precedents. In their overview of five well-established federations (United States, Canada, Germany, Argentina, and Brazil), Michael Bordo, Agnieszka Markiewicz, and Lars Jonung (2011) conclude that "institutional developments in most of the five federations were driven by exceptional events, often downturns in economic activity during deep crises . . . which affected in a fundamental way the institutions of the five federal states. In response to the economic crisis, central governments increased their power." The strengthening of central institutions at the expense of regional ones in these five federations involved, first and foremost, fiscal policy and the financing of public debts. While these five examples refer to cases where an established political union antedated monetary and fiscal unification, several arguments suggest that present-day Europe (where many functions are already transferred to the EU level and a common central bank exists) is more comparable to historical examples of national monetary unifications than to international ones (Bordo and Jonung 1999).

The second argument is that most reforms, enacted or under consideration, aimed at strengthening the euro's economic governance are also likely to promote its position in the IMS. There is, in other words, strong synergy between the *internal stability* of the euro and its *external attractiveness*. Therefore, should the more favorable scenario mentioned above materialize, the euro will probably be well positioned to assume a growing role in a multipolar currency system. Let us consider the different aspects of this argument in some detail.

Philip Lane and Gian Maria Milesi-Ferretti (2001, 2009) and Gourinchas and Hélène Rey (2005) have concluded, looking at detailed data on US balance sheets, that the dollar's international role is linked to the United States acting in many ways like a financial intermediary, issuing liabilities attractive for international portfolio holders (mainly private liquid balances and official reserve holdings) and investing in more risky assets. To extract the "exorbitant privilege" the US banking sector performs a liquidity-creating and a maturity-transforming function, much like a bank, for the rest of the world (as noted already by Charles Kindleberger 1965). In recent years this intermediation has become more extreme, as the demand for liquidity by international investors has increased while the lending side (equity and foreign direct investment, often in emerging economies) has become more risky. This interpretation seems to fit to some extent also the earlier case of the British pound; during the gold standard period, and even later in the first half of the 20th century, the City of London performed financial intermediation by supplying liquid assets to international investors (bank deposits, Treasury paper, etc.) and financing, via trade credit, the vast international trade between the United Kingdom and its empire (Eichengreen 2011, chapter 3).

The question is whether the financial and banking sector of the euro area can perform a similar function, and what the necessary conditions for their doing so would be. Will the reforms undertaken in euro area economic governance, including financial regulation, be sufficient?

Of central importance here is the stability and efficiency of the euro area banking and financial sector, including its governance and the availability of an effective safety net. The steps taken so far go some way toward providing new and sounder regulatory and supervisory structures. In particular, the European Systemic Risk Board (ESRB), an EU body of central bankers and supervisors entrusted with the responsibility of monitoring systemic risks and making policy recommendations, should ensure regular and well-informed oversight against the insurgence of systemic risks. At a more operational level, the introduction of new European supervisory authorities (or ESAs, for banks, markets, and other intermediaries) should help ensure consistent regulation across the area (a level playing field) and homogeneous implementation of rules (a single rule book)—thus addressing a major deficiency that the early institutional structure of the Economic and Monetary Union (EMU) had left unresolved (Padoa-Schioppa 2007).

This granted, much remains to be done. The new European supervisory structures need to be tested and will acquire credibility and influence gradually, building on the limited statutory powers they have. This can only be achieved through consistent and successful performance in the field. This is particularly relevant for the ESRB, which does not possess direct intervention powers but acts through nonbinding recommendations. The interplay between the ESAs and the national supervisors, a complex web of cross-country and cross-institutional interlinkages, will unavoidably have to be phased in gradually and by trial and error. In addition, there is an unresolved potential tension between two financial logics in Europe. One is financial integration associated with the internal market, the other is financial supervision associated with the single currency, with the tension coming from the fact that the former is an EU matter, whereas the latter has an important euro area dimension, as the crisis has shown. The ESRB and the ESAs are EU rather than euro area bodies, which may preclude their evolution toward euro area supervisors.

A closely related issue regards financial integration, i.e., the ability of the euro area financial system to ensure broadly uniform lending and borrowing (risk-adjusted) conditions to all market participants, especially across borders. In the early years of the EMU, cross-border financial integration, measured by volumes of cross-border flows and yield spreads, progressed steadily but unevenly (more on money markets, less in other market segments).[11] The financial crisis has very seriously impaired financial integration; at the time of writing there are parts of the euro area banking system and money markets that are cut out of regular market linkages and receive financing by the ECB, or else are in drastically different conditions than the rest of the area. This has not only endangered the monetary policy transmission process, as often emphasized by the ECB, but also generated uncertainty and opacity in market conditions within and across compartments (interbank funds, bonds, retail banking services), constituting a factor of discouragement for international investors. The new supervisory and regulatory framework will help but is not sufficient (Angeloni 2011).

We regard the integration of sovereign bond markets as a first key condition to *jointly* restore financial stability in the euro area and to enhance the euro's international role. A broad, liquid, and integrated market for public sector benchmarks plays a key role in all well-functioning financial systems. Official wealth holders (central banks and other sovereign institutions), covering a rising share of global funds under management, have a systematic preference for low-risk instruments. While the German Bund has fulfilled this role to some extent, an areawide liquid market, including benchmarks issued and guaranteed by European institutions, would contribute to financial integration (by improving the collateral pools) and to the attractiveness of the euro as an international store of value.

While the advantages of areawide bond issuances (or bond guarantees) from the point of view of fostering European financial integration and promot-

---

11. See European Central Bank, *Financial Integration in Europe* (Frankfurt, various years).

ing the international attractiveness of the euro are clear, the political and institutional conditions for their introduction, in amounts significantly beyond those already existing for specific purposes (like the issues by the European Investment Bank, the European Commission, or the European Financial Stability Facility) are not yet present. A discussion of them would lead us too far from our central theme. Adequate legal and economic basis would require new treaty provisions, including strict issuance rules and limits to guarantee the quality of the new instruments and to avoid free riding.

The second condition we see underpinning confidence in the euro both internally and internationally is an upgrade of the euro area economic performance. Area-wide price stability is not sufficient in this respect; real sector performance will be equally important. In the first decade of the euro, progress has been achieved in making euro area labor markets more responsive and in securing a reduction of unemployment rates (ECB 2008). But this has not prevented growing competitiveness gaps and external disequilibria across euro area countries. Real economic performance gaps across countries increasingly coincide with differentials in sovereign credit risks and in financial sector risks. The euro area has agreed on a new surveillance framework, the Excessive Imbalance Procedure, with the aim of triggering structural policy responses as a result of monitoring of national developments and peer pressure. The challenge will be, once again, implementation: Peer pressure can easily lose force and political bargaining produce laxity, as the experience of the Stability and Growth Pact demonstrates.

Conclusions

Our reasoning suggests three conclusions. First, the IMS is changing, partly due to the influence of the financial crisis. The stable equilibrium that prevailed for decades, characterized by a dominant US dollar and the lack of plausible alternatives, is no longer there.

Second, this situation creates opportunities and risks for the system as a whole and for individual currencies. It seems likely that the next decades will witness the emergence of a multipolar IMS, where the dollar will continue to play a crucial role but other currencies will also occupy a key role. It also seems likely that the Chinese renminbi will, sooner or later, be one of the key currencies.

Third, the prospects for the euro are less clear but by no means somber. As a result of the sovereign debt crisis, which has exposed some fundamental institutional weaknesses, the euro finds itself in a sort of knife-edge situation: regress or advance, both internally and internationally. The reforms needed to provide the euro with a stable institutional foundation largely coincide, in our view, with those likely to foster its international use. Stability, efficiency, and integration of the banking and financial system are crucial conditions for both internal and international viability, and they will require further reform of the financial supervisory framework, a broad and liquid sovereign bond market, and structural reforms on the real side of the economy. The coming months will tell whether the euro area is able to demonstrate the political cohesion and leadership necessary for such steps to materialize. If it does, internal stabilization of the euro will be achieved and is likely to be matched by a growing international role.

References

Adrian, Tobias, and Hyun Song Shin. 2008. Liquidity, Monetary Policy, and Financial Cycles. *Current Issues in Economics and Finance* 14, no. 1: 1–7.

Angeloni, Ignazio. 2011. Policy Perspectives on Financial Integration After the Crisis. In *Post-Crisis Growth and Financial Integration in Europe*, ed. E. Nowotny, P. Mooslechner, and D. Ritzberger-Grünwald. Cheltenham, UK and Northampton, MA: Edward Elgar.

Angeloni, Ignazio, Agnès Bénassy-Quéré, Benjamin Carton, Zsolt Darvas, Christophe Destais, Jean Pisani-Ferry, André Sapir, and Shahin Vallé. 2011. *Global Currencies for Tomorrow: A European Perspective*. Bruegel Blueprint 13. Brussels: Bruegel.

Bordo, Michael D., and Lars Jonung. 1999. *The Future of EMU: What Does the History of Monetary Unions Tell Us?* NBER Working Paper 7365. Cambridge, MA: National Bureau of Economic Research.

Bordo, Michael D., Agnieska Markiewicz, and Lars Jonung. 2011. *A Fiscal Union for the Euro: Some Lessons from History*. NBER Working Paper 17380. Cambridge, MA: National Bureau of Economic Research.

Camdessus, Michel, Alexandre Lamfalussy, and Tommaso Padoa-Schioppa. 2011. *Reforms of the International Monetary System: A Cooperative Approach for the Twenty First Century*. Palais-Royal Initiative final report (February). Available at http://global-currencies.org/smi/gb/telechar/news/Rapport_Camdessus-integral.pdf.

Cheung, Yin-Wong, Guonan Ma, and Robert N. McCauley. 2010. *Renminbising China's Foreign Assets*. CESifo Working Paper 3009. Munich: CESifo.

de Larosière, J. 2009. *Report of the High-Level Group on Financial Supervision in the EU*. Brussels. available at http://ec.europa.eu/internal_market/finances/docs/de_larosiere_report_en.pdf.

Dooley, M., D. Folkerts-Landau, and P. Garber. 2004. The Revived Bretton Woods System. *International Journal of Finance and Economics* 9: 307–13.

Dorucci, E., and J. McKay. 2011. *The International Monetary System After the Financial Crisis*. ECB Occasional Paper 123 (February). Frankfurt: European Central Bank.

ECB (European Central Bank). 1999. *Monthly Bulletin* (August). Frankfurt.

ECB (European Central Bank). 2008. *Monthly Bulletin: 10th Anniversary of the ECB*. Frankfurt.

Eichengreen, Barry. 2009. The Financial Crisis and Global Policy Reforms. Paper presented at Federal Reserve Bank of San Francisco conference on Asian economic policy, Santa Barbara, October 19–21.

Eichengreen, Barry. 2010. The Renminbi as an International Currency. University of California, Berkeley. Available at www.econ.berkeley.edu (accessed on January 22, 2012).

Eichengreen, Barry. 2011. *Exorbitant Privilege*. New York: Oxford University Press.

Eichengreen, Barry, and Marc Flandreau. 2009. The Rise and Fall of the Dollar (or When Did the Dollar Replace Sterling as the Leading Reserve Currency?). *European Review of Economic History* 13, no. 3 (December): 377–411.

Eichengreen, Barry, and Marc Flandreau. 2010. *The Federal Reserve, the Bank of England and the Rise of the Dollar as an International Currency, 1914–39*. BIS Working Paper 328. Basel: Bank for International Settlements.

Flandreau, Marc, and Clemens Jobst. 2009. The Empirics of International Currencies: Network Externalities, History and Persistence. *Economic Journal* 119, no. 537: 643–64.

Fouré, Jean, Agnès Bénassy-Quéré, and Lionel Fontagné. 2010. *The World Economy in 2015: A Tentative Picture.* Working Paper 2010-27. Paris: CEPII.

Fratzscher, Marcel, and Arnaud Mehl. 2011. *China's Dominance Hypothesis and the Emergence of a Tripolar Global Currency System.* ECB Working Paper 1392. Frankfurt: European Central Bank (October).

Gourinchas, Pierre-Olivier. 2010. US Monetary Policy, "Imbalances" and the Financial Crisis. Remarks prepared for the Financial Crisis Inquiry Commission Forum, Washington, February 26–27.

Gourinchas, Pierre-Olivier, and Hélène Rey. 2005. *From World Banker to World Venture Capitalist: US External Adjustment and the Exorbitant Privilege.* NBER Working Paper 11563. Cambridge, MA: National Bureau of Economic Research.

Gourinchas, P.-O., N. Govillot, and H. Rey. 2010. Exorbitant Privilege and Exorbitant Duty. University of California, Berkeley. Photocopy.

IMF (International Monetary Fund). 2011. *World Economic Outlook: Tensions from the Two-Speed Recovery: Unemployment, Commodities, and Capital Flows* (April). Washington.

Kenen, Peter B. 2011. Beyond the Dollar. Paper presented at the AEA Allied Social Science Association Meetings, Denver, January.

Kindleberger, Charles. 1965. *Balance of Payments Deficits and the International Market for Liquidity.* Princeton Essays in International Finance 46. Princeton, NJ: Princeton University Department of Economics.

King, Mervyn. 2010. Speech at the University of Exeter, January 19. Available at http://www.bankofengland.co.uk/publications/Documents/speeches/2010/speech419.pdf (accessed on May 24, 2012).

Kubelec, C., and F. Sá. 2010. *The Geographical Composition of National External Balance Sheets: 1980–2005.* Bank of England Working Paper 384 (March). London: Bank of England.

Lane, P., and G. M. Milesi-Ferretti. 2001. The External Wealth of Nations: Measures of Foreign Assets and Liabilities for Industrial and Developing Countries. *Journal of International Economics* 55: 263–94.

Lane, P., and G. M. Milesi-Ferretti. 2009. *The External Wealth of Nations Mark II: Revised and Extended Estimates of Foreign Assets and Liabilities.* IMF Working Paper WP/06/09. Washington: International Monetary Fund.

Padoa-Schioppa, T. 2007. Progressing Within the Lamfalussy Framework. Note prepared for the Informal Ecofin Council. Available at www.tesoro.it (accessed on January 24, 2012).

Portes, Richard. 2009. *Global Imbalances.* PEGGED Policy Brief 3. Available at http://pegged.cepr.org (accessed on January 24, 2012).

Subramanian, Arvind. 2011. *Eclipse: Living in the Shadow of China's Economic Dominance.* Washington: Peterson Institute for International Economics.

Triffin, Robert. 1960. *Gold and the Dollar Crisis: The Future of Convertibility.* New Haven, CT: Yale University Press.

Turner, A. 2009. *The Turner Review: A Regulatory Response to the Global Banking Crisis.* London: Financial Services Authority. Available at www.fsa.gov.uk/pubs/other/turner_review.pdf.

Vallée, S. 2011. The Path of Internationalisation of the RMB. Background paper prepared for *Global Currencies for Tomorrow: A European Perspective*, Angeloni et al. Bruegel Blueprint 13. Brussels: Bruegel.

Zhou, Xiaochuan. 2009. *Reform the International Monetary System* (March 23). Beijing: People's Bank of China. Available at www.pbc.gov.cn.

10

European Monetary Unification

Precocious or Premature?

JOSEPH E. GAGNON

Prior to the formation of the euro area, in a process formally known as European Economic and Monetary Unification (EMU), research suggested that potential participants in EMU were less economically integrated than regions of the United States. Subsequent research held out the hope that countries within the euro area were becoming more integrated because of the formation of the "single market" in 1992 and the creation of the common currency in 1999. This chapter finds only weak evidence of an increase in euro area integration since 1999. Countries in the euro area remain considerably less integrated than regions or states within the United States, particularly in the area of labor markets.

Previous Studies

In a widely cited paper, Tamim Bayoumi and Barry Eichengreen (1992) found that the precursor to the European Union, the European Community, was less economically integrated—and thus less well suited as a common currency area—than the United States. However, they also noted that a core group of countries centered on Germany was roughly as integrated as the United States.[1] Bayoumi and Eichengreen based their conclusions on measures of the correlation of inflation and economic activity across members of the

Joseph E. Gagnon has been a senior fellow at the Peterson Institute for International Economics since September 2009. He thanks Anders Åslund, Otmar Issing, Jacob Kirkegaard, Juan-Carlos Martinez Oliva, Adam Posen, Ted Truman, and John Williamson for helpful comments and Marc Hinterschweiger for gathering the data.

1. The core group was Belgium, Denmark, France, Germany, Luxembourg, and the Netherlands.

European Community and across regions of the United States over the period 1960–88. Their guiding principle was that regions that share common economic movements are better suited to share a common monetary policy than regions with highly different economic movements.

Jeffrey Frankel and Andrew Rose (1998) argued that currency union may increase the synchronization of business cycles across member economies, in part because of increased trade links. Andrew Rose and Eric van Wincoop (2001) predicted that trade of euro area countries would rise "in excess of 50 percent." Richard Baldwin (2006) subsequently estimated that currency union had increased trade among euro area countries by 5 to 15 percent. Joseph Gagnon and Marc Hinterschweiger (2011) found results consistent with Baldwin's estimate.

Phillip Lane (2006) surveyed research on several dimensions of integration within the euro area, including price differentials, labor mobility, financial integration, fiscal coordination, and trade. Lane found strong evidence of integration in financial markets and trade; he found little evidence of increased integration of labor markets, and only weak evidence of integration in fiscal policy and inflation.

Rose (2008) found that EMU had increased trade of member countries between 8 and 23 percent. Using meta-analysis of 20 studies of the effect of trade on business cycle correlation, he estimated that the increased trade caused by EMU may have increased the correlation of detrended real output across euro area members from about 0.2 to at least 0.4.

Jean-Claude Trichet argued that measures of dispersion of inflation, GDP growth, and labor costs across members of the euro area are comparable to those across states of the United States.[2]

A Fresh Look

This chapter presents updated analysis similar in spirit to, though somewhat simpler than, that of Bayoumi and Eichengreen (1992). Bayoumi and Eichengreen decomposed shocks into supply and demand shocks. They focused more on supply shocks than on demand shocks because differences in monetary policy across European countries prior to EMU contributed to dispersion in demand shocks that presumably would not be present after EMU. This chapter does not decompose shocks in this way because it focuses on the period after EMU in which the euro area had a common monetary policy.

In addition to looking at GDP growth and inflation, this chapter examines the unemployment rate. The importance of labor market integration for a currency union was first advanced by Robert Mundell (1961) in his Nobel prize–winning research on optimum currency areas. The experience of Texas within the United States over the past few years confirms Mundell's insight.

---

2. Jean-Claude Trichet, The Euro, Its Central Bank, and Economic Governance, Stamp Memorial Lecture, London School of Economics and Political Science, June 13, 2011.

Table 10.1 Data description

Data	United States	Euro area
Real GDP, GDP deflator, and unemployment rate (annual, 1980–2010); data on US regional GDP and GDP deflator begin in 1987	9 Census divisions (main): New England, Middle Atlantic, East North Central, West North Central, South Atlantic, East South Central, West South Central, Mountain, and Pacific	10 countries (main): Original members except Luxembourg
		13 countries (alternate): Original members plus Denmark and Greece (statistics weighted by nominal GDP)
	51 states (alternate): 50 states plus District of Columbia (statistics weighted by nominal GDP)	Core (alternate): Austria, Belgium, Denmark, France, Germany, Luxembourg, and the Netherlands

Sources: IMF, *World Economic Outlook* database; US Bureau of Economic Analysis; and US Bureau of Labor Statistics.

The rise of world oil prices since 2003 has greatly boosted the growth rate of Texas GDP, yet the Texas unemployment rate remains close to the US average as a large inflow of workers has arrived from other states. This labor market flexibility has reduced the cost to Texas and the rest of the United States of having a common monetary policy. Because unemployment is more closely linked to the unobservable output gap than real GDP, divergences in the unemployment rate across regions may be a better indicator of the cost of a common monetary policy than divergences in GDP growth.

Data Description

Table 10.1 describes the data and the definition of regions. The variables are the rates of real GDP growth, inflation, and unemployment. Inflation is measured using the GDP deflator.[3] Because the regional breakdowns for the euro area have different geographic coverage, the areawide data for the euro area are calculated as nominal GDP-weighted averages of data for the regions that are included in each breakdown. Table 10.2 displays summary statistics for both the 12 years since the launch of EMU, 1999–2010, and for periods prior to EMU, which differ according to availability of data.

The main regional breakdown for the United States consists of the nine Census divisions. An alternate breakdown consists of the 50 states plus the District of Columbia. Statistics for this alternate breakdown are weighted

---

3. Consumer price inflation is not available on a state or regional basis in the United States. It is available for selected metropolitan areas. Bayoumi and Eichengreen (1992) used the GDP deflator.

Table 10.2   Summary statistics

Statistic	United States		Euro area	
Real GDP growth rate	**1988–98**	**1999–2010**	**1981–98**	**1999–2010**
Area average	3.2	2.0	2.1	1.5
Area standard deviation	1.7	1.9	1.2	2.0
Standard deviation of regional averages	0.9	0.6	0.7	0.8
Average of regional standard deviations	1.9	2.0	2.0	2.6
Inflation rate				
Area average	2.5	2.2	4.8	1.8
Area standard deviation	0.9	0.8	2.6	0.5
Standard deviation of regional averages	0.2	0.2	2.7	0.6
Average of regional standard deviations	1.0	0.9	3.5	1.4
Unemployment rate	**1980–98**	**1999–2010**	**1980–98**	**1999–2010**
Area average	6.6	5.8	9.2	8.5
Area standard deviation	1.4	1.9	1.3	0.7
Standard deviation of regional averages	0.9	0.6	4.1	2.4
Average of regional standard deviations	1.6	1.8	2.3	1.8

Note: Regional statistics are based on the main regional breakdowns defined in table 10.1.

by nominal GDP in order to damp the effect of idiosyncratic shocks in small regions.

The main regional breakdown for the euro area consists of the 11 original members minus Luxembourg. Luxembourg is excluded because it has a population barely one-tenth that of the next smallest member (Ireland). Very small regions are prone to idiosyncratic shocks that bias downward their correlation with the rest of the currency union. One alternate breakdown consists of the 11 original members plus Denmark, which has maintained a tightly pegged exchange rate to the euro since its inception, and Greece, which joined the euro area in 2001. As in the case of the alternate breakdown in the United States, statistics for this alternate breakdown are weighted by nominal GDP. Another alternate breakdown, referred to as the core group, consists of the core countries identified by Bayoumi and Eichengreen (1992) plus Austria.

Real GDP Growth

According to Table 10.2, real GDP growth was moderately higher in the United States than in the euro area during 1999–2010 but variability of this growth was roughly equal in the two areas. Differences in growth rates across regions (the third line) were slightly larger in the euro area than in the United States, but the opposite was true in the years before 1999. The variability of

Table 10.3 Regression analysis of GDP growth rates

	United States			Euro area			
	9 Census divisions		51 states (weighted)	10 countries		13 countries (weighted)	Core
	1999–2010	1999–2007	1999–2010	1999–2010	1999–2007	1999–2010	1999–2010
β_1	0.02	0.10	0.08**	0.01	0.11	0.01	−0.07
	(.06)	(.09)	(.03)	(.07)	(.08)	(.05)	(.06)
β_2	−0.05	−0.07	−0.04	0.19*	0.07	0.12	0.03
	(.07)	(.08)	(.04)	(.10)	(.07)	(.08)	(.09)
β_3	0.96***	0.89***	0.98***	1.13***	1.10***	1.02***	1.20***
	(.05)	(.10)	(.04)	(.07)	(.10)	(.05)	(.07)
Regression Standard deviation	0.95	0.95	1.68	1.32	0.78	1.01	0.95
	1990–98				1983–98		
β_1		0.15**	0.11***		0.44***	0.29***	0.20**
		(.06)	(.04)		(.07)	(.05)	(.08)
β_2		−0.04	−0.02		−0.05	−0.09*	0.10
		(.06)	(.04)		(.07)	(.05)	(.08)
β_3		0.93***	0.94***		0.80***	0.86***	0.83***
		(.07)	(.05)		(.10)	(.07)	(.13)
Regression Standard deviation		0.92	1.60		1.44	1.04	1.44

$$\Delta y_{it} = \alpha_i + \beta_1 \Delta y_{it-1} + \beta_2 \Delta y_{it-2} + \beta_3 \Delta y_{(EA|US)t}$$
(α_i are regional fixed effects)

Notes: *, **, *** denote statistical significance at 10, 5, and 1 percent levels, respectively. Standard errors are in parentheses. Weighted statistics are weighted by regional nominal GDP. See table 10.1 for data description and sources.

real GDP growth over time in each region (the fourth line) was somewhat greater on average in the euro area than in the United States after 1999.

Table 10.3 presents results of panel regressions of real GDP growth in the United States and the euro area. The top half of the table focuses on the post-EMU period and the bottom half focuses on the pre-EMU period. Real GDP growth in each region is regressed on two lags of itself plus the current value of GDP growth for the area as a whole.[4] In addition, there is a complete set of regional fixed effects that allows each region to have a different average growth rate. Δy denotes the growth rate of GDP. α and β are coefficients to be estimated. The subscript i in the regression equation denotes regions and the subscript t denotes years. The subscripts EA and US denote areawide data for the euro area or the United States, respectively.

$$\Delta y_{it} = \alpha_i + \beta_1 \Delta y_{it-1} + \beta_2 \Delta y_{it-2} + \beta_3 \Delta y_{(EA|US)t}$$

4. Additional lags are never significant in tables 10.3, 10.4, and 10.5.

Figure 10.1   Magnitude and persistence of region-specific real GDP shocks

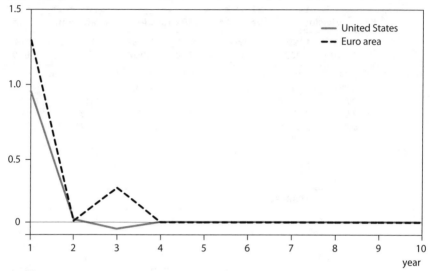

percentage points

Source: Author's calculation based on regression standard deviation and regression coefficients for the main regional breakdowns in 1999–2010 from table 10.3.

The coefficient β_3 indicates the extent to which the regions share common shocks; a value of β_3 near zero means regions do not share common shocks, whereas a value of β_3 near one means regions fully share common shocks. The coefficients β_1 and β_2 indicate the extent to which idiosyncratic, or region-specific, shocks are persistent or transitory. Large values indicate that regional differences persist for a long time, whereas small values indicate that regional differences die out quickly. Finally, the standard deviation of the regression is a measure of the size of the typical region-specific shock (in percentage points).

According to the top half of table 10.3, shocks to real GDP growth rates in the post-EMU period are highly shared across regions, as shown by the estimates of β_3 close to one. Region-specific shocks are not persistent, as shown by the estimates of β_1 and β_2 close to zero, although there is a slight indication of greater persistence in the euro area 10-country and 13-country breakdowns. These results are not sensitive to excluding the Great Recession years (2008–10) from the analysis, as shown in the second column for each area. Figure 10.1 displays the magnitude and persistence of region-specific GDP shocks for the main regional breakdowns in the post-EMU period based on these regression results. Region-specific GDP shocks are moderately larger in the euro area and have slightly greater persistence.

In the pre-EMU period, regional coherence (β_3) was roughly the same in the United States, but noticeably lower in the euro area. Persistence of regional

GDP shocks (β_1) was slightly larger in the United States and considerably larger in the euro area prior to EMU. These results may reflect the adoption of a common monetary policy in the euro area, which replaced region-specific monetary policies with a common monetary policy.

Overall, the GDP regressions display similar degrees of economic integration in the United States and the euro area since 1999.

Inflation

As can be seen in the middle section of table 10.2, inflation was a little higher in the United States than in the euro area over the past 12 years. In addition, the volatility (standard deviation) of US inflation was somewhat higher than that of euro area inflation. However, the dispersion of average inflation rates across regions was much higher in the euro area than in the United States.[5] The volatility of regional inflation is also higher in the euro area than in the United States, despite the lower volatility for the euro area as a whole.

Table 10.4 presents regressions of regional inflation similar in structure to those shown for GDP growth in table 10.3. For the United States, the results are similar for both regional breakdowns and for the shorter sample period. The estimates of β_3 imply that inflation in each region moves roughly one-for-one with national inflation. The estimates of the lag coefficients (β_1 and β_2) imply that idiosyncratic regional shocks to inflation are very short-lived.

The estimates are different for the euro area. For the main breakdown (10 countries), regional inflation moves a bit more than half of areawide inflation (β_3) and idiosyncratic regional shocks are strongly persistent—two-thirds of any increase in regional inflation carries over into the next year (β_1). In the sample that ends in 2007, the persistence of region-specific inflation is a bit lower and the coherence of regional inflation rises a bit; but the coherence is still notably lower, and persistence considerably higher, than in the United States. For the 13-country breakdown, the coherence of regional inflation (β_3) also is somewhat higher, probably reflecting the high weights on French and German inflation, which dominate the euro area average. For the core group, persistence (β_1 and β_2) drops essentially to zero, similar to that in the United States, but coherence remains notably lower than in the United States.

Figure 10.2 displays the magnitude and persistence of region-specific inflation shocks based on the regressions for the main regional breakdowns in 1999–2010. Region-specific inflation shocks (even after allowing for different regional mean rates of inflation) are much larger and more persistent in the euro area than in the United States.

The bottom half of table 10.4 shows results for the pre-EMU period. For the United States, the results are essentially the same as for the post-EMU

---

5. Surprisingly, this dispersion is even greater for the core of the euro area, at 0.8 (not shown in the table).

Table 10.4 Regression analysis of inflation rates

	United States			Euro area			
	9 Census divisions		51 states (weighted)	10 countries		13 countries (weighted)	Core
	1999–2010	1999–2007	1999–2010	1999–2010	1999–2007	1999–2010	1999–2010
β_1	−0.07	0.08	−0.14***	0.65***	0.45***	0.39***	−0.07
	(.08)	(.08)	(.04)	(.09)	(.10)	(.08)	(.10)
β_2	0.09	0.01	0.03	−0.04	−0.07	0.00	−0.10
	(.07)	(.06)	(.04)	(.10)	(.10)	(.09)	(.10)
β_3	0.94***	0.90***	1.07***	0.60***	0.73**	0.81***	0.71***
	(.08)	(.09)	(.06)	(.13)	(.18)	(.12)	(.18)
Regression Standard deviation	0.59	0.37	1.12	0.90	0.77	0.75	1.09

	1990–98			1983–98			
β_1	−0.02		−0.07	0.53***		0.37***	0.36***
	(.10)		(.05)	(.08)		(.06)	(.09)
β_2	−0.03		−0.29***	0.05		0.06	−0.00
	(.12)		(.06)	(.08)		(.06)	(.09)
β_3	1.04***		1.28***	0.30***		0.60***	0.38***
	(.13)		(.08)	(.10)		(.08)	(.12)
Regression Standard deviation	0.45		0.85	1.86		1.76	1.67

$\Delta p_{it} = \alpha i + \beta_1 \Delta p_{it-1} + \beta_2 \Delta p_{it-2} + \beta_3 \Delta p_{(EA|US)t}$
(α_i are regional fixed effects)

Notes: **, *** denote statistical significance at 5 and 1 percent levels, respectively. Standard errors are in parentheses. Weighted statistics are weighted by regional nominal GDP. See table 10.1 for data description and sources.

period.[6] For the 10-country and 13-country euro area breakdowns, the regressions find similar persistence and lower coherence before EMU than after. For the core of the euro area, the differences before and after EMU are somewhat greater.

Note that all of these regressions include regional fixed effects, which allow each region to have a different average inflation rate. One objective of a monetary union may be to have the same average inflation rate across the regions. The summary statistics show that regional inflation rates are very similar in the United States but much less so in the euro area. Regressions without regional fixed effects (not shown) display similar results to those of table 10.4 for the United States, but less coherence and greater persistence for the euro area. Different mean rates of inflation might arise if euro area regions

---

6. The negative second lag in the 51-state regression is probably spurious. Owing to lack of data, the sample for the United States is rather short.

Figure 10.2   Magnitude and persistence of region-specific inflation shocks

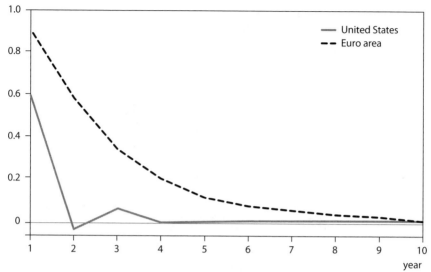

percentage points

Source: Author's calculation based on regression standard deviation and regression coefficients for the main regional breakdowns in 1999–2010 from table 10.4.

had different price levels prior to EMU and were converging toward a common level of prices. Before the Great Recession, it was commonly argued that higher inflation in the periphery of the euro area reflected such a convergence process. Now, however, many argue that different inflation rates across euro area regions during the past decade led to a divergence of prices from long-run equilibrium.

Overall, the inflation data and regressions for the post-EMU period display greater economic integration in the United States than in the euro area, although the differences are notably smaller between the United States and the core of the euro area. The euro area has narrowed some of the large integration gap that existed before EMU, especially in the core.

Unemployment

The bottom section of table 10.2 compares statistics on unemployment. The average unemployment rate for the United States is considerably lower than that for the euro area, but unemployment was a lot more volatile in the United States during the past 12 years. It is widely accepted that US firms are both more willing and more able to fire workers in downturns and thus feel greater freedom to hire in upturns. Differences in average rates of unemployment across regions are much larger in the euro area than in the United States. This finding is true even within the core of the euro area (not shown). The volatility

Table 10.5 Regression analysis of unemployment rates

	United States			Euro area			
	9 Census divisions		**51 states (weighted)**	**10 countries**		**13 countries (weighted)**	**Core**
	1999– 2010	**1999– 2007**	**1999– 2010**	**1999– 2010**	**1999– 2007**	**1999– 2010**	**1999– 2010**
β_1	0.22***	0.46***	0.37***	1.29***	1.15***	1.25***	1.01***
	(.08)	(.11)	(.04)	(.08)	(.10)	(.07)	(.11)
β_2	−0.04	−0.20**	−0.09*	−0.62***	−0.42***	−0.62***	−0.47***
	(.10)	(.09)	(.05)	(.07)	(.08)	(.07)	(.10)
β_3	0.83***	0.67***	0.77***	0.19**	0.05	0.19*	0.25**
	(.05)	(.09)	(.03)	(.09)	(.09)	(.11)	(.13)
Regression Standard deviation	0.45	0.27	0.63	0.93	0.59	0.85	0.55
		1982–98			**1982–98**		
β_1		0.69***	0.77***	1.38***		1.21***	1.28***
		(.08)	(.03)	(.07)		(.06)	(.07)
β_2		−0.21***	−0.24***	−0.60***		−0.54***	−0.61***
		(.06)	(.03)	(.06)		(.05)	(.06)
β_3		0.54***	0.50***	0.07		0.27***	0.15**
		(.05)	(.02)	(.07)		(.06)	(.08)
Regression Standard deviation		0.66	0.74	0.91		0.62	0.50

$u_{it} = a_i + \beta_1 u_{it-1} + \beta_2 u_{it-2} + \beta_3 u_{(EA|US)t}$
(a_i are regional fixed effects)

Notes: *, **, *** denote statistical significance at 10, 5, and 1 percent levels, respectively. Standard errors are in parentheses. Weighted statistics are weighted by regional nominal GDP. See table 10.1 for data description and sources.

of unemployment by region (after subtracting region-specific means) is broadly similar in the United States and the euro area.

Table 10.5 presents results of regressions of the regional unemployment rates on their own lagged values and on the value of the areawide unemployment rate. As in the regressions of GDP growth and inflation, fixed effects are included for each region to control for differences in the average unemployment rates across regions. In the United States, about 80 percent of national movements in unemployment are shared across the regions (β_3). Idiosyncratic regional shocks to unemployment die out quickly (β_1 and β_2). These results are not particularly sensitive to ending the sample in 2007.

The results for the euro area are strikingly different. Only about 20 percent of areawide movements in unemployment are shared across the regions; even in the core, this coherence is only 0.25. These differences are not greatly changed by restricting the sample to the period before the Great Recession. The estimates of β_1 around 1.3 imply that idiosyncratic regional shocks are

Figure 10.3 Magnitude and persistence of region-specific unemployment shocks

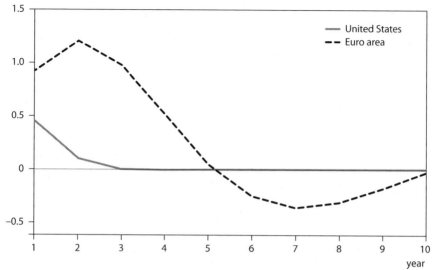

percentage points

Source: Author's calculation based on regression standard deviation and regression coefficients for the main regional breakdowns in 1999–2010 from table 10.5.

not only persistent but actually tend to grow in the near term before slowly dying out. In the core, idiosyncratic shocks do not grow over time, but they are still more persistent than in US regions. Figure 10.3 shows that region-specific unemployment shocks in the euro area are both larger and more persistent than in the United States.

The bottom half of table 10.5 presents results for unemployment prior to EMU. For both the United States and the euro area, the sample is 1982–98. For the United States, the coherence of unemployment shocks across regions appears to have been somewhat lower in the earlier sample and the persistence of regional shocks moderately greater. For the euro area, there is little difference in the coherence of unemployment shocks before and after EMU. In both samples, coherence is far lower in the euro area than in the United States. Persistence appears to have decreased a bit over time in the core of the euro area, but remained well above that in the United States over the past 12 years. For the overall euro area, there is little change in the persistence of region-specific unemployment shocks, with persistence remaining far above that in US regions.

Overall, the unemployment data and regressions for the post-EMU period display much greater economic integration in the United States than in the euro area, and the differences are nearly as large when comparing the United States to the core of the euro area. The euro area has made little progress in integrating its labor markets since the launch of EMU.

Conclusion

These results suggest that countries in the euro area are less economically integrated than states or regions in the United States, but the degree of integration varies across markets. Specific findings include the following:

- Progress toward integration in the euro area is greatest in terms of real GDP growth. Countries in the euro area now have GDP growth rates that are nearly as closely connected as those of US regions.

- Inflation rates are less closely linked in the euro area than in the United States, although the core of the euro area has correlations not far from US levels.

- There has been little progress in linking unemployment rates within the euro area. Labor markets in euro area countries are far less integrated than in US regions, and these divergences are nearly as great for the core of the euro area as for the entire euro area.

References

Baldwin, Richard. 2006. *In or Out: Does It Matter? An Evidence-Based Analysis of the Euro's Trade Effects.* London: Center for Economic Policy Research.

Bayoumi, Tamim, and Barry Eichengreen. 1992. *Shocking Aspects of European Monetary Unification.* NBER Working Paper 3949. Cambridge, MA: National Bureau of Economic Research.

Frankel, Jeffrey, and Andrew Rose. 1998. The Endogeneity of the Optimum Currency Area Criteria. *Economic Journal* 108: 1009–25.

Gagnon, Joseph, and Marc Hinterschweiger. 2011. *Flexible Exchange Rates for a Stable World Economy.* Washington: Peterson Institute for International Economics.

Lane, Phillip. 2006. The Real Effects of European Monetary Union. *Journal of Economic Perspectives* 20, no. 4: 47–66.

Mundell, Robert. 1961. A Theory of Optimum Currency Areas. *American Economic Review* 51: 509–17.

Rose, Andrew. 2008. Is EMU Becoming an Optimum Currency Area? The Evidence on Trade and Business Cycle Synchronization. University of California, Berkeley. Manuscript (October 21).

Rose, Andrew, and Eric van Wincoop. 2001. National Money as a Barrier to International Trade: The Real Case for Currency Union. *American Economic Review* 91, no. 2: 386–90.

Europe's Growth Emergency

ZSOLT DARVAS and JEAN PISANI-FERRY

In the 20th century it was common to joke that "Brazil is a country of the future, and always will be." In the same way it is tempting to say that growth is Europe's agenda for the future, and always will be. This goal has been emphasized as a priority at least since the 1980s, and it seems that each decade makes it even more elusive.

It was therefore bold for the Polish presidency of the EU Council to put economic growth at the core of its agenda (Polish Presidency 2011), and it was brave for the World Bank to undertake an in-depth examination of the "luster" of European growth (Gill and Raiser 2011). Both should be congratulated on their initiatives, because growth in Europe is both more important and more difficult to achieve now than at any point in recent decades.

The reasons why restoring growth has become paramount are not hard to grasp. Until the global crisis, Europe's disappointing growth performance could be seen as a merely relative concern vis-à-vis more successful countries. It meant that the continent would not reach the US level of GDP per capita, but it enjoyed already high living standards, and benefited from longer holidays and earlier retirement. As Olivier Blanchard (2004) put it in a (controversial) paper, Europe's lower income per capita was perhaps the result of a

Zsolt Darvas has been a research fellow since January 2009 at Bruegel, which he joined as a visiting fellow in September 2008. He is also a research fellow at the Institute of Economics of the Hungarian Academy of Sciences and associate professor at the Corvinus University of Budapest. Jean Pisani-Ferry is the director of Bruegel and professor of economics at Université Paris-Dauphine. Earlier versions of this chapter were presented at the BEPA-Polish Presidency of the European Union Council conference "Sources of Growth in Europe," Brussels, October 6, 2011. The authors are grateful to Dana Andreicut and Silvia B. Merler for excellent research assistance and to several colleagues for useful comments and suggestions.

social choice. Furthermore, as pointed out by Indermit Gill and Martin Raiser (2011), Europe successfully fostered the catching up of its least developed areas, where there was the most pressing need for growth.

The global crisis has however altered this benign landscape in three fundamental ways:

- First, growth is of utmost importance for both public and private deleveraging and for reducing the fragility of the banking sector. History shows that in addition to growth and fiscal consolidation, previous rounds of financial repression, inflation, and occasional default helped achieve the deleveraging of the public sector. Europe does not want to have to fall back on the latter three. Without growth, Europe is at risk of struggling permanently with debt sustainability and is at the mercy of stagnation and a debt overhang. Without growth the sustainability of the (already precarious) European social model would be further brought into question.

- Second, the convergence machine has brutally stopped in the southern part of the European Union—and has moved into reverse in Greece, Portugal, and Spain, with little chance of short-term improvement. Italy, meanwhile, has been falling behind since the early 1990s.

- Third, the euro area sovereign debt crisis may put Europe at risk of being seen by investors as a place where there are very few reasons to invest. This may trigger an accelerated weakening of its economic performance.

It is of the highest importance to assess the seriousness of these threats and the possible policy responses. With this goal in mind and with a focus on the medium term, we have organized this chapter as follows: we first explain why we think growth should now be given higher priority; we next investigate if the seeds of future growth have been sown during the recession; we then discuss the policy responses and finally offer some conclusions.

To simplify matters, throughout this chapter we use five groups of countries as the basis for discussion of the diverse challenges. Appendix 11A presents the classification.

Why Growth Is So Important

Overall Performance

After the Second World War, European countries embarked on a rapid convergence with the United States in terms of GDP per capita (figure 11.1). This was in part based on the rebuilding of the capital stock lost during the war, in part on technological catching up, and in part on economic integration efforts.

By the late 1970s, however, convergence with the United States had stopped in most countries of "older" Europe—though with significant exceptions, such as Ireland. Countries in the North group (Denmark, Finland, Sweden, Ireland, United Kingdom; see appendix 11A) and South group

Figure 11.1 GDP per capita at purchasing power parity, 1950–2016

index, United States = 100

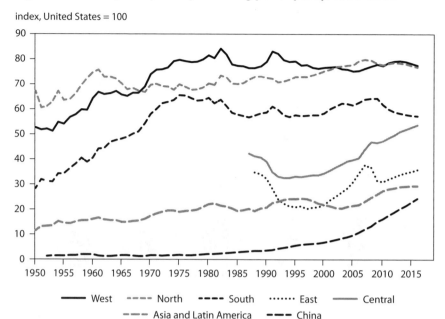

Note: Figure shows median values. Data for most countries in Central and Eastern Europe are available only starting the late 1980s. For makeup of country groups, see appendix 11A.

Source: Bruegel calculations using data from IMF (2011d); Penn World Tables; and European Bank for Reconstruction and Development.

(Greece, Italy, Portugal, Spain) in particular had apparently settled for levels corresponding to 80 and 60 percent, respectively, of US GDP per capita. The central and eastern countries by contrast were catching up beginning in the mid-1990s, though from a much lower base.

Figure 11.1 also shows International Monetary Fund (IMF) projections up to 2016 suggesting that the positions of the West and North country groups relative to the United States should remain broadly stable, while southern Europe is expected to fall behind and the convergence of the Central and East groups is projected to continue (after the major shock of recent years in the latter case).[1]

Judging from figure 11.1 it seems that the potential for naturally catching up with the United States has been exhausted in three of the five groups, and the gap remains noteworthy. Only significant economic reforms and/or a change in social preferences would lead to a change in this diagnosis.

Europe should look not only at the United States but also at the new emerging powers. Figure 11.1 underlines the extremely rapid development of

---

1. By 2016, the relative position of the East group is forecast to reach only pretransition level. Note that data for the late 1980s and early 1990s should be interpreted with caution given the differences in statistical methodology, changes in relative prices, and measurement errors.

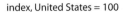

Figure 11.2   GDP per hour worked and per capita at purchasing power parity, 2010

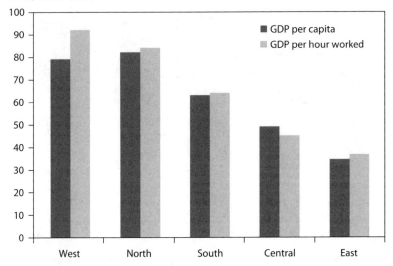

index, United States = 100

Note: For makeup of country groups, see appendix 11A.

Source: Bruegel calculations using data from Eurostat database (for GDP per hour for four East group countries excluding Estonia) and Organization for Economic Cooperation and Development (for the rest).

China and shows that smaller countries in Asia and Latin America are also converging.

But there is some good news. As figure 11.2 shows, Western European countries are closer to the United States in terms of GDP per hour worked. Belgium and the Netherlands are even at the US level. From the North group, Ireland is only 3 percent below. Therefore, these European countries were able to catch up with the United States in terms of productivity; lower per capita output is in part a reflection of social preferences (more leisure), and in some cases higher unemployment. The four South group countries have mixed records in this respect: Spain and Italy are closer to the United States than Greece and Portugal.

Deleveraging

The period in the run-up to the crisis was characterized by a rapid increase in private debt in several countries, such as the Baltic countries, Ireland, the Netherlands, Spain, and the United Kingdom, while in many other countries, such as Austria, the Czech Republic, and Germany, private debt accumulation was less pronounced. In most of Europe, public debt ratios (as a percent of

GDP) were generally stable or slowly declining. Some countries, such as Ireland, Spain, and Bulgaria, had even achieved sizeable debt reductions.

The postcrisis landscape is very different. Public debt ratios in the European Union have increased by 20 percentage points on average, and in some cases they have reached alarming levels. Market tolerance of high public debt has diminished severely, especially for the members of the euro area. The challenge of public deleveraging is therefore paramount. At the same time, several European countries face the challenge of bringing down household or corporate debt.[2]

Let us start with public debt. Carmen Reinhart and Kenneth Rogoff (2011) summarize five major ways in which high debt ratios were reduced in past episodes of deleveraging: (1) economic growth; (2) substantial fiscal adjustment, such as austerity plans; (3) explicit default or restructuring of public and/or private sector debt; (4) a sudden surprise burst in inflation (which reduces the real value of the debt); and (5) a steady dose of financial repression accompanied by an equally steady dose of inflation.[3]

Of these, economic growth is by far the most benign. There are three main channels through which it aids deleveraging in both the public and private sectors:

■ First, higher growth results in higher government primary balances and higher private sector incomes—which can be used to pay off the debt.

■ Second, higher growth results in a reduction of the relative burden of past debt accumulation. Other things being equal, a one percentage point acceleration of the growth rate reduces the required primary surplus by 1/100 of the debt ratio. With the debt ratio approaching or in certain cases exceeding 100 percent of GDP, this is a meaningful effect.

■ Third, by improving sustainability, higher growth makes future threats to solvency less probable and for this reason is likely to result in lower risk premia. It is not by accident that the potential growth outlook is often mentioned by market participants and rating agencies as a key factor in their solvency assessments.

---

2. McKinsey Global Institute (2010) assessed the likelihood of deleveraging in five EU countries (among others). Concerning the household sector, it found high probability for Spain and the United Kingdom, but low probability for Germany, France, and Italy. In the case of the non-real estate corporate sector the likelihood of deleveraging is low in the United Kingdom and France, moderate in Germany and Italy, and mixed in Spain.

3. According to Reinhart, Kirkegaard, and Belén Sbrancia (2011, box 1, 22), "financial repression occurs when governments implement policies to channel to themselves funds that in a deregulated market environment would go elsewhere." At the current juncture, these authors and Reinhart and Rogoff (2011) foresee a revival of financial repression—including more directed lending to government by captive domestic audiences (such as pension funds), explicit or implicit caps on interest rates, and tighter regulation on cross-border capital movements.

Box 11.1 illustrates the point by decomposing factors behind the impressively fast reduction of the UK general government and the US federal debt ratios in the first three postwar decades. Growth and primary surpluses made sizeable contributions to deleveraging, and primary surpluses were partly the result of growth. There were several years with negative real interest rates (and whenever the real interest rate was positive, it was small), which also helped deleveraging. As pointed out by Reinhart and Belén Sbrancia (2011), financial repression was the major reason for low real interest rates.

Another reason why public debt deleveraging, and hence growth, is paramount is that without it the European social model is not sustainable. This was observed by André Sapir et al. (2004) and is a major reason why they advocated an agenda for a growing Europe.

Turning to the private side, credit developments show that deleveraging has started: As a result of both credit demand and supply factors, credit aggregates have started falling in several EU countries (figure 11.3). These credit developments help private sector deleveraging on the one hand. But on the other hand, the simultaneity of public and private deleveraging is a major challenge that could hinder economic growth and could even lead to a vicious circle of lower growth and lower credit—even for those companies and households that are not overly leveraged.[4] Furthermore, the banking sector in Europe is itself highly leveraged and will need to undergo sizeable corrections, not least because of the Basel III regulations.

There are therefore major concerns on both the supply and the demand sides. On the supply side, potential growth in the coming years could weaken further after the financial crisis; on the demand side, the combination of public and private deleveraging may result in slow growth of private aggregate demand.

In this context, improving potential growth in the long run remains of paramount importance, but at the same time policymakers cannot afford to ignore the interplay between supply and demand or between short-term and longer-term developments.

---

4. There is a growing literature about "creditless" recoveries (see Abiad, Dell'Ariccia, and Li 2011 and references therein), which finds that such recoveries are not rare, but growth and investment are lower than in recoveries with credit; industries more reliant on external finance seem to grow disproportionately less during creditless recoveries; and such recoveries are typically preceded by banking crises and sizeable output falls. But there are at least two important caveats in applying these results to Europe. First, financing of European firms is predominantly bank based and the level of credit to output is much higher than in other parts of the world. Therefore, lack of new credit or even a fall in outstanding credit could drag growth more in Europe than elsewhere. Second, the literature has not paid attention to real exchange rate developments during creditless recoveries. But Darvas (2011) found that creditless recoveries are typically accompanied by real effective exchange rate depreciations, which can boost the cash flow from tradable activities, thereby reducing the need for bank financing. But the southern members of the euro area and the eastern countries with fixed exchange rates cannot rely on nominal depreciation and hence this effect cannot work.

Box 11.1   Decomposition of post–World War II UK and US public debt reduction

In the United Kingdom and the United States, the public debt ratio (general government for the United Kingdom, federal government for the United States) fell rapidly after the Second World War. In 1946, the public debt was 257 percent of GDP in the United Kingdom and 122 percent in the United States. By 1976 it had been brought down to 52 percent and 36 percent, respectively. Table B11.1.1 shows average annual growth, interest rates, and primary surpluses during these three decades. GDP growth was robust and both countries had primary surpluses (especially sizeable in the United Kingdom), but real interest rates were very low—always below the growth rate of GDP and even negative in several years.

Table B11.1.1   Average annual growth, interest rate, and primary surplus in the United Kingdom and the United States, 1947–76

Period	Real GDP growth rate (percent)	Real ex post interest rate (percent)	Primary surplus (percent of GDP)
United Kingdom			
1947–56	2.3	–3.0	7.4
1957–66	2.9	0.2	4.8
1967–76	2.4	–4.6	3.0
United States			
1947–56	3.6	–1.5	2.0
1957–66	4.2	1.7	1.2
1967–76	3.0	1.0	0.6

Note: Ex post real interest rate is calculated with the so-called implicit interest rate (i.e., interest expenditures in a given year divided by the stock of debt at the end of the previous year) and the change in the GDP deflator.

Sources: UK data are from HM Treasury (debt); Office for National Statistics (budget balance, interest payments, GDP from 1948); and measuringworth.com (GDP for 1946–48). US data are from White House, Office of Management and Budget, Historical Tables, www.whitehouse.gov (debt, budget balance); Bureau of Economic Analysis, Table 3.1: Government Current Receipts and Expenditures, www.bea.gov (interest payments); and Bureau of Economic Analysis, www.bea.gov (GDP).

Our decomposition is based on the well-known, simple accounting identity for the change in the debt ratio:

$$d_t - d_{t-1} = \left(\frac{r_t - g_t}{1 + g_t + \pi_t} \right) d_{t-1} - s_t + sf_t,$$

where d_t is the gross public debt (percent of GDP), r_t is the real interest rate (percent), g_t is the real GDP growth rate (percent), π_t is the inflation rate (percent), s_t

(box continues next page)

is primary surplus (percent of GDP), and sf_t is a stock flow adjustment (percent of GDP). Many of these variables are interlinked; for example, faster growth and higher surprise inflation improve the primary balance, a connection that complicates a causal decomposition of the change in the debt ratio. Therefore, we use this simple accounting identity to decompose the changes, i.e., we report $(r_t/(1 + g_t + \pi_t))d_{t-1}$ as "real ex post interest rate," $(-g_t/(1 + g_t + \pi_t))d_{t-1}$ as "growth," $-s_t$ as "primary surplus," and sf_t as "stock/flow adjustment." We calculate these values for each year and sum them up for each decade considered, in order to get their cumulative impacts over decades.

As table B11.1.2 indicates, growth was an important factor in bringing down debt, and it has always more than counterbalanced the impact of the real interest rate whenever the latter was positive. But the real interest rate was sometimes negative, which is labeled as financial repression by Reinhart and Belén Sbrancia (2011).

Table B11.1.2   Contributions to postwar UK and US public debt deleveraging, 1947–76 (percent of GDP)

Period	Reduction in debt ratio	Real ex post interest rate	Growth	Primary surplus	Stock/flow adjustment
United Kingdom					
1947–56	−128	−58	−37	−74	41
1957–66	−45	3	−29	−48	30
1967–76	−32	−22	−15	−30	35
United States					
1947–56	−58	−15	−28	−20	6
1957–66	−20	9	−21	−12	4
1967–76	−7	4	−11	−6	6

Note: See the explanation of the methodology and the interpretation of the numbers in the main text.

Source: Bruegel calculations based on data sources of table B11.1.1.

Developments During the Crisis

Growth policies are generally and rightly regarded as medium-term oriented. However, the impact of the Great Recession of 2009 and the current crisis in the euro area are more than mere cyclical phenomena that could be overlooked in a medium-term analysis. In this section we analyze and discuss the behavior of European countries during this episode and assess implications for medium-term growth.

Figure 11.3 Outstanding stock of loans to nonfinancial corporations, January 2007–July 2011

index, September 2008 = 100

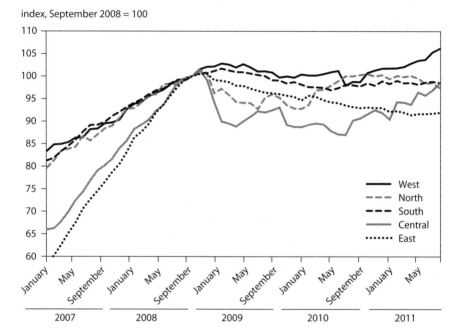

Note: Figure shows median values. For makeup of country groups, see appendix 11A.

Source: Bruegel calculations using data from European Central Bank.

Shock and Recovery

A telling measure of the economic impact of the crisis can be obtained by comparing precrisis and postcrisis forecasts. While forecasts certainly contain errors, they reflect the views about the future that are used for economic decisions. In figure 11.4, we therefore compare forecasts to 2012 made by the IMF in October 2007 and September 2011.[5]

Figure 11.4 shows that the crisis had a moderate impact on West group countries. There, as in the United States, output fell and recovered at a broadly unchanged pace, therefore not closing the gap created by the recession. The impact on the North group was more significant, owing to the greater trade openness of the countries of this group, but the recovery pattern is similar. The situation is worse in the South group, where the recession was mild in

---

5. Our purpose is not to assess the IMF's forecasting ability, but rather to use forecast changes as indicative of changes in economic perspectives. Comparison of forecasts by the IMF (2007) to those of the European Commission (2007) and the OECD (2007) made in late 2007 indicate that the latter two institutions' forecasts were broadly similar to the IMF's.

Figure 11.4 GDP forecasts to 2012: October 2007 versus September 2011

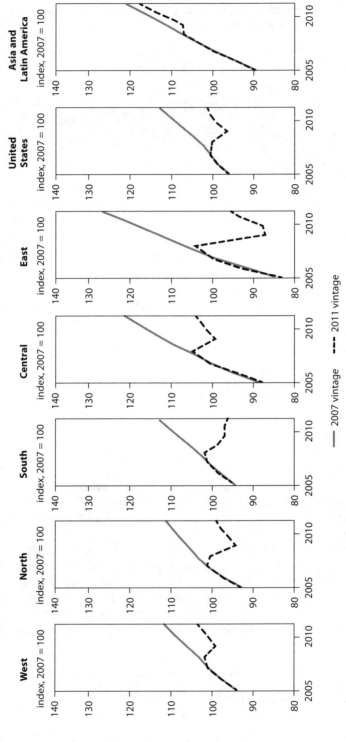

Note: For makeup of country groups, see appendix 11A.

Source: Bruegel calculations using IMF (2007, 2011d).

230

2009, but output decline has continued and is forecast to last at least until 2012. This widening gap is very worrying. Finally, Central European economies (with the exception of Poland) also suffered significantly from the crisis, and those of the East group suffered a major shock in 2009, from which they have started to recover but which leaves a major gap amounting to more than 30 percent of the 2007 GDP trajectory.

European developments are similar to those in the United States but contrast sharply with the experience of the 14 emerging countries of Asia and Latin America (see appendix 11A), where the impact was mild. In China (not shown in the figure), pre- and postcrisis growth trajectories are almost identical. These emerging countries were primarily impacted by the global trade shock, but did not suffer from a financial crisis and started to recover when global trade recovered.

Adjusting to the Shock

At the time of economic hardship, firms relied on different strategies to survive and to sow the seeds of future growth. The strategies depended on initial conditions (firms that were not competitive enough before the crisis had no choice but to improve), credit constraints (liquidity-constrained firms had no choice but to cut costs), expectations about future growth (firms looking forward to recovery had an incentive to hoard labor), economic policies (countries devised policies such as Germany's *Kurzarbeit*, designed to support part-time work and keep workers employed during the recession[6]), and other factors, such as exchange rate changes (countries that experienced depreciation faced less pressure to adjust).

To get a better picture of productivity developments in the private sector, we exclude construction and the public sector from GDP and compare patterns of adjustment across countries. The reason for excluding construction is that it is a highly labor-intensive and low-productivity sector that suffered heavily in some countries. The shrinkage of construction may therefore give rise to a misleading improvement in productivity data due to a composition effect, i.e., the disappearance of construction increases average productivity of the economy even when productivity has not improved in other sectors.

Figure 11.5 shows output (at constant prices), hours worked, and the ratio of these two indicators, average productivity.

It is interesting to observe that there was a prompt and significant productivity surge in the United States—as a result of reducing labor input by more than the output fall. In Western and Northern Europe, by contrast, productivity initially fell while employment did not, which is evidence of labor hoarding. Only after a lag did productivity start to recover, but only to a level barely above the precrisis level. In Central Europe productivity started to improve from mid-2009 and the gains have been impressive. In Southern Europe

---

6. See Brenke, Rinne, and Zimmermann (2011).

Figure 11.5 Output, hours worked, and productivity in the nonconstruction business sector, 2008Q1–11Q2

a. EU groups and the United States

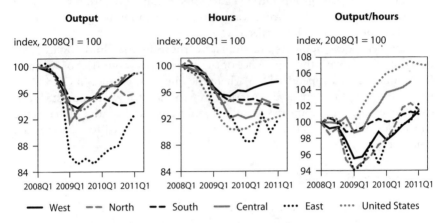

b. Best-performing EU countries

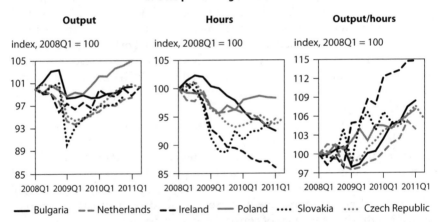

Note: Panel A shows median values. For makeup of country groups, see appendix 11A. US data are for the whole business sector.

Sources: Bruegel calculations using data from Eurostat database, Organization for Economic Cooperation and Development, and US Bureau of Labor Statistics.

the fall in output and labor input went broadly hand in hand. Productivity essentially remained flat for the group as a whole.

Interpreting these differences is not straightforward. The broad evidence is that the supply side was more damaged in Europe than in the United States, at least if one assumes that the largest part of US unemployment is cyclical. Labor hoarding by European firms seems to have resulted in lasting effects on aggregate output per hour.

There are significant variations within our groups as well. Panel B of figure 11.5 shows data for the six best-performing EU countries, most of which outperformed the United States in terms of the cumulative productivity increase in the last three years. The sharp increase in Irish productivity is remarkable and suggests a brighter growth outlook.[7] Bulgaria ranks second, followed by three Central European countries (the Czech Republic, Slovakia, and Poland) and the Netherlands.

The worst performers in terms of productivity increase are found in all regional groups. These are Greece from the South group, Romania from the East group, Hungary from the Central group, the United Kingdom from the North group, and Germany from the West group. Hungary, Romania, and the United Kingdom have floating exchange rates that depreciated in 2008–09 and have remained weak since then, which improved external competitiveness. However, Poland, another floater that benefited from an exchange rate depreciation, was among the best performers in terms of productivity increase. German firms were already highly competitive before the crisis, and weak productivity developments to date are not necessarily worrying. What is much more worrying is the weak performance of Greece, as its real overvaluation would call for major improvements.

With respect to manufacturing unit labor costs, before the crisis there was a surge in the South and the East groups but not in the other three regions (figure 11.6). Postcrisis, there is almost no adjustment in the South group, but the adjustment is impressive in the East group. In the West and North groups, after a temporary increase in 2008, unit labor costs have fallen. Ireland again is the best performer: Unit labor costs fell by 25 percent from the first quarter of 2008 to the first quarter of 2011.

Finally, another major aspect of the adjustment is the impact on external accounts. Figure 11.7 shows that there was an abrupt adjustment in the East group, due to a sudden stopping of capital inflows, but that the adjustment in the South group is slow. Private capital also stopped flowing into Southern European countries. The main reason for the lack of faster adjustment is the massive European Central Bank (ECB) support to Southern European banks, which has offset the sudden stop in private capital flows and contributed to financial stability. But at the same time, ECB financing has made it possible for these countries to delay the adjustment, as noted by Hans-Werner Sinn.[8]

---

7. Note that total economy Irish GDP fell by 10 percent between the first quarter of 2008 and 2009–10, and recovery started in 2011, but the nonconstruction business sector shown in figure 11.5 fell only by 3 percent and the recovery started in 2010.

8. Hans-Werner Sinn, "The ECB's Stealth Bailout," VoxEU, June 1, 2011, www.voxeu.org (accessed on January 29, 2012).

Figure 11.6   Unit labor cost in manufacturing, 2000Q1–2011Q1

index, 2000Q1 = 100

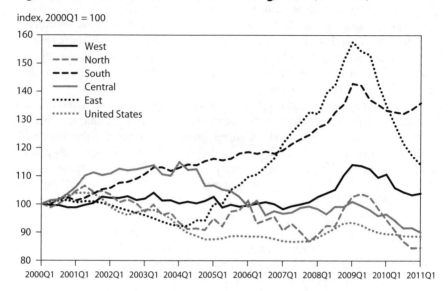

Note: Figure shows median values. For makeup of country groups, see appendix 11A.

Sources: Bruegel calculations using data from the Organization for Economic Cooperation and Development and Eurostat database.

Figure 11.7   Current account as percent of GDP, 1995–2016

percent of GDP

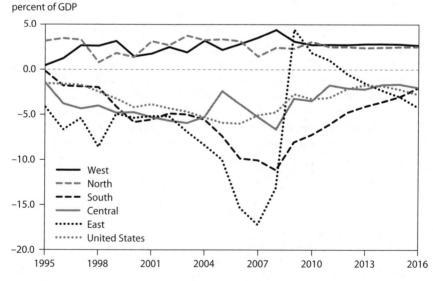

Note: Figure shows median values. For makeup of country groups, see appendix 11A.

Source: Bruegel calculations using data from IMF (2011d).

Figure 11.8   Unemployment rate, 2000–10

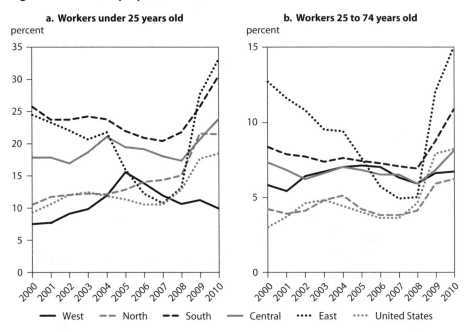

a. Workers under 25 years old

b. Workers 25 to 74 years old

— West   – – North   –– South   — Central   •••• East   ••••• United States

Note: Figures show median values. For makeup of country groups, see appendix 11A.

Source: Bruegel calculations using data from Eurostat database.

The Special Challenges of Southern Europe

The evidence presented thus far confirms that Southern European countries face special challenges. Their economic convergence has reversed, their unit labor costs have failed to improve following a steady rise in the precrisis period, and their current account deficits have hardly improved. Most Southern European countries are under heavy market pressure and face a vicious circle of low and even worsening confidence and weak economic performance. This combination necessitates a greater fiscal adjustment, which again leads to a weaker economy, thereby lowering public revenues and resulting in additional fiscal adjustment.

The social consequences of fiscal adjustment and the weaker economy make it more difficult to implement the adjustment programs and escape the vicious circle. Figure 11.8 shows that unemployment has increased, especially youth unemployment (which is also very high in the East group). Such a high youth unemployment rate is already leading to widespread frustration and the rise of anti-EU political movements.

It is interesting to contrast South group countries with Ireland, because the latter seems to have been able to avoid this vicious circle through a greater flexibility to adjust to the shock, specifically by improving competitiveness

Table 11.1   Program assumptions and recent forecasts for Greece and Ireland

Indicator	Date of forecast	2009	2010	2011	2012	2013	2014	2015
			Greece					
GDP (percent change)	May 2010	−2.0	−4.0	−2.6	1.1	2.1	2.1	2.7
	September 2011	−2.3	−4.4	−5.0	−2.0	1.5	2.3	3.0
Gross public debt as percent of GDP	May 2010	115	133	145	149	149	146	140
	September 2011	127	143	166	189	188	179	165
Budget balance as percent of GDP	May 2010	−13.6	−8.1	−7.6	−6.5	−4.8	−2.6	−2.0
	September 2011	−15.5	−10.4	−8.0	−6.9	−5.2	−2.8	−2.8
			Ireland					
GDP (percent change)	December 2010	−7.6	−0.2	0.9	1.9	2.4	3.0	3.4
	September 2011	−7.0	−0.4	0.6	1.9	2.4	2.9	3.3
Gross public debt as percent of GDP	December 2010	66	99	113	120	125	124	123
	September 2011	65	95	109	115	118	117	116
Budget balance as percent of GDP	December 2010	−14.4	−32.0	−10.5	−8.6	−7.5	−5.1	−4.8
	September 2011	−14.2	−32.0	−10.3	−8.6	−6.8	−4.4	−4.1

Sources: Greece: May 2010 projections are from IMF (2010b); September 2011 projections are from IMF (2011d) for GDP percent change and from IMF (2011e) for gross public debt as percent of GDP and budget balance as percent of GDP. Ireland: December 2010 projections are from IMF (2010c); September 2011 projections are from IMF (2011a) for GDP percent change and gross public debt as percent of GDP and from IMF (2011e) for budget balance as percent of GDP.

and unit labor costs. The fundamentals of the Irish economy, which are much better than those of the South group economies (see Darvas et al. 2011), have likely played important roles in this development. The Irish program is broadly on track (table 11.1), but the outcomes and recent forecasts for Greece are significantly worse compared with the May 2010 assumptions of the initial program.

What Should Be Done?

The European growth agenda traditionally focuses on horizontal structural reforms that have the potential to improve potential output growth. Much of this agenda is indisputable, but policymakers must also reflect on whether it is still enough. In particular, two issues deserve attention in the policy discussion: the pace and composition of fiscal adjustments, and the potential for more-active policies.

Revisiting the Europe 2020 Agenda

Against the background presented in the previous sections, what can be said of the Europe 2020 agenda?[9] Most of it clearly still makes sense. Education, research, and employment are perfectly sensible areas on which to focus in the current context, and the goals of ensuring climate-friendly and inclusive growth are also appropriate.

Implementing this agenda requires a significant stepping up of efforts. Progress so far is very uneven within the European Union. While indicators related to the five main Europe 2020 targets are readily available (see, e.g., Eurostat), in table 11.2 we construct a scoreboard, based on the methodology of IMF (2010a) and also used in Allard and Everaert (2010), that assesses the various structural indicators in 2005 and currently. These indicators do not relate to all five main Europe 2020 targets, but to certain aspects of growth that could be improved with structural reforms. In its progress with structural reforms, the North group is unsurprisingly much further ahead than the West group and, especially, the South group, which is severely lagging on all criteria. While countries under a program face very strong external pressure to reform, the main challenge is to foster improvements in countries such as Italy, which are performing poorly but are not under IMF/EU programs.

Composition of Fiscal Adjustments

The vast majority of European countries are facing major fiscal challenges. Assessments of the details vary, but for most countries reaching sustainable budgetary positions will require exceptionally large and sustained adjustments amounting to more than 10 percentage points of GDP in Greece, Ireland, Portugal, Spain, and the United Kingdom (IMF 2011e). A large number of European countries are expected to need adjustments on the order of 5 to 10 percent of GDP.

There is a broad consensus that these adjustments should be as growth friendly as possible. This implies, first, striking the right balance between revenue-based and spending-based adjustments; and second, selecting from revenue and spending measures the least detrimental to growth. Although there is no ready-made general metric to design growth-friendly adjustment packages, it is widely accepted that revenue measures tend to involve more adverse supply-side effects than spending measures; that tax measures that broaden the tax base or do not directly distort incentives to work and invest are preferable; and that spending cuts should preserve public investment in infrastructure, education, and research.

---

9. See European Commission (2011) for the Europe 2020 targets.

Table 11.2 Structural reform scoreboard

Reform area	West										North										South								Central										East											
	Austria		Belgium		France		Germany		Nether-lands		Denmark		Finland		Ireland		Sweden		UK		Greece		Italy		Portugal		Spain		Czech Republic		Hungary		Poland		Slovakia		Slovenia		Estonia		Latvia		Lithuania		Bulgaria		Romania		United States	
	Old	New	Old	New	Old	New	Old	New	Old	New	Old	New	Old	New	Old	New	Old	New	Old	New	Old	New	Old	New	Old	New	Old	New	Old	New	Old	New	Old	New	Old	New	Old	New	Old	New	Old	New	Old	New	Old	New	Old	New	Old	New
Medium term																																																		
Labor market inefficiency																																																		
Business regulation																																																		
Network regulation																																																		
Retail sector regulation																																																		
Professional services regulation																																																		
Long term																																																		
Institutions and contracts																																																		
Human capital																																																		
Infrastructure																																																		
Innovation																																																		

Legend:
- ■ Above average by more than one standard deviation
- ▨ Above average by no more than one standard deviation
- ░ Below average by no more than one standard deviation
- ▤ Below average by one to two standard deviations
- ■ Below average by more than two standard deviations

Note: The scoreboard is relative to the "advanced" OECD countries, i.e., those apart from Mexico and the Central European member states.

Source: Bruegel calculations. The new indicators are based on 2008–10 data from World Economic Forum (2011), OECD (2011), Fraser Institute, and World Bank Doing Business database. The old indicators are based on 2003–05 data from the same sources. Each indicator shown is constructed from a large number of more detailed indicators; see IMF (2010a) and Allard and Everaert (2010) for details.

These simple criteria can be used to assess the measures planned and implemented in EU countries. An appropriate starting point is a late 2010 IMF survey of country exit strategies conducted for G-20 members and a group of countries (including Greece, Ireland, Portugal, and Spain) facing exceptionally high adjustments (IMF 2010d, 2011c). This comprehensive survey suggested that virtually all countries facing medium-scale adjustment (between 5 and 10 percent of GDP starting from 2009 positions) were planning expenditure-based adjustment, whereas countries facing large-scale adjustments (above 10 percent of GDP) were relying more on mixed strategies. Interestingly, no country was planning a revenue-based adjustment. Second, most countries were envisaging structural reforms of the government sector aimed at reducing the size of the public service and limiting the growth of social transfers. Overall, cuts in public investment amounted to about one-seventh of total spending cuts. Third, planned tax measures gave priority to broadening tax bases as opposed to increasing taxes, especially in the field of direct taxation of labor and capital, and to increased consumption taxes. This was prima facie evidence of the governments' intention to make fiscal adjustment as growth friendly as possible.

The worsening conditions in government bond markets changed the course of events completely. Under increasing pressure, governments had to front-load planned measures, or even to adopt emergency measures in an attempt to meet markets' apparently insatiable demand for fiscal consolidation. The belt tightening was not limited to program countries (Greece, Ireland, and Portugal) but also extended to Italy, Spain, and France, which all approved extraordinary fiscal consolidation measures in August and September 2011.

Table 11.3 shows the composition of the recent consolidation measures. It is apparent that giving priority to growth has often given way to expediency. In all countries surveyed, recent adjustments are either mixed or revenue based. It is probable that they are also markedly growth friendly in the choice of detailed measures.

Evidence thus indicates that the growth-adverse impact of the precipitous adjustment plans being implemented in response to market strains are likely to go beyond standard Keynesian effects and also result in potentially adverse supply-side effects. This is in part unavoidable. But good intentions are of little help if they are reneged on under the pressure of events. Whereas there is no magic bullet to address this problem, at least a close monitoring of national plans within the context of the Economic and Financial Affairs Council is called for.

Growth Policy under Constraints

A key challenge for several euro area countries is how to implement growth strategies in the context of "wrong" prices. When prices perform their economic role they convey information to agents about the profitability of working or investing in various sectors; this in principle leads to socially optimal

Table 11.3   Composition of recent fiscal adjustments in selected euro area countries

Country	Program	Adjustments
Greece	Original version of IMF/EU program (May 2010)	11.1 percent GDP, of which: 47.8 percent expenditure 36 percent revenues 16.2 percent structural reforms[a]
	Reinforced Medium-Term Fiscal Strategy (June 2011)	12 percent GDP (on top of what was already implemented), of which: 52.50 percent expenditure 47.50 percent revenues
	Second emergency round (September 2011)	1.1 percent GDP (property tax on electricity-powered buildings), of which: 100 percent revenues
Portugal	IMF/EU Extended Fund Facility (May 2011)	10.6 percent GDP, of which: 67 percent expenditure 33 percent revenues
	Emergency measures due to fiscal slippages (August 2011)	1.1 percent of GDP, of which: 100 percent revenues
Spain	Emergency measures (August 2011)	0.5 percent GDP, of which: ~50 percent expenditure ~50 percent revenues
	Emergency measures (September 2011)	0.2 percent GDP, of which: 100 percent revenues
Italy	Fiscal Consolidation Package (August 2011)	3.6 percent GDP, of which: < 50 percent expenditure > 50 percent revenues
France	(August 2011)	0.6 percent of GDP, of which: > 80 percent revenues

a. In the case of Greece, in addition to direct revenue and expenditure measures, IMF (2010b) included a third category called structural reforms, which comprise lower expenditures resulting from improvements from budgetary control and processes and higher revenues due to improvements in tax administration.

Sources: IMF (2010b, 2010d, 2011a, 2011b); Greek Ministry of Finance (2011); ECB (2011); Spanish Ministry of Finance (2011a, 2011b); news reports in *Financial Times, Sole 24 Ore,* and LaVoce.info.

choices. In this context the main task of policies is to boost the supply of labor and capital and to create a level playing field for employees and firms.

Things are different, however, when prices are "wrong,"[10] which is particularly relevant in the European context because of real exchange rate misalign-

---

10. This traditionally happens when they fail to take account of externalities. Environmental costs here are a well-known example but there are other externalities, either positive (when firms contribute to knowledge) or negative (when they fail to take into account the impact of individual decisions on aggregate financial stability). In this type of context, a more hands-on approach, specifically one that includes industrial policies, can be advisable, as argued in Aghion, Boulanger, and Cohen (2011).

Figure 11.9 Real exchange rate misalignments in euro area countries in 2009 and subsequent adjustments

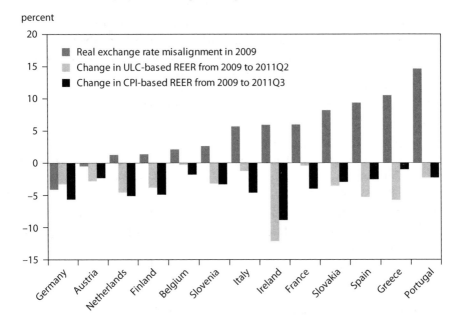

percent

Legend:
- Real exchange rate misalignment in 2009
- Change in ULC-based REER from 2009 to 2011Q2
- Change in CPI-based REER from 2009 to 2011Q3

Countries (x-axis): Germany, Austria, Netherlands, Finland, Belgium, Slovenia, Italy, Ireland, France, Slovakia, Spain, Greece, Portugal

ULC = unit labor costs
REER = real effective exchange rate
CPI = consumer price index

Sources: Bruegel calculations using data from European Commission (2010) for misalignment and European Central Bank for real effective exchange rate. Data on the ULC-based exchange rate of Portugal are from Eurostat database and available only through 2010Q4.

ments within the euro area and in countries in a fixed exchange rate regime. Countries that experienced major domestic demand expansion in the first 10 years of Economic and Monetary Union must reallocate capital and labor to the traded good sector in spite of a still overvalued real exchange rate. Without policy-driven incentives, private decisions are likely to lead to suboptimal factor allocation in this sector, ultimately hampering growth.

Figure 11.9 gives European Commission (2010) estimates of real exchange rate misalignments in the euro area for 2009—the latest available estimate—and the changes in real effective exchange rates since then. The figures presented for the misalignment are the average of two measures, one based on current account norms and the other based on the stabilization of the net foreign asset positions. Estimates for 2009 provide lower misalignment than estimates for 2008, so we are erring on the side of caution. What is apparent is that significant misalignments prevail, because the real depreciation from 2009 to mid-2011 in the most overvalued countries (except Ireland) was limited and broadly similar to or less than the depreciation in Germany, the biggest euro area country that already had an undervalued real exchange rate in 2009. Real exchange rate misalignments result in meaningful distortions in private decisions.

Furthermore, the correction of these imbalances is exceedingly slow. In the previous section we looked at the evolution of unit labor costs and concluded that with the exception of Ireland, correction has barely started. The persistence of inadequate prices is bound to be detrimental to efficient capital accumulation and to weigh on potential output growth.

In this context policies that help correct distortions are an integral part of the growth agenda. Such policies may involve

- product and labor market reforms (i.e., improvements in several areas assessed in table 11.2) that increase the responsiveness of the wage-price system to market disequilibria and help bring about the required correction in relative prices;

- tax-based internal devaluations that foster an adjustment in relative prices;

- temporary wage-price subsidies or tax breaks targeted at the traded goods sector that help restore competitiveness; and

- industrial policy measures such as sectoral subsidies that favor accumulation in certain sectors.

EU/IMF-sponsored adjustment programs in Greece, Portugal, and Spain include structural components, some of which include some of the measures listed above. In the context of heightened bond market tensions the focus of policymakers' attention tends to be budgetary consolidation. Growth will return, however, only if the structural agenda is given sufficient weight and if means are mobilized to support it. In countries that benefit from Structural Funds, especially Greece and Portugal, where they are sizeable, we follow Marzinotto (2011) and advocate temporary reallocations to support the growth and competitiveness aspects of the programs. Examples of growth-friendly policies that could be supported through this channel include credit for small and medium enterprises and temporary wage subsidies aimed at restoring competitiveness.

Conclusions

In this chapter we revisited the European growth issue in the light of recent developments. We agree with the World Bank (Gill and Raiser 2011) that Europe can build on its past achievements, but we emphasize that it cannot afford to remain complacent about its recent and current economic performance. For most of the continent, business-as-usual policies are likely to deliver insufficient growth to ensure the viability of the social model, which is in any case under threat because of aging populations. The challenge of reviving growth is heightened by the deteriorating performance of Southern Europe and the very limited, or even disappointing, adjustment these countries were able to achieve during the last three years. The single most remarkable success of the European Union, its ability to foster convergence, is under threat. In "new Europe," convergence is still happening, but it should be strengthened.

On this basis our main policy conclusions are these:

- The growth agenda is of paramount importance in the current context. The Polish EU presidency should be commended for having selected it as a priority, and the detailed proposals in Polish Presidency (2011) should be considered seriously.

- The Europe 2020 agenda remains broadly appropriate, but its governance should be improved to achieve more rapid progress on structural reform in countries that are under threat of falling behind, making use of the new instruments embodied in the European semester;[11] structural reforms in general, and reforms of product and labor markets in particular, are of paramount importance, especially in countries with weak scores and over-valued real exchange rates.

- Tax-based internal devaluations, temporary wage-price subsidies, or tax breaks could help restore competitiveness.

- The European Union should urgently speed up the reallocation of Structural and Cohesion Funds in countries under program to support growth and competitiveness; there may be a general political will for these, but action is lacking. Special legislation is needed to turn principles into swift action.

- The proposals for issuing "European project bonds" by the European Commission or increasing the capacity of the European Investment Bank (EIB) in order to fund investment throughout Europe should be considered and implemented.

- The growth agenda needs to be put in context. It is of little use to set objectives for the medium term if governments depart from them under the pressure of events. The composition of fiscal adjustments is a case in point in this respect.

- The policy tool kit should be broadened to include policies that help direct resources to the traded goods sectors in a situation when prices give inadequate signals to economic agents. This implies a more hands-on approach, including to industrial policies, than under the traditional agenda.

Europe is so integrated that domestic measures may not be sufficient to restore growth in particular countries when the rest of the European Union is sinking, even when supported by EU-level initiatives. The euro area's lingering sovereign debt and banking crisis is the most important factor in driving confidence down, even in those countries where fiscal sustainability has not been questioned. There is a negative feedback loop between the crisis and growth, and without effective solutions to deal with the crisis, growth is unlikely to resume.

---

11. See an assessment of the first European semester in Hallerberg, Marzinotto, and Wolff (2011).

Appendix 11A
Country Groups

Precrisis developments, current difficulties, and prospects vary widely across EU countries. To simplify matters, we define five major groups, named according to the cardinal points, and discuss the diverse challenges along them.

West: Austria, Belgium, France, Germany, and the Netherlands
South: Greece, Italy, Portugal, and Spain
North: Denmark, Finland, Sweden, Ireland, and the United Kingdom
Central: Czech Republic, Hungary, Poland, Slovakia, and Slovenia
East: Estonia, Latvia, Lithuania, Bulgaria, and Romania

We leave aside the three least populous EU countries, Luxembourg, Cyprus, and Malta, because they have some unique features and do not fit well in our groups. To control for relative sizes, we use medians for each country group.

Certainly, our groups are heterogeneous. For example, Ireland faces different challenges than does Sweden, and more generally the Scandinavian and Anglo-Saxon economic and social models are different. Yet the North group countries share similarities, such as good governance indicators and low structural reform gaps (see table 11.2). These countries were also affected worse by the initial phase of the crisis than countries in our West group, before bouncing back faster (figure 11A.1).

Figure 11A.1 GDP growth in EU-15 countries, 2007–13

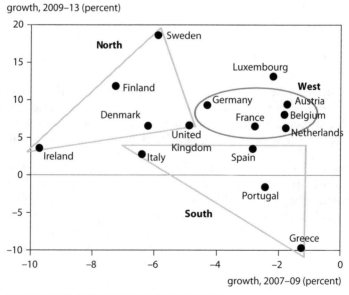

Sources: Bruegel calculations using data from IMF (2011d).

The countries that joined the EU in 2004–07 are also heterogeneous. But by analyzing in detail their growth model, presented in Becker et al. (2010), we came to the conclusion that the five Central European countries had developments remarkably different from countries in the East group (the three Baltic countries, Bulgaria, and Romania) and that their challenges also differ.

For comparison, in some figures we also show data for the United States, China, and a group of 14 countries from Asia and Latin America (not including China and India).

Asia and Latin America 14: Six countries from Asia—Indonesia, Korea, Malaysia, Philippines, Taiwan, and Thailand; and eight from Latin America—Argentina, Brazil, Chile, Colombia, Ecuador, Mexico, Peru, and Uruguay.

References

Abiad, Abdul, Giovanni Dell'Ariccia, and Bin Li. 2011. *Creditless Recoveries*. IMF Working Paper WP/11/58. Washington: International Monetary Fund.

Aghion, Phillipe, Julian Boulanger, and Elie Cohen. *2011. Rethinking Industrial Policy*. Bruegel Policy Brief 2011/04. Brussels: Bruegel.

Allard, Celine, and Luc Everaert. 2010. *Lifting Euro Area Growth: Priorities for Structural Reforms and Governance*. IMF Staff Position Note 10/19. Washington: International Monetary Fund.

Becker, Torbjorn, Daniel Daianu, Zsolt Darvas, Vladimir Gligorov, Michael A. Landesmann, Pavle Petrović, Jean Pisani-Ferry, Dariusz K. Rosati, André Sapir, and Beatrice Weder di Mauro. 2010. *Whither Growth in Central and Western Europe? Policy Lessons for an Integrated Europe*. Bruegel Blueprint 11. Brussels: Bruegel.

Blanchard, Olivier. 2004. *The Economic Future of Europe*. NBER Working Paper 10310. Cambridge, MA: National Bureau of Economic Research.

Brenke, Karl, Ulf Rinne, and Klaus F. Zimmermann. 2011. *Short-Time Work: The German Answer to the Great Recession*. CEPR Discussion Paper 8449. London: Center for Economic Policy Research.

Darvas, Zsolt. 2011. Growing Without Credit. Bruegel, Brussels. Photocopy.

Darvas, Zsolt, Christophe Gouardo, Jean Pisani-Ferry, and André Sapir. 2011. *A Comprehensive Approach to the Euro-Area Debt Crisis: Background Estimates*. Bruegel Working Paper 2011/05. Brussels: Bruegel.

ECB (European Central Bank). 2011. *Monthly Bulletin* (September). Frankfurt.

European Commission. 2007. *Economic Forecast, Autumn 2007 (European Economy 7/2007)*. Brussels.

European Commission. 2010. *Surveillance of Intra-Euro-Area Competitiveness and Imbalances (European Economy 1/2010)*. Brussels.

European Commission. 2011. *Europe 2020*. Brussels. Available at http://ec.europa.eu.

Gill, Indermit, and Martin Raiser. 2011. *Golden Growth: Restoring the Lustre of the European Growth Model*. Washington: World Bank.

Greek Ministry of Finance. 2011. *Greece, Medium-Term Fiscal Strategy 2012–2015*. Athens. Available at www.minfin.gr.

Hallerberg, Mark, Benedicta Marzinotto, and Guntram B. Wolff. 2011. *How Effective and Legitimate Is the European Semester? Increasing the Role of the European Parliament*. Bruegel Working Paper 2011/09 Brussels: Bruegel.

IMF (International Monetary Fund). 2007. *World Economic Outlook* (October). Washington.

IMF (International Monetary Fund). 2010a. *Cross-Cutting Themes in Employment Experiences During the Crisis*. Report prepared by the Strategy, Policy, and Review Department. Washington.

IMF (International Monetary Fund). 2010b *Greece: Staff Report on Request for Stand-By Arrangement.* Washington.

IMF (International Monetary Fund). 2010c. *Ireland: Request for an Extended Arrangement—Staff Report, Staff Supplement, Staff Statement, and Press Release on the Executive Board Discussion.* Washington.

IMF (International Monetary Fund). 2010d. *A Status Update on Fiscal Exit Strategy.* IMF Working Paper WP/10/272. Washington.

IMF (International Monetary Fund). 2011a. *Ireland: Third Review Under the Extended Arrangement— Staff Report.* Washington.

IMF (International Monetary Fund). 2011b. *Regional Economic Outlook 2011: Europe.* Washington.

IMF (International Monetary Fund). 2011c. *Portugal: Request for a Three-Year Arrangement Under the EFF.* Washington.

IMF (International Monetary Fund). 2011d. *World Economic Outlook* (September). Washington.

IMF (International Monetary Fund). 2011e. *Fiscal Monitor* (September). Washington.

Marzinotto, Benedicta. 2011. *A European Fund for Economic Revival in Crisis Countries.* Bruegel Policy Contribution 2011/01. Brussels: Bruegel.

McKinsey Global Institute. 2010. *Debt and Deleveraging: The Global Credit Bubble and Its Economic Consequences* (January). McKinsey and Company.

OECD (Organization for Economic Cooperation and Development). 2007. *OECD Economic Outlook,* volume 2007/2, no. 82. Paris.

OECD (Organization for Economic Cooperation and Development). 2011. *Going for Growth.* Paris. Available at www.oecd.org.

Polish Presidency. 2011. *Towards a European Consensus on Growth.* Report of the Polish Presidency of the Council of the European Union. Warsaw.

Reinhart, Carmen M., and Kenneth Rogoff. 2011. *Decade of Debt.* NBER Working Paper 16827. Cambridge, MA: National Bureau of Economic Research.

Reinhart, Carmen M., Jacob F. Kirkegaard, and M. Belén Sbrancia. 2011. Financial Repression Redux. *Finance & Development* 48, no. 1 (June): 22–26.

Reinhart, Carmen M., and M. Belén Sbrancia. 2011. *The Liquidation of Government Debt.* NBER Working Paper 16893. Cambridge, MA: National Bureau of Economic Research.

Sapir, André, Philippe Aghion, Giuseppe Bertola, Martin Hellwig, Jean Pisani-Ferry, Dariusz Rosati, and José Viñals. 2004. *An Agenda for a Growing Europe: The Sapir Report.* New York: Oxford University Press.

Spanish Ministry of Finance. 2011a. *Additional Austerity Measures August 2011.* Available at www.thespanisheconomy.com.

Spanish Ministry of Finance. 2011b. *Nota de Prensa: El Gobierno aprueba la recuperación del gravamen del Impuesto de Patrimonio.* (September). Available at www.meh.es.

World Economic Forum. 2011. *The Global Competitiveness Report 2011–2012.* Geneva.

12

Challenges to Economic Recovery in the United States and Europe

MICHAEL MUSSA

After a quarter century of generally moderate economic growth, interrupted by only relatively mild recessions, the United States and Western Europe suffered their most severe economic contractions of the postwar era during the great global recession of 2008–09. Thanks to the strong performances of most emerging-market and developing countries, the subsequent recovery has been moderately vigorous for the world economy on average, even though it has been notably sluggish and disappointing for most of the advanced economies. This chapter will examine the reasons for the sluggish recoveries so far in the United States and Western Europe and the prospects for their economic growth looking forward.

I will take a medium-term perspective on growth prospects—the next 5 to 10 years covering both the United States and Western Europe, with somewhat more emphasis on the United States. Issues of short-term macroeconomic policy management and factors underlying long-term economic growth will get some attention, insofar as they are relevant to economic performance over the medium term. For Western Europe, the main focus will be on the euro area. The United Kingdom will get some attention, as it provides a useful contrast with countries in the euro area. Sweden and Switzerland will also get brief mention primarily for the same reason.

The main conclusion of this chapter is that both the United States and most of Western Europe, especially the euro area, face significant and persis-

Michael Mussa (1944–2012) was a senior fellow at the Peterson Institute for International Economics from 2001 to 2012. He served as economic counselor and director of the Department of Research at the International Monetary Fund from 1991 to 2001.

tent problems in significantly and rapidly reducing large existing margins of slack and in restoring their economies to growth paths similar to those that prevailed on average for the quarter century before the Great Recession. There are important similarities between the problems facing the United States and the euro area, notably in the need for medium-term fiscal consolidation, but there are also important differences. In particular, wide disparities in the economic problems faced by different euro area members, the constraints implied by a unified currency, and the absence of other powerful policy instruments to address regional disparities make the achievement of adequate medium-term economic growth especially difficult. I do not have a magical solution for these difficulties; they exist and to a considerable extent will need to be endured.

More generally, I will argue that sound economic policies can play only a limited role in improving medium-term growth prospects, in either the United States or Western Europe—although it is always possible for bad policy to make matters worse. Central banks must still act to help potential financial crises, but there is little room for traditional monetary policy (or quantitative easing) to affect the course of economic activity; and, at some point within the medium term, monetary policies will need to move to significantly less accommodative stances. The public deficit and debt situations of the United States and most West European countries do not permit significant and sustained fiscal easing to promote economic expansion, and in many countries the immediate and continuing priority is fiscal consolidation. Structural reforms are often touted as the third and critical tool for promoting noninflationary growth. No doubt, such reforms could be quite helpful in some cases. However, after 30 years of listening to and participating in discussions of structural reform, I remain skeptical about how much can be accomplished, and how well, to boost meaningful growth in either the United States or Western Europe.

Recent Histories of Comparatively Sluggish Economic Growth

To set the stage for the discussion and establish some benchmarks for what might normally be expected for growth in the United States and Western Europe, it is useful to examine key data concerning the economic performance in the period from 1999 through 2007, preceding the Great Recession; see table 12.1. This nine-year period is selected because statistics for the euro area are conveniently available starting in 1999 and because the business cycles in the United States and Western Europe were at similar stages at the beginning and end of this period.[1] The two key conclusions from this examination are

---

1. It makes virtually no difference if the 10-year period from 1998 through 2007 is used. Similarly, the expansion of the euro area after 1999 to include five small countries (Greece, Cyprus, Malta, Slovakia, and Slovenia) makes no appreciable difference for growth of the area as a whole.

Table 12.1 Real growth and unemployment rates for the United States and Europe (percent)

Country/economy	Real GDP growth (annual average rate, 1999–2007)	Unemployment rate	
		1999	2007
United States	2.8	4.2	4.6
United Kingdom	2.8	4.1	2.7
Euro area	2.2	9.3	7.6
Germany	1.6	10.5	7.8
France	2.2	10.4	7.8
Italy	1.5	10.6	6.1
Spain	3.6	15.9	8.3

that (1) growth rates in this nine-year period were not particularly impressive by postwar standards, and (2) except for the United States, unemployment rates declined over the period, suggesting that growth rates of potential GDP were somewhat lower than growth rates of actual real GDP.

With this as background, experiences in the Great Recession of 2008–09 and the initial stages of recovery through end-2010 are discussed, and developments in different countries and regions compared and contrasted. The general observation is that all countries suffered deep recessions, and recoveries were generally disappointing in their initial stages, but that there were some meaningful differences in the depth and timing of recessions and in the early pace of recoveries. For most countries, sluggishness in the initial stages of recoveries reflects factors that are likely to keep future growth rates relatively low.

Medium-Term Prospects for the US Economy

Recoveries that followed deep US recessions earlier in the postwar era (1957–58, 1973–75, and 1980–82) were typically quite vigorous, especially in their early stages. The recovery from the combined recessions of 1980–82 is particularly noteworthy in this regard. During the six quarters from the beginning of 1983 to the middle of 1984, real GDP rebounded at a 7.5 percent average annual rate and by almost 12 percent cumulatively. During this period the civilian unemployment rate fell from a postwar high of 10.7 percent to 7.2 percent. By the end of 1988, after six years of expansion, real GDP was up cumulatively by almost one-third and the unemployment rate had fallen to one-half of its peak level.

The recovery from the Great Recession of 2008–09 has been very sluggish by these earlier standards. After a sharp drop of 5 percent from its level at the end of 2007, real GDP began to recover in the summer of 2009. This was sooner than most forecasters had anticipated at the start of that year, including many who feared that the recession would continue to deepen well into 2010. Even for the relative optimists (like myself), however, the pace of the recovery since mid-2009 has been disappointingly slow. At the top end of all forecasters, I had anticipated that annualized real GDP growth during the first six quarters of the present recovery would average 4 percent, barely half of the pace in the initial six quarters of the Reagan recovery. Current estimates place real GDP growth at only a 3 percent annual rate over this period, and real GDP growth for the first half of 2011 is estimated at only a meager 0.7 percent annual rate.

For employment, the story is even more discouraging. During the recession, employment fell by even more than would normally be expected from the decline in real GDP, by 8.8 million (according to the Establishment Survey) from December 2007 to March 2010. The unemployment rate almost doubled, from 5.3 percent in December 2007 to a peak of 10.1 percent in October 2009. In the recovery so far, employment is up by 1.9 million from its low, and the unemployment rate is now running at 9.1 percent. Initially, the recovery of employment seemed somewhat sluggish in view of the sluggish recovery of output, but the results for the first half of 2011 show moderate employment growth despite exceptionally sluggish output growth. In related developments, estimates of labor productivity growth have turned negative in 2011 and unit labor costs have shown significant increases.

Growth of US Aggregate Demand

Many of the reasons why the present recovery has been so sluggish are reasonably well understood and have implications for the likely continued sluggishness over the medium term. Before turning to the reasons for sluggishness, however, it is useful to mention factors that weigh in the other direction.

Inventory investment has already staged its usual cyclical bounce-back from sharply negative to moderately positive levels. Further significant contributions to aggregate demand growth from this factor may not be expected. Also on the plus side, business investment in equipment and software has recovered fairly strongly in accord with its usual cyclical pattern, and further contributions to demand growth from such investment may reasonably be expected so long as overall economic growth remains at least moderately positive. Investment in nonresidential structures has, as usual, lagged in the initial stages of recovery, but may be expected to pick up again as the recovery proceeds, aided by a low cost of capital. US exports have grown strongly as volumes of world trade bounced back from very large declines during the global recession.

US imports have also increased during the recovery, but the rise in exports has been sufficiently strong that the deterioration of real net exports subtracted only one-quarter of a percentage point from real GDP growth—significantly less than in most US recoveries. The competitive foreign exchange value of the US dollar, along with continued fairly strong growth in key emerging-market economies, will support US export growth. Meanwhile, continued subdued growth of domestic demand will slow growth of imports relative to what normally happens during a US economic expansion. The result will likely be that US real net exports will deteriorate less than in past expansions, implying less of a drag on US real GDP growth, and retarding the reemergence of one of the important imbalances that characterized past expansions.

Turning to factors that have retarded the recovery, consumption spending has grown quite slowly in the present expansion. During the expansion from 2001 through 2002, consumption spending was boosted (beyond gains in disposable income) by rising household net worth, especially that coming from rising home prices—which doubled in real terms between 2001 and their peak in mid-2006. The drop in home prices since their peak (mainly during the recession) has reversed two-thirds of their earlier unsustainable increase. The decline in this important component of household net worth, along with more moderate declines in equity values, has weighed down consumption and helped to prompt an increase in household saving rates from about 2 percent just before the recession to 5 to 6 percent recently.

Looking ahead, it may be anticipated that consumption spending will rise as GDP rises but at a somewhat lower percentage rate, implying that the ratio of consumption to GDP will decline at a modest pace. Home prices are unlikely to rise significantly and the value of other components of household net worth will probably not rise sufficiently rapidly to drive increases in the ratio of consumption to disposable income. The old practice of extracting equity from homes through mortgage refinancing in order to support consumption spending will not revive any time soon. Meanwhile, household disposable income will rise more slowly than GDP because governments will be increasing tax collections and reducing transfer payments as part of their efforts to reestablish fiscal sustainability.

The collapse of the housing bubble has also been reflected in the depression of residential investment, which fell by 57 percent from its peak at end-2005 to mid-2009. Moreover, unlike past recessions that have seen strong rebounds of residential investment in their initial stages, the present recovery has featured no such rebound. Indeed, at mid-2011, two years after the general recession trough, real residential investment was off by a further 3 percent. In comparison, during the combined recessions of the early 1980s, real residential investment fell by 42 percent from its peak in late 1978 to the end of 1982, and then over the next two years recovered 85 percent of the ground lost.[2]

The prolonged depression of residential investment in the present recovery reflects primarily the consequence of the bubble in house prices and its subsequent collapse—developments that were not a significant feature of earlier boom and bust cycles of residential investment at the national level. The drop in home prices since mid-2006 (by about one-third, according to the

---

2. I place the trough of the recession of the early 1980s in the fourth quarter of 1982. This is consistent with the dating of the cyclical trough in November 1982 and with original estimates that real GDP (in 1972 dollars) fell between the third and fourth quarters of 1982. Later estimates of real GDP (using different bases for real dollars) generally show a small increase in real GDP between the third and fourth quarters of 1982. In accord with the usual cyclical pattern the peak for residential investment came significantly before the general peak in economic activity preceding the 1980 recession.

Case-Shiller index) left millions of homeowners with mortgage debt greater than the value of their properties. This, together with the rise of unemployment and drop in incomes associated with the recession, led to widespread defaults and to foreclosures and threatened foreclosures on a scale not seen since the Great Depression of the 1930s. Significant reductions in mortgage interest costs engineered by the Federal Reserve and by the Treasury through its control of the mortgage giants Fannie Mae and Freddie Mac have been unable to propel recovery in the housing market as would otherwise have been expected. Other official efforts to ease problems for distressed homeowners have enjoyed only modest success.

All of this is painful and costly to the millions caught up in the housing crisis, including the holders of mortgages on distressed properties. There was, however, no viable alternative to most of this pain and cost once the housing bubble had been inflated. House prices needed to decline substantially to realistic levels, and the process of foreclosure, with all of its inefficiency and messiness, is the principal means available to deal with situations where homeowners are unable to meet their mortgage commitments. On the whole, it is positive that this necessary correction is occurring much more rapidly during the present episode in the United States than during a similar necessary correction in Japan in the 1990s. Nevertheless, the correction in the United States still has a considerable distance to go and it will be a burden on recovery of residential investment for some years to come.

That said, it is important not to be too gloomy about the contribution that recovery of residential investment can make to overall recovery in the medium term. At the present rate of about 600,000 units per year, new home building is barely sufficient to keep up with the rate of depreciation of units out of the existing housing stock. Normally, formation of new independent households adds 1.0 to 1.2 million per year to demand for the housing stock. During the Great Recession, this situation reversed as economic pressures led some independent households to combine (e.g., young adults moving back in with their parents) and some households that would ordinarily have separated not to do so. As economic conditions gradually improve, we may expect the number of independent households to resume growing, thereby absorbing homes presently vacant and adding to the demand for new housing units. Looking ahead six to eight years, it is reasonable to expect that annual new home building will recover to 1.5 to 1.8 million units, although perhaps not to the peak of over 2 million in 2005. This would add about 3 percentage points to aggregate demand (plus any multiplier effects).

As US households slow their own consumption, their demand for government services (such as permits, approvals, and safety rulings) is decreasing. This is a key force behind the continuing downward pressure on expenditures and employment in state and local governments. During the first two years of recovery, increased transfers from the federal government have helped to blunt the decline in state and local spending, but these transfers are eroding and will erode further in the context of efforts to reduce the federal deficit.

Purchases of goods and services by the federal government, including those for national security, will likely be on a downward path under the pressures for substantial deficit reduction.

During the long expansion from late 1982 to the summer of 1990, real government purchases rose by 31 percent, making a significant contribution to aggregate demand growth during that expansion. During the long expansion from early 1991 through 2000, pressures for deficit reduction helped to contain the cumulative rise in real government purchases to 11.7 percent. In the present expansion, the most recent GDP data indicate that real government purchases reached a peak (for total government and separately for federal and state and local) in mid-2010 and have been declining for the past year. Such declines will probably continue for a while, but in the medium term we are likely to see a resumption of positive growth, at least in the state and local sector. Nevertheless, it is reasonable to project that growth rate of government purchases over the medium term will be less than 1 percent and possibly not much greater than zero.

In sum, looking at the forces driving growth of aggregate demand over the medium term, it seems extremely unlikely that the present expansion could match the 4.2 percent annual growth rate of the long expansion from late 1982 through the summer of 1990, or even match the 3.6 percent average annual growth rate of the long expansion from early 1991 through 2000. Indeed, even a projection of average annual real GDP growth of 3 percent over an expansion lasting another six to eight years seems a little on the optimistic side.

The simple arithmetic supporting this conclusion works out as follows: If real GDP is growing at 3 percent per year, then it is reasonable to suppose (consistent with a gradually declining share of consumption) that real consumption spending would rise at 2.5 percent per year. This implies that consumption would contribute 1.9 percent per year to aggregate demand growth. Real government purchases rising on average at a very sluggish 0.5 percent annual rate contribute 0.1 percent to aggregate demand growth. With an eventual recovery in residential investment, it is reasonable to suppose that real fixed investment would rise at an annual average rate of 8 percent over the medium term. This implies a contribution of 1 percent to the annual growth rate of aggregate demand. With inventory investment making no net contribution, all this would imply aggregate demand growth of 3 percent per year—assuming that real net exports remained flat. Powerful export growth might achieve this latter result, but a more plausible assumption is that real net exports would subtract a modest amount from annual average aggregate demand growth.

Behavior of US Aggregate Supply

Consideration must also be given to likely developments on the supply side of the US economy. This involves assessments of (1) the size of the present output gap (the difference between potential output and actual output result-ing from underutilization of productive resources), (2) possible restraints on or enhancements to the speed at which the output gap might be closed, and (3) the underlying rate of potential output growth implied by trend labor force growth and by the rate of productivity increase.

The large declines in output and employment during the Great Recession and their subsequent very sluggish recoveries would normally suggest a large remaining output gap. In other words, there should be a great deal of room for the US economy to expand in response to rising demand, without raising concerns about supply constraints and associated increases in inflation pres-sures. Unfortunately, there are significant problems on the supply side of the US economy that work against this normal expectation, implying that the continued likely sluggishness of the US expansion is not exclusively a problem of weak demand growth.

These supply-side problems include the mismatch between the skills of workers who are unemployed (or have left the labor force and would normally plan to return) and the skill needs in areas where the US economy will now be expanding. Most prominent in this regard is the displacement of large num-bers of construction workers. Employment for construction workers (season-ally adjusted) peaked at 7.72 million in early 2007 and was down modestly to 7.49 million by December 2007. It fell to 6 million during the recession (to June 2009) and has subsequently fallen by 470,000. In comparison, total employment, which was 138.0 million at the start of the recession, fell to a low of 129.2 million in early 2010, and has subsequently recovered by 1.9 mil-lion. Thus, out of a total employment decline of 6.7 million from the start of recession to date, fully one-third (2.2 million) is accounted for by construction workers—a sector that accounted for only 5.7 percent of total employment at the start of the recession.

The loss of jobs in the construction sector varies considerably across sub-sectors. Employment in residential construction (including specialty trades) has fallen 42 percent from its peak of 3.4 million in 2007. Employment in con-struction of nonresidential buildings (including specialty trades) has fallen 21 percent from its peak of 3.6 million in 2008 to date. Employment in heavy construction and civil engineering has fallen 15.5 percent from its peak during 2008 to date (including a small gain over the past year).

This subsector breakdown is important because many construction work-ers are fairly highly skilled and highly paid and are not especially mobile across subsectors. The carpenters, electricians, painters, plasterers, and plumbers who predominate in residential construction are not the same as the steel workers and crane operators who erect tall buildings or the heavy equipment operators used in civil engineering projects. A key policy implication is that while federal financing to help support public investments by state and local governments have been effective in reducing job losses among some categories of construc-tion workers (especially in heavy construction and civil engineering), they do not provide a useful solution for many construction workers who are no longer

Table 12.2   Employment for US adults 25 years and older, by educational attainment

Education level	December 2007	December 2008	December 2010	June 2011
Less than high school				
Number employed (thousands)	11,358	10,144	9,963	9,768
Unemployment rate (percent)	7.6	15.3	15.3	14.3
High school only				
Number employed (thousands)	37,034	33,649	34,465	33,863
Unemployment rate (percent)	4.7	10.5	9.8	10.0
Some college				
Number employed (thousands)	34,924	33,560	33,821	33,708
Unemployment rate (percent)	3.7	9.0	8.1	8.4
BA degree or higher				
Number employed (thousands)	43,476	43,707	44,095	44,894
Unemployment rate (percent)	2.2	5.0	4.8	4.4

employed. General recovery of employment in construction will need to await recovery of private investment in residential and nonresidential structures—a process that will take considerable time.

Another noteworthy feature of the employment situation in the United States is the distribution of employment losses among workers with different levels of educational attainment. Data on this subject, as reported in table 12.2, come from the Household Survey and refer to adult workers 25 years of age and older. Comparing the situation today with that on the eve of the Great Recession, it is notable that employment for those with a college degree or higher has risen by 3.3 percent, while employment in less-educated categories is down significantly (by 3.5 percent for those with some college, by 8.6 percent for those with only a high school degree, and by 13.1 percent for those with less than a high school education). Unemployment rates are up for all levels of educational attainment, but at 4.4 percent the rate for those with a bachelor's degree or higher suggests that margins of slack are moderate. In contrast, unemployment rates of 8.4 percent, 10.0 percent, and 14.3 percent for the other three groups (in descending order of educational attainment) indicate that most of the labor market slack is among such workers.

These facts raise three related concerns. First, as the US economy recovers and the aggregate demand for labor rises, shortages may develop in supplies of highly educated workers, while substantial slack remains for those less well educated. This will tend to constrain the pace of expansion. Second, as total employment expands with reemployment of the unemployed and those who have left the labor force, the productivity of the workers who are added is likely to be lower on average than that of those already employed. This will tend to lower overall labor productivity growth and hence the potential growth rate of the economy. Third, holding wages constant, slower labor productivity growth implies direct upward pressure on unit labor costs. Also, the quest to employ more-educated workers will likely place upward pressures on wages for such workers, adding to upward pressures on unit labor costs. And all of these problems will likely be exacerbated by the deterioration in work skills often associated with prolonged unemployment, as well as by the unusual impediments to geographic labor mobility arising from the housing crisis.

Economic policies can help to address some of these supply-side concerns, but one should not expect a great deal in this regard. Workers need to adapt to the changing needs of employers, and employers need to provide training or adapt work demands to take account of the skills of the available labor force. These processes have been ongoing throughout the history of the US economy, and in general they have functioned effectively to align worker skills with job requirements. The displacement of large numbers of workers during the Great Recession and the transformation of the US economy under way in the present expansion obviously put greater than normal strain on these essential adjustment processes. But the existing mechanisms (which involve substantial government involvement especially at the state and local levels) will continue to function and may be expected to perform reasonably well.

The policy issue is, What else might usefully be done? The usual recommendation is more federal programs to retrain unemployed workers for jobs in the expanding areas of the economy. Unfortunately, the history of federal programs to train the unemployed (extending back to the 1960s) is not a very happy one. Part of the reason probably is that those who are most likely to benefit from retraining seek and obtain it through other means, leaving the federal programs with those for whom retraining is least likely to be successful.

Supply-side concerns also have important implications for the usefulness of demand-side policies, especially monetary policy. The Federal Reserve eased monetary policy aggressively and appropriately to combat the Great Recession and the financial panic of late 2008 and early 2009. Fears that low core inflation might turn into deflation and concern about the sluggish pace of recovery motivated further easing in the QE2 operation (second quantitative easing) begun in the autumn of 2010. More recently, the Federal Reserve has indicated its intention to keep the federal funds rate near zero at least to the middle of 2013 and has announced measures to lengthen the maturity of its holdings of US Treasury obligations. In taking these latest actions the Fed has taken the view that, although core inflation has recently risen to near its implicit target, large margins of slack and continued sluggish recovery imply that inflation is unlikely to accelerate to a worrying rate any time soon. Supply-side developments raise questions about the wisdom of this policy.

Weakness in residential investment, which has been a key impediment to more rapid recovery, has not responded as it has in the past to monetary easing because of the structural problems in the housing sector. Further monetary easing is unlikely to provide much stimulus through residential investment for the same reason. Other components of aggregate demand have typically not been very responsive to movements in interest rates, suggesting that there is little that further monetary easing can contribute to enhanced output and employment growth. On the other hand, problems with aggregate supply may mean that significant inflationary pressures are nearer at hand than models relating inflation primarily to the output gap would suggest. Indeed, over the past year, the core inflation rate has picked up from under 1 percent to nearly 2 percent despite a continued large margin of slack—contradicting directly the model of inflation used by the Federal Reserve. Clearly, the output gap does not always dominate the determination of the inflation rate (or changes in the inflation rate). Perhaps the downturn of labor productivity and the increase in unit labor costs during the first half of 2011 have something to do with the rise in core inflation. If so, we may be seeing early evidence that supply-side concerns will constrain monetary policy.

Supply-side issues reinforce the earlier conclusion that the pace of growth of the US economy over the medium term is likely to be significantly more sluggish than during the long expansions of 1982–90 and 1991–2000. Specifically, consideration of demand-side factors suggests that if the recovery is sustained over the next six to eight years, we might reasonably expect an annual real GDP growth rate of a little below 3 percent.

Supply-side considerations suggest that we might reasonably expect annual employment growth of 1.6 percent per year, about half from the increase in the working-age population and about half from reemployment of the unemployed and of those who have left the labor force. Over eight years, this would be consistent with a rise of almost 19 million in (the Household Survey measure of) employment and with a gradual reduction of the unemployment rate to about 5 percent.

Problems on the supply side of the economy suggest that labor productivity growth will be more sluggish than in recent expansions. Specifically, in the expansion from 1982 to 1990, overall labor productivity defined as the ratio of real GDP to total (household) employment increased at a 1.7 percent average annual rate. During the expansion from 1991 through 2000, this measure of labor productivity advanced at a 2.1 percent average annual rate. During the expansion from 2001 through 2007, labor productivity advanced at a 1.5 percent rate. In view of the supply-side problems already discussed, it is plausible to suppose that if the present expansion survives for another six to eight years, labor productivity will advance at a 1.2 percent average annual rate. This implies that potential GDP would rise at about a 2 percent annual rate—given by the sum of normal labor force growth and labor productivity growth. The implied growth rate of aggregate supply, which includes the effect of a declining output gap, would be 2.8 percent. Thus the story told about aggregate supply over the medium term is broadly consistent with the story about aggregate demand.

Of course, the numbers describing likely medium-term growth rates for aggregate demand and aggregate supply of slightly below 3 percent are subject to significant margins of error. And there is no guarantee that the present expansion will proceed uninterrupted for another six to eight years. Nevertheless, I believe that these estimates are consistent with the most reasonable expectation that medium-term growth for the US economy will be somewhat more sluggish than in recent expansions but not catastrophically so.

Medium-Term Growth Prospects for Western Europe

The advanced economies of Western Europe face many of the same challenges for medium-term growth as the United States, plus others. As noted earlier, real GDP growth in Western Europe and the United States during the reference period 1999 through 2007 was already slower than the growth rates achieved earlier in the postwar era. It is reasonable to expect that most of the factors that contributed to this general slowing of growth will continue to operate in the period ahead for Western Europe as well as for the United States. Gradual elimination of large margins of slack will likely provide some boost to growth rates over the medium term, but other forces impeding economic progress will weigh against and possibly outweigh this effect.

The United Kingdom, Sweden, and Switzerland

Before turning to the euro area, it is useful to examine the situation in the United Kingdom, followed by a brief discussion of Sweden and Switzerland. The United Kingdom enjoyed sustained economic expansion from 1993 through 2007, achieving a 2.8 percent average annual growth rate (the same as during the nine-year reference period from 1999 through 2007). Although inflation remained well contained over this period, other important imbalances developed in the UK economy. Even with the benefit of long expansion, the structural fiscal deficit reached about 3 percent of GDP in 2007. Rapid growth of the financial services industry became a key driver of general economic expansion, as well as of a housing boom focused in the area around London. The real effective foreign exchange value of sterling appreciated considerably, contributing to persistent weakness in the manufacturing sector. Despite substantial net earnings from financial services, the current account deficit stood at 3 percent in 2007.

With the great global recession and the associated financial crisis, the imbalances that developed during the long expansion have come to the fore. The financial services industry has suffered a serious setback from which it will not soon recover. The housing boom has ended, and although the situation is not as dire as in the United States (or, even more so, Ireland and Spain), recovery in this sector will be a painful and drawn-out process. The fiscal deficit ballooned as the economy fell into recession and the old Labor government initially resorted to significant fiscal stimulus. Aggressive reversal of this policy by the new Conservative/Liberal coalition has clearly put significant (temporary) downward pressure on economic activity. One bright spot (at least from the perspective of the United Kingdom) is the substantial real effective depreciation of sterling since 2007. On the other hand, inflation since 2007 has been running above its announced target and appears likely to continue to do so for at least another year. The Bank of England has essentially ignored this problem and has maintained an exceptionally easy monetary policy to support the economy. Before much longer, however, monetary policy will need to respond to concerns about inflation, lest the whole notion of an "inflation target" for UK monetary policy become a bad joke.

Looking to the medium term, fiscal consolidation will continue to depress aggregate demand for at least the next year or two, but then should become essentially a neutral factor. For some of the same reasons as in the United States, growth of consumption spending is likely to remain subdued (but still positive) in the United Kingdom. Business investment should do relatively well as the manufacturing sector continues to expand, but with some worries about the impact on the United Kingdom of a prolonged slowdown in most of the rest of Western Europe. As with the United States, it is reasonable to assume that real net exports will not make a significant contribution, positive or negative, to real GDP growth in the United Kingdom. All told, after the substantial output losses during the Great Recession and the stagnation of the past two years, it is probably reasonable to expect a medium-term growth rate of about 2.5 percent. This is broadly consistent with a potential growth rate of about 2 percent and with a gradual reduction of the unemployment rate toward 5 percent.

Sweden is interesting in that its economy has performed quite well relative to most of Western Europe since the mid-1990s. The economy grew at a 3 percent annual rate during the reference period 1999 through 2007, almost a percentage point better than the euro area. With its relatively large manufacturing sector, the Swedish economy was hit fairly hard during the Great Recession, but the subsequent recovery has been reasonably strong, and the unemployment rate is already down 1.7 percentage points from its recession peak and barely 1 percent above its prerecession level.

The relatively good performance of the Swedish economy reflects, to an important degree, the sound management of economic policy before, during, and after the Great Recession. Lessons were well learned from the trauma following the collapse of the credit and housing bubbles in the early 1990s and the attendant need to rein in the excesses of Sweden's welfare state. Since then, the government has run a very responsible fiscal policy, leading to budget surpluses in the years before the Great Recession. This allowed some room for fiscal support at the depths of the recession, and did not create a need for aggressive fiscal consolidation in the present recovery (a need now felt by many other European countries). Sound management and supervision of Swedish banks (recognizing the bitter lessons of earlier experience) allowed them to avoid much of the distress that affected financial institutions in other countries. Also, the flexible exchange rate of the Swedish krona, especially against the euro, allowed the exchange rate to absorb some of the stress from the great recession and the associated collapse of world trade—an adjustment mechanism not available to members of the euro area. Recent upward pressures on the exchange rate of the krona suggest that this may become more of an impediment to economic growth. Looking at the supply side of the Swedish economy, we might expect that because the margin of slack in the Swedish economy is not very large, growth over the medium term will be near the potential growth rate, plausibly about 2.5 percent.

Switzerland provides a useful comparison with Sweden. Economic growth was quite good (at a 3 percent annual rate) during the four years immediately preceding the Great Recession, but was somewhat disappointing before that. Fiscal policy was soundly managed, and there is no need now for significant fiscal consolidation. Swiss banks (especially the two very large banks) did absorb major losses during the global financial crisis, but these losses were primarily associated with their international operations—not their operations inside Switzerland. The Swiss authorities dealt with these problems without significant cost to the taxpayer or to the Swiss economy. Subsequently, bank regulation (especially capital standards) has been improved to an extent that significantly exceeds the accomplishments of other countries. Quite rightly, the Swiss authorities are not worried that this strengthening of bank regulation will impede growth of the Swiss economy.

Like that of the Swedish krona, the exchange rate of the Swiss franc has been flexible, at least until quite recently. Switzerland gained some room for maneuver from this exchange rate flexibility, which helped to shield its economy from the Great Recession. More recently, however, the exchange rate has become a problem, as the Swiss franc has appreciated very strongly against other currencies, most notably the euro. It remains to be seen how much this appreciation will slow the growth of the Swiss economy, but it seems prudent to suppose growth in the period ahead will not match that immediately preceding the Great Recession but will instead be in the 1.5 to 2.0 percent range.

The Euro Area: Demand- and Supply-Side Considerations

Turning finally to the situation in the euro area, as reported in table 12.1, real GDP grew at a rather sluggish 2.2 percent average annual rate during the nine years preceding the Great Recession. France (the second-largest economy) performed at this average, but Germany and Italy (the largest and third-largest economies) grew one-half percentage point below the average. Spain (the fourth-largest economy) enjoyed stronger-than-average growth at a 3.6 percent annual rate. Some of the smaller members of the euro area (Finland and especially Ireland) also grew more rapidly than the average, while Portugal lagged behind.

During the reference period 1999 through 2007, real domestic demand in the euro area grew at essentially the same average annual rate as real GDP; see table 12.3. Correspondingly, there was relatively little change in the current account of the euro area, which improved from a modest deficit of 0.5 percent of GDP in 1999 to balance in 2007. For individual members of the euro area, however, differentials between growth of output and growth of domestic demand were significant. Germany shows very weak growth of domestic

Table 12.3   Output, demand growth, and current accounts (percent)

Country/economy	Real GDP growth rate, 1999–2007	Domestic demand growth rate, 1999–2007	Current account share of GDP 1999	Current account share of GDP 2007
United States	2.8	3.1	−3.2	−5.1
United Kingdom	2.8	3.2	−2.4	−2.6
Sweden	3.0	—	3.5	8.6
Switzerland	2.1	—	11.6	9.9
Euro area	2.2	2.2	−0.5	0.1
Germany	1.6	1.1	−1.3	7.5
France	2.2	2.5	3.1	−1.0
Italy	1.5	1.7	0.7	−2.5
Spain	3.6	4.2	−2.1	−10.0
Netherlands	2.3	—	4.3	7.6
Belgium/Luxembourg	2.6	—	4.2	1.6
Austria	2.3	—	−2.8	3.1
Finland	3.5	—	5.9	4.1
Greece	4.1	—	−4.1	−14.2
Portugal	1.4	—	−8.7	−9.4
Ireland	7.5	—	0.6	−5.6

demand, only 1.1 percent per year, reflecting primarily very weak growth of consumption. Italy has slightly stronger growth of domestic demand than of output, whereas France has modestly stronger growth of domestic demand than of real GDP. Spain recorded 4.2 percent annual growth of real domestic demand versus 3.6 percent annualized growth of real GDP.

These differentials between the growth of real GDP and real domestic demand are reflected, of course, in the evolution of current account balances. In 1999, the euro area as a whole had a small (about 0.5 percent of GDP) current account deficit, and in 2007 the current account was essentially balanced. Germany had a moderate current account deficit in 1999, amounting to 1.3 percent of GDP. In 2007, this had been transformed into a large surplus equivalent to 7.5 percent of GDP. This rise in Germany's surplus was offset by deterioration of the current account balance of the rest of the euro area. In particular, France went from a surplus of 3.1 percent of GDP to a deficit of 1.0 percent of GDP. Italy went from a surplus of 0.7 percent of GDP to a deficit of 2.5 percent of GDP. Spain's current account deteriorated massively from a deficit of 2.1 percent of GDP to a deficit of 10.0 percent of GDP.

Closely related to these developments was the rapid gain in cost competitiveness of German manufacturing relative to manufacturing in the rest of the euro area. Comparatively rapid increases in labor productivity in German manufacturing, combined with comparatively sluggish wage growth, induced about a 20 percent decline in unit labor costs in Germany relative to those in the rest of the euro area. These gains in Germany's cost competitiveness were more modest vis-à-vis France, but were greater than the average vis-à-vis Italy and Spain. Taking account of the real exchange rates among national precursor currencies when the euro was introduced in 1999, it is fair to say that Germany's real exchange rate started out somewhat overvalued, while the real exchange rates of Italy and Spain were initially somewhat undervalued. Developments in the current account balances of euro area members, as well as in labor productivity and wages, indicate that this initial disequilibrium was more than reversed by 2007.

The euro area as a whole was hit fairly hard during the Great Recession, with real GDP falling about 5 percent. The subsequent recovery has in general been quite sluggish, but substantial disparities in the performances of different countries exist. Clearly, there are important issues about medium-term growth prospects for each of the member countries. Greece's problems, in particular, have been a central focus of concern since early 2010. More generally, fears about the fiscal sustainability of several euro area members and the spillover effects onto European banks and more broadly to the world economy and financial system have dominated recent debates about economic policies and even about the future of the euro area itself.

The purpose here, however, is not to delve deeply into these very important and immediate concerns. Instead, it will be assumed that current difficulties are resolved without a major systemic breakdown of the euro system or the euro area financial system. Even with continued substantial official assistance, Greece will need to restructure its sovereign debt (but will not leave the euro), and the Greek economy will face a long and painful adjustment to gradually restore its competitiveness and return to reasonable rates of economic growth. Ireland and Portugal, the two other euro area countries now receiving official assistance, may well be able to avoid sovereign debt restructuring and the more extreme difficulties of the Greek economy, but will nevertheless face prolonged periods of adjustment before economic activity comes substantially back toward its previous growth path. Beyond these three countries (which accounted for about 8 percent of euro area GDP in 2007), the considerations relevant for assessing medium-term growth prospects are more within the normal range.

Looking at the prospective growth of aggregate demand, it is important to focus first on growth of domestic demand, which was 2.2 percent during the reference period 1999–2007, the same as the growth rate for real GDP. Growth of domestic demand over the next six to eight years is likely to fall significantly below this figure. Several members of the euro area, most notably Italy and Spain (in addition to Greece, Ireland, and Portugal), will need to establish and maintain quite austere fiscal policies in order to persuade markets of fiscal rectitude. Elsewhere there is little or no room for fiscal expansion. Hence, we may expect both that increases of government purchases will contribute little to demand growth and that efforts of fiscal consolidation will weigh upon private spending.

In the period following the advent of the euro, interest rates converged downward toward German rates. This boosted spending (especially for residential investment) in those countries benefiting from this downward convergence. Reduction of fiscal deficits and public debt levels was also made easier. This process will not be repeated in the period ahead. Indeed, there will be a continuing need to work off the excesses of housing booms in some countries (especially Ireland and Spain), and the likelihood is that at least some of the recent increases of interest rate spreads vis-à-vis Germany will prove durable, except in the unlikely event that the euro area becomes a full fiscal union.

Focusing next on the likely contribution of the external sector to medium-term growth of aggregate demand, it is reasonable to expect something positive, though not much. Import growth will be somewhat restrained by the weak growth of domestic demand, while euro area exports participate in the general expansion of world trade. However, unlike the first five years of the reference period, when the real exchange rate of the euro was highly competitive against the US dollar and the UK pound, today the euro area enjoys no such competitiveness advantage. Slight improvement of the euro area current account from a deficit of about 0.5 percent of GDP to a surplus of 0.5 percent of GDP may be reasonable. But this implies a contribution of only 0.1 to 0.2 percentage points to the annual average growth rate of aggregate demand in the medium term. Adding in a reasonable projection for growth of domestic demand suggests that the annual average growth rate of aggregate demand for the euro area in the medium term will be below 2.0 percent and perhaps as low as 1.5 percent.

Consideration of aggregate supply generally supports the conclusion of medium-term growth below 2 percent. Between 1999 and 2007, the unemployment rate fell from 9.2 to 7.6 percent, indicating that output and employment growth were absorbing significant slack during these nine years. The implication is that the potential growth rate in that period was below 2.2 percent, plausibly about 1.7 percent.

Growth of the euro area labor force arising from population growth and immigration looks likely to be no higher than in the reference period. There is no persuasive reason to believe that labor productivity growth will be any higher than previously, and there are forces operating in the other direction. At 9.9 percent, the present euro area unemployment rate is somewhat above the 1999 level, but it will likely prove difficult to reduce it rapidly to near its 2007 low. Germany's unemployment rate (now 7.0 percent) is already below its 2007 level (7.8 percent) and further significant reductions of German unemployment will be difficult to achieve. Despite its weak recovery, Italy's unemployment rate is now not much above its 2007 low. Exceptionally high unemployment in Spain (now 21 percent) reflects to a considerable degree the collapse in construction, and reducing unemployment to near 8 percent again will be a very daunting task. Similarly, reduction of the very high unemployment rates in Greece and Ireland to near their prerecession lows is likely to be a very slow process at best. Altogether, it seems unlikely that reducing unemployment and margins of slack will add much more than 0.3 to 0.4 percent per year to the growth rate of aggregate supply over the growth rate of potential output.

Critical Divergences Within the Euro Area

Beyond the normal considerations of aggregate demand and aggregate supply, further important concerns about medium-term growth prospects for the euro area arise from disparities among members in their economic situations. In the debates that preceded the formation of the euro, it was emphasized (especially by skeptics of the euro) that the introduction of a common currency would eliminate exchange rate adjustments as a means for accommodating differing requirements for economic growth in different members, especially differing requirements for adjustments in international competitiveness. Proponents of the common currency generally argued that these problems would be limited by economic convergence before and after the introduction of the euro and by rules ensuring appropriate and coop- erative behavior among the governments of the euro area. Experience before the Great Recession generally appeared to support the position of the euro's proponents. Subsequently, serious problems have arisen that appear likely to hamper economic growth.

Current account imbalances are not always a sign of trouble but they can be. In particular, the (previously described) widening of current account imbal- ances among members of the euro area between 1999 and 2007—notably the large improvement in Germany's current account and the offsetting deteriora- tion in the current accounts of other members (especially Spain)—should have been seen as symptomatic of considerable potential trouble. Developments in the relative cost competitiveness of different euro members should have been seen as a related concern. Instead, euro area officials tended to emphasize that the overall current account of the euro area remained near balance and that questions of (real) exchange rates or payments imbalances among members were not really relevant for a common currency area.

During the Great Recession, the current account of the euro area moved briefly into moderate deficit, but most recently this deficit has shrunk to only about 0.5 percent of area GDP—the same as in 1999. The German surplus has fallen from its 2007 peak but is still about 5 percent of GDP. Spain's deficit has shrunk dramatically to about 4.5 percent of GDP, while France's deficit has remained essentially constant at 2.5 percent of GDP and Italy's deficit has grown to almost 4 percent of GDP.

By themselves, present payments imbalances of euro area members are not especially disturbing, but they are much more so when viewed in the con- text of other economic developments. With its large manufacturing sector, the German economy was hard hit by the global recession and the associated collapse in world trade, and real GDP fell 6 percent. However, unlike most of the rest of the euro area, Germany has enjoyed a fairly strong recovery, with real GDP rising above its previous peak by early 2011 and the unemployment rate now below its prerecession low. Strong gains in German exports and associated gains in real net exports have driven this recovery, along with an important contribution from domestic demand. For the rest of the euro area real GDP is still about 2 percent below its prerecession peak, and the unemployment rate is up modestly from its peak during the recession and almost 3 percent above its prerecession low. Domestic demand growth has been quite modest, and real export growth has been significantly less buoyant than for Germany. The cost competitiveness advantage of German manufacturers vis-à-vis the rest of the euro area has not diminished. The real exchange rate for Germany appears to be significantly undervalued relative to that of the rest of the euro area, especially Italy, Spain, Ireland, and Greece.

Starting from this situation, the question is, How can the euro area reasonably be expected to achieve a medium-term growth rate as high as 2 percent? Already operating near potential, sustained growth of 2 percent or better may not be achievable for Germany. To achieve whatever is its maximum sustainable growth rate, growth of demand for German output will need to come primarily from rising domestic demand, not from rising net exports as was the case from 1999 to 2007. Indeed, for the rest of the euro area to achieve medium-term growth that modestly exceeds potential growth and allows for gradually falling margins of slack, it will probably be necessary for weak domestic demand growth to be supplemented by improvements in real net exports. Such improvement would clearly not be consistent with little change in the real trade balance of the euro area and continued significant growth of Germany's real trade surplus.

Significant adjustments in the relative competitiveness of different euro area economies will clearly be essential to achieving something close to medium-term growth of 2 percent for the euro area. The relative cost competitiveness of most euro area countries needs to improve vis-à-vis Germany, in some cases very substantially. This will be required to redistribute improvements in net exports toward those member countries where margins of slack are high and constraints on the growth of domestic demand are likely to be tight. Germany and the Netherlands (and possibly Austria and Finland) will have to be on the other side of this adjustment process, with domestic demand growth somewhat outstripping output growth and with relative cost competitiveness gradually eroding versus other euro area members.

How might this adjustment process operate? David Hume suggested a key part of the necessary mechanism two and a half centuries ago. In those countries already operating near potential, with relatively buoyant growth of domestic demand, wages (and, to a lesser extent, prices) will be pushed up. In other countries where margins of slack are considerable and domestic demand growth is relatively weak, wages will decline or rise less rapidly. Over time, the necessary adjustments in relative cost competitiveness will be achieved. Economic policies should promote or, at a minimum, not impede these adjustments. However, even with the best of policies, medium-term economic growth is still likely to be impeded by the need for substantial adjustments to correct critical divergences among members of the euro area.

13

The Euro Area Crisis and Future Global Implications

WOLFGANG SCHÄUBLE

Keynote address at the PIIE-Bruegel conference in Berlin, September 27, 2011

For more than two decades, economic policy in industrialized countries has tried to avoid recessions—sacrificing fiscal prudence and monetary rectitude in the process. When financial markets crashed, central banks, particularly in Anglo-Saxon countries, cut interest rates. And when growth declined, governments plundered the public's purse—even worse, they robbed children's piggy banks—to make up for the private sector's reluctance to spend freely.

One result of such misguided policies was a series of debt-financed asset bubbles. It seems to me no coincidence that the most recent of these financial crises started in the United States and its real estate sector. US policymakers attempted to support high levels of growth via monetary policy. They tried to promote homeownership of poorly skilled workers through less-stringent lending practices. The former International Monetary Fund (IMF) chief economist, Raghuram Rajan, has analyzed that problem lucidly and argues in his recent book that America's growing inequality and thin social safety net create tremendous political pressure to encourage easy credit and keep job creation robust—no matter what the consequences are for the US economy or the world economy.

My purpose here is not to blame US economic policy. And helping the poor and undereducated is a worthy goal. But lax monetary and lending policies are no replacement for good education and social policies. And while

---

Wolfgang Schäuble has been federal minister of finance of Germany since 2009. He was federal minister for the interior from 2005 to 2009.

there are indeed adverse incentives in the social market economy, I would argue that—as a system partially designed to alleviate social inequity by a mix of income redistribution and accessible education—that model is superior to the US model, which uses monetary and lending policies to soften inequality.

To return to the financial crisis: When the last of those debt-financed bubbles burst three years ago, governments had to up the ante and use massive fiscal stimuli, and central banks had to resort to unprecedented measures of easing monetary policy to avoid the breakdown of financial markets and an ensuing depression.

To be fair, those measures were necessary to avoid a depression. But Keynesian deficit spending has had unfortunate consequences: Governments' debts and deficits are on the verge of spiraling out of control. At least markets think so, withdrawing their confidence and demanding higher risk premia, i.e., interest rates.

Governments are now faced with a predicament. There is little political or market appetite for more fiscal and monetary stimuli. But markets and citizens do not crave tighter fiscal and monetary policies, either, for fear of their economies heading back into recession.

There is a feeling that politics is at wit's end. And in a sense that is true: Governments and central banks have used up much of their fiscal and monetary firepower. I think it is no accident that unemployment in the United States has remained stubborn despite all the efforts by the Federal Reserve and the United States government to promote growth. We will not spend our way out of the current predicament, nor will it work to lower the debt burden by inflating the problem away. Loosening monetary and fiscal policies in the short term while promising monetary and fiscal tightening in the medium term might have worked in the past. Today, however, as market reactions demonstrate, it lacks credibility with investors as well as with citizens.

The key question today is this: What is the alternative to those boom and bust cycles of the past, caused by and in turn causing overleveraged public and private sectors? Is there an alternative economic policy framework?

I would argue that we can establish an alternative economic policy framework—a framework that does not encourage the laissez-faire economic policies of the recent past nor the discretionary meddling in economic affairs of the 1970s, but nevertheless will not lead to marginal economic growth in tightly regulated markets but will instead foster sustainable growth.

I am convinced that we can establish fiscal and financial policy frameworks that encourage long-term sustainable growth of the economy instead of short-term volatile growth bursts or long-term economic decline. But for such frameworks to be established, immediate fiscal consolidation and structural reforms in highly indebted countries are of the essence. Public debts and deficits in a number of industrialized countries are too high, and we need to bring them down fast. Markets no longer accept current debt and deficit levels, and they no longer accept that governments put economic reform off until after the next election.

Recent studies—most prominently the book by Carmen M. Reinhart and Kenneth S. Rogoff (2009), *This Time Is Different*[1]—have shown that once government debt burdens reach thresholds perceived to be unsustainable, more debt will stunt rather than stimulate growth. Investors as well have reached the conclusion that debt and deficit levels in a number of countries are unsustainable, and they expect governments to bring them down—now.

There are some who argue that fiscal consolidation, a smaller public sector, and more-flexible labor markets will lead to a decrease in consumption in these countries in the immediate future. I am not sure that's necessarily the case, but even if it were, there is a tradeoff between short-term pain and long-term gain in these countries: I would argue that an increase in consumer and investor confidence and a shortening of unemployment lines will in the medium term cancel out any short-term dip in consumption. I am not deluding myself, however, and neither should anyone else: It will take not months but years before these efforts bear fruit.

Given the time necessary to bring public debts and deficits down to sustainable levels in Europe, we will have to provide strictly conditional financial assistance to highly indebted and less competitive member countries. In essence we are buying those countries the time they need to put their public finances on a sustainable footing and improve their competitiveness.

One of the major problems of most of these countries is their large current account deficit, exposing their lack of competitiveness and strong dependency on imports. A key question therefore is this: What effect would fiscal adjustments have on countries' external balances? The IMF looked at fiscal policy changes over the past 30 years in advanced economies. What it found was that fiscal policy has a large and long-lasting effect on the current account. And the improvement in the current account takes place not just because imports fall as a result of lower consumption and investment. Exports also rise as the real exchange rate depreciates.

That finding is true for countries where the exchange rate is fixed as well. Of course, as the real exchange rate depreciates, domestic wages and prices will have to adjust. And these adjustments are painful, no doubt. But that is why we are providing financial assistance to Greece and allowing it to prolong the adjustment period to accommodate social hardships. Now there are a number of economists who argue that it will be easier politically to deal with nominal real exchange rate adjustments. Well, they should not fool themselves.

No, the key question for the eurozone is, Can we establish and adhere to a framework for the economic governance of the eurozone that encourages long-term sustainable growth of our economies instead of short-term volatile growth bursts or long-term economic decline? I think we can. But every journey starts with the first step: For this to happen, immediate fiscal

---

1. Carmen M. Reinhart and Kenneth S. Rogoff, *This Time Is Different: Eight Centuries of Financial Folly* (Princeton, NJ: Princeton University Press, 2009).

consolidation and structural reforms in Italy, Spain, Portugal, and Greece are of the essence.

Merely calling for more budgetary discipline will be insufficient. We have to repair public finances, but we have to do so in a way that encourages rather than hinders future growth. Governments need to demonstrate their commitment not only to fiscal consolidation but also to increasing competitiveness in order to restore the confidence of markets as well as their citizens.

This bears repeating: The challenge for governments today is not to repair public finances. It is not even to start doing so immediately. It is to restore the trust of investors and citizens in the sustainability of their governments' fiscal policies and foster sustainable growth in the long run. Otherwise the financial, economic, social, and political consequences of an ensuing crisis of confidence would be dramatic and difficult to contain.

Some argue that such a demand for sustainable growth is eurocentric and something only wealthy European countries can afford. Others even argue that it is a sinister strategy by well-off nations to stop developing nations from gaining ground.

Nothing could be further from the truth. Developed and developing nations alike—at least most of them—learned a hard lesson the last three years, namely, that long-term gains have been consistently postponed or forsaken for short-term gratification, that fiscal and financial policies are off track and unsustainable. This time we will have to take the long view: Developed economies need—and are in the process of—deleveraging. It is not only households that have to live within their means, that—at least in the long run—cannot spend more than they earn. It is countries and their citizens as well.

Recent events have shown that a common currency cannot survive without solidarity among its members. But such solidarity has its limits. It can only accompany a country's reform efforts, not replace them. A member state has to be willing to deal with the root causes of its problems itself. In other words, European solidarity cannot replace a government's own resolve. But it is not only highly indebted countries that have to change. Brussels has to change its bureaucratic ways as well. Perhaps it is no accident that enthusiasm for the European idea has been fading while the European Commission's staff—and their pay—have been steadily increasing. But for Europe and its members to become more efficient, their bureaucracy has to become more effective and less self-absorbed. Helping those countries most in need by realigning their spending priorities to foster sustainable growth could be a start.

It is indeed vital that we look at more than just government budgets, debt, and deficit figures. We must consider an individual member's economic performance, too, and improve competitiveness and better coordinate economic policy.

On the subject of improving competitiveness: We do have to avoid overly large imbalances between member states. But this avoidance cannot take the form of successful countries voluntarily limiting their competitiveness. The only workable course is for the somewhat weaker eurozone countries to become stronger. We can help them, but we cannot do their job. One does not resolve one's own problems of competitiveness by asking others to become less competitive, and one cannot permanently close the gap between expenditure and income by asking others for money.

I am well aware that growth rates in Europe will vary, notwithstanding our best efforts to improve competitiveness. While not a zero-sum game, growth in the more mature economies of Western Europe will not keep pace with growth rates in a number of Eastern European countries, not least for demographic reasons, but also because of pent-up demand in those countries. But that is not a bad thing at all: If you ask me, What is Europe's contribution to global prosperity? It is our emphasis on long-term, stable, and sustainable growth. I would even argue that gearing economic policies toward that goal is worthy of consideration even in those economies in Asia and South America that are more dynamic than the mature economies in Europe.

I think the core lesson from the past crises is that highly cyclical, credit-fueled growth, which is driven by the financial market, does more harm than good. Instead, we need to create the preconditions for lasting and sustainable growth, defined as steady, environmentally friendly, and socially compatible growth propelled by the industry and productivity of the real economy and not by an overleveraged financial sector.

I am convinced that, if we stick with our policy of fiscal and structural reforms, we will put the economies of the eurozone on a sustainable footing and prevent the debt crisis of some countries from becoming a crisis threatening the eurozone as a whole and in turn the world economy.

There are some who are not satisfied with the way European politicians are dealing with the crisis, who are now calling for the supposed structural faults in European Monetary Union to be corrected once and for all by building up the political and fiscal union. But that is an approach that does not reflect the genesis of European integration. Europe always moved forward one step at a time. And it will do so in the future as well. I am a great fan of Karl Popper and his concept of an open society, which improves through a constant process of trial and error. If we want to draw the right lessons from the recent crisis, then that is how we have to proceed.

But there is time for small steps and there is a time for bold ones. And the time for bold steps is now. Governments in the eurozone need not just to commit to fiscal consolidation and improved competitiveness and governance, they have to deliver. And they will. We will strengthen the institutional links between the common European monetary policy and the national responsibilities of member states for fiscal policies.

I believe that it will become increasingly necessary for European democracies to strengthen the bond between their citizens and Europe by strengthening the democratic mandate of European institutions. However, that does not mean that the fiscal and monetary policy decisions taken by these democratically legitimated institutions need the public's continual approval. As I understand it, that squares with an insight of constitutional economics: That you establish and legitimate their principal monetary—and fiscal—institutions with a strong democratic mandate, but then entrust them to conduct monetary and fiscal policy as independently from politics as possible. Of course these institutions will still make mistakes, but at least mistakes based on error-prone interpretations of the public mood should not be one of them.

To sum up: To regain credibility, immediate fiscal consolidation and structural reforms in highly indebted and noncompetitive countries are of the essence, even as the returns on that investment are one or perhaps two election cycles away. Europe has begun to create a framework that promotes the sustainable growth of the real economy—a framework that encourages more responsible behavior on the part of European governments (as well as financial market participants). Strengthening the institutions of the eurozone may need treaty changes and will take time. But make no mistake about it: The direction is undisputed, as is the decisiveness of all member states to defend the common European currency. We will form an ever closer European Union, contributing to European prosperity and global stability in the process.

14

The Debt Challenge in Europe

ALAN AHEARNE and GUNTRAM B. WOLFF

At the heart of the ongoing crisis in the euro area are market concerns about the sustainability of sovereign debt in some Economic and Monetary Union (EMU) countries. Standard equations of public debt dynamics show that if the interest rate on the debt exceeds the nominal growth rate of GDP, then stabilization of the debt-to-GDP ratio requires that the country run a sufficiently large primary (that is, noninterest) budget surplus. Based on this analysis, fiscal consolidation to reduce primary budget deficits is an important part of the prescription for EMU countries with sovereign debt difficulties. Fiscal consolidation is expected to increase investor confidence in the sustainability of public debt, thereby lowering interest rates on sovereign debt. Lower interest rates further improve the debt dynamics.

An issue that has not received the attention it deserves in the debate over sovereign debt sustainability is the interaction between public debt and private debt. Rising fiscal deficits can support aggregate demand and thereby facilitate private sector deleveraging in cases where businesses and households find themselves overindebted. It follows that as governments implement needed fiscal consolidation programs, the accompanying increases in taxes and cuts in spending may frustrate the efforts of the private sector to reduce the debt overhang (Eggertsson and Krugman 2010). This suggests a potential policy dilemma involving whether to emphasize public or private sector debt reduction. For that reason, it is important to understand how overindebted

Alan Ahearne lectures in economics at the National University of Ireland in Galway. He is also a nonresident research fellow at Bruegel and a member of the Board of the Central Bank of Ireland. Guntram B. Wolff is the deputy director of Bruegel.

businesses and households might respond to planned fiscal policy actions in the current crisis.

A second potential policy dilemma relating to private sector debt results from the fact that the EMU countries with sovereign debt problems also often have overvalued real exchange rates. To pay down external debt, these countries require real exchange rate depreciation through cuts in prices and wages to boost net exports. However, it usually takes time for improvements in competitiveness to translate into faster export and income growth. In particular, empirical evidence suggests that declines in export prices relative to import prices may in the short run reduce net exports.[1] In heavily indebted countries, therefore, required depreciation of the real exchange rate may in the short term push up debt relative to net exports and income, thereby temporarily exacerbating the overindebtedness problem.

Against this background, this chapter discusses corporate and household debt and the related adjustment process. Our discussion relies particularly on flow of funds (or financial account) data that have recently become popular.[2] The remainder of the chapter is structured as follows. In the next section we provide a horizontal overview and discuss the interaction between the processes of debt reduction and real exchange rate adjustment. The following two sections discuss corporate debt and household debt, respectively. The last section develops policy recommendations.

Debt and Competitiveness: An Overview

Figure 14.1 documents the net external financial assets (as a percentage of GDP) of Greece, Portugal, Ireland, Spain, and Italy. As can be seen, net external liabilities currently exceed 100 percent of GDP in Greece and Portugal. Ireland's net external liabilities are close to 100 percent, though some caution is required in interpreting the data for Ireland.[3] In Spain, the figure is around 90 percent. Only in Italy are the net external liabilities relatively low, at less than 20 percent of GDP. Net external liabilities, of course, find their counterpart in net external assets in surplus countries, which have increased over the past decade, in particular in Germany.

---

1. Backus, Kehoe, and Kydland (1994) note that the negative effect of such a terms-of-trade deterioration usually reverses itself after two to eight quarters, giving rise to a J-shaped pattern.

2. Be Duc and Le Breton (2009); Castren and Kavonius (2009); Dirk Bezemer, "No One Saw This Coming—Or Did They?" VoxEU, September 30, 2009, www.voxeu.org (accessed on January 30, 2012).

3. Gros (2011) estimates that based on accumulated current account balances over the past 25 years, Ireland's external liabilities are about 20 percent of GDP, compared with the figure of nearly 100 percent reported by Eurostat. The differences in estimates may in part reflect distortions in the data associated with the presence of the large International Financial Services Center (IFSC) in Dublin. In addition, Lane (2011) argues that a substantial component of the increase in net external liabilities since 2008 reflects the internationally leveraged structure of the financial portfolios of domestic Irish residents.

Figure 14.1 Net external financial assets, 2009

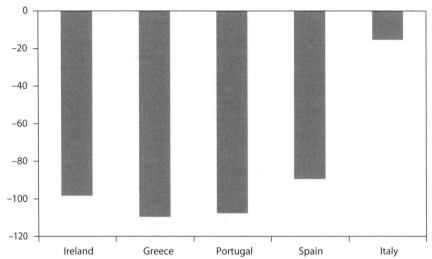

percent of GDP

Source: Eurostat database, http://epp.eurostat.ec.europa.eu.

Large external liabilities reflect past increases in domestic net liabilities, which have increased differently in different sectors of the economies. Figure 14.2 provides data on net assets of the different sectors of the economy. Households are typically holders of net assets, while corporations and governments have a net debt position. The figure also reveals that in Greece the main driver of the large liability position is the government sector, while in Spain, Portugal, and Ireland the large accumulation of liabilities results from the corporate and household sectors. In Italy, large government debt is offset by large asset holdings of the household sector so that the net position of the economy is more balanced.

These net positions conceal very large gross financial asset and liability positions (figure 14.3). Ireland stands out with financial assets and financial liabilities of around 18 times GDP, though these figures are distorted by the inclusion of activities in the International Financial Services Center.[4] But the gross positions for the other countries are also large, easily constituting stocks of assets and liabilities exceeding several years' worth of income.

Such large stocks can render countries' net external positions vulnerable to changes in the prices of assets and liabilities. Suppose that asset values react

---

4. According to the International Monetary Fund (IMF), Ireland's reported gross external liabilities are around 1,100 percent of GDP (end-2010), but most of these liabilities are related to IFSC activities and are largely offset by external assets. Excluding the IFSC, gross external liabilities are estimated to be about 330 percent of GDP. See IMF Country Report 11/276, September 2011, www.imf.org (accessed on January 30, 2012).

Figure 14.2 Net financial assets in domestic sectors, 2009

percent of GDP

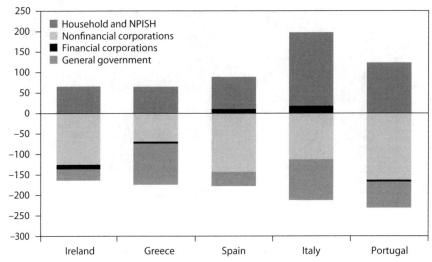

Legend:
- Household and NPISH
- Nonfinancial corporations
- Financial corporations
- General government

NPISH = Nonprofit institutions serving households

Source: Eurostat database, http://epp.eurostat.ec.europa.eu.

Figure 14.3 Gross assets and liabilities, 2009

percent of GDP

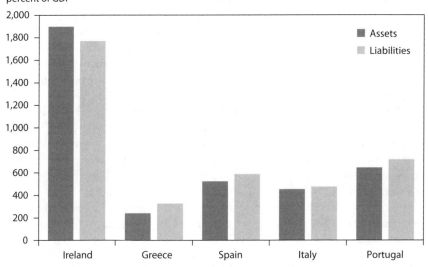

Legend:
- Assets
- Liabilities

Note: Assets and liabilities obtained as the sum of three categories—securities other than shares, loans, and shares and other equity.

Source: Eurostat database, http://epp.eurostat.ec.europa.eu.

Figure 14.4   Net assets and liabilities across categories, 2009

percent of GDP

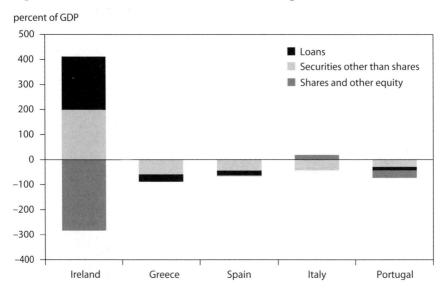

Source: Eurostat database, http://epp.eurostat.ec.europa.eu.

differently to changes in economic circumstances than liabilities. In that case, an economic or financial shock has the potential to change markedly the net asset position of a country.[5]

A large part of the increase in net liabilities is in the form of debt—that is, securities other than shares (bonds) and loans (figure 14.4).[6] This may put a heavy burden on the economies concerned in a recession as the value of the debt remains unchanged while income and the values of nonfinancial assets can fall markedly.

These high external and internal debt burdens must be seen in the light of the significant competitiveness adjustments that are required in these economies. Figure 14.5 summarizes the divergence in competitiveness based on unit labor costs for these economies. It shows that there has been a continuous divergence in relative unit labor costs since 1999. This divergence in competitiveness has not been corrected to any great extent during the crisis, except for the case of Ireland and to a lesser degree Spain.

The loss in price competitiveness has gone hand in hand with a significant decline in the share of the manufacturing sector in total value added (see figure 14.6). The value-added share has fallen by as much as 25 percent,

---

5. An extensive discussion of valuation effects can be found in European Commission (2008).

6. Again, the data for Ireland are distorted by Ireland's role as an international financial center. In particular, the breakdown between equity, loans, and bonds in large part reflects Ireland's relatively large mutual funds industry.

Figure 14.5   Divergence in competitiveness, 1994–2010
(unit labor cost–adjusted real effective exchange rate)

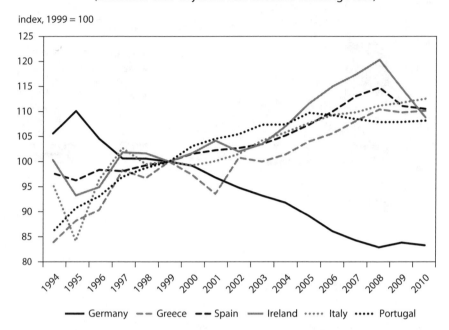

index, 1999 = 100

Source: European Commission, Directorate General for Economic and Financial Affairs, Price/Competitiveness Database.

highlighting a tendency of deindustrialization of the euro area periphery. To pay back external debt, these economies will have to grow their exports. This probably means that the peripheral economies will have to strengthen their manufacturing export base, although in the case of Ireland strong export growth over recent years has been driven by exports of services.

The ability of these economies to adjust through growth in exports also depends on the size of the export base in each country. In this regard Ireland is in a potentially strong position, since gross exports exceed GDP (table 14.1) and net exports account for more than 20 percent of GDP. In contrast, the export sectors are considerably smaller in the other peripheral countries relative to GDP, so a given increase in exports has less effect on overall economic activity.

The discussion above suggests that most of the economies that are the focus of this chapter face a double challenge. On the one hand, they have to deal with large debt burdens. These debt burdens can be difficult to cope with when interest rates on public and private debt are rising and when incomes are falling because of the recession. Needed fiscal consolidation further depresses incomes, both directly through budgetary measures such as tax hikes and indirectly by aggravating the recession.

Figure 14.6 Manufacturing share of value added, 1995–2007

index, 1995 = 100

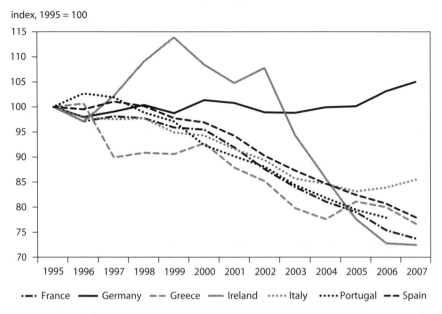

Source: Organization for Economic Cooperation and Development.

Table 14.1 Size of the export sector, 2007 and 2011 (gross exports as percent of GDP)

Country	2007	2011
Ireland	80.5	110.0
Portugal	32.2	34.6
Italy	29.0	29.1
Spain	26.9	28.4
Greece	22.7	24.0

Source: European Commission, Directorate General for Economic and Financial Affairs, Annual Macroeconomic (AMECO) Database, http://ec.europa.eu/economy_finance/db_indicators/ameco/index_en.htm.

On the other hand, the economies in question need to increase their competitiveness in order to grow and in order to service their foreign debt. This is particularly relevant for those economies that hold large external debt positions. Repaying external debt means that a country needs to run current account surpluses. The combination of the two factors—the need for a competitiveness adjustment and the debt overhang—makes the current situation delicate. While downward wage adjustments help on the competitiveness and export side in the long term, in the short term an effect similar to the J-curve effect may worsen the trade balance. In addition, the wage cuts may also reduce the overall income in the near term (depending on the time profile of job creation), making debt repayment more difficult.

The evidence for Italy (and possibly for Ireland) reveals a somewhat better picture. Italy's export performance and price competitiveness indicators are poor. However, this is less of an issue in Italy as the external debt problem is more limited and the large public sector debt is matched by large household assets. In principle, the Italian public debt problem could therefore be solved by taxing Italian households and corporations that hold large financial assets. In fact, many of those assets are government bonds issued by the Italian government. Overall, a large part of the solution to Italy's problems thus appears to be in the control of the Italian government.

Corporate Debt

As was shown earlier, corporate debt has been an important contributor to the overall increase in debt in a number of countries. At some stage, corporations will wish to correct their debt levels. In this section, we document this process of balance sheet adjustment and its economic causes and consequences. We start by showing a simple measure of balance sheet adjustment for the five peripheral euro area economies. We then reference previous research (Ruscher and Wolff 2010, 2012), which analyzed the typical economic consequences of such adjustment.

A simple measure of balance sheet adjustment is the net lending of the nonfinancial corporate sector.[7] Corporate net lending measures corporations' net financial investments (if positive) or, alternatively, their net needs in terms of external finance (if negative). When corporate net lending increases, savings increase relative to investment in the corporate sector, leading to a reduction in domestic demand. Indeed, corporate net lending is negatively associated with the business cycle and positively associated with the current account balance, showing that large increases in corporate net lending are not fully offset by other domestic sectors' net lending.

---

7. An important literature investigates the determinants of corporate balance sheet adjustment. The finance literature offers two competing models of financing decisions and balance sheet structure. In the tradeoff model, firms identify their optimal leverage ratio by weighing the costs and benefits of additional debt. The benefits of debt include, for example, the tax deductibility of interest and the disciplining effect of debt in case of agency problems between managers and shareholders (Jensen 1986). The costs of debt include potential bankruptcy costs and others. In the pecking order model (Myers and Majluf 1984), equity issuance and, to a lesser degree, debt issuance come with a cost due to asymmetric information between managers and investors. In this model, companies prioritize their sources of financing, using internal funds first before resorting to debt and ultimately equity. The pecking order model predicts that a firm's debt issuance is an inverted function of its net cash flows (cash earnings minus investment layouts). Fama and French (2002) test both models with firm-level data and find supporting and contradicting evidence for both models, suggesting that both models partially hold.

Table 14.2 Net lending of nonfinancial corporations and government (percent of of GDP)

Country/economy	Corporate sector	Government sector	Start year
Euro area 17	2.7	−3.9	2008
Ireland	3.0	−11.9[a]	2007
Greece	4.0	−3.7	2007
Spain	8.9	−11.2	2007
Italy	1.9	−3.0	2007
Portugal	5.4	−5.6	2008

a. Excludes banking-sector support.

Note: Adjustment in net lending since the year in which corporate borrowing was largest.

Source: Eurostat database, http://epp.eurostat.ec.europa.eu.

Table 14.2 shows the percentage adjustment in corporate net lending for the euro area as a whole and for the five peripheral euro area economies since the beginning of the recent adjustment processes. Spain has seen by far the largest adjustment of corporate net lending with an adjustment of close to 9 percent of GDP, but adjustments in Portugal, Greece, Ireland and even Italy have also been sizeable. This strong balance sheet adjustment will be accompanied by a significant recession unless the shortfall in domestic demand is offset by an increase in demand in other sectors of the economy, typically the public or external sector.

To address these large drops in corporate net borrowing and make up for the fall in aggregate demand, several governments have significantly increased their public deficits. Obviously, the increase in public borrowing has been most pronounced in Spain, as is shown in table 14.2. The adjustment in corporate borrowing has thus come at the expense of an increase in government borrowing.

How much have corporate debt and leverage adjusted? Figure 14.7 plots the debt-to-GDP ratio and reveals that corporate debt levels have barely started to decline.[8] Similarly, corporate leverage ratios continue to remain high and have not adjusted much (figure 14.8).

How long will the corporate deleveraging process last? This is one of the central questions for policymakers today, as the deleveraging process goes hand in hand with depressed domestic demand and weak economic activity. It becomes particularly relevant when the international growth prospects are weak and export opportunities are subdued.

Previous research in Ruscher and Wolff (2010) shows that past balance sheet adjustment episodes may have lasted between five and ten years. The recent corporate balance sheet adjustment in Germany has lasted seven years. In

---

8. The jump in Ireland's corporate debt in 2007 may reflect the move of one or more multinational companies' corporate headquarters to Ireland.

Figure 14.7 Debt-to-GDP ratio in the nonfinancial corporate sector, 1999–2010

percent

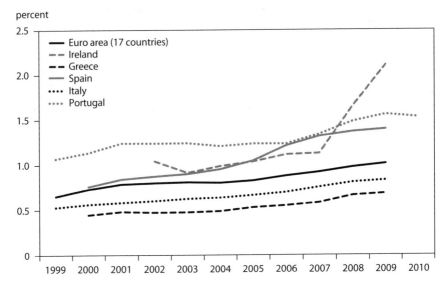

Source: Eurostat database, http://epp.eurostat.ec.europa.eu.

Figure 14.8 Leverage in the nonfinancial corporate sector, 1999–2010

percent

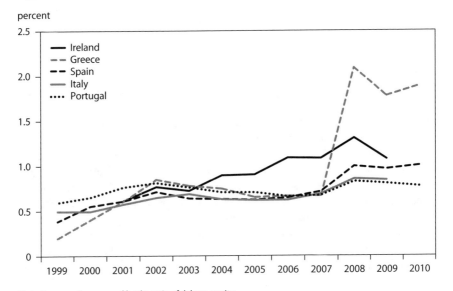

Note: Leverage is measured by the ratio of debt to equity.

Source: Eurostat database, http://epp.eurostat.ec.europa.eu.

Table 14.3   Consequences of corporate balance sheet adjustment

	$t = 0$[a] (A)	$t = 4$ (B)	Actual change[b] (C) = (B) – (A)	Average change in entire sample (D)	Effect of balance sheet adjustment (E) = (C) – (D)	Number of episodes (F)
Debt/GDP	60.3	58.4	–1.9	5.2	–7.1	12
Leverage[c]	101.2	85.3	–15.9	–1.2	–14.7	12
Liquidity/value added[d]	30.0	33.4	3.4	0.9	2.5	10
Investment/value added	26.1	23.2	–2.9	–0.2	–2.8	16
Savings/value added	17.2	22.3	5.0	0.4	4.6	16
Compensation of employees/value added	60.2	55.6	–4.6	–0.9	–3.7	20
Real growth			6.6	9.9	–3.3	24

a. Period $t = 0$ is the year prior to the balance sheet adjustment.
b. In the case of "real growth," the actual change is the difference between the cumulated growth during the four-year adjustment period and the cumulated growth in the broader sample during an average four-year period.
c. Leverage is measured by the ratio of debt to equity (data are from the balance sheet section of national accounts).
d. Liquidity is measured by corporations' holdings of currency and deposits (data are from the balance sheet section of national accounts).

Note: To ensure a constant size of the sample for every year, the table covers only events that lasted more than four years and for which data are available. The number of observations per variable differs depending on data availability.

Source: Ruscher and Wolff (2010).

a larger sample of Organization for Economic Cooperation and Development (OECD) countries analyzed in Ruscher and Wolff (2010), the average balance sheet adjustment period lasted 8.3 years.

This long balance sheet adjustment is typically accompanied by large changes in macroeconomic variables. Table 14.3 is taken from Ruscher and Wolff (2010) and provides the statistics related to the adjustment of corporate balance sheets. The authors show the development in time of a number of central variables, starting from the year prior to the balance sheet adjustment episode ($t = 0$) to the year $t = 4$.[9]

A number of key features of corporate balance sheet adjustment can be discerned from table 14.3 and are highlighted in Ruscher and Wolff (2012):

1. Debt-to-GDP ratios are significantly reduced, in particular when compared with the overall sample in which debt increases on average. Similarly, corporate leverage (i.e., the ratio of debt to equity) is reduced significantly, by almost 16 percentage points.

---

9. The set of countries is kept constant during this period so that changes in the values are not driven by changing samples. For different variables, the data availability is different and this explains the different number of observations per variable considered.

2. Corporate balance sheet adjustments are associated with significant increases in the holdings of liquid funds. The increase in the sample averages 3.4 percent of corporate value added.

3. Compensation of employees as a share of corporate value added falls by almost 5 percentage points and is therefore much more significant than the fall in the overall sample.

4. At the same time, corporate savings as percent of corporate value added increases substantially, by 5 percentage points. The increase in savings thus corresponds very much to the decrease in labor compensation.

5. Investment as percent of corporate value added falls substantially, by around 3 percentage points.

The descriptive evidence from a large sample of corporate balance sheet adjustment episodes thus confirms that corporate balance sheet adjustments have very large and significant effects on wages, investment, savings, and corporate balance sheets themselves. Indeed, the descriptive evidence supports the notion that corporate balance sheet adjustments have strong income effects as they are associated with persistent periods of wage moderation. Increased corporate gross savings are therefore partly achieved by weakening labor remunerations. Moreover, the results highlight that investment is subdued during episodes of corporate balance sheet adjustment. Corporate balance sheets are thus adjusted by reducing investment and increasing savings on the back of falling labor cost. The corporate balance sheet adjustment is found to be associated with significant decreases in leverage and debt as well as sizeable increases in liquidity held by the corporations.

Ruscher and Wolff (2012) also analyze the drivers of this corporate balance sheet adjustment. They find that large debt levels, a weak liquidity situation, and negative stock market shocks can trigger adjustment. Christoffer Sorensen, David Marques Ibanez, and Carlotta Rossi (2009) estimated that by end-2006, the debt overhang in the euro area corporate sector was as much as 15 percent (that is, corporate debt was as much as 15 percent above its estimated equilibrium level). Judging by intra–euro area differences in the pace of debt accumulation over the past decade, the overhang could have been considerably larger in some member states. This large overhang may explain the rapid increase in corporate net lending.

Household Debt

Large-scale fiscal consolidation in crisis countries requires measures to raise taxation revenues and cut spending. Other things being equal, such policies reduce household disposable income and could result in financial distress when households are highly indebted. Widespread financial distress would not only weigh on consumer spending in crisis countries, thereby hurting prospects for growth, but could also threaten the stability of the banking system. In turn, banking problems could dampen confidence and restrict the supply of credit to viable businesses, further depressing economic growth and exacerbating the crisis (Fisher 1933).

As discussed earlier, there is also an interaction between needed improvements in competitiveness and high levels of indebtedness. Depreciation of the real exchange rate through cuts in nominal wage rate should eventually boost net exports and employment as the country gains global market share. As such, falling wage rates do not necessarily mean lower aggregate disposable incomes, and in time should boost disposable incomes as employment rises in export sectors. However, there may be a timing issue here. Economic theory suggests that this so-called competitiveness channel of adjustment in a currency union operates gradually and with a lag (European Commission 2008). Therefore, in the near term, the capacity of households to absorb large wage cuts may be limited by high levels of indebtedness. Moreover, as discussed in the previous section, the empirical evidence shows that corporate balance sheet adjustment also puts downward pressure on wages.

For these reasons, it is important to look at the facts on household debt in EMU countries, especially in the crisis countries where many households may find themselves overindebted and where large-scale budgetary and competitiveness adjustments are required. As in our study of corporate deleveraging earlier, we examine the process of household deleveraging in crisis countries. In particular, we explore previous episodes of household deleveraging and what lessons these past experiences might offer about what EMU membership implies for the process of deleveraging.

How Much Debt Did Households Take on During EMU?

In most European economies, household indebtedness has risen sharply since the late 1990s. As shown in figure 14.9, the ratio of household debt to disposable income in the euro area on average increased from 73 percent in 1999 to 97 percent in 2009. The rise in household indebtedness during EMU marks the continuation of a broader trend across advanced countries in which average household debt as a percentage of GDP in the OECD as a whole has doubled from about 40 to 80 percent over the period 1985–2005.

The largest increases in household indebtedness in the euro area were recorded in Ireland (where household debt jumped roughly 90 percentage points of disposable income during 2002–09), the Netherlands, Spain, and Portugal. The most muted increases were registered in Austria, Belgium, and France. Household indebtedness fell in only one country, Germany, bringing German household debt to nearly 10 percentage points of disposable income below the euro area average in 2009, from more than 30 percentage points above average in 1999.

Outside the euro area, the increases in household debt in Sweden and the United Kingdom matched those in Spain and Portugal, while indebtedness of the household sector in Denmark managed to outpace even Ireland.

Figure 14.9   Household debt as a percent of disposable income, 1999 and 2009

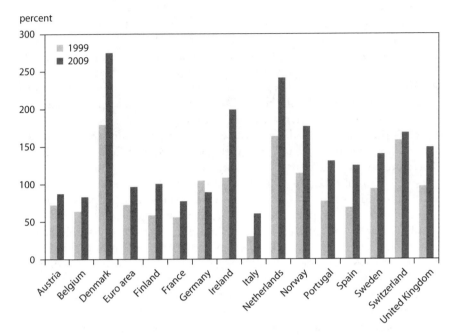

percent

■ 1999
■ 2009

Note: For Ireland and the Netherlands, earlier data are from 2002; for Spain, earlier data are from 2000; and for Norway and Switzerland, later data are from 2008.

Source: Eurostat database, http://epp.eurostat.ec.europa.eu.

Why Has Household Indebtedness Risen?

Economic theory provides a useful starting point for understanding the rise in indebtedness over the past couple of decades. The well-known permanent income (or life cycle) model of consumption and saving relates decisions on savings and borrowings to life cycle factors.[10] Savings are typically low or negative during an individual's early working years and during retirement when income is low. Households save at a higher rate during late working years when income is highest. Standard economic theory suggests several factors that might account for the rise in household indebtedness across countries during EMU and for differences in indebtedness across countries.

- *Real interest rates.* For many EMU countries, real interest rates fell after 1999. This is especially true for Ireland and Spain (figure 14.10), which recorded some of the largest increases in indebtedness after the creation of the single

---

10. The life cycle model was developed in the 1950s and is closely associated with Franco Modigliani, Albert Ando, and Milton Friedman. Modigliani (1986) provides a useful summary.

Figure 14.10 Real short-term interest rates, 1997–2010

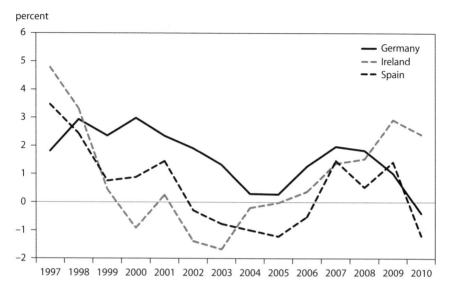

Note: Figure shows nominal three-month interbank interest rates deflated by harmonized index of consumer price inflation.

Source: Eurostat database, http://epp.eurostat.ec.europa.eu.

currency. Negative real interest rates in Ireland and Spain contributed to housing bubbles and rapid increases in household indebtedness.

- *Future income expectations.* Prolonged periods of relatively fast economic growth like those experienced by several EMU economies during the so-called Great Moderation can lead households to believe that disposable incomes are likely to continue to rise at a strong pace well into the future. Permanent income considerations would then encourage households to borrow against these expected future income gains.

- *Demographics.* Ireland and Spain have a relatively large proportion of the population in their early working years, which could explain some of the high indebtedness in these countries. Moreover, the young workforce in Ireland is highly educated and well qualified, so expectations of future real income growth were high during the boom.[11] In addition, the young work-force in Ireland and Spain was boosted by large inward migration during the boom years.

A major driver of the rise in indebtedness has been the growth in mortgage debt. The marked expansion of mortgage credit reflects rapid increases

---

11. According to Eurostat data, more than 80 percent of the population aged 20-24 years are educated to at least upper secondary level, marking the highest proportion in the EU-15. On the other end of the scale are Portugal (55 percent) and Spain (60 percent).

in house prices in many countries since the mid-1990s, increased household formation and home ownership rates in some countries, and deregulation in the mortgage markets (which boosted borrowing by previously credit-constrained households). Indeed, rising house prices themselves help to ease credit constraints, since these constraints are related to collateral values, and housing acts as collateral for mortgage debt. Mortgage debt now accounts for over 70 percent of household indebtedness across the OECD on average, up more than 5 percentage points over the past decade.

Housing is typically the largest asset owned by a household. So although rapidly rising house prices have been accompanied by large increases in gross household indebtedness, the net wealth of households has generally increased. However, in countries that experienced house price booms and busts over the past decade or so (Ireland and Spain), net wealth is now deteriorating because of the ongoing declines in housing values.

Though debt-to-income ratios have increased sharply, the household debt service burden—that is, households' debt service payments relative to their disposable income—has been relatively stable. This suggests that the rise in indebtedness has been roughly offset by the decline in interest rates on household loans. Of course, lower interest rates were a factor in boosting asset prices during the last decade, including the price of housing. Higher house prices, in turn, required households to take on increased mortgage debt.

Other things equal, declines in disposable incomes push up households' debt burdens. In countries with large public debt levels, necessary fiscal consolidation will reduce disposable incomes through higher taxation burdens and lower social transfer payments. Therefore EMU countries with higher levels of both public and household debt would appear to be most vulnerable. Figure 14.11 presents gross household and general government debt for euro area economies in 2011.[12] Both Ireland and Portugal have levels above the euro area average for both household and public debt, strikingly so in the case of Ireland. Spain has above average levels of household debt, but below average public debt, while in Italy, the opposite is true.

Another perspective on the interaction of public debt and household debt is offered by Stephen Cecchetti, M. S. Mohanty, and Fabrizio Zampolli (2011). They find that beyond a certain level, debt is bad for economic growth. They estimate the threshold is in the range of 80 to 100 percent of GDP for public debt and around 85 percent of GDP for household debt, though they caution that their estimate of the effect on growth of household debt is very imprecise. Relating these estimates to the data presented in figure 14.11, it can be seen that Ireland and Portugal exceed both thresholds; Spain exceeds the threshold for housing indebtedness but not for public debt, while Italy and Greece exceed the threshold for public debt but not for housing indebtedness. This approach might suggest a need for household deleveraging in Ireland, Portugal, and Spain to better position these countries for sustained economic recovery.

---

12. Latest IMF (2011) projections for public debt and most recent data for household debt.

Figure 14.11   Government and household gross debt, 2011

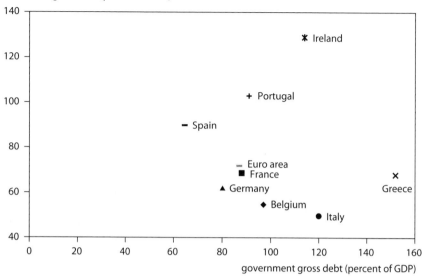

household gross debt (percent of GDP)

Source: IMF, *World Economic Outlook*.

So far we have considered only gross measures of indebtedness. Of course households and governments also hold stocks of financial assets, so net indebtedness can be considerably lower than gross measures. In fact, gross financial assets for the household sector exceed gross liabilities in all countries, so that net financial assets are positive (or net debt is negative), as shown in figure 14.12. Moreover, our measure of assets excludes the value of housing, meaning that the true net worth of the household sector is even greater. The ranking of countries when the net debt measure is used is similar to the pattern for gross debt, though one striking change is that Portugal's household sector has markedly higher gross indebtedness than the euro area average but is close to the euro area average for net indebtedness.

It should be noted that in the discussion of a country's household debt, households are treated as an aggregate. Even where, on average, net household financial assets for a country are positive, a large cohort of households may have substantial net indebtedness and find it difficult to meet debt obligations. In other words, the distribution of financial assets and liabilities across households in a country is important for the degree of financial distress that households may experience. Unfortunately, reliable data on financial conditions at the individual household level are not yet available for the euro area crisis countries.[13]

---

13. The Eurosystem of Central Banks recently launched an initiative to produce and publish surveys of consumer finances across euro area countries, similar to the Survey of Consumer Finances in the United States sponsored by the Federal Reserve Board.

Figure 14.12   Government and household net debt, 2011

household net debt (percent of GDP)

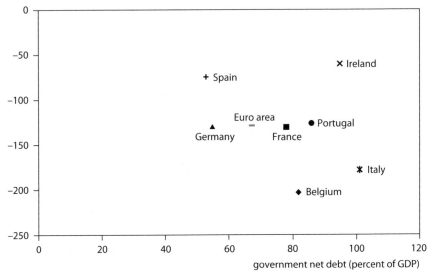

Source: IMF, *World Economic Outlook.*

Recognizing the heterogeneous features of household indebtedness is also important in examining what constitutes a sustainable level of indebtedness. Many older workers have little or no debt, so indebtedness tends to be concentrated in younger workers, consistent with the life cycle model. Moreover, younger workers tend to have lower disposable incomes than older workers. So although aggregate indebtedness may look manageable, ongoing declines in disposable income may cause significant financial distress for many younger highly indebted workers.

Household Deleveraging During the Current Crisis

Table 14.4 shows the evolution of household indebtedness during the current economic and financial crisis. In most countries, indebtedness continued to move up, possibly reflecting consumption-smoothing motives during the recession. In Spain and the United Kingdom, household indebtedness was lower in 2009 than at the start of the crisis in 2007, as rising disposable income outpaced household debt. The trend of declining indebtedness continued in Germany.

Our data end in 2009, but other sources of data can help to update the picture. In Ireland, banking data show that loans outstanding to households were down 3.3 percent in the first quarter of 2011 compared with the same period a year earlier. Indeed, annual credit growth to the household sector in Ireland has been negative since late 2009. Irish households are now paying down debt. However, although data for 2010 are not yet available, it is

Table 14.4 Household debt, 2007–09 (percent of disposable income)

Country	2007	2008	2009
Austria	86	87	87
Belgium	77	79	83
Denmark	255	262	275
Euro area	94	95	97
Finland	97	98	101
France	73	76	77
Germany	93	89	89
Ireland	194	198	199
Italy	57	57	61
Netherlands	222	230	241
Norway	177	177	n.a.
Portugal	128	129	131
Spain	130	127	125
Sweden	131	133	140
Switzerland	170	168	n.a.
United Kingdom	152	153	149

n.a. = not available

Source: Eurostat database, http://epp.eurostat.ec.europa.eu.

expected that household disposable income in Ireland dropped sharply in both 2009 and 2010. As a result, it is not clear that the paying down of nominal debt has actually reduced indebtedness (that is, the level of debt relative to disposable income). But it does appear that households are trying to reduce indebtedness or at least attempting to stem its rise, even though these efforts are being frustrated by continuing declines in disposable income.

In Spain, data from the National Financial Accounts show that total loans outstanding to households peaked in 2008 at €913 billion, up from €450 billion in 2003. Loans outstanding to households subsequently edged down to €907 billion in 2009 and €902 billion in 2010. In Portugal, the National Financial Accounts show that loans to households rose from €161 billion in 2009 to €164 billion in 2010. In both countries, it will turn out that household indebtedness will have risen in 2010 if disposable income fell, even though households are paying down loans.

Other Countries' Experiences with Household Deleveraging

Unlike nonfinancial corporate debt, episodes in which household indebtedness shows annual declines have been rare in Europe over the past few decades. This means that we do not have a broad sample of episodes of household deleveraging to study.

The remainder of the section focuses on the three cases we can identify from our data in which household debt (as a percentage of disposable income) recorded negative annual growth in one or more years. These cases are Finland

**Table 14.5 Real GDP growth during the previous and current crises
(percent)**

Country	1989	1990	1991	1992	1993	1994
Finland	5.4	0.1	−6.0	−3.6	−0.9	3.7
Sweden	2.8	1.0	−1.1	−1.2	−2.1	3.9
United Kingdom	2.3	0.8	−1.4	0.1	2.2	4.3
	2007	2008	2009	2010	2011f	2012f
Greece	4.3	1.0	−2.3	−4.4	−5.0	−2.0
Ireland	5.2	−3.0	−7.0	−0.4	0.4	1.5
Italy	1.5	−1.3	−5.2	1.3	0.6	0.3
Portugal	2.4	0.0	−2.5	1.3	−2.2	−1.8
Spain	3.6	0.9	−3.7	−0.1	0.8	1.1

f = forecast

Source: Organization for Economic Cooperation and Development (for Finland, Sweden, and the United Kingdom); IMF, World Economic Outlook, September 2011 (for the rest).

(1990–97), the United Kingdom (1991–97), and Sweden (1993–95).[14] Each of these episodes was associated with the bursting of large housing and credit bubbles as well as with recessions, currency crises, and (in the case of Finland and Sweden) severe banking crises.

As shown in table 14.5, Finland, Sweden, and the United Kingdom suffered recessions in the early 1990s. The recession was especially deep in Finland, where real GDP dropped more than 10 percent over the period 1991–93.

For comparison with the current crisis, the recent economic performance of the five most stressed countries are also presented in table 14.5. The data are arranged so that the table is centered on the most acute year of the recession, which is 1991 in the previous crisis and 2009 in the current one. The cumulative loss in real GDP in Ireland is expected to be similar to Finland's experience in the early 1990s. Spain and Italy look much closer to Sweden on this score. The striking difference between the current and previous episodes is that Finland, Sweden, and the United Kingdom rebounded strongly in 1994—three years after the worst year of growth—while projected growth rates for the troubled EMU countries for 2012 are very weak. These projections underscore how much more difficult it is to adjust balance sheets in the current crisis compared with the Nordic-UK crisis in the 1990s.

As in Spain and Ireland today, the large rise in household indebtedness in the episode countries in the previous crises was associated with booms in house prices (figure 14.13). In the Nordic-UK crisis, real house prices stabilized about four to five years after their peak and began to rise again about three to four years later.

---

14. Data for household indebtedness in Sweden are available only from 1993. It is likely that household deleveraging began a few years earlier, along the lines of what happened in Finland.

Figure 14.13 Real house prices, 1980–99

index, 1995 = 100

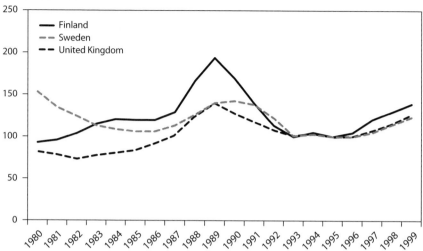

Source: Bank for International Settlements, www.bis.org.

During the housing market booms in the late 1980s, household indebtedness rose sharply in Finland, Sweden, and the United Kingdom (figure 14.14). Following the bursting of the bubbles, the household sector in each of these countries began to deleverage. The reduction in indebtedness was most pronounced in Finland, which had suffered the most severe crisis and where debt relative to disposable income dropped from a peak of 88.5 percent in 1989 to a low of 60 percent in 1997. Indebtedness peaked in the United Kingdom at 110 percent in 1990 and drifted down to 100 percent by 1997, before edging back up. Data for Sweden are incomplete, but deleveraging ended two years earlier than in Finland and the United Kingdom.

How did households in these countries deleverage? Table 14.6 decomposes the drop in indebtedness in the three episodes into changes in nominal household debt and nominal disposable income. It shows the change in the indebtedness ratio, measured as the change in the natural log of the ratio over the indicated period. This change is then decomposed into the change in the (natural log of the) stock of debt and the change in the (natural log of) disposable income. For example, the Finnish indebtedness ratio fell by approximately 39 percent between 1989 and 1997, of which about one-third resulted from a fall in debt and two-thirds from a rise in disposable income. Tables 14A.1 to 14A.3 in appendix 14A provide detailed data on debt, disposable income, and the indebtedness ratio.

Several aspects of the Finnish experience are worthy of comment. First, household debt continued to rise through 1991, even though real economic

Figure 14.14 Household debt, 1987–99

percent of disposable income

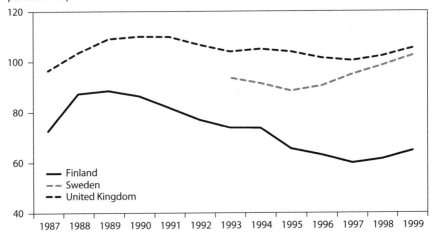

Note: Data for Sweden are not available for all the years shown in this figure.

Sources: Statistics Finland, www.stat.fi/index_en.html; Statistics Sweden, www.scb.se; UK Office for National Statistics, www.ons.gov.uk/ons/index.html.

Table 14.6 Decomposition of changes in indebtedness ratio

Country	Period	Change in debt (A)	Change in disposable income (B)	Change in indebtedness ratio (C) = (A) – (B)
Finland	1989–97	–0.13	0.26	–0.39
Sweden	1993–97	0.07	0.08	–0.01
United Kingdom	1991–97	0.27	0.36	–0.10

Source: Authors' calculations based on data from Statistics Finland, UK Office for National Statistics, and Statistics Sweden.

activity slumped that year. This suggests that it may take a while for households to realize that the boom is over. Second, households managed to pay down about 7.5 billion markka of debt between 1992 and 1996, equivalent to about 20 percent of the stock of debt in 1991. Third, disposable incomes rose in most years of the adjustment, with the exception of 1993 and 1994. By 1995, disposable income was markedly higher than at the height of the boom in the late 1980s.

What is most striking about the UK experience is that in no year did UK households pay down nominal debt. In fact, debt levels were markedly higher in 1997 than in 1991, when the indebtedness ratio peaked. The reduction in indebtedness after 1991 was achieved by continuous increases in disposable incomes. The role of rising disposable income in helping overindebted households to deleverage in all three countries is an important feature of the earlier experiences.

Policy Options and Conclusions

The indebtedness of the corporate and household sectors in the peripheral euro area economies rose markedly over the first decade of EMU. Recent data suggest that these sectors have responded to the financial crisis, deterioration in access to finance, and weakening growth prospects by beginning a process of balance sheet adjustment. These efforts to deleverage have contributed to a large drop in domestic demand in these economies. Large fiscal deficits and low or negative GDP growth rates have led to a sharp increase in the ratios of public debt to GDP. Financial markets in turn have grown increasingly worried about the underlying solvency of governments, and risk premia have risen. These high risk premia are now forcing governments into fiscal adjustments that are further depressing economic growth.

These efforts to reduce indebtedness are likely to continue, but progress will be slow because weak GDP growth will hinder the deleveraging process. Of course, GDP growth is weak in part because the private sector is attempting to deleverage. That is the catch-22 situation facing the euro area. Peripheral euro area economies are encumbered with high private and public sector debt, intense market pressure, and a need for significant adjustments in competitiveness. We have argued that the situation in Italy appears to be less problematic as external debt is small and structural problems can in principle be solved. However, determined policy action is required in Italy to reverse the weak growth prospects and the structural difficulties in the economy.

The EU policy response to this dilemma has so far focused on supporting the public sector by alleviating market pressure and providing rescue programs at concessionary interest rates to Greece, Portugal, and Ireland. Markets, however, remain unconvinced. A number of further policy options therefore need to be discussed, some relating to domestic policies and others to policies for the euro area as a whole.

Domestic Policies

1. Ongoing fiscal consolidation is necessary in countries with large fiscal deficits, especially in countries with sizeable structural deficits.[15] However, fiscal adjustments should be done in a way that minimizes negative effects on growth. Zsolt Darvas and Jean Pisani-Ferry (2011) have shown that this approach has often not been used in recent years. A policy rethink on the composition of fiscal adjustment is necessary. In addition, in making budgetary adjustments policymakers should be cognizant of the unequal distribution of assets and liabilities across households. To facilitate private sector deleveraging, the burden of fiscal consolidation in countries with

---

15. According to IMF estimates, the general government structural deficit (as a percentage of potential GDP) in 2011 stood at 6.9 percent in Greece, 6.8 percent in Ireland, 4.4 percent in Spain, 4 percent in Portugal, and 2.6 percent in Italy (IMF 2011).

overindebted household sectors should, where possible, weigh more heavily on households with little or no debt than on the highly indebted cohorts.

2. Reducing external debt burdens requires improvements in external balances in the peripheral economies. These economies therefore must improve competitiveness to increase market share. Indeed, given the expected slowing of growth in Europe in 2012, increasing market share is increasingly important. However, internal devaluation to restore competitiveness takes time. Importantly, there are policy measures that can accelerate this process without increasing the indebtedness of the private sector. Benedicta Marzinotto, Pisani-Ferry, and Wolff (2011) argued that unused structural funds could be spent on targeted wage subsidies in the tradable sector to promote the creation of jobs in the export sector. Increased competition in goods and services markets to boost productivity and bring down prices in the nontraded sector would also contribute to improved competitiveness. More generally, policymakers could usefully focus on structural reforms that facilitate the reallocation of the workforce to the tradable sector. Similarly, in surplus countries, policymakers should not resist freely set wage increases resulting from tight labor market conditions.

3. Structural factors that impede domestic investment and consumption should be removed in countries with large current account surpluses. The tax and regulatory system should avoid discouraging investment in the corporate sector.

Euro Area Policies

The past experiences of corporate and household deleveraging studied in this chapter highlight the key role of overall economic growth in facilitating private sector deleveraging. But there is a policy dilemma because domestic fiscal adjustments, although necessary to reduce structural deficits, drag economic growth in the short term and therefore hinder the deleveraging. Necessary real exchange rate depreciation may in the short term even lead to a deterioration of the current account balance due to the usual delayed pickup of export volumes. As a result, the deleveraging process will likely be prolonged, and this in turn will delay economic recovery. The key point is this: Along with fiscal consolidation and competitiveness improvements at home, the countries concerned need favorable external conditions. Strong growth in the euro area as a whole will help the peripheral countries to increase their exports in a more robust manner. An important lesson we draw from the analysis in this chapter is that policymakers must ensure that the euro area as a whole does not enter a deep or prolonged recession and that the overall euro area macroeconomic stance is appropriate.

Room for fiscal expansion by other members of the euro area is limited because budget deficits are sizeable and market pressures could increase rapidly. Germany has more room than most to support growth using fiscal policy, but large-scale fiscal expansion by Germany is not a realistic proposition, not least because of concerns about unfavorable demographics. The European Central Bank has reduced policy interest rates over recent months and could cut rates further given recent declines in inflation expectations. Additional monetary policy support to the euro area economy would probably need to rely on more unconventional monetary policy tools, which have so far been ruled out.

Given the current constraints on traditional fiscal and monetary policy in the euro area, what can policymakers in the euro area do to address the dilemma facing the overindebted countries?

1. A targeted euro area–wide strategy centered on European investment should be envisaged. A natural area for common public expenditure is where clear European spillovers and externalities exist. The ongoing energy transition is such an area where an ambitious European strategy would be beneficial. Raising tax revenues at the European level—for example by taxing the financial services industry—to help leverage borrowing for a European energy network could be an efficient way of supporting the euro area economy. While it takes time to define such a program and begin actual spending, it should be recognized that debt adjustment will take many years. Moreover, simply announcing such a strategy may give a boost to the euro area economy even in the short term via positive expectation effects.

2. Overindebtedness in the (nonfinancial) corporate sector and in the household sector puts severe strains on the banking system. Bad assets in the banking system should be recognized and dealt with promptly so that credit provision to growing sectors of the economy is not curtailed. Banks should be rigorously stress tested to detect such bank balance sheet problems and recapitalized if necessary. The current arrangement allows European funds (via the European Financial Stability Facility, EFSF) to be loaned to countries for bank recapitalization. Governments should request European funds where necessary rather than delay bank restructuring. EFSF loans for bank recapitalization should be given at no extra charge, that is, at EFSF borrowing costs, so that the banking-sovereign feedback loop that is contributing to financial fragility does not get aggravated. Better still, the rules of the EFSF could be changed to allow the EFSF to inject capital directly (not via loans to governments) into European banks in exchange for ordinary equity in the banks and increased supervisory powers at the euro area level.

3. Debt relief may be required in some cases. If public and/or private debt levels cannot be managed by the debtors, creditors will have to accept losses. This is not the place to review how such debt reduction can be achieved in a way that results in the lowest damage to the euro area as a whole and the individual country. What is clear, however, is that if the euro area suffers a deep and prolonged recession in 2012 and 2013, debt relief for private and public creditors may be needed in some member countries.

Appendix 14A
Data on Household Indebtedness in Finland, Sweden, and the United Kingdom

Table 14A.1 Household indebtedness in Finland, 1989–97

Year	Debt (billions of Finnish markka)	Disposable income (billions of Finnish markka)	Indebtedness ratio (percent)
1989	36.6	41.4	88.5
1990	38.5	44.6	86.4
1991	39.2	47.9	81.7
1992	37.7	49.0	77.0
1993	35.5	48.0	73.8
1994	34.0	46.2	73.7
1995	32.7	50.0	65.4
1996	31.6	50.2	63.0
1997	32.1	53.6	59.8

Source: Statistics Finland, www.stat.fi/index_en.html.

Table 14A.2 Household indebtedness in the United Kingdom, 1989–97

Year	Debt (billions of pounds)	Disposable income (billions of pounds)	Indebtedness ratio (percent)
1989	353	324	109
1990	402	365	110
1991	439	400	110
1992	459	431	107
1993	478	460	104
1994	499	475	105
1995	523	503	104
1996	545	537	101
1997	575	573	100

Source: UK Office for National Statistics, www.ons.gov.uk/ons/index.html.

Table 14A.3 Household indebtedness in Sweden, 1993–97

Year	Debt (billions of Swedish kronor)	Disposable income (billions of Swedish kronor)	Indebtedness ratio (percent)
1993	889	832	93.6
1994	910	831	91.4
1995	939	830	88.4
1996	942	851	90.3
1997	950	901	94.9

Source: Statistics Sweden, www.scb.se.

References

Backus, David, Patrick J. Kehoe, and Finn E. Kydland. 1994. Dynamics of the Trade Balance and the Terms of Trade: The J-Curve? *American Economic Review* 84, no. 1 (March): 84-103.

Be Duc, Louis, and Gwendael Le Breton. 2009. *Flow-of-Funds Analysis at the ECB: Framework and Applications.* ECB Occasional Paper 105. Frankfurt: European Central Bank.

Castren, Olli, and Ilja K. Kavonius. 2009. *Balance Sheet Interlinkages and Macro-Financial Risk Analysis in the Euro Area.* ECB Working Paper 1124. Frankfurt: European Central Bank.

Cecchetti, Stephen, M. S. Mohanty, and Fabrizio Zampolli. 2011. The Real Effects of Debt. Paper presented at a symposium sponsored by the Federal Reserve Bank of Kansas City, Jackson Hole, WY, August 25-27, 2011.

Darvas, Zsolt, and Jean Pisani-Ferry. 2011. *Europe's Growth Emergency.* Bruegel Policy Contribution 2011/13. Brussels: Bruegel.

Eggertsson, Gauti, and Paul Krugman. 2010. Debt, Deleveraging, and the Liquidity Trap. Princeton University, Princeton, NJ. Photocopy.

European Commission. 2008. *EMU@10: Successes and Challenges After 10 Years of Economic and Monetary Union.* European Economy 2. Brussels.

Fama, E., and K. French. 2002. Testing Trade-Off and Pecking Order Predictions about Dividends and Debt. *Review of Financial Studies* 15, no. 1: 1-33.

Fisher, Irving. 1933. The Debt-Deflation Theory of the Great Depression. *Econometrica* 1, no. 4: 337-57.

Gros, Daniel. 2011. *How to Make Ireland Solvent.* CEPS Commentary (May). Brussels: Center for European Policy Studies.

IMF (International Monetary Fund). 2011. *World Economic Outlook* (September). Washington.

Jensen, M. 1986. Agency Costs of Free Cash Flow, Corporate Finance and Takeovers. *American Economic Review* 76, no. 2: 323-29.

Koo, R. C. 2008. The Age of Balance Sheet Recessions: What Post-2008 U.S., Europe and China Can Learn from Japan 1990-2005. Presentation at the Nomura Research Institute, Tokyo, October.

Lane, Philip. 2011. *The Dynamics of Ireland's Net External Position.* IIIS Discussion Paper 388. Dublin: Institute for International Integration Studies.

Marzinotto, Benedicta, Jean Pisani-Ferry, and Guntram B. Wolff. 2011. *An Action Plan for Europe's Leaders.* Bruegel Policy Contribution 2011/09 (July). Brussels: Bruegel.

Modigliani, F., and M. Miller. 1958. The Cost of Capital, Corporation Finance and the Theory of Investment. *American Economic Review* 48: 261-97.

Modigliani, Franco. 1986. Life Cycle, Individual Thrift, and the Wealth of Nations. *American Economic Review* 76, no. 3: 297-313.

Myers, S. C., and N. S. Majluf. 1984. Corporate Financing and Investment Decisions When Firms Have Information that Investors Do Not Have. *Journal of Financial Economics* 13: 187-221.

Ruscher, E., and G. B. Wolff. 2010. Balance Sheet Adjustment in the Corporate Sector. *Quarterly Report on the Euro Area* 9, no. 3. Brussels: DG ECFIN, European Commission.

Ruscher, E., and G. B. Wolff. 2012. *Corporate Balance Sheet Adjustment: Stylized Facts, Causes and Consequences.* Bruegel Working Paper 2012/03 (January). Brussels: Bruegel.

Sorensen C. K., D. Marques Ibanez, and C. Rossi. 2009. *Modelling Loans to Non-financial Corporations in the Euro Area.* ECB Working Paper 989 (January). Frankfurt: European Central Bank.

15

General Government Net Indebtedness
Is There a Role for the Asset Side?

JACOB FUNK KIRKEGAARD

> *A national debt, if it is not excessive, will be to us a national blessing.*
> —Alexander Hamilton, letter to Robert Morris, April 30, 1781

> *It shows nobility to be willing to increase your debt to a man to whom you already owe much.*
> —Marcus Tullius Cicero

Since the beginning of the Great Recession in 2008, government debt levels in the United States and Europe have risen to unprecedented peacetime levels, approaching 100 percent of GDP. The focus of political and debt-market concerns has generally been on rising general government gross debt levels. This chapter takes a broader approach to government debt and considers two things in addition: the scope of contingent liabilities from public interventions to support financial institutions and financial markets since 2007[1] and (especially) the asset side of governments' balance sheets. I ask whether "forgotten government assets" hold the answer to today's high general government gross debt levels and attempt to estimate government financial and nonfinancial assets; consider the political and economic possibilities of disposing of recently acquired distressed assets by governments on both sides of the Atlantic; and look at the wider-ranging prospects for renewed privatization drives to reduce government debt levels.

Jacob Funk Kirkegaard has been a research fellow at the Peterson Institute for International Economics since 2002 and is also a senior associate at the Rhodium Group, a New York–based research firm.

1. The chapter addresses only the direct actions by national governments. Financial market interventions carried out by the European Central Bank and US Federal Reserve in support of financial stability and economic growth are not considered, as central banks are not deemed part of the general government for statistical and accounting purposes. Government support measures for nonfinancial institutions and general economic stimulus support are also not included.

The New Debt Reality in Europe and the United States

The Great Recession, which caused the largest decline in economic activity in 50 years in both the United States and Western Europe,[2] has through resulting declines in government revenues and necessary countercyclical stimulus spending generated the highest transatlantic peacetime general gross government debt levels in modern history.[3] This trend is summarized in table 15.1.

Table 15.1 shows that in recent years general government gross debt levels in the United States have for the first time surpassed levels in the EU-27 and euro area, as well as all individual EU-15 and euro area members except Greece, Italy, Belgium, and Ireland. Going back further in time, it is evident that general government debt in all countries (except the United Kingdom under Margaret Thatcher) rose rapidly from relatively low levels during the 1980s before beginning to decline—from a combination of rapid economic growth and spending restraints—in the United States, Belgium, and Ireland during the 1990s. After 2000, this transatlantic trend, however, reversed itself, as US general government debt levels began rising, while those of the EU-27 and euro area declined slightly. In Europe, therefore, the dramatic increase in general government indebtedness after 2007 marked a reversal of longer-term trends, while in the United States the Great Recession merely accelerated what was already rising indebtedness.

Table 15.1 further illustrates that low government debt levels going into the Great Recession provided no ex ante guarantee for countries to escape its effects. This is most evident in Ireland, where a debilitating construction and real estate collapse and an ensuing banking crisis have caused general gross government debt levels to explode from just 25 percent of GDP in 2007 to an estimated 109 percent in 2011, pushing the country into the arms of the International Monetary Fund (IMF). But it is also evident in Spain, which in August 2011 required secondary market bond purchases by the European Central Bank (ECB) to shore up confidence[4] and which as late as 2008 had less than 40 percent of debt to GDP. This issue will be further explored in the next section.

---

2. International Monetary Fund, *World Economic Outlook,* April 2009, Washington, www.imf.org.

3. Comparing debt levels at the general government level, i.e., including all subnational governmental levels at state, regional, and local levels, allows for more accurate comparisons between different countries irrespective of whether they have a unitary or federal governmental structure. Regretably, for most countries debt data at the general government level are available only for recent decades.

4. See European Central Bank, Statement by the President of the ECB, press release, Frankfurt, August 7, 2011, www.ecb.int (accessed on January 30, 2012).

Table 15.1 General government gross debt levels, 1980–2012p (percent of GDP)

Country	1980	1990	2000	2007	2008	2009	2010	2011p	2012p
United States	42.3	63.9	54.8	62.3	71.6	85.2	94.4	100.0	105.0
EU-27	n.a.	n.a.	62.4	59.4	63.7	73.9	79.5	81.8	82.8
Euro area 17	n.a.	54.1	69.1	66.2	69.7	79.1	85.4	87.9	88.7
Germany	n.a.	n.a.	59.7	65.0	66.4	74.1	84.0	82.6	81.9
France	20.7	35.2	57.3	64.2	68.2	79.0	82.3	86.8	89.4
Netherlands	n.a.	n.a.	53.8	45.3	58.2	60.8	63.7	65.5	66.5
Belgium	74.1	125.8	107.9	84.2	89.6	96.2	96.7	94.6	94.3
Austria	n.a.	56.1	66.5	60.7	63.8	69.6	72.2	72.3	73.9
Finland	10.8	13.9	43.8	35.2	33.9	43.3	48.4	50.2	50.3
Slovakia	n.a.	n.a.	50.3	29.6	27.8	35.4	41.8	44.9	46.9
Slovenia	n.a.	n.a.	26.8	23.4	22.5	35.5	37.3	43.6	47.2
Luxembourg	n.a.	n.a.	6.2	6.7	13.6	14.6	18.4	19.7	21.5
Estonia	n.a.	n.a.	5.1	3.7	4.6	7.2	6.6	6.0	5.6
Cyprus	n.a.	n.a.	48.7	58.3	48.3	58.0	60.8	64.0	66.4
Malta	n.a.	n.a.	55.9	61.8	61.3	67.3	67.1	66.3	66.1
Countries supported by the ECB									
Italy	n.a.	94.7	109.2	103.6	106.3	116.1	119.0	121.1	121.4
Spain	16.6	42.5	59.3	36.1	39.8	53.3	60.1	67.4	70.2
IMF program countries									
Greece	22.6	73.3	103.4	105.4	110.7	127.1	142.8	165.6	189.1
Portugal	n.a.	57.3	48.5	68.3	71.6	83.0	92.9	106.0	111.8
Ireland	65.2	93.5	37.8	24.9	44.4	65.2	94.9	109.3	115.4
Noneuro "old EU members"									
United Kingdom	46.1	32.6	40.9	43.9	52.0	68.3	75.5	80.8	84.8
Denmark	n.a.	n.a.	60.4	34.1	42.2	41.8	43.7	44.3	45.8
Sweden	n.a.	n.a.	53.2	40.2	38.8	42.8	39.7	36.0	32.6
Other OECD countries									
Australia	n.a.	16.2	19.3	9.6	11.7	16.9	20.5	22.8	23.8
Japan	51.4	68.0	142.1	187.7	195.0	216.3	220.0	233.1	238.4
Korea	n.a.	12.8	16.7	30.7	30.1	33.8	33.4	32.0	30.0
Canada	n.a.	75.2	82.1	66.5	71.1	83.3	84.0	84.1	84.2
Switzerland	n.a.	38.2	61.1	57.2	54.8	54.8	54.5	52.4	51.2

n.a. = not available

ECB = European Central Bank; IMF = International Monetary Fund; OECD = Organization for Economic Cooperation and Development

Note: Data for 2011 and 2012 are projected.

Source: IMF, *World Economic Outlook,* September 2011.

Transfer of Private "Distressed Assets" to the Public Sector During the Crisis

The scale of the drop in economic output during the Great Recession (reducing the denominator) and the associated drops in government revenues and scaled-up stimulus spending (increasing the numerator) are responsible for the majority of the deterioration in general government debt levels.

As seen in table 15.1, Ireland, Spain, and the United Kingdom, which as late as 2007–08 had general government debt levels below or close to 40 percent of GDP, had far higher levels by 2011. Levels in Ireland surpassed 100 percent of GDP and forced the country to seek conditional financial assistance from the IMF and the European Union. In all three countries, the Great Recession exposed the relative procyclicality of government revenues—buoyed precrisis by strong revenues related to booms in the construction, real estate, or financial services industries[5]—and showed how even their very low precrisis general government debt levels were no reliable indicator of their ultimate debt sustainability. Low gross debt levels precrisis are no panacea, and general government revenue sources reliable through the business cycle and robust to real estate and construction decelerations in particular are an important additional source of long-term fiscal stability.

However, the public policy response to the global financial crisis, which has since 2007 required US and EU government interventions in the private financial sector of an unparalleled magnitude, has played a critical role in the debt buildup, too.

In the absence of operating distressed assets/debt markets, substantial amounts of impaired or illiquid privately owned financial assets and liabilities[6] have during the course of the crisis been transferred to the general government to support individual institutions and the financial system as a whole.[7] Notable examples of entire institutions taken over by governments

---

5. See OECD (2009, 2011a, 2011b) for discussions of the high government revenue volatility in the United Kingdom, Ireland, and Spain and the need for less cyclically sensitive revenue sources.

6. Some definitions: Impaired assets are assets in a balance sheet valued in excess of their long-term fair value and consequently expected to incur future losses, while illiquid assets are assets that cannot be disposed of in the short term due to the lack of a properly functioning market (Eurostat 2011a). Distressed assets or debt typically refers to assets or debt put on sale, usually at a highly attractive price, because the owner is compelled to sell at short notice. Multiple reasons for such sales can be envisioned, including seller bankruptcy, excessive debts, or prudential and regulatory constraints.

7. Activities of central banks are outside the scope of this chapter. However, while central banks for reasons of risk control in normal times would probably never engage in transactions involving distressed assets and lend only against high-quality collateral, the global financial crisis has led to numerous examples of such transactions. On May 3, 2010, the ECB suspended its application of the minimum credit rating threshold in the collateral eligibility requirements in open market operations for the Greek government and guaranteed collateral, a suspension subsequently extended also to Ireland and Portugal. The ECB has since May 2010 been engaged in purchases of euro area government bonds through its Securities Market Program (today €152.5 billion) and the ECB

are Anglo Irish Bank, the Irish National Building Society, and Allied Irish Bank (AIB) in Ireland; Bradford & Bingley (B&B) and Northern Rock in the United Kingdom; Hypo Real Estate (HRE) and IKB Deutsche Industriebank in Germany; Caja Castilla–La Mancha (CCM) and CajaSur in Spain; and AIG, Fannie Mae, and Freddie Mac in the United States. Asset transfers from private financial institutions to the general government have also taken the form of partial guarantees of high-risk assets in some institutions[8] or the transfer of only part of the risky asset of an institution to the general government sector.[9]

The complexity of many government financial rescues and associated uncertainty about how such operations are recorded in governments' accounts raise questions about the ultimate effect on the same governments' reported indebtedness of such measures to stabilize the financial system. Two principal issues cloud the outlook.

First, there is the question of the correct sector classification—inside or outside the general government sector—of the entities created during the crisis (see box 15.1). In the European Union, where the rules concerning the Stability and Growth Pact's Excessive Deficit Procedure create an obvious incentive for national governments to seek to place any financial defeasance entity created during the crisis outside the general government sector to eliminate any potential adverse effect on annual deficit levels, this is a particular concern and has prompted a series of Eurostat statistical decisions to clarify the issue.[10]

However, this issue has also emerged in the United States, likely because the government doesn't wish to permanently take onto its books the government-sponsored enterprises (GSEs) taken into conservatorship in 2008.[11] Today, while the US executive branch continues to treat Fannie Mae and Freddie Mac as outside the US federal government for budgetary purposes,

covered bond purchase program (today €59.4 billion). See the ECB website at www.ecb.int. The US Federal Reserve in June 2008 extended credit to Maiden Lane I LLC to acquire certain assets from Bear Stearns; in November and December 2008 it extended credit to Maiden Lane II LLC and III LLC to purchase assets from AIG; it made similar moves during the operation of the Term Asset-Backed Securities Loan Facility (TALF). See the Federal Reserve website at www.federalreserve.gov.

8. An example is the loss-sharing agreement between Citigroup, the US Treasury, Federal Reserve, and FDIC involving $301 billion in Citigroup assets under the US Treasury TARP-funded Asset Guarantee Program. The guarantee was in place from January to December 2009, but did not result in any losses to the US government. See US Treasury (2010, 30f) for details.

9. An example is the transfer of €77.5 billion of WestLB assets to the government-controlled Erste Abwicklungsanstalt (EAA) in 2009. For details, see Erste Abwicklungsanstalt, Erste Abwicklungsanstalt Annual Report 2010, Düsseldorf.

10. See Eurostat (2009, 2011a, 2011b); see also related publications at http://epp.eurostat.ec.europa.eu.

11. GSEs are federally chartered but established to be privately owned and operated financial institutions; they are authorized to make loans or loan guarantees for limited purposes. GAO (2009) lists three GSEs—Fannie Mae, Freddie Mac, and the Federal Agricultural Mortgage Corporation (Farmer Mac)—while the US Office of Management and Budget typically includes the Farm Credit System and the Federal Home Loan Bank System among GSE-type entities.

Box 15.1 Accounting treatment of the public sector

Comprehensively accounting for the economic activities of governments is a complex affair, as the public sector makes up a sizeable chunk of modern economies. The *Government Finance Statistics Manual* (GFSM) of the International Monetary Fund (IMF 2001) breaks the public sector into several constituent parts, as depicted in figure B15.1.1.[1]

Figure B15.1.1 Components of the public sector

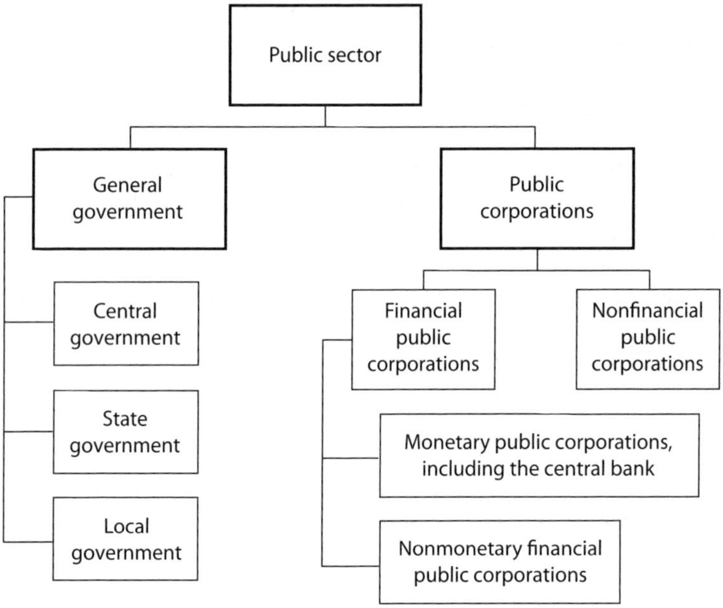

Source: IMF (2001).

The "general government" consists of all legal and administrative levels in a country, which are typically (though not exhaustively) comprised by the central, state, and local government subsectors. What is not included in the general government sector is also important, namely public corporations and quasi-corporations owned by the general government. Such corporations may carry out governmental operations and specific transactions on behalf of their general government owners in a variety of forms with fiscal policy implications, including lending to special parties at preferential interest rates, selling power to select customers at reduced rates, employing more staff than required, purchasing additional inputs at above-market prices, or selling outputs at less than market determined prices. Changes in

(box continues next page)

Box 15.1 Accounting treatment of the public sector
(continued)

the value of public corporations will moreover affect the value of the equity-type assets held by the general government.

In figure B15.1.1, the GFSM lists two separate analytical subgroupings for public corporations: (1) nonfinancial public corporations, including all resident nonfinancial corporations controlled by general government units; and (2) financial public corporations, divided into (a) monetary public corporations, including the central bank and all resident depository corporations controlled by the general government;[2] and (b) nonmonetary financial public corporations. For the purposes of this chapter, the classification of the central bank outside the general government is of particular importance.

Like private corporations, the public sector and its constituent parts also have a balance sheet, or stock compilation, as a statement of the value of the assets owned at a specific time and the financial claims, or liabilities, held by other entities against it. As with private entities, assets included on the public sector balance sheet must be economic assets over which ownership rights are enforced and from which economic benefits are derived from use over a period of time.

However, due to the sovereign character of governments, their balance sheets will invariably incorporate a wider range of assets than do private organizations. Such assets contain "infrastructure assets"—i.e., immovable nonfinancial assets with no alternative use and whose benefits accrue to the public in general, including such items as streets, highways, bridges, communication networks, military assets, and canals or dikes. Governments also own "heritage assets," generally intended to be preserved indefinitely due to historic, cultural, or educational significance. Lastly, governments by exercising their sovereign powers can create new assets for themselves by asserting ownership over naturally occurring assets that would otherwise not be subject to ownership. Such "nonproduced assets" include electromagnetic spectrum, subsoil natural resources, fresh water and hydro resources, and fishing resources in exclusive economic zones.

Table B15.1.1 presents a simplified version of a public sector entity balance sheet. In principle, the GFSM demands that the valuation of all government assets at any given time be their current market value. However, given the character of many—especially nonfinancial—government assets, in reality no functioning market for price discovery exists for most items on the public sector's balance sheet asset side. Correspondingly, the statistical reporting of general government balance sheet values is extremely limited and invariably not consistent even across industrialized countries.[3]

(box continues next page)

Box 15.1   Accounting treatment of the public sector
(continued)

Table B15.1.1   Public-sector balance sheet items

Assets	Liabilities
Financial assets	Domestic
Domestic	Currency and deposits
Currency and deposits	Securities other than shares
Securities other than shares	Loans
Loans	Shares and other equity
Shares and other equity	(public corporations only)
Insurance technical reserves	Insurance technical reserves
Financial derivatives	Financial derivatives
Other accounts receivable	Other accounts payable
Foreign	Foreign
Currency and deposits	Currency and deposits
Securities other than shares	Shares and other equity
Loans	(public corporations only)
Shares and other equity	Loans
Insurance technical reserves	Shares and other equity
Financial derivatives	Insurance technical reserves
Other accounts receivable	Financial derivatives
Monetary gold and special drawing rights	Other accounts payable
Nonfinancial assets	
Fixed assets	
Buildings and structures	
Machinery and equipment	
Other fixed assets	
Inventories	
Nonproduced assets	
Land	
Subsoil assets	
Other naturally occurring assets	

Source: IMF (2001).

Due to these data deficiencies and to differences in the collection methodologies of government financial asset data, probably no truly comparable data exist today for transatlantic net general government debt levels.[4,5] At the same time, it is evident from the composition of governments' nonfinancial assets that their value can never be an objective or exact number, but will always be a "political number." In other words, net general government debt levels are invariably wholly dependent on the political willingness of a sovereign government to make its financial and especially nonfinancial assets available for purchase by private investors, and on the conditions of the process at a given point in time.

(box continues next page)

Box 15.1 Accounting treatment of the public sector
(continued)

Dramatic political reorientations of government policy concerning the scope of the general government emerging from an urgent sovereign debt crisis (as in Greece currently) or political revolutions (1989 and after in the former communist countries) can consequently have a direct and material impact on governments' net debt levels. The launch of privatization drives from similar shifts in governments' political orientation can have the same effects.

Due to the large stock of government nonfinancial assets that could potentially be sold to private entities (at least in industrialized nations with solid governmental institutions), sovereign debt crises in the OECD countries inevitably therefore revolve around a sovereign's "willingness to pay" at least as much as its objective "capacity to pay."

---

1. This box builds extensively on the second edition of the GFSM (IMF 2001).

2. The central bank includes the central bank itself, currency boards or other independent authorities that issue national currency backed by foreign exchange reserves, and any other entity that primarily performs central bank activities.

3. This is illustrated by the fact that no country in the IMF membership reports data values for nonfinancial governmental assets to the IMF GFSM.

4. See notes to OECD, *Economic Outlook Annex*, Table 33: General Government Net Financial Liabilities (defined by the OECD here as the general government gross liabilities subtracted from general government financial assets) for a discussion of the large differences in data collection methodologies for OECD countries' general government financial asset data. OECD, Economic Outlook Sources—Notes to Statistical Annex Tables 25–33: Fiscal Balances and Public Indebtedness, www.oecd.org (accessed on January 31, 2012).

5. The general government net debt data presented in the IMF's *World Economic Outlook* are calculated in a simplified manner as gross debt minus financial assets corresponding to debt instruments. The included financial assets are monetary gold and Special Drawing Rights, currency and deposits, debt securities, loans, insurance, pension and standardized guarantee schemes, and other accounts receivable. IMF net general government debt data do not take nonfinancial government assets into account. See IMF, *World Economic Outlook* database, April 2011, www.imf.org.

the Congressional Budget Office (CBO) considers that the two GSEs should be treated in the federal budget as government entities. Neither the executive branch nor the CBO, though, incorporates debt securities or mortgage-backed securities issued by Fannie Mae and Freddie Mac in estimates of federal debt held by the public (CBO 2010).

Second, there is the broader matter of accounting for the gross and net debt effects of transfers to the general government sector of impaired or illiquid assets during the crisis. Public interventions to support private financial institutions during the crisis that involved the government's taking majority or full ownership of the rescued entity (i.e., nationalization) invariably resulted in the transfer of both assets and liabilities to the general government sector. Often, the value of liabilities assumed by the general government is easily established (assuming that for purposes of instilling financial stability the general government does not pursue default on such assumed obligations) and can be added to the general government's existing gross debt levels.

However, as described in box 15.1, the concept and extent of general government assets and their valuation is generally surrounded by considerable uncertainty. The asset value uncertainty of impaired or illiquid assets taken over in a crisis is often acute, since their long-term value is by definition uncertain. Correspondingly, the net debt effects of financial rescues are unclear, but invariably (as the recovery value of assumed assets will almost always be above zero) they are considerably smaller than the gross debt effects for the general government.

In the European Union, for the purposes of ensuring evenhanded enforcement of the Stability and Growth Pact's Excessive Deficit Procedure, Eurostat has collected a series of data covering the statistical recording of general government interventions to support financial institutions and markets during the crisis.[12] Based on statistical decisions for each reported instance of intervention, the Eurostat data classify the resulting transactions as inside or outside the general government sector and categorize their effects on general government net revenues/costs and general government assets, liabilities, and contingent liabilities.[13] Contingent liabilities are liabilities that may contribute to general government liabilities in the future, even if they are not presently recorded as government debt. In the European Union, such contingent liabilities have come predominantly in the form of government guarantees granted to private financial institutions' assets and liabilities, securities issued by the general government under liquidity schemes for banks, and the operations of special purpose vehicles.

In the United States, no comparable comprehensive official collection of data covering the impact of financial interventions on the US general government books has been found by this author. However, COP (2011) and US Treasury (2010) provide material sufficient for at least a partial replication of US data comparable to those of Eurostat. US data for incurred contingent liabilities, however, are not available. Figure 15.1 brings together Eurostat and compiled US data.

---

12. Eurostat data cover seven types of transactions particularly relevant in this regard: general government–led recapitalization operations, lending, guarantee issuance, purchase of assets and defeasance, exchange of assets, new bodies created during the crisis, and transactions carried out by public corporations. See Eurostat (2009, 2011a).

13. General government liabilities here refer to liabilities incurred by the general government to finance its interventions. Such liabilities come in the form of new government bond issuance or direct loans taken out. See Eurostat (2011a, 8f).

Figure 15.1 General government assets, liabilities, and contingent liabilities from public interventions to support financial institutions, end-2010

percent of GDP

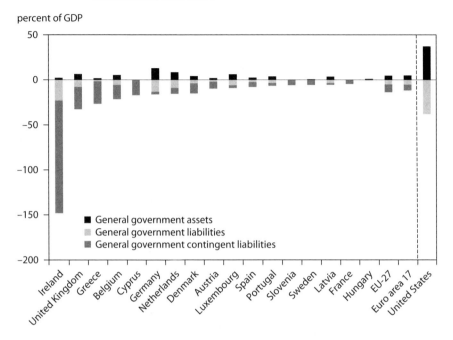

Sources: Eurostat (2011a); US Treasury (2010); Fannie Mae, *Annual Report 2010*, www.fanniemae.com; Freddie Mac, *Annual Report 2010*, www.freddiemac.com.

Figure 15.1 shows the impact on general government assets and liabilities of interventions by the 17 EU members (where such interventions were recorded by Eurostat) and by the United States.[14] It is noteworthy that in almost all countries, the relative magnitude of assets and liabilities transferred to the general government sector roughly correspond. As such, there could be a relatively limited impact of financial market interventions since 2007 on transatlantic general government net debt levels.

Only in Ireland, where very large capital injections into the country's banking sector have been financed with new general government liabilities, and where relatively few assets have been transferred directly to it in return, have public crisis interventions led to sizeable increases in net debt levels. The Irish government's National Asset Management Agency (NAMA) is not part of

---

14. There were 10 EU members with no changes to general government assets, liabilities, or contingent liabilities stemming from reported crisis interventions: Bulgaria, the Czech Republic, Finland, Estonia, Italy, Lithuania, Malta, Poland, Romania, and Slovakia. In three of these (Finland, Italy, and Lithuania) interventions affected general government deficits, but not directly the assets, liabilities, and contingent liabilities of the general government.

the Irish general government and is thus excluded from these data.[15] Yet when NAMA purchased €71.2 billion in loan assets from five financial institutions involving 850 debtors with more than 11,000 individual loans collateralized by 16,000 individual properties, it paid only €30.2 billion for them, implying an average 58 percent haircut on transferred private assets. Consequently, the just-over €30 billion in bonds (19 percent of GDP) issued by NAMA is offset by assets acquired at a very substantial discount. Consolidating NAMA into the general government of Ireland will therefore in all likelihood have a relatively limited impact on general government net debt, and depending on the ultimate value of the asset acquired may even serve to reduce Ireland's net debt.

Ireland's outlier status in Europe is further illustrated by the magnitude of the Irish government's contingent liabilities, which even after already incurred losses remain at 125 percent of GDP,[16] or five times the level of contingent liabilities in second- and third-placed Britain and Greece, and far in excess of the EU and euro area average of 7 to 9 percent of GDP.

The largest EU private asset (and liability) transfer directly to the general government, at 13 percent of GDP, has occurred in Germany; the next-largest in the Netherlands, at 8 percent, and then the United Kingdom and Luxembourg at 6 percent of GDP. This illustrates the scale of the private financial sector crisis in Germany, where the collapse of several financial institutions has seen €318 billion in distressed German bank assets transferred to the German general government,[17] accounting for nearly 75 percent of all asset transfers in the euro area (€440 billion at end-2010) and amounting to almost three times the level of distressed assets transferred from UK banks to the British government (€109 billion excluding the value of now majority-owned Royal Bank of Scotland).

In terms of distressed assets, therefore, Germany has by a substantial margin had the second-worst banking crisis in Europe. As an instructive comparison, it should be noted that even if the Spanish government uses up all the available €99 billion in its bank rescue fund to comprehensively recapitalize its Caja sector, Madrid will still likely end up spending less to clean up its failed banks than the German government. Obviously, the German banking crisis has not occurred on the back of a domestic housing slump and hence is not accompanied by the same macroeconomic downturn as seen in Ireland or

---

15. The decision to exclude NAMA from the Irish general government was taken by Eurostat. See National Asset Management Agency, Annual Report 2010, Dublin; and NTMA (2011).

16. Ireland's contingent liabilities were 196 percent of GDP at the end of 2008 and 176 percent at the end of 2009.

17. The majority of transferred distressed assets in Germany are associated with the Hypo Real Estate group, in relation to which in late 2010 €175 billion of assets was transferred to the German federal government's FMS Wertmanagement "wind-up company." See FMS Wertmanagement Annual Report 2010, Berlin. Meanwhile, at the German state level, Erste Abwicklungsanstalt, which was controlled by the state government of North Rhein–Westphalia, in 2010 saw the transfer €77.5 billion of assets from the troubled WestLB Landesbank. See Erste Abwicklungsanstalt Annual Report 2010, Düsseldorf.

Spain; but as a standalone banking crisis, Germany's is proving very expensive indeed.

The two principal German "wind-up companies"—the federal government's FMS Wertmanagement (FMS) and the state of North Rhein–Westphalia's Erste Abwicklungsanstalt (EAA)—have been reclassified by Eurostat (2011a) as part of the general government; thus these transfers have led to an increase in reported German gross general government debt of 9.5 percentage points of GDP from 2009 to 2010, accounting for the vast majority of the total 2010 German debt increase to a level of 82.3 percent of German GDP. The troubled German banking sector therefore accounts for essentially all the deterioration in 2010 of recorded gross general government debt in Germany. Without transfers of impaired assets and liabilities, Germany's 2010 real growth rate of 3.5 percent and general government deficit of 3.3 percent would otherwise have meant an essentially stable debt-to-GDP ratio. With FMS and EAA already consolidated into the German general government sector, in the event that the companies are successful in their goal of liquidating transferred portfolios while limiting the costs to the German taxpayer, a future downward revision of reported German general government gross debt is plausible.[18]

Figure 15.1 illustrates that the scale of assets and liabilities transferred from the private sector to the general government sector in the United States is considerably larger than in Europe. The US data included in figure 15.1 refer to the outstanding balance of Troubled Asset Relief Program (TARP) funds and the transfer of GSEs Fannie Mae and Freddie Mac to conservatorship in the US Treasury. While, as mentioned above, the US executive branch does not consider the two GSEs part of the federal (and thereby general) US government for budgetary or debt recognition purposes, the logic and outcome of their financial rescue by the US Treasury in 2008 should demand such treatment, and the rescue certainly is similar to those recorded by Eurostat in the European Union.[19]

Figure 15.1 shows how the consolidation of roughly comparable private assets and liabilities transferred to the US government during the crisis would add little to the net US general government debt position by end-2010.[20] On

---

18. The recent discovery of a €55.5 billion "accounting error" in FMS Wertmanagement, leading to a likely 2.6 percent downward revision in German government debt, is illustrative of this potential. See *Financial Times*, "Germany €55bn Richer After Error at Hypo 'Bad Bank,'" October 29, 2011.

19. The notion that entities financially guaranteed and managerially completely controlled by the US federal government should not be considered a part of the general government sector defies economic logic and common sense, especially considering that Ginnie Mae (the Government National Mortgage Association), which performs the same tasks from within the Department of Housing and Urban Development, is so considered. See www.ginniemae.gov.

20. As the US Treasury has since 2008 guaranteed the two companies' positive cash position, deteriorations of the asset quality in Fannie Mae and Freddie Mac will lead to an ongoing increase in the US federal government debt. The US Treasury has already provided the two GSEs with over

the other hand, such a consolidation of transferred assets and liabilities would have added materially to the reported gross US general government debt levels reported above in table 15.1. US gross general government debts would rise to 129 percent of GDP in 2010, below only Japan (220 percent) and Greece (142 percent), but significantly above Italy (119 percent) and more than 50 percent higher than the euro area average.[21]

The United States stands in contrast to Germany (and several other EU countries), where the effects of financial rescues have largely been consolidated onto the government balance sheet and are already reflected in reported gross government debt numbers. The lack of such recognition in reported US general government gross debt levels means that there can be no future improvement in reported US government gross debt levels arising from the US government's successful unwinding of its rescued GSEs.

Future General Government Consolidation Requirements

Today's exceptional general government gross debt levels will require equally exceptional longer-term fiscal adjustment on both sides of the Atlantic to restore debt ratios to what can be considered sustainable levels. Generally a ratio of 60 percent of gross government debt to GDP is considered reasonable, as it provides governments the fiscal space to launch a forceful countercyclical fiscal stimulus program in the event of a sudden deep economic downturn without the risk of triggering immediate solvency concerns.[22] In the European Union, the 60 percent long-term debt target is of course also enshrined in the European Treaty,[23] where (following recent euro area decisions) it has taken on a new degree of policy relevance. After having been de facto ignored by the euro area to facilitate the founding euro member status of Italy and Belgium,[24]

$100 billion in new capital in this way. See Fannie Mae, Annual Report 2010, www.fanniemae.com (accessed on February 1, 2012), and Freddie Mac, Annual Report 2010, www.freddiemac.com (accessed on February 1, 2012). The CBO currently includes estimates of such future losses in its baseline budget projections for the US federal government.

21. Gross debt data for Greece, Italy, and the euro area include the effects of financial rescue operations conducted up to end-2010.

22. As will be discussed further below, very rapid increases in public liabilities related to banking crises and an economic downturn have the potential to render insufficient a precrisis level of gross government debt of 60 percent of GDP. See IMF (2011a) for a discussion of the appropriateness of a long-term gross government debt target of 60 percent of GDP.

23. Protocol #12 of the Excessive Deficit Procedure, annexed to the Treaty of the European Union; see http://eur-lex.europa.eu.

24. The original 60 percent gross debt reference value in the Maastricht Treaty was circumvented from the beginning of Economic and Monetary Union through the addition to Article 126 (formerly Article 104) in the European Treaty of the clause that debt values above 60 percent of GDP would be excessive "unless the ratio is sufficiently diminishing and approaching the reference value at a satisfactory pace." What would constitute an insufficiently diminishing ratio at an unsatisfactory pace has never been established by European leaders.

the March 2011 decision by euro area leaders to introduce an annual numerical benchmark of 1/20 reduction in debt in excess of the reference value 60 percent[25] reintroduces the 60 percent gross debt level as a key long-term policy target in the euro area.

Figure 15.2 shows the scope of required fiscal consolidation in the United States and Europe, in terms of improvements to the general government cyclically adjusted primary balance (CAPB), to achieve a 60 percent gross government debt level by 2030. It also shows the total fiscal consolidation required when taking into consideration projected aging-related increases in health care and pension spending between 2010 and 2030 (requiring offsetting fiscal measures).[26]

Figure 15.2 shows that at 19 percent of nominal GDP (black/striped bar), Greece requires the largest improvement in the general government CAPB to reach a 60 percent gross debt level by 2030, including projected rising general government health care and pension costs. The figure for Greece surpasses the 17 percent required improvement in the United States and the 13 to 14 percent in Portugal, Ireland, and the United Kingdom. Required consolidation in Greece and the United States is significantly above required levels in Spain, too, and more than twice those of France, which requires a 7.9 percent of nominal GDP improvement in the CAPB. Meanwhile, low required adjustment for Italy—at just over 4 percent—illustrates Rome's existing positive CAPB and relatively modest projected increases in pension and health care expenses.[27] Germany, Finland, and Denmark similarly face relatively modest additional future fiscal consolidation, and Sweden and Estonia none at all, to secure the 60 percent debt target by 2030.

With fiscal consolidation on both sides of the Atlantic requiring historic improvements in countries' CAPB and consequently presenting governments with sizeable political implementation challenges, the scope of required future fiscal measures relative to the existing weight of the government in the economy becomes relevant. The same amount of improvement in the CAPB in terms of GDP may be politically easier to achieve in countries with a relatively larger existing general governmental sector, as it will require a relatively smaller change in the status quo. Countries with a small existing general government share of the economy (like the United States) can be said to possess substantial "hypothetical fiscal space" from potential future revenue increases

---

25. See Conclusions of the Heads of State and Government of the Euro Area of March 11, 2011, http://consilium.europa.eu (accessed on January 31, 2012).

26. Data from IMF (2011a) rely on a modeled fiscal adjustment strategy, which assumes CAPBs improve in line with April 2011 Fiscal Monitor projections between 2011 and 2012 and gradually from 2013 until 2020, after which they are maintained constant until 2030. Data on projected health care and pension spending increases to be offset are from IMF (2011a, statistical table 9 and appendix 1).

27. See also IMF (2011c) for a discussion of Italy's relatively benign long-term debt sustainability projections.

Figure 15.2 Required fiscal adjustment to achieve 60 percent gross debt target by 2030 (change in cyclically adjusted primary balance)

percent of nominal GDP/general government revenues

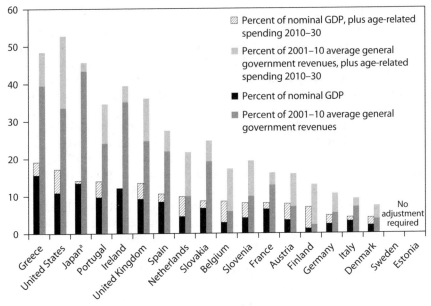

a. For Japan, a 2030 net debt target of 80 percent of GDP (200 percent gross) is assumed.

Source: IMF (2011f) and *World Economic Outlook*, September 2011.

to move the CAPB toward sustainability.[28] However, judging from the ongoing debate in the United States, it is evident that the political obstacles to accessing hypothetical fiscal space through legislating future revenue increases can be at least as high as (if not higher than) the political obstacles associated with very substantial cuts in government spending in European countries with a large existing general government sector. Ongoing coordinated fiscal austerity in Europe thus suggests—perhaps as a result of the more urgent and severe debt crisis there—that cutting spending in crises to restore fiscal sustainability in "big government" countries is today politically easier than raising revenues in "small government" countries (like the United States) to achieve the same goal.

To capture the magnitudes of required fiscal consolidation relative to the current size of countries' general government sectors, figure 15.2 also shows

---

28. Actual "fiscal space" is defined in Heller (2005) as "room in a government's budget that allows it to provide resources for a desired purpose without jeopardizing the sustainability of its financial position or the stability of the economy."

the CAPB consolidation efforts as a share of average general government revenue during the decade from 2001 to 2010.

The United States at 52.6 percent stands out as having the biggest future political challenge of fiscal consolidation relative to the status quo (measured as a share of the average 10-year general government revenues), due to its relatively smaller government sector (an average 32 percent of GDP from 2001 to 2010, compared to for instance 39 percent in Greece or 45 percent in Italy).[29] Greece at 48 percent is almost at US levels, while Ireland, Portugal, and the United Kingdom face fiscal consolidation efforts above one-third of the long-term average size of the general government. Meanwhile, by this metric, the West European countries with relatively larger general government sectors face a smaller future fiscal consolidation effort.

General Government Assets and Potential Privatization Proceeds

These future consolidation requirements to reduce gross debt levels to sustainable levels are of a truly herculean magnitude, and justifiable concerns will arise about the transatlantic political willingness to ultimately restore general government fiscal stability through traditional means of revenue increases and spending cuts. Other government policy initiatives will have to be considered to help restore the health of government finances.

As described in Reinhart and Rogoff (2010) and Kirkegaard, Reinhart, and Belén Sbrancia (2011), several other avenues to restoring fiscal sustainability apart from austerity are open to governments. These include sovereign defaults, bursts of unexpected inflation combined with financial repression, and rapid growth. Each has such large drawbacks, however, that its efficacy must be questioned. Attempting to restore fiscal sustainability through a sovereign default is patently mad, as the cure kills the patient, while creating abrupt spikes in inflation and financially repressing the private sector will also be both difficult and costly for individual governments in a relatively open and financially integrated global economy. Lastly, the long-term demographic outlook for both the United States and especially Europe will in all probability make rapid economic growth an impossible road to a sizeable reduction in the transatlantic debt burden.

Yet, as indicated above, there is a large difference between the gross and net debt implications of financial rescue operations in all countries analyzed in this chapter, due to the simultaneous transfer of sizeable assets to the general government sector. This same difference in overall gross and net debt positions exists for the entire general government sector, as recorded government assets are sizeable in several countries. The complete recording and utilization of government assets therefore offers an additional road toward

---

29. See IMF, *World Economic Outlook*, September 2011, www.imf.org (accessed on February 1, 2012).

fiscal sustainability, beyond the ongoing (generally) positive revenue return from governments' asset holdings.

As discussed in box 15.1, significant concerns about data surround the recording of comprehensive and correctly valued general government assets. Fiscal sustainability analyses of a general government net debt basis are therefore complicated to carry out. Two principal data sources exist for general government net debt information for the United States and Europe: the IMF's *World Economic Outlook* (WEO) database and the Organization for Economic Cooperation and Development (OECD) *Economic Outlook* Annex Tables.[30]

These two sources are not methodologically similar. The general government net debt data presented in the IMF's WEO are calculated in a simplified manner as gross debt minus financial assets corresponding to debt instruments. The included financial assets are monetary gold and special drawing rights, currency and deposits, debt securities, loans, insurance, pension and standardized guarantee schemes, and other accounts receivable. IMF net general government debt data do not take nondebt instrument government assets into account and therefore avoid any uncertainty concerning (for instance) the estimation of future projected earnings from equity holdings.[31]

On the other hand, OECD "net government debt" data, or more precisely data on general government net financial liabilities, include data for a wider range of government financial assets, including general government nondebt assets such as equity participation in private sector companies and holdings in public corporations.[32] OECD net financial liabilities data are estimated as simply general government financial assets minus (all recorded) financial liabilities, making the result akin to the general government's "net financial worth." The status and treatment of government prefunded assets and pension liabilities in public employee pension plans are a further very significant source of divergence across countries. The distinction in the 1993 System of National Accounts between "autonomous" (outside the general government sector) and "nonautonomous" (inside the general government sector with the funded component reflected in the books) means that some EU countries (like Finland) have prefunded pension plans reported as part of the general government and as contributing to general government assets, while most countries don't. This makes cross-country comparability of net government debts problematic.

Figure 15.3 shows available US and European gross and net debts, as well as debt assets from the IMF WEO database and "other financial assets" from the OECD *Economic Outlook* Annex Tables. The figure underlines the

---

30. These are available, respectively, at www.imf.org and www.oecd.org.

31. This simplification, however, clearly understates the assets of country governments with large listed and nonlisted equity holdings outside the general government sector. See also IMF (2011f, appendix 3).

32. See OECD, EO Sources—Notes to Statistical Annex Tables 25–33: Fiscal Balances and Public Indebtedness, www.oecd.org (accessed on January 31, 2012).

Figure 15.3   General government gross and net debt, debt assets, and other financial assets, 2010

percent of GDP

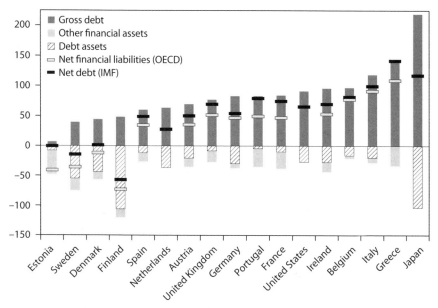

Sources: Organization for Economic Cooperation and Development, *Economic Outlook: Economic Background Annex Tables*, 2011; International Monetary Fund, *World Economic Outlook* database, September 2011.

precarious state of Greece, which according to the IMF had similar gross and net debts in 2010 and was the only country with no debt assets. OECD data meanwhile suggest that the Greek general government possesses about 33 percent of GDP in other types of financial assets.[33]

At the same time, if one believes the OECD data, Greece's actual net general government debt in 2010 was only around 109 percent of GDP. Combined with the fact that parts of the most recent Greek bailout package from July 21, 2011, will add further to general government assets, this suggests that the gross debt-to-GDP ratio projections for Greece overstate the country's solvency problem.[34] Part of the envisioned future gross debt increase for Greece is scheduled to be set aside for zero-coupon AAA-rated assets as collateral for the

33. The lack of Greek general government debt assets is partly an outcome of the country's pension system, which historically has been a wholly public PAYGO system with no prefunded or private components. OECD Global Pension Statistics show no assets in either autonomous or nonautonomous Greek pension systems. See OECD Global Pension Statistics database at www.oecd.org/daf/pensions/gps.

34. See Cline (2011) for an in-depth discussion.

private sector involvement.[35] Up to 10 percent of GDP is furthermore scheduled to be used to recapitalize the Greek banking system, a set of transactions through which—assuming the government takes ownership shares—government assets will also be accumulated.

Figure 15.3 also shows general government net debt levels, when estimated with the more inclusive OECD data, are generally lower in Europe than in the United States. Only Greece, Italy, and Belgium had net government debts higher than the United States in 2010. Meanwhile, in Denmark, Sweden, and Estonia, large general government financial assets surpassed outstanding government gross debts in 2010.

Another source of information about government assets is the value of any equity holdings in listed companies.[36] Selling such holdings to private buyers could immediately raise funds for the general government to potentially reduce gross debt. Table 15.2 contains a nonexhaustive list of EU government equity holdings in listed companies in 2011.

France is easily the country with the most equity holdings in currently listed companies, with holdings valued at €130 billion in early 2011,[37] but Italy's holdings also surpassed €50 billion. Only in Finland did equity holdings surpass 10 percent of GDP (figure 15.3 similarly showed Finland as a country with large government financial assets), while elsewhere in the euro area holdings were small as a share of the total national economy.

Government assets need not be held only in currently listed companies. Indeed, the vast number of public corporations are unlisted companies; to potentially raise revenue from them governments would have to either list them on the stock market or sell them outright to a private buyer through a privatization transaction.[38] Figure 15.4 shows the total government revenue obtained by EU-15 governments from privatizations between 1977 and 2009.[39] Just as the French government today still retains larger equity holdings than other governments in Europe or the United States (table 15.2), it is also the EU-15 country that has historically privatized most assets; its assets are valued in current dollars at over $200 billion, a level followed by Italy at around $175 billion. Meanwhile, looking at privatization measured as a share of 2010 GDP, Portugal has historically been the EU-15's most intensive privatizer, with 16 percent of 2010 GDP between 1977 and 2009, followed by Finland at 13 percent and Greece and Sweden at 10 percent.

---

35. Institute of International Finance, Private Creditor-Investor Group on Greece Forms Steering Committee to Pursue Bond Negotiations, IIF Press Release, November 28, 2011, www.iif.com.

36. Such holdings are included in the OECD but not IMF data for general government net debts.

37. Given the recent decline in European stock markets, the valuations listed in table 15.2 from February 2011 are likely to be higher than today.

38. See OECD (2011c) for older survey data breaking out the value of listed and unlisted government equity holdings.

39. Figure 15.4 is computed from current dollar transaction values and will hence underestimate the real value of transactions conducted early in the period.

Table 15.2   Government holdings of quoted shares and other equity-like holdings, February 2011 (billions of euros)

Entity	Value	Entity	Value
France		Outokumpo	1.1
Électricité de France SA	66.0	Rautaruukki Corporation	1.3
GDF Suez SA	32.0	Sponda PLC	0.2
France Telecom	16.0	Others	0.5
Aéroports de Paris	4.0	Total	23.2
Safran SA	4.0	Percent of 2010 GDP	12.9
Renault SA	3.0	**Greece**	
Thales Group	2.0		
Air France-KLM	0.9	Piraeus Bank	0.02
Dexia SA[a]	0.5	Hellenic Telecom	1.1
Dexia Belgium[a]	1.9	Public Power Corporation	1.9
CNP Assurances	0.1	OPAP SA	2.3
Areva-Ci	0.1	Hellenic Petroleum SA	1.1
European Aeronautic Defence		Athens Water & Sewage	0.4
and Space Company NV		Pireaus Port Authority	0.3
(EADS)	0.01	Others	0.5
Total	130.4	Total	7.62
Percent of 2010 GDP	6.7	Percent of 2010 GDP	3.3
Italy		**Belgium**	
Ente Nazionale per l'Energia		Dexia Belgium[a]	0.5
Elettrica SpA (ENEL)	17.0	Belgacom	6.8
Eni SpA	30.0	Total	7.3
Finmeccanica	2.2	Percent of 2010 GDP	2.1
Terna	3.7	**Austria**	
Total	52.9		
Percent of 2010 GDP	3.3	Verbund AG	3.9
Germany		Telekom Austria Group	1.8
		Österreichische Post AG	1.1
Commerzbank[a]	2.7	Total	6.8
Deutsche Telekom	18.8	Percent of 2010 GDP	2.4
Deutsche Post	6.9	**Portugal**	
Total	28.4		
Percent of 2010 GDP	1.1	Energias de Portugal	3.6
Finland		Galp Energia	1.2
		Total	4.8
Fortum OYJ	13.7	Percent of 2010 GDP	2.8
Sampo Group	2.6	**Ireland**	
Nokia Corporation	0.1		
Kone Oyj	0.1	Bank of Ireland[a]	1.0
Stora Enso Oyj	1.2	Aer Lingus	0.2
Metso Corporation	0.1	Total	1.2
Neste Oil	2.3	Percent of 2010 GDP	0.8

(table continues next page)

Table 15.2 Government holdings of quoted shares and other equity-like holdings, February 2011 (billions of euros) *(continued)*

Addendum: United States (Troubled Asset Relief Program)	
	Percent of shares
General Motors	33.3
Chrysler	9.2
Ally Financial	73.8
AIG	92.2

Addendum: Japan[b]	
	Value (trillions of yen)
Japan Post Holdings Company Limited	9.6
Japan Finance Corporation	4.5
Development Bank of Japan, Inc.	2.2
Nippon Telegraph and Telephone Corporation (NTT)	2.0
Japan Tobacco	1.7
Other corporations (15)	1.8
Total	21.8
Percent of 2010 GDP	4.6

a. Acquired via emergency capital infusion during crisis.
b. Value as of March 31, 2010.

Sources: COP (2011); UBS Investments Research (2011); Japan Ministry of Finance (2011).

Figure 15.4 illustrates that European countries—even countries today under IMF programs—have in earlier privatization campaigns been able to raise substantial amounts of revenue from divesting previously state-owned assets. Yet given that between 1977 and 2009 Greece managed to privatize just over $30 billion worth of state assets, it is equally clear that the country's commitment to divesting €15 billion ($20 billion) by end-2012 and €50 billion ($67 billion, about 20 percent of GDP) by end-2015 is extremely ambitious by the country's historical standards (IMF 2011d).[40] Less ambitious in a historical context is the Portuguese commitment to the IMF to privatize state assets totaling €5 billion (around 3 percent of GDP) by end-2013 (IMF 2011e), considering Portugal's earlier privatization revenues were $37 billion. Meanwhile, in Ireland the key privatization issue facing the government is what to do about the roughly €30 billion (acquisition cost) of private assets taken over by NAMA since the beginning of the crisis. Historically, Irish governments can be seen in figure 15.4 not to have raised much revenue of this type, but

---

40. Revenues are scheduled to come from sales of listed companies (€5 billion), unlisted companies (€2 billion), infrastructure concessions (€9 billion), and roughly €35 billion from state-owned real estate assets with clear legal title.

Figure 15.4   Total revenues from privatizations, 1977–2009

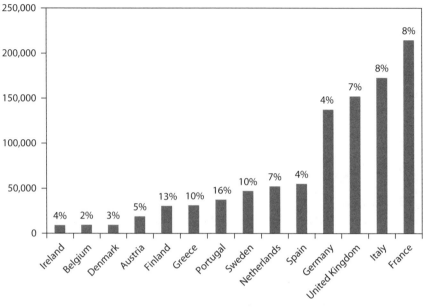

millions of US dollars

Note: No adjustments to "real dollars" has been made, meaning total sum values underestimate "real revenue values." Numbers above bars are the dollar figures as percent of the country's 2010 GDP.

Source: Privatization Barometer (2011).

the current government has nonetheless set a €7.5 billion (5 percent of GDP) NAMA asset sales revenue target by end-2013.[41]

Decisions to privatize state assets should not be dictated by either acute crisis requirements for cash (fire sales) or by a "small government is good government" ideology. Rather, they must always be evaluated against the expected value of lost future government revenue. Frequently, in addition to instant new cash revenues, privatization can secure large productivity improvements, as governments can escape the need to continuously subsidize loss-making state-owned enterprises and new private owners are better able to reallocate and restructure such assets (OECD 2011c). Yet governments should be particularly wary of selling off lucrative monopolies, such as in gambling, to private investors, both because the public sector thereby risks losing stable and sizeable future revenue streams and because private monopolies almost invariably reduce consumer welfare compared to government monopolies. Particularly during times of acute financial market stress,

41. National Asset Management Agency, Annual Report 2010, Dublin.

sudden large-scale privatization initiatives may therefore result in too little new revenue being raised right away to make up for the future loss of control of state assets.

Traditional privatization revenues (as opposed to those raised by divesting distressed NAMA assets taken over by the Irish government during the country's financial crisis) are expected to play a material role in restoring short-term fiscal sustainability only in Greece among the current IMF program countries. It seems clear that for this commitment to be successfully achieved the IMF's and European Union's new involvement in the Greek economy must usher in a political/economic revolution not dissimilar to the fall of the Berlin Wall in 1989. The demise of communist state control of East European economies was accompanied by large-scale privatization campaigns across the region during the 1990s. Only through a similarly decisive break with past political resistance to privatization will Athens be able to create a sufficiently large improvement in its business climate to attract private sector buyers for its assets. The coming years will indicate whether this is politically feasible and sufficient private risk appetite can be mobilized.

There is doom aplenty surrounding Greece and much of the rest of the euro area. Yet at the same time, recent elections in both Ireland and Portugal led to governments where strong majorities favored IMF reform in the midst of deep recessions, while in general EU national elections since the beginning of the financial crisis in late 2007 have produced fiscally conservative winning platforms.[42] Thus it cannot be ruled out that the current economic crisis in Europe has led to a lasting shift in public perceptions about the scope of government in the euro area and consequently that a new wave of privatizations might be unleashed as a result. This shift has occurred partly due to sheer economic and financial necessity, partly enabled by the associated crisis-generated shift in public opinion.

This raises the question of whether euro area governments may in the near term be able to begin to better utilize the forgotten part of their balance sheet, their real estate and other fixed assets, for new revenue-generation purposes. So far this section has focused exclusively on governments' financial assets, but as discussed in box 15.1, governments also hold an extensive portfolio of fixed assets, which crisis-induced shifts in public opinion might enable euro area governments to increasingly offload through new privatizations. In contrast to data for governments' financial assets, whose availability

---

42. The most extraordinary example is Latvia, which has now twice reelected a government that oversaw a 20 percent decline in living standards since 2007. Other noticeable election results are the historic reelection of a center-right government in Sweden in September 2010, and the UK Conservative party's victory in May 2010 after a campaign of explicit promises of tough future austerity. As of fall 2011, traditional center-left parties in Europe are part of the government in only Spain, Austria, Slovenia, Greece, Finland (junior coalition member), and non-EU Norway and Iceland.

Figure 15.5 Euro area general government net fixed assets, 2010

billions of euros

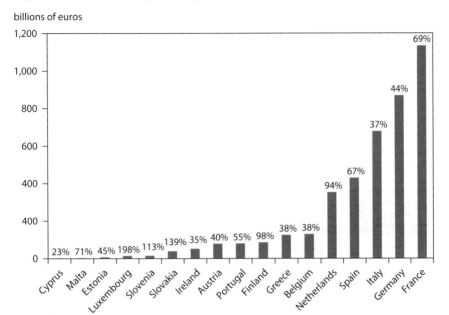

Note: Numbers above bars are the euro figures as percent of the country's 2010 general government gross debt.

Sources: Eurostat database, http://epp.eurostat.ec.europa.eu; European Central Bank, www.ecb.int.

is merely poor, reliable estimates of the scope and value of governments' fixed assets do not exist at all. The best approximation is an aggregate number for the entire euro area published regularly by the ECB, which stood at €4.1 trillion in the fourth quarter of 2010. Assuming that the ratio of total fixed assets in the euro area is the same as the available ratio for governments' annual consumption of fixed capital, this aggregate number can then be broken into approximate estimated national values. This is done in figure 15.5 for the end-2010 values.

By virtue of their size, the largest euro area members will of course have the largest holdings of net fixed assets. France again leads the euro area in this government asset measure with over €1.1 trillion in fixed assets, followed by Germany at €872 billion and Italy at €680 billion.[43] By this estimation Greece

---

43. Incomplete fixed asset data from the OECD's Detailed National Accounts Database, 2011, http://stats.oecd.org, shows general government fixed asset data values comparable to those in figure 15.5, albeit for the year 2009. Finland reports €87 billion, Belgium €126 billion, Netherlands €357 billion, Germany €1,068 billion, and France €888 billion.

has €125 billion in fixed assets, Portugal around €80 billion, and Ireland just over €50 billion. The Greek estimate of €125 billion in government fixed assets is considerably lower than an estimate, discussed by IMF staff in the spring of 2011, of over 100 percent of GDP in "potentially privatizable assets" in Greece ultimately controlled by the Greek government.[44]

However, on top of the methodological uncertainties surrounding the estimated values in figure 15.5, it must be clear that "total fixed assets" contain far more than any government could plausibly privatize under any circumstance. As discussed in box 15.1, many government assets are "heritage assets" of important national, educational, and historical value, which could never be sold off. The values in figure 15.5 (even if they were correctly estimated) thus represent substantially more fixed assets than could be converted into new revenues even under the best political and economic circumstances.

As indicated by the numbers for total fixed assets as a share of 2010 gross government debts, it is consequently not realistic to assume that even historically large new privatization drives in the EU-15 will be able to seriously erode gross debt levels in high-debt euro area countries. Total fixed asset levels between 35 and 40 percent in Greece, Italy, and Belgium are evidence of the futility of such hopes.[45]

The sudden emergence of new "created fixed assets" on euro area balance sheets, similar to the large auction revenues from the sale of electromagnetic spectrum to telecommunication carriers in the early 2000s, cannot be ruled out in the future. Likewise, governments might find innovative ways to securitize future revenue streams with investors for immediate cash payments, or engage in leaseback arrangements by selling real estate assets and leasing them immediately back. Substantial longer-term productivity improvements, which almost always emerge from outright privatization transactions, may also be feasible from this type of government fixed asset management operation (Nicoletti and Scarpetta 2003, OECD 2011c).

Yet the magnitudes in figure 15.5 ultimately suggest that such "asset sweating" measures will play at most a peripheral role in returning today's high-debt countries to more long-term sustainable net debt levels in the future. The asset side of general governments' balance sheets on both sides of the Atlantic cannot credibly substitute for required new revenue, spending, and most importantly growth-enhancing structural reforms to address current gross debt levels.

---

44. See IMF, Transcript of a Press Briefing with IMF European Department Director Antonio Borges, Washington, April 15, 2011, www.imf.org (accessed on January 31, 2012).

45. In the European Union under the Stability and Growth Pact rules, privatization proceeds moreover do not generally count toward reducing annual deficits, even if they reduce government total gross debt levels. In accounting terms, large privatization proceeds would consequently reduce annual deficits only through reduced government interest expenses.

A final straightforward way to illustrate the finding above—that the asset side of government balance sheets can play only a relatively modest role in restoring transatlantic fiscal sustainability—is to estimate what impact assets could have on the primary surplus required to stabilize different levels of government debt. The general debt sustainability criterion stipulates that the government primary surplus (PS) required to stabilize debt levels is given by $PS = d\ (r - g)/(1 + g)$, where d = debt/GDP ratio, g = nominal growth ratio, and r = interest rate on government debt.[46] Usually, such sustainability estimates are based on governments' gross debt levels, but they may also be estimated using net debt levels. Doing so implies assuming that all recorded government assets can be converted into cash and used to service or pay off parts of outstanding gross debt. As discussed in box 15.2 for the United States, this is an implausible assumption, but for the purposes of illustrating the relative scope of the impact government assets could potentially have on debt sustainability, this exercise nonetheless has heuristic value. Table 15.3 shows debt sustainability estimates for selected countries based on general government gross debt levels, IMF net debt levels, and OECD net financial liability levels.

Table 15.3 shows that in most countries, the primary balance required for debt sustainability is only marginally lower when relying on net debt data instead of higher gross debt levels. Rows 6 to 8 show that in Germany, the difference is just 0.2 percent of GDP, in Italy and Spain 0.3 percent, and in the United Kingdom and the United States 0.2 percent. Meanwhile, only in Portugal and Greece, at 0.8 and 1.5 percent respectively in the required primary balance, is the difference of a politically and fiscally meaningful size. Relying on net debt levels for Portugal instead of gross levels thus reduces the required improvement in the primary balance from 1.3 percent of GDP (row 10) to 0.5 percent of GDP (row 12), while in Greece the same reduction is from 3.2 to 1.7 percent of GDP. In other words, only in countries with low nominal growth and high interest costs does the gross versus net debt difference make a real difference and do government assets have any substantive relevance.

In countries like the United States, Japan, France, Germany, and the United Kingdom, the (impossible) assumption that all recorded government assets could be used to reduce outstanding gross debt makes just a few decimal points' difference in the required primary balances for debt sustainability.

Concluding Remarks

Beginning with present-day high general government debt levels, this chapter has analyzed both the effects of government interventions to support financial markets during the Great Recession and the scope and character of the

---

46. See also Goldstein (2003) and Cline (2011) for a discussion of debt sustainability.

Box 15.2   US federal government debt: Different holders, different impact?

In June 2011, the total federal government outstanding debt was $14.3 trillion, amounting to 95.8 percent of nominal second quarter 2011 GDP. Thus the vast majority of general US government debt is evidently issued by the central federal government, while US state and local governments, due to their balanced state budget clauses, have historically not accumulated much independent debt.

Several important conceptual subcategories of US federal debt exist.

- *Debt held by the public.* This is federal debt held by all investors outside of the federal government, including individuals, corporations, state or local governments, the Federal Reserve, and foreign governments.
- *Debt held by government accounts (intragovernmental debt).* This is federal debt owed to government accounts, primarily to federal trust funds such as Social Security and Medicare. The cumulative surpluses, including interest earnings, of these trust funds and other government accounts have been invested in Treasury securities, almost always nonmarketable. Whenever a government account needs to spend more than it takes in from the public, the Treasury must provide cash to redeem debt held by the government account.
- *Marketable treasury securities.* These consist of treasury bills, notes, bonds, and treasury inflation-protected securities (TIPS), which can be resold by whoever owns them.
- *Nonmarketable treasury securities.* These are nontransferable securities issued by the government and registered to the owner. While the securities cannot be sold in the financial market, they can be redeemed at any time after they have been held for one year.

Almost all US federal debt is issued in marketable securities, with only $427 billion (less than 3 percent) outstanding in nonmarketable securities at the end of June 2011. The distinction between total outstanding debt, debt held by the public, and debt held by government accounts, however, is far larger. At end-June 2011, $9.7 trillion (65 percent) of total federal debt was held by the public, while $4.6 trillion (35 percent) was held by government accounts.

From the definition of debt held by government accounts, it can be seen that under the International Monetary Fund/Organization for Economic Cooperation and Development (IMF/OECD) definitions of net government debt, this debt would count as "debt assets" for the general government and thus be subtracted from general government gross debt in the estimation of general government

(box continues next page)

Box 15.2   US federal government debt: Different holders, different impact? *(continued)*

net debt. Consequently, debt held by the public is quite close to the definition of general government net debt.

Table B15.2.1 shows the different government account holders of outstanding federal debt as of end-June 2011. Social Security, federal employees, and health care insurance funds account for over 80 percent of this category. It is important to note that most of these "government accounts" were trivial in size or did not exist the last time the US federal government had debt levels approaching today's levels, right after World War II. Consequently, at that point in time, there was very little difference between total debt and "debt held by the public." Once the Social Security and Hospital Insurance Trust Funds cash flows turn negative (given the

Table B15.2.1   Government account holders of federal debt, June 2011

Account holder	Billions of US dollars	Percent of debt
Federal Old-Age and Survivors Insurance Trust Fund (Social Security)	2,498.2	54
Federal Employees Retirement System	696.6	15
Federal Hospital Insurance Trust Fund (Medicare/Medicaid)	267.2	6
Federal Disability Insurance Trust Fund	171.0	4
Federal Supplementary Medical Insurance Trust Fund	80.4	2
Employees Life Insurance Fund	39.1	1
Deposit Insurance Fund	37.2	1
Exchange Stabilization Fund	22.8	0
Highway Trust Fund	22.1	0
Unemployment Trust Fund	21.1	0
National Service Life Insurance Fund	7.8	0
Airport and Airway Trust Fund	7.6	0
Federal Savings and Loan Corporation, Resolution Fund	3.4	0
Federal Housing Administration	2.2	0
Postal Service Fund	0.6	0
Railroad Retirement Account	0.5	0
Treasury Deposit Funds	0	0
Other	742.7	16
Total	4,620.4	100

Source: US Treasury (2011).

(box continues next page)

Box 15.2 US federal government debt: Different holders, different impact? *(continued)*

labor market crisis in the United States since 2008 and temporary payroll tax breaks, this turning point has already been reached) and more federal employees begin retiring, today's difference will again begin to narrow rapidly.

Which of the different US subcategories of debt is most relevant from a debt sustainability perspective is a hotly contested issue. On the one hand, it is clear that since US debt held by government accounts is overwhelmingly held by entities created to finance the US social safety net, this debt reflects a future burden on the US economy and the US Treasury. On the other hand, it can be argued that while debt holders outside the government sector enjoy strong legal protections against unilateral actions by the US federal government, this is not true for government account debt holders. Or put another way, in an emergency the federal government could legally (though not of course politically) default against intragovernmental entities much more easily than against the public.

"Defaults" against intragovernmental holders of debt can come in multiple forms through future changes in laws governing such entities. Ultimately, this possibility indicates the difference between "political promises for the future" and legally protected "government debt commitments." A cut in retirement benefits, for instance, would amount to a "default" against the "political promises for the future" to retirees, against which they will have no recourse except to try to elect another government.

Yet the US social safety net and its associated pension and health care trust funds are already severely underfunded, when measured against the actual costs of the "political promises for the future" made by US politicians concerning the social services to be provided. Far-reaching reforms of (especially) Medicare/Medicaid will therefore be required merely to reduce the current scope of future underfunding. What this means is that unless the US government decides to essentially eliminate the provision of any future social services, it will not be able to avoid the costs of servicing the debt already held today by government accounts, as the debt is earmarked for the purpose of future social services.

Cuts in social "entitlements" of such magnitude are politically implausible, and the costs of the debt held by government accounts thus amount to a lasting future economic burden for the US Treasury. Since according to both the IMF and OECD the US federal government owns very few other "financial assets" to offset its gross liabilities, valid debt sustainability analyses for the United States should be carried

(box continues next page)

out using the total outstanding debt levels and not merely the levels for debt held by the public.

Taking any comfort in the large, but temporary, difference between total US outstanding debt and debt held by the public is misguided. Government debt held by government accounts, accelerated by recent US payroll tax cuts, will soon largely disappear and almost all US debt will be held by the public again.

---

1. All debt data in this box are from US Treasury (2011). GDP data are from Bureau of Economic Analysis, Current-Dollar and "Real" Domestic Product, www.bea.gov (accessed on February 1, 2012).

2. Definitions are from the Government Accountability Office (GAO) website, www.gao.gov/special.pubs/longterm/debt/glossary.html.

3. In liberal democracies, interest groups obviously may also try street protests and other nonviolent demonstrations to try to put pressure on their government. They need not wait for the next election to push their case.

asset side of general government balance sheets. Among EU countries, Ireland has seen by far the largest fiscal effects of financial market interventions, while (excluding Ireland) Germany has seen the highest amount of distressed private financial assets/liabilities transferred to the general government. Meanwhile, through the takeover of Fannie Mae and Freddie Mac, the scope of the US federal government's reception of previously private financial assets during the crisis significantly surpasses interventions in Europe (excluding Ireland).

Required future fiscal consolidation efforts on both sides of the Atlantic are of a historic scale. But this chapter's investigation into countries' historical record of generating new revenues from government assets through privatizations, and into the potential magnitude of new privatization campaigns in the future, suggests that the "asset side of governments' balance sheets" can provide only nonessential assistance to this effort. Neither the high-debt general governments of Europe nor the government of the United States seems to possess the assets today to materially reduce gross indebtedness through asset divestments. In the case of Greece, this could have potentially large effects on its current IMF-led rescue program.

In the end, today's highly indebted governments will not be able to rely on their currently held assets to service their liabilities, but must instead trust to their future austerity and structural reform actions and to the lower deficits and higher growth these will generate.

Table 15.3 Debt sustainability estimates, by gross and net debt levels (percent)

Debt	Germany	France	Italy	Spain	Portugal	Ireland	Greece	Japan	United Kingdom	United States
General government gross debt, 2011 (percent of GDP, projected)	83	87	121	67	106	109	166	233	81	100
General government net debt, 2011 (IMF) (percent of GDP, projected)	57	81	100	56	102	99	153	131	73	73
General government net financial liabilities, 2011 (OECD) (percent of GDP, projected)	50	60	101	46	75	70	125	128	62	75
Average nominal growth rate, 2011–16 (projected)	2.5	3.6	2.6	3.3	2.0	3.6	1.0	1.2	5.2	3.9
General government implicit interest rate[a] (projected)	3.0	3.5	4.4	3.7	4.7	4.2	4.8	1.2	4.2	3.1
Primary balance required for debt sustainability, gross debt	0.4	-0.1	2.0	0.3	2.8	0.7	6.2	0.03	-0.8	-0.8
Primary balance required for debt sustainability, IMF net debt	0.3	-0.1	1.7	0.3	2.7	0.6	5.7	0.02	-0.7	-0.6
Primary balance required for debt sustainability, OECD net financial liabilities	0.2	-0.1	1.7	0.2	2.0	0.4	4.7	0.02	-0.6	-0.6
Average projected primary balance, 2011–16[b]	1.4	-0.9	3.5	-2.2	1.5	-1.2	3.0	-6.4	-1.8	-4.7
Implied required improvement in projected average primary balance 2011–16, gross debt	-1.0	0.8	-1.4	2.5	1.3	1.9	3.2	6.4	1.0	3.9
Implied required improvement in projected average primary balance, 2011–16, IMF net debt	-1.2	0.8	-1.8	2.4	1.2	1.8	2.8	6.4	1.1	4.2
Implied required improvement in projected average primary balance, 2011–16, OECD net financial liabilities	-1.2	0.8	-1.8	2.4	0.5	1.6	1.7	6.4	1.2	4.1

IMF = International Monetary Fund; OECD = Organization for Economic Cooperation and Development

a. Annual interest expense as percent of gross general government debt of preceding year.

b. The five-year 2011–16 average value covers a period during which very large improvements in the primary balance in several countries are projected. As such, it is inherently an optimistic value, which assumes that governments do as projected in the IMF September 2011 *World Economic Outlook*.

Note: Values in italics are estimated, while 2011 data are projected.

Sources: IMF, *World Economic Outlook*, September 2011; OECD, *Economic Outlook*, November 2011; European Commission, Directorate General for Economic and Financial Affairs, Annual Macroeconomic (AMECO) Database, 2011.

References

Cline, William. 2011. *Sustainability of Greek Public Debt.* Policy Briefs in International Economics 11–15. Washington: Peterson Institute for International Economics.

CBO (Congressional Budget Office). 2010. *CBO's Budgetary Treatment of Fannie Mae and Freddie Mac.* Washington.

COP (Congressional Oversight Panel). 2011. *The Final Report of the Congressional Oversight Panel* (March 16). Washington.

Eurostat. 2009. *Eurostat Guidance Note: The Statistical Recording of Public Interventions to Support Financial Institutions and Financial Markets During the Financial Crisis.* Brussels.

Eurostat. 2011a. *Eurostat Supplementary Table for the Financial Crisis: Background Note, April 2011.* Brussels.

Eurostat. 2011b. *Eurostat Guidance on Accounting Rules for EDP: Financial Defeasance Structures Manual on Government Deficit and Debt—Chapter IV.5.* Brussels.

GAO (Government Accountability Office). 2009. *Federally Created Entities: An Overview of Key Attributes.* GAO-10-97. Washington.

Goldstein, Morris. 2003. *Debt Sustainability, Brazil, and the IMF.* Working Paper 03-1. Washington: Institute for International Economics.

Heller, Peter. 2005. Back to Basics—Fiscal Space: What It Is and How to Get It. *Finance and Development* 42, no. 2 (June). Available at www.imf.org (accessed on February 1, 2012).

IMF (International Monetary Fund). 2001. *Government Finance Statistics Manual,* 2nd edition. Washington.

IMF (International Monetary Fund). 2011a. *IMF Fiscal Monitor* (April). Washington.

IMF (International Monetary Fund). 2011b. *IMF Fiscal Monitor Update* (June). Washington.

IMF (International Monetary Fund). 2011c. *Italy—Article IV Review 2011.* Washington.

IMF (International Monetary Fund). 2011d. *Greece—Fourth Review Under the Stand-By Arrangement and Request for Modification and Waiver of Applicability of Performance Criteria.* Washington.

IMF (International Monetary Fund). 2011e. *Portugal: First Review Under the Extended Arrangement.* Washington.

IMF (International Monetary Fund). 2011f. *IMF Fiscal Monitor* (September). Washington.

Japan Ministry of Finance. 2011. *What Do You Know About National Properties?* Tokyo: Ministry of Finance. Available at www.mof.go.jp/english.

Kirkegaard, J., C. Reinhart, and M. Belén Sbrancia. 2011. Financial Repression Redux. *Finance & Development* 48, no. 1 (June): 22–26.

NTMA (National Treasury Management Agency). 2011. *Information Note on Ireland's Debt.* Available at www.ntma.ie (accessed on February 1, 2012).

Nicoletti, G., and S. Scarpetta. 2003. *Regulation, Productivity and Growth: OECD Evidence.* OECD Economics Department Working Paper 347. Paris: OECD Publishing.

OECD (Organization for Economic Cooperation and Development). 2009. *Economic Survey of the United Kingdom.* Paris.

OECD (Organization for Economic Cooperation and Development). 2011a. *Economic Survey of Ireland.* Paris.

OECD (Organization for Economic Cooperation and Development). 2011b. *Economic Survey of Spain.* Paris.

OECD (Organization for Economic Cooperation and Development). 2011c. *The Size and Composition of the SOE Sector in OECD Countries.* OECD Corporate Governance Working Paper 5. Available at www.oecd.org (accessed on February 1, 2012).

Privatization Barometer. 2011. *The PB Report 2010*. Available at www.privatizationbarometer.net.

Reinhart, Carmen M., and Kenneth S. Rogoff. 2010. *From Financial Crash to Debt Crisis*. NBER Working Paper 15795. Cambridge, MA: National Bureau of Economic Research.

UBS Investments Research. 2011. *How Can Governments Sweat Their Assets?* European Economic Monitor (July 20). London.

US Treasury. 2010. *The Troubled Asset Relief Program: Two Year Retrospective*. Washington.

US Treasury. 2011. *U.S. Treasury Bulletin* (June). Washington.

About the Contributors

Alan Ahearne lectures in economics at the National University of Ireland in Galway. He is also a nonresident research fellow at Bruegel and a member of the Board of the Central Bank of Ireland. Ahearne was recruited as a special advisor to Irish Minister for Finance Brian Lenihan in March 2009 and was a senior economist at the Federal Reserve Board's Division of International Finance. He holds a master's degree from University College Dublin and a PhD from Carnegie Mellon University.

Ignazio Angeloni has been a visiting fellow at Bruegel since June 2008 and is an advisor to the European Central Bank's Executive Board on European financial integration, financial stability, and monetary policy. He is the coordinator of and contributor to Bruegel's G-20 monitor. He was director for international financial relations at the Italian Ministry of Economy and Finance, deputy director general of research at the European Central Bank, and director of monetary and financial research at the Bank of Italy. His research interests include macroeconomics, central banking, financial markets, and the economics and politics of European integration. He has published books and articles in top international journals. He holds a degree from Bocconi University and a PhD in economics from the University of Pennsylvania.

Marco Buti has been director-general for economic and financial affairs at the European Commission since December 2008, before which he was acting director-general for six months. He joined the European Commission in 1987 and has held various positions, including economist in the Directorate General of Economic and Financial Affairs (DG ECFIN) and the commissioner's private office before becoming economic advisor to the Commission president in 2002–03. In September 2003 he returned to DG ECFIN as director of the Directorate for Economies of the Member States. In September 2006 he was appointed deputy director-general of DG ECFIN. Buti has been a visiting professor at the Université libre de Bruxelles, the University of Florence, and the European University Institute and has published extensively on Economic and Monetary Union, macroeconomic policies, welfare state reforms, and European unemployment. He completed his education at the Universities of Florence and Oxford.

William R. Cline has been a senior fellow at the Peterson Institute for International Economics since its inception in 1981. While on leave during 1996–2001, he was deputy managing director and chief economist of the Institute of International Finance. Since 2002 he has held a joint appointment with the Center for Global Development. He has been a senior fellow at the Brookings Institution (1973–81); deputy director for development and trade research, US Treasury Department (1971–73); Ford Foundation visiting professor in Brazil (1970–71); and lecturer and assistant professor of economics at Princeton University (1967–70). He is the author of 24 books, including *Resolving the European Debt Crisis* (2012), *Financial Globalization, Economic Growth, and the Crisis of 2007–09* (2010), *Global Warming and Agriculture* (2007), and *The United States as a Debtor Nation* (2005). He graduated summa cum laude from Princeton University and received his PhD in economics from Yale University.

Zsolt Darvas has been a research fellow at Bruegel since January 2009, which he joined as visiting fellow in September 2008. He is also a research fellow at the Institute of Economics of the Hungarian Academy of Sciences and associate professor at the Corvinus University of Budapest. From 2005 to 2008, he was research advisor to the Argenta Financial Research Group in Budapest. He has worked at the research unit of the Central Bank of Hungary (1994–2005), where he served as deputy head. His research interests include macroeconomics, international economics, central banking, and time series analysis. He holds a PhD in economics from Corvinus University of Budapest, where he teaches courses in econometrics.

Mario Draghi has been the president of the European Central Bank since November 2011. Before taking up this position, he had been the governor of the Bank of Italy since December 2005 and the head of the Financial Stability Board, formerly the Financial Stability Forum, since 2006. He was vice chairman and managing director of Goldman Sachs International, London (2002–05), director-general of the Italian Treasury (1991–2001), and executive director at the World Bank (1984–90). He earned a PhD in economics from Massachusetts Institute of Technology, where he studied under Franco Modigliani and Robert Solow. He also holds a degree in economics from Università degli Studi, Rome.

Joseph E. Gagnon, senior fellow at the Peterson Institute for International Economics since September 2009, was visiting associate director, Division of Monetary Affairs (2008–09) at the US Federal Reserve Board. Previously he served at the US Federal Reserve Board as associate director, Division of International Finance (1999–2008), and senior economist (1987–1990 and 1991–97). He has also served at the US Treasury Department (1994–95 and 1997–1999) and has taught at the University of California's Haas School of Business (1990–91). He is author of *Flexible Exchange Rates for a Stable World Economy* (2011) and *The Global Outlook for Government Debt over the Next 25 Years: Implications for the Economy and Public Policy* (2011). He has published numerous articles in economics journals, including the *Journal of International Economics*, the *Journal of Monetary Economics*, the *Review of International Economics*, and the *Journal of International Money and Finance*, and has contributed to several edited volumes. He received a BA from Harvard University and a PhD in economics from Stanford University.

Vítor Gaspar has been the finance minister of Portugal since June 2011. Before taking up this position, he had been advisor to the Bank of Portugal since February 2010 and director-general at the Bureau of European Policy Advisers (BEPA) with the President of the European Commission since 2007. He was director-general for research at the European Central Bank for six years. He earned a PhD in economics from Universidade Nova de Lisboa and a degree in economics from the Faculdade de Ciências Humanas of the Universidade Católica Portuguesa.

Morris Goldstein, senior fellow at the Peterson Institute for International Economics, has held several senior staff positions at the International Monetary Fund (1970–94), including deputy director of its Research Department (1987–94). From 1994 to 2010, he was the Dennis Weatherstone Senior Fellow at the Peterson Institute. He has written extensively on international economic policy and on international capital markets. He is the author of *Managed Floating Plus* (2002), *The Asian Financial Crisis: Causes, Cures, and Systemic Implications* (1998), *The Case for an International Banking Standard* (1997), *The Exchange Rate System and the IMF: A Modest Agenda* (1995), coeditor of *Debating China's Exchange Rate Policy* (2008), *Private Capital Flows to Emerging Markets after the Mexican Crisis* (1996), coauthor of *The Future of China's Exchange Rate Policy* (2009) with Nicholas R. Lardy, *Controlling Currency Mismatches in Emerging Markets* (2004) with Philip Turner, *Assessing Financial Vulnerability: An Early Warning System for Emerging Markets* with Graciela Kaminsky and Carmen Reinhart (2000), and project director of *Safeguarding Prosperity in a Global Financial System: The Future International Financial Architecture* (1999) for the Council on Foreign Relations Task Force on the International Financial Architecture.

Jacob Funk Kirkegaard has been a research fellow at the Peterson Institute for International Economics since 2002 and is also a senior associate at the

Rhodium Group, a New York–based research firm. Before joining the Institute, he worked with the Danish Ministry of Defense, the United Nations in Iraq, and in the private financial sector. He is author of *The Accelerating Decline in America's High-Skilled Workforce: Implications for Immigration Policy* (2007) and co-author of *US Pension Reform: Lessons from Other Countries* (2009) and *Transforming the European Economy* (2004) and he assisted with *Accelerating the Globalization of America: The Role for Information Technology* (2006). His current research focuses on European economies and reform, pension systems and accounting rules, demographics, offshoring, high-skilled immigration, and the impact of information technology. He is a graduate of the Danish Army's Special School of Intelligence and Linguistics with the rank of first lieutenant; the University of Aarhus in Aarhus, Denmark; and Columbia University in New York.

Michael Mussa (1944–2012) was a senior fellow at the Peterson Institute for International Economics from 2001 to 2012. He served as economic counselor and director of the Department of Research at the International Monetary Fund from 1991 to 2001, where he was responsible for advising the management of the Fund and the Fund's Executive Board on broad issues of economic policy and for providing analysis of ongoing developments in the world economy. By appointment of President Ronald Reagan, Mussa served as a member of the US Council of Economic Advisers from August 1986 to September 1988. He was a member of the faculty of the Graduate School of Business of the University of Chicago (1976–91) and was on the faculty of the department of economics at the University of Rochester (1971–76). During this period he also served as a visiting faculty member at the Graduate Center of the City University of New York, the London School of Economics, and the Graduate Institute of International Studies in Geneva, Switzerland. Mussa's main areas of research were international economics, macroeconomics, monetary economics, and municipal finance. He published widely in these fields in professional journals and research volumes. He is author of *Argentina and the Fund: From Triumph to Tragedy* (2002) and editor of *C. Fred Bergsten and the World Economy* (2006).

Jean Pisani-Ferry is the director of Bruegel, the Brussels-based economics think tank, and professor of economics at Université Paris-Dauphine. He was executive president of the French prime minister's Council of Economic Analysis (2001–02); senior economic advisor to the French minister of finance (1997–2000); director of Centre d'Études Prospectives et d'Informations Internationales (CEPII), the French institute for international economics (1992–97); and economic advisor to the European Commission (1989–92). His current research interests are economic policy in Europe and global macroeconomics. He has regular columns in *Le Monde, Handelsblatt, The FT A-List, Project Syndicate,* and the Chinese magazine *Century Weekly*.

Adam S. Posen is an external member of the Monetary Policy Committee of the Bank of England and a senior fellow at the Peterson Institute for International Economics. His research and policy expertise focuses on macro-economic policy and forecasting, European and Japanese political economy, central banking issues, and the resolution of financial crises. He was a visiting scholar and consultant at central banks across Europe and the Asia-Pacific prior to joining the Bank of England and has also been a consultant to several US government agencies, the European Commission, the Japanese Ministry of Economy, Trade, and Industry, the UK Cabinet Office, and the International Monetary Fund. Posen is author or editor and coauthor of seven books including *The Euro at 10: The Next Global Currency?* (2009).

André Sapir is a senior fellow at Bruegel and professor of economics at the Université libre de Bruxelles, where he teaches international economics and European integration at the Solvay Brussels School of Economics and Management. He is also a research fellow at the Centre for Economic Policy Research. In addition, he currently (2011–14) serves as co-chair of the Advisory Scientific Committee and a voting member of the General Board of the European Systemic Risk Board (ESRB). From 2005 to 2009 he was a member of the Economic Advisory Group to European Commission President José Manuel Barroso. Previously, he worked for 12 years for the European Commission, first serving as economic advisor to the director-general for economic and financial affairs, then as economic advisor to President Romano Prodi. Sapir holds a PhD in economics from the Johns Hopkins University. He has written extensively on various aspects of European and global integration.

Wolfgang Schäuble has been federal minister of finance of Germany since 2009. He was federal minister for the interior from 2005 to 2009. From 1984 to 1991 he was a member of Helmut Kohl's cabinet, first as federal minister for special tasks and head of the Federal Chancellery and then as federal minister of the interior. Between 1991 and 2000, he was chairman of the Christian Democratic Union/Christian Social Union of Bavaria (CDU/CSU) Parliamentary Group in the German Bundestag and from 1998 to 2000 also CDU party chairman. From 2002 to 2005 he was deputy head of the CDU/CSU Parliamentary Group in the German Bundestag with responsibility for foreign, security, and European policies. He studied law and economics at the Universities of Freiburg and Hamburg.

Garry J. Schinasi joined the International Monetary Fund (IMF) in 1990, where he has focused on global finance and financial stability issues. He comanaged the IMF's surveillance of international capital markets, including the IMF's flagship publication *International Capital Markets: Developments, Prospects, and Key Policy Issues* (from 1994 to 2001) and later the *Global Financial Stability Report*. After taking a one-year sabbatical to write a book on financial stability, Schinasi returned to the IMF's Finance Department, where he managed the development of the department's framework for assessing financial risk in the Fund, with an emphasis on credit risk. He is currently on sabbatical from the IMF and is working as an independent researcher and consultant on global financial stability issues. He has also held staff positions at the Board of Governors of the US Federal Reserve System. He has published articles in the *Review of Economic Studies, Journal of Economic Theory, Journal of International Money and Finance,* and other academic and policy journals. His book *Safeguarding Financial Stability: Theory and Practice* was published by the IMF in January 2006. He received his PhD in economics from Columbia University.

Edwin M. Truman, senior fellow at the Peterson Institute for International Economics since 2001, served as assistant secretary for international affairs at the US Treasury from December 1998 to January 2001 and returned as counselor to the secretary March–May 2009. He directed the Division of International Finance of the Board of Governors of the Federal Reserve System from 1977 to 1998. He has been a member of numerous international groups working on economic and financial issues and also a visiting economics lecturer at Amherst College and a visiting economics professor at Williams College. He has published on international monetary economics, international debt problems, economic development, and European economic integration. He is the author, coauthor, or editor of *Sovereign Wealth Funds: Threat or Salvation?* (2010), *Reforming the IMF for the 21st Century* (2006), *A Strategy for IMF Reform* (2006), *Chasing Dirty Money: The Fight Against Money Laundering* (2004), and *Inflation Targeting in the World Economy* (2003).

Nicolas Véron is a senior fellow at Bruegel and a visiting fellow at the Peterson Institute for International Economics. His research focuses on financial systems and financial regulation around the globe, including current developments in the European Union. He has been involved in the creation and development of Bruegel since 2002 and has divided his time since 2009 between the United States and Europe. A graduate of France's École Polytechnique and École des Mines, his earlier experience combines policy work as a French civil servant and corporate finance as a junior investment banker, chief financial officer of a small listed company, and independent strategy consultant. In 2006 he coauthored *Smoke & Mirrors, Inc.: Accounting for Capitalism* (Cornell University Press). He is also the author of several books in French. He writes a monthly column on European finance, which is published by leading newspapers and online media in most Group of Twenty (G-20) countries.

Reinhilde Veugelers is a senior fellow at Bruegel, where she coordinates research on competition, innovation, and sustainable growth. She is a professor at KU Leuven (Belgium) in the Faculty of Economics and Business, where she teaches international business economics and game theory. She is also visiting faculty at the MSI program of the Barcelona Graduate School of Economics and a research fellow at the Center for Economic and Policy Research. From 2004 to 2008, she was on academic leave as advisor at the European Commission's Bureau of Economic Policy Advisers (BEPA). She was a visiting scholar at Northwestern University's Kellogg Graduate School of Management; MIT's Sloan School of Management; New York University's Stern Business School; Université catholique de Louvain (UCL), Belgium; European Center of Advanced Research in Economics and Statistics (ECARES), Université libre de Bruxelles, Belgium; Paris 1 (France); Universitat Pompeu Fabra and Universitat Autònoma de Barcelona (Spain); and Maastricht University (Netherlands). She has authored numerous publications in leading international journals on industrial organization, international economics and strategy, and innovation and science.

Guntram B. Wolff is the deputy director of Bruegel. His research focuses on the euro area economy and governance, fiscal policy, global finance, and Germany. Prior to joining Bruegel, he worked at the European Commission, where he focused on the macroeconomics of the euro area and reform of euro area governance. He was an economist at the Deutsche Bundesbank, where he coordinated the research team on fiscal policy. He was also an advisor to the International Monetary Fund. He taught economics at the University of Pittsburgh. He has published numerous papers in leading academic journals. His columns and policy work have been published and cited in leading international media such as the *Financial Times, New York Times, Wall Street Journal, El País, La Stampa, Frankfurter Allgemeine Zeitung, Financial Times Deutschland,* BBC, ZDF, WDR, *Die Welt,* and CNBC. He is coeditor (with William R. Cline) of *Resolving the European Debt Crisis* (2012). He holds a PhD from the University of Bonn and has studied economics at the Universities of Bonn, Toulouse, Pittsburgh, and Passau.

Index

Congressional Budget Office (CBO)
  accounting treatment of GSEs, 309
  budget projections, 34
  climate change policy costs, 51
  supply-side assessment, 15
construction industry, unemployment in, 254
consumption, life cycle model of, 286
consumption spending, 251, 259, 269
Continental Illinois National Bank and Trust Company, 89
contingent capital (CoCos), 119–20
contingent liabilities, 310
Copenhagen Accord, 45
  US pledges, 46–50, 47t
Copenhagen Convergence (CopCon), 48
  abatement costs, 49–50, 50t
  global abatement under, 48, 49t
corporate debt, 280–84, 281t
  deleveraging, 13–14, 14t, 36, 281–84, 296–97
corporations, loans to, 229, 229f
credit default swap (CDS) spreads, 105
credit developments, 226
credit easing, 22–28, 267–68
creditless recoveries, 226n
Credit Lyonnais, 90
credit rating agencies, 80
credit unions, 93
crisis management
  differing strategies, 2
  postcrisis reforms, 143–44, 173
  precrisis system, 130, 131t, 133
cross-border oversight, 80
currency. See exchange rates; specific currency
current account balance, 40–41
  as percent of GDP, 233, 234f
  postcrisis recovery and, 264
cyclically adjusted primary balance (CAPB), 315
Cyprus, 103

debt
  corporate, 280–84, 281t
    deleveraging, 13–14, 14t, 36, 281–84, 296–97
  private (See also household debt)
    deleveraging, 13–14, 14t, 36, 224–26
    public debt interaction with, 273–74
  public (See public debt)
debt-financed bubbles, 267–68
demand growth
  euro area, 260–63, 261t
  US, 250–53

demographic outlook, 35–36
  climate change policy and, 54
  household debt and, 287
Denmark, banking sector, 93, 99
Deutsche Bank, 90
Dexia, 99
Directorate General for Competition (DG COMP), 90, 114
discretionary stimulus estimates, 31–32, 32f
distressed assets, 304–14
Dodd-Frank Act (2010), 94, 96, 108
  European criticism of, 172
  ex ante tax, 138
  size cap, 113, 120
  special resolution regimes, 115, 117
DSB Bank, 92
Dunfermline Building Society, 92

early warning systems, 80, 143, 168
ECB. See European Central Bank
Economic and Monetary Union (EMU), 204, 209
economic developments, policy reactions, 11–19
economic growth. See also specific country
  household debt and, 288–89, 289f, 290f, 292t
  monetary system and, 206
  monetary unification and, 211–15, 213t, 214f
  policy reactions, 11–13, 15
  postcrisis recovery (See economic recovery)
  sustainable, 7, 268–72
  fiscal space and, 33–36, 35f, 42
Economic Outlook (OECD), 318
economic power, distribution of, 1, 185–87, 192, 194–96
economic recovery, 247–65
  medium-term prospects
    European Union, 258–65
    United States, 249–58
  recent histories of, 248–49, 249t
emerging-market economies. See also specific country
  capital flows, 145
  climate change policy, 48–50, 58
  exchange rate policies, 193
  FSB representation, 160, 163
  IMF assistance to, 148–49
Emissions Trading System (ETS), 54, 56–57, 63, 74
employment. See also unemployment
  by educational attainment, 255, 255t
  labor costs, 233, 234f
  labor market integration, 210

Other Publications from the Peterson Institute for International Economics

WORKING PAPERS

* = out of print

POLICY ANALYSES IN INTERNATIONAL
ECONOMICS Series

Global Corporations and National
Governments   Edward M. Graham
May 1996   ISBN 0-88132-111-7
Global Economic Leadership and the Group of
Seven   C. Fred Bergsten and
C. Randall Henning
May 1996   ISBN 0-88132-218-0
The Trading System after the Uruguay Round*
John Whalley and Colleen Hamilton
July 1996   ISBN 0-88132-131-1
Private Capital Flows to Emerging Markets
after the Mexican Crisis*   Guillermo A. Calvo,
Morris Goldstein, and Eduard Hochreiter
September 1996   ISBN 0-88132-232-6
The Crawling Band as an Exchange Rate
Regime: Lessons from Chile, Colombia, and
Israel   John Williamson
September 1996   ISBN 0-88132-231-8
Flying High: Liberalizing Civil Aviation in the
Asia Pacific*   Gary Clyde Hufbauer and
Christopher Findlay
November 1996   ISBN 0-88132-227-X
Measuring the Costs of Visible Protection
in Korea*   Namdoo Kim
November 1996   ISBN 0-88132-236-9
The World Trading System: Challenges Ahead
Jeffrey J. Schott
December 1996   ISBN 0-88132-235-0
Has Globalization Gone Too Far?   Dani Rodrik
March 1997   ISBN paper 0-88132-241-5
Korea-United States Economic Relationship*
C. Fred Bergsten and Il SaKong, eds.
March 1997   ISBN 0-88132-240-7
Summitry in the Americas: A Progress Report
Richard E. Feinberg
April 1997   ISBN 0-88132-242-3
Corruption and the Global Economy
Kimberly Ann Elliott
June 1997   ISBN 0-88132-233-4
Regional Trading Blocs in the World Economic
System   Jeffrey A. Frankel
October 1997   ISBN 0-88132-202-4
Sustaining the Asia Pacific Miracle:
Environmental Protection and Economic
Integration   Andre Dua and Daniel C. Esty
October 1997   ISBN 0-88132-250-4
Trade and Income Distribution
William R. Cline
November 1997   ISBN 0-88132-216-4
Global Competition Policy
Edward M. Graham and J. David Richardson
December 1997   ISBN 0-88132-166-4
Unfinished Business: Telecommunications
after the Uruguay Round
Gary Clyde Hufbauer and Erika Wada
December 1997   ISBN 0-88132-257-1
Financial Services Liberalization in the WTO
Wendy Dobson and Pierre Jacquet
June 1998   ISBN 0-88132-254-7
Restoring Japan's Economic Growth
Adam S. Posen
September 1998   ISBN 0-88132-262-8

Measuring the Costs of Protection in China
Zhang Shuguang, Zhang Yansheng, and Wan
Zhongxin
November 1998   ISBN 0-88132-247-4
Foreign Direct Investment and Development:
The New Policy Agenda for Developing
Countries and Economies in Transition
Theodore H. Moran
December 1998   ISBN 0-88132-258-X
Behind the Open Door: Foreign Enterprises
in the Chinese Marketplace   Daniel H. Rosen
January 1999   ISBN 0-88132-263-6
Toward A New International Financial
Architecture: A Practical Post-Asia Agenda
Barry Eichengreen
February 1999   ISBN 0-88132-270-9
Is the U.S. Trade Deficit Sustainable?
Catherine L. Mann
September 1999   ISBN 0-88132-265-2
Safeguarding Prosperity in a Global Financial
System: The Future International Financial
Architecture, Independent Task Force Report
Sponsored by the Council on Foreign Relations
Morris Goldstein, Project Director
October 1999   ISBN 0-88132-287-3
Avoiding the Apocalypse: The Future of the
Two Koreas   Marcus Noland
June 2000   ISBN 0-88132-278-4
Assessing Financial Vulnerability: An Early
Warning System for Emerging Markets
Morris Goldstein, Graciela Kaminsky, and
Carmen Reinhart
June 2000   ISBN 0-88132-237-7
Global Electronic Commerce: A Policy Primer
Catherine L. Mann, Sue E. Eckert, and Sarah
Cleeland Knight
July 2000   ISBN 0-88132-274-1
The WTO after Seattle   Jeffrey J. Schott, ed.
July 2000   ISBN 0-88132-290-3
Intellectual Property Rights in the Global
Economy   Keith E. Maskus
August 2000   ISBN 0-88132-282-2
The Political Economy of the Asian Financial
Crisis   Stephan Haggard
August 2000   ISBN 0-88132-283-0
Transforming Foreign Aid: United States
Assistance in the 21st Century   Carol Lancaster
August 2000   ISBN 0-88132-291-1
Fighting the Wrong Enemy: Antiglobal
Activists and Multinational Enterprises
Edward M. Graham
September 2000   ISBN 0-88132-272-5
Globalization and the Perceptions of American
Workers   Kenneth Scheve and
Matthew J. Slaughter
March 2001   ISBN 0-88132-295-4
World Capital Markets: Challenge to the G-10
Wendy Dobson and Gary Clyde Hufbauer,
assisted by Hyun Koo Cho
May 2001   ISBN 0-88132-301-2
Prospects for Free Trade in the Americas
Jeffrey J. Schott
August 2001   ISBN 0-88132-275-X

Toward a North American Community: Lessons from the Old World for the New
Robert A. Pastor
August 2001   ISBN 0-88132-328-4

Measuring the Costs of Protection in Europe: European Commercial Policy in the 2000s
Patrick A. Messerlin
September 2001   ISBN 0-88132-273-3

Job Loss from Imports: Measuring the Costs
Lori G. Kletzer
September 2001   ISBN 0-88132-296-2

No More Bashing: Building a New Japan–United States Economic Relationship
C. Fred Bergsten, Takatoshi Ito, and Marcus Noland
October 2001   ISBN 0-88132-286-5

Why Global Commitment Really Matters!
Howard Lewis III and J. David Richardson
October 2001   ISBN 0-88132-298-9

Leadership Selection in the Major Multilaterals
Miles Kahler
November 2001   ISBN 0-88132-335-7

The International Financial Architecture: What's New? What's Missing?   Peter B. Kenen
November 2001   ISBN 0-88132-297-0

Delivering on Debt Relief: From IMF Gold to a New Aid Architecture   John Williamson and Nancy Birdsall, with Brian Deese
April 2002   ISBN 0-88132-331-4

Imagine There's No Country: Poverty, Inequality, and Growth in the Era of Globalization   Surjit S. Bhalla
September 2002   ISBN 0-88132-348-9

Reforming Korea's Industrial Conglomerates
Edward M. Graham
January 2003   ISBN 0-88132-337-3

Industrial Policy in an Era of Globalization: Lessons from Asia   Marcus Noland and Howard Pack
March 2003   ISBN 0-88132-350-0

Reintegrating India with the World Economy
T. N. Srinivasan and Suresh D. Tendulkar
March 2003   ISBN 0-88132-280-6

After the Washington Consensus: Restarting Growth and Reform in Latin America
Pedro-Pablo Kuczynski and John Williamson, eds.
March 2003   ISBN 0-88132-347-0

The Decline of US Labor Unions and the Role of Trade   Robert E. Baldwin
June 2003   ISBN 0-88132-341-1

Can Labor Standards Improve under Globalization?   Kimberly Ann Elliott and Richard B. Freeman
June 2003   ISBN 0-88132-332-2

Crimes and Punishments? Retaliation under the WTO   Robert Z. Lawrence
October 2003   ISBN 0-88132-359-4

Inflation Targeting in the World Economy
Edwin M. Truman
October 2003   ISBN 0-88132-345-4

Foreign Direct Investment and Tax Competition   John H. Mutti
November 2003   ISBN 0-88132-352-7

Has Globalization Gone Far Enough? The Costs of Fragmented Markets
Scott C. Bradford and Robert Z. Lawrence
February 2004   ISBN 0-88132-349-7

Food Regulation and Trade: Toward a Safe and Open Global System   Tim Josling, Donna Roberts, and David Orden
March 2004   ISBN 0-88132-346-2

Controlling Currency Mismatches in Emerging Markets   Morris Goldstein and Philip Turner
April 2004   ISBN 0-88132-360-8

Free Trade Agreements: US Strategies and Priorities   Jeffrey J. Schott, ed.
April 2004   ISBN 0-88132-361-6

Trade Policy and Global Poverty
William R. Cline
June 2004   ISBN 0-88132-365-9

Bailouts or Bail-ins? Responding to Financial Crises in Emerging Economies
Nouriel Roubini and Brad Setser
August 2004   ISBN 0-88132-371-3

Transforming the European Economy
Martin Neil Baily and Jacob Funk Kirkegaard
September 2004   ISBN 0-88132-343-8

Chasing Dirty Money: The Fight Against Money Laundering   Peter Reuter and Edwin M. Truman
November 2004   ISBN 0-88132-370-5

The United States and the World Economy: Foreign Economic Policy for the Next Decade
C. Fred Bergsten
January 2005   ISBN 0-88132-380-2

Does Foreign Direct Investment Promote Development?   Theodore H. Moran, Edward M. Graham, and Magnus Blomström, eds.
April 2005   ISBN 0-88132-381-0

American Trade Politics, 4th ed.   I. M. Destler
June 2005   ISBN 0-88132-382-9

Why Does Immigration Divide America? Public Finance and Political Opposition to Open Borders   Gordon H. Hanson
August 2005   ISBN 0-88132-400-0

Reforming the US Corporate Tax
Gary Clyde Hufbauer and Paul L. E. Grieco
September 2005   ISBN 0-88132-384-5

The United States as a Debtor Nation
William R. Cline
September 2005   ISBN 0-88132-399-3

NAFTA Revisited: Achievements and Challenges   Gary Clyde Hufbauer and Jeffrey J. Schott, assisted by Paul L. E. Grieco and Yee Wong
October 2005   ISBN 0-88132-334-9

US National Security and Foreign Direct Investment   Edward M. Graham and David M. Marchick
May 2006   ISBN 978-0-88132-391-7

Accelerating the Globalization of America: The Role for Information Technology
Catherine L. Mann, assisted by Jacob Funk Kirkegaard
June 2006   ISBN 978-0-88132-390-0

Delivering on Doha: Farm Trade and the Poor
Kimberly Ann Elliott
July 2006   ISBN 978-0-88132-392-4
Case Studies in US Trade Negotiation, Vol. 1:
Making the Rules   Charan Devereaux,
Robert Z. Lawrence, and Michael Watkins
September 2006   ISBN 978-0-88132-362-7
Case Studies in US Trade Negotiation, Vol. 2:
Resolving Disputes   Charan Devereaux,
Robert Z. Lawrence, and Michael Watkins
September 2006   ISBN 978-0-88132-363-2
C. Fred Bergsten and the World Economy
Michael Mussa, ed.
December 2006   ISBN 978-0-88132-397-9
Working Papers, Volume I   Peterson Institute
December 2006   ISBN 978-0-88132-388-7
The Arab Economies in a Changing World
Marcus Noland and Howard Pack
April 2007   ISBN 978-0-88132-393-1
Working Papers, Volume II   Peterson Institute
April 2007   ISBN 978-0-88132-404-4
Global Warming and Agriculture: Impact
Estimates by Country   William R. Cline
July 2007   ISBN 978-0-88132-403-7
US Taxation of Foreign Income
Gary Clyde Hufbauer and Ariel Assa
October 2007   ISBN 978-0-88132-405-1
Russia's Capitalist Revolution: Why Market
Reform Succeeded and Democracy Failed
Anders Åslund
October 2007   ISBN 978-0-88132-409-9
Economic Sanctions Reconsidered, 3d ed.
Gary Clyde Hufbauer, Jeffrey J. Schott, Kimberly
Ann Elliott, and Barbara Oegg
November 2007
          ISBN hardcover 978-0-88132-407-5
     ISBN hardcover/CD-ROM 978-0-88132-408-2
Debating China's Exchange Rate Policy
Morris Goldstein and Nicholas R. Lardy, eds.
April 2008   ISBN 978-0-88132-415-0
Leveling the Carbon Playing Field:
International Competition and US Climate
Policy Design Trevor Houser, Rob Bradley, Britt
Childs, Jacob Werksman, and Robert Heilmayr
May 2008   ISBN 978-0-88132-420-4
Accountability and Oversight of US Exchange
Rate Policy   C. Randall Henning
June 2008   ISBN 978-0-88132-419-8
Challenges of Globalization: Imbalances and
Growth   Anders Åslund and
Marek Dabrowski, eds.
July 2008   ISBN 978-0-88132-418-1
China's Rise: Challenges and Opportunities
C. Fred Bergsten, Charles Freeman, Nicholas R.
Lardy, and Derek J. Mitchell
September 2008   ISBN 978-0-88132-417-4
Banking on Basel: The Future of International
Financial Regulation   Daniel K. Tarullo
September 2008   ISBN 978-0-88132-423-5
US Pension Reform: Lessons from Other
Countries   Martin Neil Baily and
Jacob Funk Kirkegaard
February 2009   ISBN 978-0-88132-425-9

How Ukraine Became a Market Economy and
Democracy   Anders Åslund
March 2009   ISBN 978-0-88132-427-3
Global Warming and the World Trading
System   Gary Clyde Hufbauer,
Steve Charnovitz, and Jisun Kim
March 2009   ISBN 978-0-88132-428-0
The Russia Balance Sheet   Anders Åslund and
Andrew Kuchins
March 2009   ISBN 978-0-88132-424-2
The Euro at Ten: The Next Global Currency?
Jean Pisani-Ferry and Adam S. Posen, eds.
July 2009   ISBN 978-0-88132-430-3
Financial Globalization, Economic Growth, and
the Crisis of 2007–09   William R. Cline
May 2010   ISBN 978-0-88132-4990-0
Russia after the Global Economic Crisis
Anders Åslund, Sergei Guriev, and Andrew
Kuchins, eds.
June 2010   ISBN 978-0-88132-497-6
Sovereign Wealth Funds: Threat or Salvation?
Edwin M. Truman
September 2010   ISBN 978-0-88132-498-3
The Last Shall Be the First: The East European
Financial Crisis, 2008–10   Anders Åslund
October 2010   ISBN 978-0-88132-521-8
Witness to Transformation: Refugee Insights
into North Korea   Stephan Haggard and
Marcus Noland
January 2011   ISBN 978-0-88132-438-9
Foreign Direct Investment and Development:
Launching a Second Generation of Policy
Research, Avoiding the Mistakes of the First,
Reevaluating Policies for Developed and
Developing Countries   Theodore H. Moran
April 2011   ISBN 978-0-88132-600-0
How Latvia Came through the Financial Crisis
Anders Åslund and Valdis Dombrovskis
May 2011   ISBN 978-0-88132-602-4
Global Trade in Services: Fear, Facts, and
Offshoring   J. Bradford Jensen
August 2011   ISBN 978-0-88132-601-7
NAFTA and Climate Change
Meera Fickling and Jeffrey J. Schott
September 2011   ISBN 978-0-88132-436-5
Eclipse: Living in the Shadow of China's
Economic Dominance   Arvind Subramanian
September 2011   ISBN 978-0-88132-606-2
Flexible Exchange Rates for a Stable World
Economy   Joseph E. Gagnon with
Marc Hinterschweiger
September 2011   ISBN 978-0-88132-627-7
The Arab Economies in a Changing World,
2d ed.   Marcus Noland and Howard Pack
November 2011   ISBN 978-0-88132-628-4
Sustaining China's Economic Growth After the
Global Financial Crisis   Nicholas Lardy
January 2012   ISBN 978-0-88132-626-0
Who Needs to Open the Capital Account?
Olivier Jeanne, Arvind Subramanian, and John
Williamson
April 2012   ISBN 978-0-88132-511-9

Australia, New Zealand,
and Papua New Guinea
D. A. Information Services
648 Whitehorse Road
Mitcham, Victoria 3132, Australia
Tel: 61-3-9210-7777
Fax: 61-3-9210-7788
Email: service@dadirect.com.au
www.dadirect.com.au

India, Bangladesh, Nepal, and Sri Lanka
Viva Books Private Limited
Mr. Vinod Vasishtha
4737/23 Ansari Road
Daryaganj, New Delhi 110002
India
Tel: 91-11-4224-2200
Fax: 91-11-4224-2240
Email: viva@vivagroupindia.net
www.vivagroupindia.com

Mexico, Central America, South America,
and Puerto Rico
US PubRep, Inc.
311 Dean Drive
Rockville, MD 20851
Tel: 301-838-9276
Fax: 301-838-9278
Email: c.falk@ieee.org

Asia (*Brunei, Burma, Cambodia, China,*
Hong Kong, Indonesia, Korea, Laos, Malaysia,
Philippines, Singapore, Taiwan, Thailand,
and Vietnam)
East-West Export Books (EWEB)
University of Hawaii Press
2840 Kolowalu Street
Honolulu, Hawaii 96822-1888
Tel: 808-956-8830
Fax: 808-988-6052
Email: eweb@hawaii.edu

Canada
Renouf Bookstore
5369 Canotek Road, Unit 1
Ottawa, Ontario KlJ 9J3, Canada
Tel: 613-745-2665
Fax: 613-745-7660
www.renoufbooks.com

Japan
United Publishers Services Ltd.
1-32-5, Higashi-shinagawa
Shinagawa-ku, Tokyo 140-0002
Japan
Tel: 81-3-5479-7251
Fax: 81-3-5479-7307
Email: purchasing@ups.co.jp
For trade accounts only. Individuals will find
Institute books in leading Tokyo bookstores.

Middle East
MERIC
2 Bahgat Ali Street, El Masry Towers
Tower D, Apt. 24
Zamalek, Cairo
Egypt
Tel. 20-2-7633824
Fax: 20-2-7369355
Email: mahmoud_fouda@mericonline.com
www.mericonline.com

United Kingdom, Europe
(*including Russia and Turkey*)**, Africa,**
and Israel
The Eurospan Group
c/o Turpin Distribution
Pegasus Drive
Stratton Business Park
Biggleswade, Bedfordshire
SG18 8TQ
United Kingdom
Tel: 44 (0) 1767-604972
Fax: 44 (0) 1767-601640
Email: eurospan@turpin-distribution.com
www.eurospangroup.com/bookstore

Visit our website at:
www.piie.com
E-mail orders to:
petersonmail@presswarehouse.com